C000232015

The Nature of Reality

by

Henry Ellington

A personal survey of religious, philosophical and scientific ideas on the subject by a life-long student of 'natural philosophy' in its broadest sense.

To Graham and Joan,
with the compliments
and very best wishes
of the author.
H.S. Ellington
12/3/21

Dedication

I would like to dedicate this book to

Bryan Magee

who died in 2019, at the age of 89. During the 1970's, Bryan introduced me to the ideas of **Sir Karl Popper**; this totally transformed my view of the nature of science, and also greatly influenced my subsequent work as an educational developer.

Thirty years later, he introduced me to the wider world of philosophy, including the ideas of **Kant** and **Schopenhauer**; this made me think much more deeply about the nature of basic reality — hence this book.

Thank you, Bryan!

Acknowledgements

I would like to thank the following five people for their key contributions to the production of my book:

- My son-in-law, George Taylor, for co-ordinating all the typing (I do all my writing 'manually', using a 'Pentel' pencil, an eraser, and an endless supply of re-cycled A4 paper).
- My grand-daughter, Kirsten Gourlay, for handling all the e-correspondence with my seven 'readers' (I do not own a computer).
- My son, Kenneth Ellington, for organising the printing and publishing of the book.
- Jeanette Lowe, for preparing the final version of the book for delivery to the publisher (in addition to typing six of the chapters).
- Andy Gourlay, of Finavon Print and Design, for producing the cover for the book – and for converting my suggested idea for the front cover into a 'work of art'.

I would also like to thank all the many other people who contributed to the project in different ways during the planning stage, the actual writing, the typing, and the final preparation prior to delivery to the publisher:

Donald Addison; Lisa Cumming; Dr Frances Germain; Fred Gordon; Monica Gordon; Claire Gourlay; Louise Leiper; Dr. Alastair McLeish; Dr. David Northcroft; Jacqueline Ruddy; Rev. Gareth Powell; Pamela Taylor; Mandy Tunstall; Kate Urbaniak; Prof. John Usher.

Printed by UK Book Publishing, 2020
ISBN 978-1-914195-06-8
© Emeritus Professor Henry Ellington, 2020

List of contents

Biographical Notes on the Author

Henry Ellington was born in 1941 to working-class parents, being brought up in the Scottish city of Aberdeen, where he subsequently worked for virtually all his life. He was educated at Robert Gordon's College and Aberdeen University, where he graduated with first-class honours in natural philosophy (physics) in 1963, and later obtained an external Ph.D. in gaseous electronics. Henry has worked as a research scientist, school teacher (briefly), physics lecturer, and educational developer, becoming one of the world's leading figures in the latter field. Indeed, the ground-breaking work that he and his colleagues carried out at Robert Gordon's Institute of Technology (later to become The Robert Gordon University) during the 1970's, 1980's and 1990's probably made a significant contribution to the recognition of educational development as a serious academic discipline in its own right. In 1990, he became Britain's first Professor of Educational Development, and, in 1996, received the first Higher Doctorate (a D.Litt.) to be awarded by any of the 'new' (post-1992) Scottish Universities. He has received numerous other awards and honours during his long career.

Henry is a genuine 'polymath', someone who has published in many different fields, including physics, astronomy, general science, engineering, history and philosophy, as well as in his main specialist areas of educational simulation/gaming and the application of the educational-technology-based 'systems approach' to instructional design of all types. He has well over 350 publications in these different areas, including 20 books, over 150 academic papers and articles, over 80 booklets, and over 100 educational and training packages of a wide range of types. Throughout his glittering academic career, Henry pursued an equally-successful parallel career as a consultant, working for a wide range of prestigious organisations at home and abroad. These included Shell, Phillips Petroleum, the United Kingdom Atomic

Energy Authority, Unilever, the Scottish Education Department, and his own University, where he is now an Emeritus Professor.

Henry was happily married to Lindsay for 53 years, but she had to spend the last 3½ years of their married life in a nursing home, suffering from vascular dementia; sadly, she died of this in April, 2019. They have two grown-up children, Kenneth and Pamela, and four grandchildren, the eldest two of whom have now moved on to tertiary education. Henry still lives in the Aberdeen house that he and Lindsay moved into early in 1969; they never saw any reason to move again!

Henry wrote his autobiography, entitled 'Meeting Fresh Challenges', in 2017, and had this published as a high-quality 'paperback' by Quo Vadis Publications Ltd., a company that he and Vic Baxter had set up a year earlier. He also produced an 'e-book' version, and lodged this on the RGU Website, from which anyone interested in it can download a personal copy free of charge; many people have done so, and all readers are cordially invited to do the same.

Introduction

'There are more things in heaven and earth, Horatio,
Than are dreamt of in your philosophy.'

- William Shakespeare (Hamlet, Act 1, Scene 5)

As in so many cases. Shakespeare gets to the very heart of the matter, with his own unrivalled combination of penetrating insight and pellucid clarity. I have therefore chosen this famous quotation as the opening words of what will probably be my last book, since it sums up its contents far better than I ever could. Thank you, Shakespeare!

I have given considerable thought to the nature of reality since my mid-teens, when I started to reflect seriously about such matters for the first time - as do so many 'thinking people'. During the intervening 65-odd years, I have thought progressively more deeply about this key philosophical/scientific problem, which I discovered much later was the core subject of a branch of philosophy known as 'ontology'. (This is defined in the 1993 edition of the 'Chambers Dictionary' as' the science that deals with the principles of pure being: that part of metaphysics which deals with the nature and essence of things'.) For most of my adult life, I have used a different term for the study of reality - 'natural philosophy' - the name that is still used for physics at some Scottish universities, including the University of Aberdeen, where I studied the subject as an undergraduate between 1959 and 1963, and later completed an external Ph.D. in the same subject. As you will have seen from the (somewhat lengthy) subtitle of this book, I still think of myself as a 'natural philosopher' in the broadest sense of the word, and will always continue to do so; I think it is a **much** better name for a student of reality than 'ontologist', which very few people outside the field of professional philosophy understand anyway!

During my ten-year career as a professional physicist between 1963 and 1973, and my subsequent 34-year career as an educational and staff developer and consultant, I continued to take an interest in the nature of reality, and my views on what it entailed underwent several radical changes as I learned more and more about the subject and its wider ramifications. After I retired from full-time employment at RGU in the summer of 2001, I decided that I wanted to devote much more of my time to studying some of the subjects that my professional work had left me comparatively little time to read about in depth. I decided to concentrate on three of these subjects - **history** (which had always fascinated me ever since I had to drop the subject in favour of geography at Robert Gordon's College at the end of my third year of secondary education), **philosophy** (in which I had been interested since I was introduced to the work of Karl Popper in the mid-1970's), and **religious studies** (in which I had always had a peripheral interest but had never been able to study in a systematic way). Since my retirement, the sections of my 'serious' library on history, philosophy and religious studies have been the most rapidly-growing parts, although I still buy many books and other types of materials on various aspects of science and technology. The expansion of my professional educational library (which had hitherto been located in my large office at RGU) slowed down significantly after I retired, since my main interests had moved on to other areas. I also phased out my work as a paid consultant after I retired, stopping such work completely in 2007, since I had not found it possible to keep fully up to date with the rapidly-changing world of educational and staff development without practising in this area on a professional, full-time basis. (**All** consultants should retire before they get past their 'sell-by' dates, preferably before their **clients** realise that this is the case!)

From 2004 onwards, I also devoted an increasingly-large proportion of my time to voluntary work - giving talks and running seminars and workshops in schools, colleges and other organisations throughout

Scotland - mainly under the auspices of the local 'SATRO' , TechFest SetPoint (which I had helped to set up in 1984) and the Royal Society of Edinburgh. I also started giving increasing numbers of talks to local bodies such as Probus and Rotary Clubs. I had been giving talks on astronomy (one of my special interests) since the mid-1960's, when I joined the staff of the School of Physics at RGU, but now expanded my 'repertoire' considerably, offering sessions on a wide range of topics on the history, philosophy, sociology and environmental impact of science and technology, and also the on philosophy of religion and on the relationship between science and religion.

Soon, sessions that I ran on the (alleged) conflict between science and religion joined my 'flagship' astronomy lecture, 'A Guided Tour of the Universe' (which I have now given well over a hundred times) as my most widely-requested presentations. Preparing for all these different sessions, and presenting them to - and discussing them with - a wide range of audiences, greatly increased my already-growing appreciation of just how little we still know about the **real** nature of basic reality.

It was not until the almost-complete 'lockdown' of society that started in Britain in March, 2020 as a result of the 'Covid 19' pandemic that I started to think seriously about writing a book on the subject. I was now 78 years old, and was living with a wide range of chronic medical conditions (including angina, which was diagnosed soon after the start of lockdown), so it was very risky for me to leave my home. (I had been living alone there since my wife Lindsay was admitted to a nursing home suffering from vascular dementia in the autumn of 2015; she eventually died of this in April, 2019). Although I was allowed to leave my house for 'essential shopping' and to undertake my 'daily exercise', I had to be **very** careful in avoiding close contact with other people, since I knew that if I were unfortunate enough to catch the disease, it would probably kill me. I therefore decided to start work on this book almost immediately after the start of lockdown, since I realised that if I did not do so then, I might never have another chance to do so. I also realised that I was far better prepared to write such a book than I had ever been, since I had acquired an extremely wide range of knowledge of all three of the areas that it would have to cover - **science**, **philosophy** and **religion**.

My wide reading in numerous areas of history during the previous 19 years would also help me to bring a 'historical perspective' into my book, which, as readers will see, I decided would take the form of a broad review of how our ideas about the nature of reality have evolved and matured from the earliest prehistoric times to the present day. I had also been able to hone and develop my skills as a historical writer when I was commissioned to write the 'official history' of RGU immediately after I retired in the summer of 2001, and, four years later, was commissioned to write an 'update' of this by the recently-appointed new Principal. Because of this work, I could now regard myself as a paid 'professional historian', albeit a 'neophyte' in the field who still had a vast amount to learn.

I completed the overall planning of the book in roughly five weeks, and started work on the actual writing early in May 2020. I decided to devote at least six months of what remained of my life to this exciting project; this was clearly a major commitment.

I have now written, co-authored or co-edited 20 'serious' books, mostly as 'sole author' or 'main author', and, in the course of this work, have developed an extremely-effective approach to such writing - based on a systematic, 'top-down' methodology. I thought that readers might be interested in how I used this approach in writing the present book. (I wrote this completely on my own, but I sought the advice and help of several friends, relatives and colleagues at various stages; their contributions have all been fully acknowledged.) Let me therefore describe my methodology in some detail, since I feel it might be of help to readers who are thinking of writing an academic textbook or a 'serious' book for the general public - as this one is intended to be.

When planning to write a book of this type, I always begin by thinking about the **general idea** for the book - the **overall subject area**, and the **specific aspect(s)** of this that I would like it to cover. This can take some time, and generally involves a great deal of reflection and preliminary discussion with other people - preferably people who know something about the area(s) to be covered. Then, I plan the **large-scale structure** of the book - choosing the **provisional title** (which may subsequently be changed) and the **provisional chapter structure** (which may also subsequently be changed), again in consultation with other people, where appropriate. Next, I start to plan the **detailed structure** of all the different chapters, carrying out **preliminary research** on each, and, on the basis of this, deciding on the **main section headings** within each chapter (these may again subsequently need changing). This process can take some time, particularly in the case of chapters where I have to carry out a significant amount of preliminary research. Only when I have carried out this work to my **complete satisfaction** do I start work on the actual **writing** of the book. I always start with Chapter 1, and work my way systematically through the rest of the book, since I find that this makes cross-referencing between chapters very much easier. This is obviously by far the longest stage in the process. I often produce a provisional draft of the 'Introduction' while I am working my way through the different chapters, and may also make notes on the main things that I think I might want to include in the 'Conclusion' (if there is one); I usually leave the actual writing of this to the very end, however.

In writing this book, I was fortunate in having **all** the necessary source materials in my own personal library, which now contains over 4000 books and other types of materials. I buy **far** more books than I can ever possibly read, being extremely selective in those that I **do** read all the way through, but browsing the contents of all the others so that I can use them for reference purposes. I have an excellent memory, so I generally find any material to which I need to refer without too much difficulty. Such was the case when I was writing this book. Let me now outline the contents of each of the 20 chapters that it includes.

Chapter 1 of the book ('Early spiritual and religious ideas about reality') starts by outlining the origins of our species ('Homo sapiens') in East Africa, and its subsequent spread throughout the world. It then describes how spiritual and religious ideas became progressively more sophisticated during the various stages of the extremely-lengthy 'Palaeolithic Era', which ended around 7000 BCE. Next, it describes developments during the much-shorter 'Neolithic Era', which ended around 3000 BCE, and in the period that immediately preceded the advent of the so-called 'Axial Age' in around 800 BCE. It ends by examining the important role of 'myth' in all these developments.

Chapter 2 ('The 'Axial Age' of religious and intellectual development') is **the** pivotal chapter on which most of the remainder of the book is based, describing the 'giant leap forward' in the development of religious, philosophical and scientific ideas that took place throughout the civilised world between 800 and 200 BCE. It explains what the 'Axial Age' involved, and then looks in some detail at what happened in each of the four main areas of the world in which it manifested itself - West Asia, South Asia, East Asia and the Eastern Mediterranean and areas to the east of it.

The next four chapters then examine these various Axial-Age developments and what they subsequently led to in even greater detail.

Chapter 3 ('Pre-Socratic Greek philosophy and science') shows how the work of the amazing people that we now describe collectively as the 'Presocratics' effectively gave birth to the whole of western philosophy and science. It then describes the work of the most important of these, including the 'Milesian School' (Thales, Anaximander and Anaximenes), the highly-mathematical 'Pythagorean School', the pioneering work on metaphysics by Heraclitus and Parmenides, the ground-breaking work on physical science by Empedocles and the 'Atomists', and the outstanding work of Hippocrates, who effectively gave birth to modern western medicine almost single-handed.

Chapter 4 ('The 'Golden Age' of classical philosophy and science') then takes a detailed look at what the pioneering work of the Presocratics led to, beginning with the tremendous advances made in Athens by Socrates, Plato and Aristotle - three of the greatest creative thinkers who ever lived. It then reviews the work that took place in the classical world **after** Plato and Aristotle, culminating in the work of Plotinus, the most influential of the late-classical philosophers. It ends by looking at the key role played by Alexandria in the development of western philosophy and science during the 900 years after it was founded by Alexander the Great. Throughout this time, it was the 'intellectual centre of the Western world', a role that has never been equalled, let alone surpassed, ever since.

Chapter 5 ('Eastern religion and philosophy') then takes a much-more-detailed look at the four most important religions that developed in the eastern part of the civilised world during the Axial Age. It begins by examining **Hinduism**, which was the first to appear, and, although it was initially largely confined to India, is now one of the major world religions. Next, it looks at **Buddhism**, which was actually born in India during the Axial Age. It began as a 'break-away' from classical Hinduism, but soon spread to other parts of East Asia, and is again now a major world religion, although it takes several different forms. Finally, it looks at the two main Chinese religions - **Confucianism** and **Taoism**, both of which had their origins during the Axial Age.

Chapter 6 ('The three 'Religions of the Book') shows how one of the religions that matured and developed in the Eastern-Mediterranean area during the 'Axial Age' (**Judaism**) subsequently gave birth to the two most important and influential religions that developed during what eventually became known as the 'Common Era'. The first was **Christianity**, which originated in the Roman province of Palestine at the very start of the Common Era, and subsequently spread throughout the rest of the world. The second was **Islam**, which originated in what is now Saudi Arabia in the seventh century of the Common Era, and again subsequently spread throughout the world.

Chapter 7 ('The development of the 'Newtonian' world picture') moves us into the 'modern' era, describing the birth of modern western science during the 16th and 17th centuries of the Common Era, and showing how these led to the development of the so-called 'Newtonian paradigm' that dominated scientific thinking until the end of the 19th century. It deals in turn with the three overlapping series of events that brought this about - the 'Copernican Revolution' in astronomy, the invention of the modern 'scientific method' by Bacon, and the ground-breaking work of Newton himself; it is largely because of him that we came to believe that we live in a 'mathematical universe'. The chapter ends by reviewing the many subsequent achievements of 'Newtonian science'.

Chapter 8 ('The development of 'modern' western philosophy') describes the growth and evolution of philosophy that took place in parallel with the steady advance of science in the western world. It begins by describing the two radically-different approaches to philosophy that developed in Europe during the 17th and 18th centuries - Continental 'rationalism' and British 'empiricism' - and shows how these were effectively unified by the work of Kant and Schopenhauer between 1781 and 1818. It then outlines some of the most important philosophical developments that took place in the western world during the 200 years after the end of this unification - none of which have proved to be as important as what went on previously according to Bryan Magee, one of our most perceptive commentators on western philosophy.

Chapter 9 ('The 'European Enlightenment' and its aftermath') describes another of the world's most important and far-reaching intellectual and social developments - the 'European Enlightenment' that originated in Britain and France during the 17th and 18th centuries. It shows how this led directly to the 'French Revolution', to the progressive transformation of much of Europe from a religious to a secular society, and to the world-shattering 'Darwinian Revolution' in biology. It shows how the ideas developed during the 'Enlightenment' are still highly influential today, despite opposing 'dark forces' of various types, which very nearly destroyed the 'Enlightenment' project at the turn of the new millennium.

(Readers may be interested to know that work on the book was almost ended permanently while I was half way through writing Chapter 9. My angina had taken a distinct 'turn for the worse', and, after a 'telephone consultation' with one of the leading consultants in the Cardiac Unit at Aberdeen Royal Infirmary, I was immediately admitted to hospital as an 'emergency case', since he thought that I was in imminent danger of suffering a severe heart attack. Six days later, having undergone an 'angiogram' and been fitted with two 'stents', I returned home completely cured, went back to my desk, and completed the chapter as if nothing had happened.)

Chapter 10 ('Dualism and the 'mind-body problem') looks in detail at one of the key problems that dominated western philosophy and science during the last 400 years - the question of whether the human body and the human mind are radically different types of ontological entity, or whether the latter is simply an 'emergent feature' of the human brain. It shows how early thinking on the matter led to the pivotal work of Descartes on what became known as 'Cartesian dualism', and how this concept was subsequently challenged by the development of the modern 'neurophysiological model' of the brain-mind system. It describes some of the problems that this model gives rise to, and asks if we are now any nearer to (dis)solving the mind-body problem than we were in the time of Descartes. I suspect that we may be, but not in the way that most scientists expect.

Chapter 11 ('The 'Einsteinian Revolution' and its aftermath') describes how virtually the whole of the previously-dominant 'Newtonian' world picture was systematically demolished by the totally-unexpected advances in physics and astronomy that began at the start of the 20th century. This was probably **the** most far-reaching and wide-ranging scientific revolution that has ever taken place, and has dominated the development of physical science ever since, eventually leading to the modern 'information age'. We are still living in the aftermath of this cataclysmic 'paradigm shift'.

Chapter 12 ('The development of modern cosmology') shows how our understanding of the true scale and complexity of the universe in which we live has increased steadily during the last 400 years. It then looks in turn at the systematic study of our own Galaxy and its contents, at the investigation of the Extra-Galactic Universe, and at the development of the 'Big-Bang' theory of the origin and subsequent evolution of the Universe. It ends by identifying some of the key questions about cosmology that have still to be resolved.

Chapter 13 ('Exploring the microscopic world') shows how our understanding of the 'very small' has undergone similar tremendous developments during the last 400 years. It looks in detail at the use of the microscope in biology, at the discovery of the atom and the study of its structure, at the discovery and subsequent explanation of the 'particle zoo', at the development of the highly-successful 'standard model' of particle physics, and at the current search for 'new physics' beyond the standard model.

Chapter 14 ('The 'weirdness of the quantum world") takes a detailed look at what is by far the most successful theory that physicists have produced to date - **quantum theory**. It describes how the theory has evolved and developed during the last 120 years, and examines some of its many counter-intuitive features - the apparently 'random nature' of the quantum world, the 'principle of superposition' of quantum states, the apparent impossibility of finding the 'true nature' of quantum systems, and the evidence it provides for the 'intrinsic interconnectedness' of the Universe. It ends by discussing some of the different 'interpretations' of quantum theory, which physicists have been arguing about since the 1920's.

Chapter 15 ('The search for a 'theory of everything") follows on from Chapter 13 by looking at how physicists and mathematicians have spent the last 100 years or so trying to find a theory that explains **all** known physical phenomena - what they call a 'theory of everything'. It describes the various unsuccessful attempts to develop such a theory that have been made so far, and examines some of the reasons why we may **never** be able to develop such a theory; I am not hopeful that we ever will.

The next two chapters of my book examine two fundamental questions that have puzzled scientists and philosophers during the last 50 or 60 years - 'why is the Universe so ideally suited for the development of life?', and 'why does mathematics appear to give such an accurate description of the physical world?'

Chapter 16 ('The 'biofriendliness' of the Universe') deals with the first of these questions. It starts its investigation by examining the so-called 'anthropic cosmological principle', and shows how the 'weak' version of this can be used to specify, in some detail, some of the key features that a universe **must** have if it is to be capable of supporting the development of life. It then goes to examine some of the attempts that have been made to explain this apparent 'biofriendliness', none of which have proved to be completely plausible in the opinion of most reflective commentators - myself included.

Chapter 17 ('The 'unreasonable effectiveness' of mathematics') deals with the second of these questions. It begins by examining the 'mysterious power of mathematics' in general terms, and goes on to describe in some detail seven specific examples of this 'unreasonable effectiveness' over the last 450 years or so. It then examines some of the possible explanations of the mysterious power of mathematics, including the recent suggestion that this may be more apparent than real, since mathematics is in fact severely limited in its range of application within the scientific world - particularly in biology and in the 'social sciences'.

The final three chapters of the book deal with three largely-unrelated topics that all have a bearing on our on-going quest to discover and explain the true nature of reality.

Chapter 18, ('The spread of 'new-age thinking' and related activities') shows how many of the key beliefs that had hitherto underpinned western society were seriously challenged by developments that began during the 1960's. The first was the appearance of 'hippie culture', and the increased use of mind-altering drugs. The second was the explosive spread of Eastern meditation techniques such as 'transcendental meditation' (TM). The third was an increasing realisation that 'spiritual' and 'scientific' world pictures had much more in common than had previously been believed. The fourth was an increased interest in the 'paranormal'.

Chapter 19 ('A broad look at atheism') follows on from Chapter 9 by looking at how one of the consequences of the European Enlightenment (the decline of religious belief) led to the rise of atheism. It explains exactly what we mean by the terms 'atheism' and 'atheist', and describes the different forms that atheism has taken to date. It then describes the 'hard atheist' movement that developed during the mid-'noughties', and the inevitable 'backlash' that this provoked. I end by explaining why I now describe myself as a 'pagan'.

Chapter 20 ('Information-based pictures of reality') describes the progressive move from a 'matter-based' picture of reality to a more 'information-based' model that has taken place during the past hundred years. It then explains what we **mean** by the term 'information', before examining the various ways in which 'information' is currently assuming much greater importance in physics, biology, philosophy and theology. It ends by asking whether we live in an information-based 'holographic Universe', as has recently been suggested by some workers in the field.

The final major element of my book on the nature of reality is the 'Conclusion'. In this, I try to review what we have learned so far about the **possible** nature of reality (a great deal, as you will have seen once you have worked your way through Chapters 1-20), and what we **actually know** with **any degree of certainty** about the **ultimate underlying nature** of such reality (not a lot). I then offer some of my **personal views** of where the study of reality **might** lead in future. I will not try to summarise my ideas on these matters here; you will have to read the 'Conclusion' to find out!

When I started to plan this book, it was my intention to include a highly-detailed 'Bibliography' section at the very end. I subsequently decided that this would make the book too much like an academic textbook of the type that I and my colleagues have written on academic gaming and simulation and on the educational-technology-based 'systems approach' to instructional design (we have written 12 of these). I have therefore decided to provide much shorter, more informal 'mini-bibliographies' at the end of each chapter, listing the key books and course packages that informed my writing of these. I hope that readers will find these much more helpful and 'user-friendly' than a conventional academic bibliography located at the end of the book. Very few of you would probably read this anyway!

Readers will find that several of these 'mini-bibliographies' include references to some of the 'Great Courses' produced and marketed by 'The Teaching Company' - an American-based organisation whose courses are now used, enjoyed and admired all over the world. I first learned about them over 15 years ago, through an (unsolicited) mail shot. I was so impressed by what they were doing that I immediately ordered a few of their courses to see what they were like - all ones that were being offered at a large discount to new subscribers. I have been buying courses regularly from them ever since - all at the highly-attractive discount prices that they offer during their frequent 'sales' (I am, after all, a true Aberdonian!) At the time of writing this (May, 2020) I have purchased 112 of their excellent courses, covering a wide range of topics in science and technology, history, philosophy, religious studies and the arts. I wholeheartedly commend their 'Great Courses' to all thinking people who wish to expand their knowledge base in an enjoyable way.

Another personal innovation that I have made use of in this book is the inclusion of what I hope is a relevant quotation at the very start of each major section - the 'Introduction', the 20 individual chapters, and the 'Conclusion'. I have read several books where this was done, and always liked the idea. I have, however, extended the basic idea of the use of such quotations by including personal comments on each one, immediately after the quotation itself. I hope that readers will find these interesting and useful, and, in a few cases, amusing. As you will see, my chosen quotations are drawn from an extremely wide range of sources, ranging from Shakespeare to Douglas Adams. There is even one in French - by one of my very 'favourite people', Voltaire; I have a bust of him in my living room.

Finally, let me say a few words about the various dates that are included in this book. Some of these, particularly the ones relating to the modern world, are known with complete certainty - or at least with a high degree of accuracy. Others, particularly those relating to the 'prehistorical world' or the eras that followed soon after it, are not. Indeed, when studying the sources from which I obtained information about these early times, I often found that there was considerable disagreement between them. I therefore had to use my historical and scientific experience to decide which of my sources were likely to be most reliable. No doubt I have got many of these personal judgements wrong, in which case I rely on better-informed readers to point such errors out to me - as I hope readers will also do in respect of other errors in my book. As someone who has always tried to be a good 'Popperian' since discovering his ideas in the mid-70's, I welcome, and take full note of, all valid criticisms of my work.

Chapter 1: Early spiritual and religious ideas about reality

'As flies to wanton boys, are we to the gods;
They kill us for their sport'

- William Shakespeare (King Lear, Act 4, Scene one)

Most educated people in the western world are familiar with at least some aspects of early Greek mythology, and with the way in which the gods who they believed lived on Mount Olympus controlled and manipulated the lives of human beings. These myths were brilliantly portrayed in the highly-popular 1981 film 'Clash of the Titans', which was probably many people's first introduction to Greek mythology. We now know that the origins of spiritual and religious ideas go much further back than the ancient Greeks, however,- right back to the very start of human prehistory in fact. In this opening chapter of my personal survey of how our ideas on the nature of reality have evolved, I will review these early developments , which were followed by the world-wide explosion of novel religious, philosophical and scientific ideas that took place in the 'Axial Age' that began around 800 BCE. These will be discussed in detail in the next chapter, and will be examined in even greater detail in Chapters 3 - 6.

The origins of 'Homo sapiens', and its spread throughout the world

The biological 'species' to which we belong (**Homo sapiens**) is one member of the 'genus' **Homo**, which is part of the 'family' of **Hominids** which is itself part of the 'order' of **Primates**, which is, in turn, part of the 'class' of **Mammals** - and so on up through the highly-complicated classification system of living things that was first introduced during the 18th century by the Swedish botanist Carolus Linnaeus. According to this system, every distinct species is assigned a double-barrelled name that identifies both its **genus** (with a capital initial letter) and the specific **species** name that it has been assigned within that genus - hence that name **Homo sapiens** for our own species. (I hope I have got all this right!)

We humans were in fact a **very** late arrival on the evolutionary scene, starting to develop into a distinct species roughly 13 million years ago. Our closest-living relatives among the primates were the chimpanzees, with which we probably continued to interbreed until roughly 7 million years ago. We now know that the subsequent evolution of what became known as the 'hominid' branch of the primates took place in the Great Rift Valley in East Africa, where all the early hominid fossils have been found. This is now generally recognised as the place where modern human beings had their origins, and from which they subsequently spread throughout the rest of the world. The very first hominid fossil to be found in this area was that of 'Ardipithecus ramidus', which lived roughly 4.4 million years ago in forests surrounding the Awash River Valley in what is now Ethiopia. Around 4 million years ago, the first members of the hominid genus 'Australopithecus' (the 'southern ape') appeared in the same area, the prize fossil find being the remarkably-complete skeleton of a female of the species 'Australopithecus afarensis', which came to be known as 'Lucy' (named after the Beatles' song 'Lucy in the Sky with Diamonds', which was apparently played 'very loudly' in the excavation camp after her discovery in 1974).

By around 2 million years ago, all the hominid species of the 'Australopithecus' genus had become extinct, and our own genus, 'Homo', had emerged from them. 'Homo habilis' ('handy-man') was the first, followed by 'Homo erectus' ('erect man') which was probably the first hominid to live as a hunter-gatherer and to control fire - not just for warmth, but possibly also for cooking. By 18 million years ago, Homo erectus had spread throughout Africa, and then become the first hominid to leave Africa and spread throughout Europe and Asia, probably in several independent waves of migration. Homo erectus persisted as a species for around 2 million years, and, roughly 800,000 years ago, gave rise to 'Homo Heidelbergensis', which by roughly 250,000 years ago, had developed into 'Neanderthal Man' in Europe, and 'Denisovan Man' in Asia. The first anatomically modern human, 'Homo sapiens', ('wise man') is believed to have emerged in East Africa between 300,000 and 200,000 years ago, and gradually become the dominant species of 'Homo', with the 'Neanderthals' and the 'Denisovans' eventually becoming extinct, leaving 'Homo sapiens' to become the undisputed rulers of the world.

It is now thought that our 'Homo sapiens' ancestors began to move out of Africa roughly 60,000 years ago, in the middle of the last Ice Age, which ended roughly 10,000 years ago. As we have seen, one of the earlier species from which we eventually developed ('Homo erectus') had spread out of Africa into Europe and Asia very much earlier, giving rise to ' Homo heidelbergensis' which, in turn, evolved into 'Neanderthal Man' and 'Denisovan Man'. It is difficult to know which routes we took around the planet, or the precise times at when we reached new areas, because the fossil record is 'very patchy' (to say the least), and it is often hard to tell from archaeological evidence exactly which branch of the hominids they were left behind by. Because of this, most of what we **do** know about humanity's expansion comes from studying the genetics of indigenous populations living in different parts of the world **today**. By analysing their DNA, particularly their 'mitochondrial DNA', and being able estimate the rate at which mutations accumulate in the genetic code, we have now been able to develop a broad picture of when humans first arrived in different regions, and thus work out roughly what paths they took in order to get there when they did.

To the best of our current knowledge, our 'Homo sapiens' ancestors probably first moved out of East Africa in a single migration event involving no more than a few thousand individuals. It is thought that this started by moving directly northwards, but subsequently moved along two different routes into the Arabian Peninsula - either by walking across the Sinai Peninsula to the north of the Red Sea or by crossing the Bab-el-Mandeb strait at the southern end of the Red Sea. Those taking the northern route seem to have followed three different paths after reaching Syria, one turning left, crossing Turkey, and then moving into Western Europe across the narrow straits at the Eastern end of the Black sea. They are believed to have reached its western extremities roughly 45,000 years ago. Their second migration path took them south of the Caspian sea, after which they again took two separate paths, one moving north into what is now Russia, and the other ending up in India.

The southern migration route into the south of the Arabian Peninsula eventually took the migrants **very** much further. After crossing the plains of Northern India between 50,000 and 45,000 years ago, they again moved in two different directions. The first took them south, through the East Indies, eventually reaching Australia roughly 40,000 years ago. The second took them north-east, through the eastern part of Asia, eventually reaching what was then the Bering Land Bridge into Alaska, and hence moving into all parts of North and South America. They reached Canada roughly 20,000 years ago, spreading throughout what is now the USA afterwards. They crossed the Isthmus of Panama into South America roughly 12,500 years ago, and subsequently spread throughout the entire continent, reaching its southern tip roughly 11,000 years ago. By now, humanity had spread throughout the entire world.

As a result of all these successive migrations, which were completed in a period of roughly 50,000 years, 'Homo sapiens' not only reached all parts of the world apart from Antarctica and a number of remote islands; they also 'inherited the earth'. As we have seen, our 'cousin' hominid species, the 'Neanderthals' and the 'Denisovans', eventually 'slid into extinction'. It seems likely that they were simply outcompeted by humans rather than hunted or killed, or else succumbed to the extremely harsh conditions as the last Ice Age reached its peak. Our mastery of fire, combined with our skill in making clothes and using tools and weapons, had enabled us to inhabit every climate zone from the tropics to the tundra. We moved out of the environment that made us (East Africa), and learned how to create our own 'artificial environments' of farms, villages and cities. It may seem surprising that all this took place during the ferociously-cold climate of the last Ice Age, but it was actually these very 'icehouse' conditions that enabled us to complete our progressive spread throughout the world. The growth of the northern ice sheets drew so much water out of the world's oceans and seas that the dropping sea levels exposed large areas of continental shelves, creating 'land bridges' that enabled us to **walk** between the continents, Without these, we would probably have taken very much longer to reach all parts of the East Indies, cross the narrow sea to Australia, and, most important of all, make our way across the Bering Land Bridge into North and South America. We would almost certainly have reached all these places eventually, but the development of human civilization would probably have been very different.

Early developments during the 'Palaeolithic Era' (before 7000 BCE)

The extremely-lengthy period of pre-historic development that preceded the invention of written languages (and the production of the first written historical records) in the 'pre-Axial' period that began roughly 5000 years ago is divided into two distinct 'eras' - the 'Palaeolithic Era' ('Old Stone Age') and the much-shorter 'Neolithic Era' ('New Stone Age'). The Palaeolithic Era is itself generally divided into three successive parts - 'Lower', 'Middle' and 'Upper'. The 'Lower Palaeolithic' probably started roughly 2.5 million years ago, when the first primitive stone tools of the so-called 'Oldowan' type were produced by Homo habilis in East Africa. More advanced 'Acheulian' hand axes started to be produced by Homo erectus roughly 1.5 million years ago. The 'Middle Palaeolithic' is thought to have begun roughly 150,000 to 125,000 years ago. During this period, a much wider range of hand tools than those of the 'Lower Palaeolithic' were produced by Neanderthal people and their contemporaries. The 'Upper Palaeolithic' in Europe is associated with the appearance of the first fully-modern human beings roughly 50,000 to 30,000 years ago. These developed more-advanced stone working techniques that enabled them to produce long, narrow blades struck from a stone core. During the entire Palaeolithic Era, human beings and their hominid predecessors lived in small, tribal bands and communities of the 'hunter-gatherer' type. They only started to move away from this way of life during the Neolithic Era, as we will see in the next section of this chapter.

We know very little about how early man started to develop spiritual and religious ideas, but we believe that this must have happened fairly early on in the Palaeolithic Era. Exactly **when** it happened is extremely difficult to tell, since the only **direct** sources of evidence of how the various species of hominids that eventually evolved into Homo sapiens lived are the few surviving physical remains of these people, together with examples of the artifacts that they produced - mainly stone tools and weapons used in hunting. There is also quite a lot of **indirect** evidence about how early hominids and humans lived, however. This has been produced by anthropologists who have studied the few surviving examples of societies that, until comparatively recently, were physically and culturally isolated from the rest of the world – e.g., the Australian aboriginals, and a number of communities in Africa and South America. Anthropologists assume that such isolated, non-agricultural tribal societies resemble similar prehistoric societies in many ways. Opportunities to study such societies are rapidly disappearing, however, as the few remaining ones are progressively 'civilised' through contact with the outside world. They may soon disappear completely.

Our very earliest direct evidence of the development of spiritual ideas comes from the study of the burial practices in early prehistoric societies, which seem to indicate some belief in life after death. Many bodies were buried along with the implements and other objects associated with everyday life, and some were covered by a stone slab, indicating the 'awe' in which the dead seem to have been held. Since these very early societies were all 'hunter-gatherers' who relied heavily on hunting wild animals to obtain their food, there is also a great deal of evidence of the importance that they attached to this activity - mainly in the form of the beautiful 'cave paintings' that we have discovered in different parts of France, Spain and North Africa. These indicate the great respect that such societies clearly felt for the animals they hunted, and may also have been produced to help them achieve success in their hunts. There is also evidence that early societies placed great importance on the need to maintain harmony between humanity and the forces of nature, e.g. by appeasing the various spirits that they believed controlled their world through sacrifices of various sorts.

Some of the earliest evidence for religious behaviour in prehistoric human societies comes from the study of the 'Neanderthals', about whom we have learned a great deal since their first fossils were discovered in the Neander Valley in Germany in 1856. These lived in Europe, the Near East and Central Asia from about 130,000 to 30,000 years ago, and, during this time, probably interbred with humans. The Neanderthals buried their dead very carefully, providing them with food and implements of various types. They also removed the brains from the skulls of their dead, suggesting that they practised cannibalism, possibly in order to acquire the skills and virtues of the deceased (the first evidence of 'ancestor worship'?). Remains of early human beings from the 'Upper Palaeolithic' indicate that they had religious practices very similar to those of the Neanderthals. During this era, their dead were also buried with great care, usually with the feet pulled up into a 'contracted position', and the body was typically buried under a stone slab, along with ornaments, stone tools, weapons and food. Such burials were often made within the cave in which the group lived, or in another cave nearby; they clearly wished to remain close to their dead.

During the Upper Palaeolithic, the way in which human beings lived and expressed themselves changed in many other ways. In addition to producing cave paintings, some of which are thought to date back 15,000 - 20,000 years, they started producing moulded clay figures and carvings on antlers. The former included exaggerated female figurines, probably associated with fertility rites. It was probably during this era that the cult of the 'Earth Mother' started to develop in human societies. Their religious practices were also increasingly intended to maintain 'harmony' between disparate parties - human and spiritual; living and dead. They also became increasingly concerned with the way people live, and with the social rules and conventions that governed human behaviour. Practically all of our subsequent religions would do the same to a greater or lesser extent.

Developments during the 'Neolithic Era' (7000 - 3000 BCE)

The second era of the prehistoric 'Stone Age' (the 'Neolithic Era') began roughly 9000 years ago, after the great northern ice sheets had fully retreated following the end of the last 'Ice Age' roughly 1000 years earlier. During this era, people still relied almost entirely on **stone** to produce their tools, implements and weapons, although they started to make some early attempts to use **metals** - mainly copper, which they found in pure ingot form in a few places. The stone technology during this era became progressively more advanced and sophisticated, with polished stone axes coming into widespread use. These were increasingly used by early farmers in Asia and Europe to clear the forests, and thus create room for the fields, once they started to evolve from pure hunter-gatherer communities into agricultural communities that grew their own crops rather than relying on what nature provided. They also became increasingly dependent on domesticated animals such as goats, sheep, cattle and, in due course, horses.

It was the invention of 'agriculture' after it became warm enough for this to be carried out effectively that truly characterised the Neolithic Era. In the opinion of nearly all anthropologists and historians, this was by far **the** most important development in the whole of human history, since it changed our way of life completely. Before the development of agriculture, the entire world population probably amounted to roughly 10 million people at the very most, and **all** of these lived as hunter-gatherers. All this started to change with the increasingly-widespread use of agriculture throughout the Neolithic Era. This greatly increased the number of people that a given area of the world could support, and led to massive surges in the population in all the parts of the world where it was adopted. It also allowed these populations to settle down permanently in a particular area rather than moving round in a 'nomadic' manner, as had largely been the case previously. As we will see in the next section of this chapter, this eventually led to the appearance of large, independent cities, supported by the agriculture in the areas surrounding them ('city states'), and to the subsequent appearance of 'nation states' and 'empires' of one form or another.

Some of the other significant changes that took place during the Neolithic Era included the invention of the wheel (one of the most important technological developments of this or any other age), and the development of a wide range of skills not directly related to the acquisition or production of food. These included the rapid development of activities such as weaving, sewing and the making and use of pottery, although the latter was a comparatively late arrival in many places, eg in Jericho, one of the earliest cities to be founded in Palestine.

Religious beliefs and practices also underwent significant changes during the Neolithic Era, being increasingly concerned with the fertility of the soil and the growth of the crops on which communities were becoming almost totally reliant, and with the fertility and breeding of the rapidly-increasing numbers of domestic animals that now lived alongside them. The fertility of the earth was now being represented by figures of the 'Mother-Goddess', which became one of their main objects of worship. Aspects of the natural world such as the Sun, Moon, animals and trees also became objects of worship, often represented in religious art. Objects important in daily life, such as axes and spears, were also venerated for their spiritual power as 'fetishes'.

Neolithic religion also appears to have been strongly focussed on the relationship between human beings and spiritual beings of one form or another, but also recognized the spiritual power thought to be possessed both by live human beings and by the dead. Most Neolithic people strongly believed that life was 'meaningful', and was lived in close relationship both with other human beings and with the various divine beings which different groups of them worshipped. They also widely believed that death was simply a 'rite of passage', involving movement from one form of life to another. Because of this belief, they still looked on death as a cause for sadness for those involved, but accepted it as part of a 'natural cycle'. And funeral practices became more and more elaborate, placing increasing emphasis on the preparation, proper adornment and subsequent treatment of the body. These practices later reached a peak of importance in ancient Egypt, during the height of its power and influence between 3000 and 300 BCE, as we will see in the next section of this chapter.

Subsequent developments prior to the 'Axial Age' (3000 to 800 BCE)

It is generally agreed that the Neolithic Era gradually came to a close roughly 5000 years ago - around 3000 BCE. Around this time, human societies began to move away from an almost total reliance on **stone** to make their tools and weapons, and made a tentative start to the use of **metals** for these purposes. This took a very long time, since people had no idea of how to extract metals from the ores in which they were found, or how to process and work with them after they had been extracted. They had been using **gold**, which was sometimes found in pure metallic form, for a long time, mainly to manufacture jewellery and ornaments of various types. The only other metal which was sometimes found in pure metallic form was **copper,** which they began to hammer and work roughly 9000 years ago, using it to manufacture a wide range of ornaments, vessels and tools. The only problem was that copper was very soft, and could not retain a sharp 'edge', so was therefore not very suitable for the manufacture of tools and weapons. It also took a long time for people to develop effective processes for extracting copper and other metals from their ores, something that started to be achieved in Persia and Afghanistan around 7000 years ago, in about 5000 BCE.

The real breakthrough came when people discovered that they could convert copper into a **very** much harder metal called **bronze** by alloying it with an even-softer metal - **tin**, which (most conveniently) was often found in close proximity to copper ores. These developments eventually ushered in what became known as the 'Bronze Age'. This began in the Middle East in around 3,800 BCE, where it totally transformed the way things were made and wars were fought. Use of bronze then gradually spread eastwards, eventually reaching China. Here, bronze-age technology reached its highest level at the start of the 'Shang' Dynasty, shortly before 1500 BCE or thereabout. This high period of bronze-age culture was also the start of Chinese civilisation as we think of it today. After around 2500 BCE, people started to make use of **iron** for the manufacture of tools and weapons, eventually ushering in the 'Iron Age', which we believe was initiated by the Hitties near the Black Sea around 1500 BCE. The use of bronze for weapons continued for a long time in many parts of the world, however; it was the use of such weapons that enabled the Greeks to defeat the Persians in the key battles fought around the start of the 6th century BCE, for example. Had the Greeks **lost** these battles, the world would be a **very** different place today.

Modern civilisation in the 'western' part of the world started in the so-called 'fertile crescent'. This stretched from the lower part of the Nile Valley in Egypt, through the areas beyond the east coast of the Mediterranean Sea, and all the way down the valleys of the Tigris and Euphrates Rivers from Assyria in the North, though Mesopotamia, to the northern shores of the Persian Gulf. Two specific parts of the Fertile Crescent played particularly important roles in this development - **Egypt** and **Mesopotamia**. Let us therefore take a detailed look at what happened in each of these.

Egyptian civilisation began as a series of Neolithic agricultural settlements along the lower part of the River Nile, whose regular annual floods in late summer deposited highly-fertile soil along its banks and in its extensive delta. These settlements were gradually brought together as two distinct 'kingdoms' - the 'Delta' kingdom ('Upper Egypt') and 'Thebes' ('Lower Egypt'); these eventually merged to form the 'United Kingdom of Upper and Lower Egypt' in around 3050 BCE. This lasted for roughly 2700 years, before it was conquered by Alexander the Great in 332 BCE and effectively became a 'Greek colony'. During this time, it went through various stages of development, but remained remarkably stable throughout these despite occasional 'hiccups'. Following the 'Archaic Period' in the three centuries immediately following the final unification, the 'Old Kingdom' began in around 2700 BCE and ended in around 2200 BCE. This was the great age of pyramid building. It was followed by the 'First Intermediate Period', marked by internal dissent, civil war, and the temporary breaking up of the kingdom. This was reunited in around 2050 BCE, forming the 'Middle Kingdom', which lasted till around 1750 BCE, and was the 'golden age' of Egyptian art and craftsmanship. The 'Second Intermediate Period' followed it, ending in around 1550 BCE with the establishment of the 'New Kingdom'. This lasted until roughly 1050 BCE, and saw a great expansion of Egyptian power and influence, with Egyptian civilization reaching its zenith under Pharaoh Amenhotep III. It was during the early part of the 'New Kingdom' that the spectacular Temples of Karnak and Luxor were built, and a 'new religion' based on worship of the sun was founded by Akhenaten, arguably their greatest-ever Pharaoh. (This 'new religion' did not long survive his death, however.) The end of the New Kingdom was followed by the 'Third Intermediate Period' (1050-650 BCE) and the 'Late Period' (650-332 BCE). Following the death of Alexander the Great in 323 BCE, his vast empire was divided up among his senior generals, with one of these, Ptolemy, being appointed 'Satrap of Egypt'. He proclaimed himself 'King' in 304 BCE, and established the 'Ptolemaic Dynasty', which ruled Egypt until it was conquered by the Romans in 30 BCE. It then became a 'Roman Province', effectively becoming the 'bread-basket' of the rapidly-growing Roman Empire.

So much for the basic history of ancient Egypt. Let us now look at how its religion developed during the 3000-odd years when it was an independent kingdom of one form or another.

In the very early, pre-unification years, each 'nome' (or small regional unit) had its own god or gods, usually identified with different animals, but once the 'nomes' were united into a single kingdom, religion became progressively more unified and centralized, although there were still significant regional variations. Egyptian religion also became progressively more 'Institutionalised', requiring more and more professional priests, administrators and support staff to keep it running smoothly and efficiently, It also became progressively more expensive, with vast civic projects such as the building of pyramids, tombs and temples eating up more and more of the country's considerable national wealth.

Basically, Egyptian religion was founded on two key principles- dependence on the annual floods of the Nile to sustain its vast agricultural output, and dependence on the power of its 'divine kings' - the 'Pharaohs'. Its 'gods' were thought of primarily in 'anthropomorphic' terms, carrying out 'human functions', and also having 'human weakness'. There were also two conflicting 'stories' in Egyptian religious culture - one about life under 'divine control', and one about life constantly threatened by 'chaos'. Being a highly hierarchical and well-ordered society, they lived in constant dread of the latter. Such dichotomies reflected the ancient Egyptian way of understanding the 'created world'; they saw these as the expression of the 'temporal' in the 'eternal', and the 'eternal' in the 'temporal'.

Like their Neolithic predecessors, the ancient Egyptians also believed firmly in an 'afterlife', and showed more concern for this than any other civilisation before or since. It was for this reason that they devoted very large proportions of their 'national wealth' and the efforts of their labour force on building elaborate tombs, including the vast 'pyramids' erected during the 'Old Kingdom'. These are some of the most impressive structures ever built by man, and are still held in awe and wonder today. It is doubtful that any of **our** structures will last anything like as long! They also built magnificent 'temples', in which their gods were worshipped. They were truly an amazing and highly-impressive people, and we should all be very proud of them and of what they achieved.

Historical studies suggest that there were two essentially-different 'faces' to religious practice in ancient Egypt - the face of the 'official religious culture', centred in the temple and the tomb, and the face of 'popular religion', which sought the 'intercession of the gods' through prayers and votive offerings. Both 'faces' represented the 'spirit of Egyptian religion' as it was experienced by its devotees. Similar dichotomies were found in the religious practices of many subsequent civilisations.

Mesopotamia is the 'land between the rivers' Tigris and Euphrates, roughly equivalent to modern Iraq. It lies in the eastern part of the 'Fertile Crescent', and it was subject to frequent invasions and ethnic migrations. The climate is semi-arid, so that the land had to be continuously irrigated in order to remain agriculturally productive, the waters of its two main rivers being used for this purpose. Along with ancient Egypt, Mesopotamia is regarded as one of the two key 'cradles' of western civilisation, because of the many ancient civilisations that arose there following the invention and spread of agriculture during the Neolithic Era. By the end of the fourth millennium BCE, a number of 'city-states' had been established by the Sumerians in the south, where agriculture, industry and trade flourished. The first Mesopotamian empire was centred on **Akkad** in around 2350 BCE, and lasted for roughly 150 years. The second was founded in **Ur** in around 2150 BCE, and again lasted for roughly 150 years. The region then came under the increasing influence of Amorites from Canaan, a new empire based in **Babylon** being established in 1894 BCE. Northern Mesopotamia had by this time been occupied by the Assyrians, who eventually created a great empire that extended as far as Egypt; this lasted from 744 BCE to 609 BCE, when it was defeated by the Babylonians, who also established an empire extending to the Mediterranean. During the latter part of the 6th century BCE, the Persians started to build what eventually became the first genuine 'world empire', occupying much of South-West Asia, and making successive failed attempts to spread into Europe, through Greece, early in the 5th-century BCE.

The various civilisations that flourished in Mesopotamia between 3000 BCE and their conquest by the Persians towards the end of the 6th-century BCE made many notable contributions to the development of the modern world. Along with ancient Egypt, they were the first to develop written languages, thus allowing them to produce detailed records of their activities, including financial and other economic activities, and, eventually, accurate accounts of historical events. One of the most prominent and long-lasting of their city-states, Babylon, was also the first to produce a written system of law - the 'Code of Hammurabi', which was developed during the 18th-century BCE. Babylon was also the first civilisation to produce written 'creation stories' such as the 'Enuma Elish', and written 'epic poems' such as the 'Epic of Gilgamesh'. They also made significant contributions to the development of religion, as I will now show.

The religious systems and beliefs that developed in the various civilisations that succeeded one another in Mesopotamia following the end of the Neolithic Era were in some ways very similar to those that developed in ancient Egypt during the same period, but were in other ways very different. Both were 'polythestic', in that a large number of different gods, responsible for different aspects of the created world, and different aspects of human behaviour, were worshipped by different groups of people. 'Polytheism' only started to be replaced by 'henotheism' (in which the existence of a large number of gods was recognised, but only one was worshipped by a particular group), and by 'monotheism' (which maintained that there was only one 'true' god, and that no others existed) much later. Indeed, 'monotheism' really only 'took off' during the 'Axial Age'. Within these polytheistic systems, both Egypt and Mesopotamia came to recognise large 'pantheons' of gods- **extremely** large in the case of Mesopotamian religions (the earliest list of such gods, produced around 2600 BCE, listed no fewer than **560 gods** by their Sumerian names!) The main differences between the religions of these two cultures were numerous and profound, however, covering basic 'theological' disagreements, different interpretations of the nature of reality and of man's relationship to this, and very different ways in which they worshipped their respective gods. One of the most fundamental of these was their very different views on the nature of the afterlife. As we have seen, the ancient Egyptians took a very 'optimistic' view of this, believing that death was simply a natural move from one 'form of life' to another, and was nothing for people to fear. The Mesopotamians, on the other hand, believed that the 'Underworld' to which **everyone** moved (whether they were good or evil) after death was a much more unpleasant place, They believed that this underworld was located 'somewhere beneath the earth's surface', and that the 'dead' lived on there in a shadowy, semi-conscious state. (This view of the underworld clearly influenced later Greek ideas on the nature of the 'underworld', as reflected in their religion and mythology.)

Their actual **practice** of religion was also very different from that of the ancient Egyptians. Here, the most important religious building was the **Ziggurat,** a massive, multi-layered, 'Pyramid-like' structure intended to represent the 'sacred mountain', and to be a physical manifestation of the intersection of 'heaven' and 'earth'. At the pinnacle, and on terraces built all the way up, were temples dedicated to various gods, and, in some cases, a site for the annual ritual of 'sacred marriage' between the 'king' and one of the leading 'priestesses' (clearly one of the 'perks' of being a King in Mesopotamian society!) The two cultures also had significant differences in their understanding of the nature of the 'sacred', but these are too complex to go into here. (Interested readers can find details in my main reference source cited at the end of the chapter).

The role of 'myth' in all these developments

From the earliest prehistoric times, during which human beings and their hominid predecessors developed spoken languages and began to **talk** to one another rather than communicating through 'grunts' and other forms of non-verbal signalling, **myths** of one form or another have become increasingly important in the development of society, and, in particular, in the development of our ideas regarding the nature of reality and our relationship with this. As far as we know, such myths have appeared in **all** human societies, in **all** parts of the world, and continue to play a key role today. Most of them fall into one of four main categories - 'creation' myths of one form or another, myths about 'gods and goddesses', myths about 'heroes', and myths about 'tricksters'. In this final section of Chapter 1, I will concentrate on the first two of these categories, since these are the ones most closely related to our study of reality. (Readers interested in the other two categories can find detailed information about these in the 'Teaching Company' course on 'Myth in Human History' cited at the end of the chapter.)

Myths are narratives that ask 'big questions' about human existence - 'How did the universe come to be?' ; 'Who are we?' ; 'How should we behave?'; 'What are the forces that are larger than we are, and, in many ways, regulate our lives?'. Myths are not the only human constructions that deal with these questions, and there is considerable overlap between myth and religion, myth and philosophy, myth and science, and myth and history - all important subjects that play key roles in this book. In many ways, myths embody the 'wisdom of the lived experience of all our ancestors', but contain 'truth' of a different order from that of other human constructs.

I could easily devote all the rest of this book to a detailed discussion of myths and their role in the investigation of the nature of reality, but, as you will have seen from the 'List of contents' and the 'Introduction', I have a great deal of other material to cover. I will therefore restrict myself to a few broad remarks about 'creation' myths and myths about 'gods and goddesses', as I indicated in the first paragraph of this final section of Chapter 1. I hope that these whet your appetite for more detailed study of the topic later.

First, **creation myths,** the technical name for which is **cosmogony** (which derives from two Greek words meaning 'order' and 'beginning'). In many of these myths, a god or gods act upon pre-existing chaos of some sort, imposing order on this. Paradigm examples are the Babylonian 'Enuma Elish', which most biblical historians believe to be the inspiration for the description of the creation of the world given at the start of the book of 'Genesis' in the 'Old Testament' of the Bible. (Both accounts are also superb literature.) Cosmogonies are sometimes divided into five different types. The first is creation 'ex nihilo', in which a deity literally creates the cosmos 'out of nothing', by an act of divine 'fiat'. The second involves so-called 'earth diver' stories, in which a deity sends an animal or a bird down into the 'primeval waters' to bring up (typically) a 'bit of mud', from which the earth is then made. The third involves creation by the breaking up of a 'primal unity', such as 'Mother Earth' from 'Father Sky', or 'form' from 'chaos'. The fourth is that of creation by 'dismemberment' of a 'primordial being', out of whose 'body' the universe is made. The fifth and last is the 'emergence' type, in which creation is a gradual process, typically featuring human-like creatures who must travel through many worlds before reaching this one. All five types of creation myth have been used by different cultures and civilisations in all parts of the world.

Second, **myths about gods and goddesses**, probably the most common type. Gods and goddesses are generally 'immortal beings', 'personified projections of the human dream of overcoming disintegration and death'. Historically, gods and goddesses seem to begin as 'generalities' such as the 'Great Mystery' or the 'Absolute'. Their first concrete embodiments are usually in animal form, as in the religions of the ancient Egyptians and Mesopotamians, typically that of a serpent, as 'part animal' and 'part human', or as giants. Over time, these often lose their 'monstrous' qualities, and take on 'specialist' duties or roles of one form or another. They are often also 'anthropomorphised' as male and female. A 'pantheon' literally means 'all gods', and refers to the deities of a people or civilisation considered 'collectively'. The extensive pantheons of the ancient Egyptians, early Mesopotamian civilisations, Greeks and Romans are typical examples, with the last two being familiar to most educated people in the western world. Other cultures in other parts of the world had (and sometimes still have) their own distinctive pantheons, the 'Hindu' pantheon being one of the best-known today. Such pantheons make a fascinating field of study for anthropologists and students of religion, and also for 'thinking' members of the general public. I wish I had space to tell you more about them here!

Some of the sources of information on material covered in Chapter 1

I have drawn this information from a wide range of sources in my personal library. They have included three of my key historical reference books:
- The 'Larousse Encyclopaedia of Ancient and Medieval History' (of which I own the 1965 edition)
- The 'Oxford Encyclopaedia of World History' (of which I own the original 1988 edition)
- The 'Times Concise History of the World' (of which I own the 2015 edition)

I also obtained a great deal of 'deep background' information by re-reading the early chapters of the outstanding book on 'The Ascent of Man' that Jacob Bronowski wrote to accompany the ground-breaking television series that was broadcast by the BBC during the early 1970's.

Most of the information that informed my writing of Chapter 1 came from the following three sources, however.

- 'Origins', by Lewis Dartnell, which looks in great detail at how the development of human society has been shaped by the environment in which we live. Virtually all the material in the first section of the chapter comes from this source.
- 'Religions in the Ancient Mediterranean World', a 'Teaching Company' course written and presented by Professor Glen S. Holland. This is the source of the great majority of the material in the middle three sections of the chapter.
- 'Myth in Human History', another 'Teaching Company' course, written and presented by Professor Grant L. Voth. This was the source of virtually all the material in the final section of Chapter 1.

Chapter 2: The 'Axial Age' of religious and intellectual development

'The years 800 - 200 BCE comprise one of the most creative and influential eras in world history'

- Mark Muesse (Religions of the Axial Age)

The term 'Axial Age' was first used by the 20th-century German philosopher Karl Jaspers, in Part 1 of his 1953 book 'The Origin and Goal of History'. In this, he identified this extraordinary period as 'die Achsenzeit'- the pivotal era in which he believed that 'the spiritual foundations of humanity were laid simultaneously and independently in many widely-separated parts of the world, and were 'the foundations upon which humanity still subsists today'. It is now recognized that the foundations of western philosophy and science were also laid down during this remarkable era, so that Jaspers' 'Axial Age' may be justifiably regarded as 'the birthplace of the modern world'. Many highly- intelligent and highly- educated people are still unfamiliar with the term, however, as I discovered when I was discussing the possible chapter structure of this book with some of my friends, relatives and colleagues. I hope that this chapter, and the four that follow on from it, will help to increase general familiarity with this key turning point in our religious, philosophical and scientific development, and in our general understanding of the nature of reality.

What was the 'Axial Age'?

The 'Axial Age' designates a period of roughly six centuries in the middle of the first millennium before the 'Common Era, starting around 800 BCE and ending around 200 BCE. During this period, unprecedented developments in religion, philosophy and science took place in four separate centres of civilisation - West Asia (centred in Persia), South Asia (centred in India), East Asia (centred in China), and the areas around the Eastern Mediterranean (particularly in the parts where Greek civilisation started to develop and where the Jews made their home). Just to mention some of the key figures who lived in these different areas during the period alerts us to the importance of this age: Zoroaster in Persia, Vardhamana Mahavira and the Buddha in India, Confucius and Lao Tzu in China, 'Second Isaiah' in Judah and numerous outstanding Greek philosophers such as Pythagoras, Heraclitus, Socrates, Plato and Aristotle. In different ways, these individuals responded to a wide range of new issues and challenges, brought to the fore by things like increased urbanisation, political instability, the emergence of self-consciousness, and the wish to understand the world and our place in it as fully as possible. As a consequence of their creative engagement with these and other important issues, the 'sages' of the Axial Age produced the 'intellectual and moral matrix' out of which virtually all major religions were born, and in which rational philosophy and empirical science burgeoned and thrived.

It is possible to identify a number of key social and political developments that contributed to the onset of the Axial Age.

First, the Axial Age occurred at a time and in places of increasing urbanisation and social mobility. This trend had significant effects on social structures and the human psyche, since changing to urban living after living in much smaller communities often disrupts people's 'sense of identity', and challenges their 'traditional values and beliefs.'

Second, the main Axial centres were generally characterized by political and social upheaval of one form or another. In China, for example, the Axial Age overlapped with the end stages of a particularly brutal epoch in Chinese history known as the 'Period of Warring

States', with Persia, India and Judah undergoing similar periods of turmoil and transformation. Such 'interesting times' (to borrow the words from the old Chinese curse) invariably generate uncertainty and insecurity, but are also often the most creative for religious and philosophical thought.

Third, sages in the Axial centres became progressively more anxious about death, and preoccupied with what, if anything, lay beyond death. As we saw in Chapter 1, early humans had always been concerned with such issues, but, during the Axial Age, they assumed more and more importance in people's minds. Increasingly, death was regarded with dread, and speculation about what might lie beyond it was filled with both hope and terror. (Shakespeare's 'Hamlet' later expressed similar fears in his famous 'third soliloquy' - 'To be, or not to be...')

Fourth, the growing sense of 'selfhood' and anxiety about life's 'transience' also stimulated conjectures about 'the nature of the person', and spurred the search to discover something within the human individual that might survive the 'dissolution of the body', something 'eternal' and 'immortal' - what eventually became known as the 'soul' in some cultures. In some cases, the Axial 'sages' were not content to accept the old 'anthropomorphic gods' with all their faults and weaknesses as the 'highest realities or powers' governing the universe; they were looking for 'something better'. They eventually found this in the various religions that were born in or were triggered by the 'Axial Age'.

Finally, the onset of the Axial Age marked a dramatic change in the 'role' and 'place' of religion in human life. During this era, the basic purpose of religion shifted from what the theologian John Hick calls 'cosmic maintenance' to 'personal transformation'. Prior to the Axial Age, the main purpose of religion was to collaborate with the divine powers in keeping the world in 'good working order'. During the Axial Age, however, it took on an unprecedented new role in human life - providing the means for the individual to undergo change in order to achieve immortality or happiness. This was particularly so in the case of the main 'eastern' religions that appeared during the axial Age, and also in two of the most important religions that appeared after it had ended - Christianity and Islam.

Let us now look in some detail about how the Axial Age manifested itself in the four different parts of the world in which these five developmental factors had their greatest influence - West Asia, South Asia, East Asia and the regions around the eastern end of the Mediterranean.

Axial developments in West Asia

Linguistic and textual analysis has conclusively shown that the people who occupied northwestern India and Eastern Iran (Persia) prior to the Axial Age were closely related, spoke common languages, and held largely-common religious beliefs. Most scholars believe that these 'Indo-Iranians' were descended from the same stock of pastoral nomads, who originally lived in the Central-Asian steppes, although some think they were indigenous to India. What we know of their culture comes almost entirely from two sources, originally preserved in oral tradition - the 'Rig Veda' (the oldest extant Indo-European text), and the 'Avesta' (a slightly-later text from Iran). These later became the 'foundational scriptures' of Hinduism (in India) and Zoroastrianism (in Persia). Essentially, their traditional religion served to provide the means to attain the things necessary for a stable and prosperous life on earth. Their gods were entreated to help maintain productivity and harmony in the 'here-and-now' rather than to secure 'other-worldly salvation'. The Indo-Iranians referred to themselves as the 'Noble Ones'. It seems that they were essentially peaceful people, with a static society that, for centuries, underwent few significant cultural changes.

The 'Avesta' suggests that the Indo-Iranians who had moved into Persia prior to the onset of the Axial Age had eventually degenerated into 'widespread lawlessness'. It is believed that 'Zoroaster', one of the most enigmatic of the founders of the 'Axial' religions, was originally a priest in the traditional religion that they had brought with them. We know very little about the man himself, and there is considerable debate about when he actually lived. Some scholars place him a few centuries **before** the start of the Axial age, but others think that there is fairly convincing evidence for including him in the line-up of 'Axial sages', not the least of which was his deep concern with morality, and the ultimate destiny of the individual. It seems that his ethical sensitivities led him to 'reinterpret' the deities of the traditional Iranian pantheon, making them partisans of either good or evil. Be that as it may, it is generally accepted that his 'reforms' eventually led to development of a new religious tradition bearing his name ('Zoroastrianism'), and to its eventual adoption as the new 'state religion' of the Persians. Zoroaster is also sometimes referred to as 'Zarathustra'. (This was the form of his name later used by the late-19th-century German philosopher Nietzsche in his philosophical masterwork 'Also Sprach Zarathustra', and by the 20th-century German composer Richard Strauss in his 'tone poem' of the same name. The spectacular opening of this was used to great effect at the start of Stanley Kubrick's 1968 film '2001: A Space Odyssey', one of the iconic films of the mid-20th century.)

At the age of 30, it is said that Zoroaster had an impressive 'visionary experience' in which he was led into the presence of the 'Ahura Mazda' and six other 'radiant beings', known collectively as the 'heptad' (the 'seven'), from whom he received a 'special revelation'. He now had a purpose - to 'teach men to seek the 'right' ('asha')'.

Though he continued to have revelations, this was clearly a turning point of his life, similar to that allegedly experienced by Paul on the 'road to Damascus'. It transformed him from a 'priest' to a 'prophet', a critic of traditional religious practices, and a 'mouthpiece' for a god. There were two main 'thrusts' in his reformed theology, both movements in the direction of 'simplification'.

First, Zoroaster wanted the Ahura Mazda to be seen as superior to **all** the other 'ahuras', and became a passionate advocate of worshipping him as the foremost deity. Indeed, in his interpretation of the 'heptad', he suggested that **all** the other 'ahuras' and lesser divinities were actually 'emanations' or 'partial manifestations' of Ahura Mazda. Zoroaster believed him to be the only 'uncreated god', who himself created the world in seven stages. This was clearly a move towards 'monotheism', and made a significant contribution to the development of a religious culture that would ultimately champion the idea. The subsequent adoption of monotheism by Judaism, Christianity and Islam thus had their roots in this key aspect of Zoroastrianism.

Second, Zoroaster assigned clear 'moral qualities' to the gods. **All** the spirits in his new pantheon were now plainly either 'good' or 'evil'. The principal gods and spirits in this new pantheon were the 'ahuras' (all of which were 'good) and the 'daevas' (all of which were regarded as 'evil'). He identified two 'superior gods' as 'leaders' of these two groups, 'Mazda' and 'Ahriman', one completely 'good' and the other completely 'evil', who were eternally locked in 'mortal combat', each struggling for triumph. Thus, Zoroaster also clearly prepared the ground for the Christian idea of eternal conflict between 'God' and 'Satan', and for what became known as the 'Manichaean Heresy' in the early Christian Church (read about this for yourselves!).

45

Zoroaster also anticipated other 'Axial sages' by connecting 'human destiny' with 'moral behavior'. He imagined history as moving in a 'linear' fashion towards a final conclusion, in which 'good' would at last triumph over 'evil'. At this key eschatological moment, those whose lives had been devoted to Ahura Mazda, the 'god of good', would be rewarded with an everlasting life of happiness, whereas those who had served Ahriman, the 'god of evil', would be utterly annihilated. These Zoroastrian doctrines clearly served as models for the remarkably-similar doctrines that were subsequently adopted by the Christian Church.

Although Zoroastrianism was a major religion in Persia and surrounding areas for a long time, it has not survived as an important 'world religion', and there are comparatively few practising Zoroastrians around today. Nevertheless, the legacy of Zoroaster's teachings lives on in other religions. Although it is still a controversial issue, many modern religious scholars believe that the three principal 'Western' monotheistic religions - Judaism, Christianity and Islam - absorbed many important aspects of Zoroastrian thought, and incorporated these into their own doctrines. These include concepts such as the devil, the 'Day of Judgment', heaven and hell, angels, and the idea of a 'divine saviour'. The modern religious world thus owes a great deal to Zoroaster and the religion that he effectively founded in Persia Back in 'Axial' times.

Axial developments in South Asia

India had a long cultural and religious history before the advent of the Axial Age. The earliest Indian civilisation that we know about was the so-called 'Indus Culture', which flourished along the Indus River valley at least 1500 years before the Indo-Aryans entered what is now Pakistan and the Punjab area. This was first discovered during the 19th century, when archaeologists found extensive ruins which indicated that it was probably the largest civilisation of the ancient world, with some cities containing as many as 50,000 people. We know very little about their society or their religion, since the Indus language has not yet been deciphered. We know that the Indus culture was already in decline by around 1500 BCE, and came to an end when the 'Indo' branch of the Indo-Iranian people began to arrive in the region. Until comparatively recently, most historians believed that these 'Indo-Aryans' conquered the 'Indus Culture' people by military force, but many contemporary scholars of ancient India now think that the Indo-Aryans migrated slowly and relatively peacefully into the Indus valley, coexisting for a time with the remaining Indus peoples, and gradually assimilating them into their culture. As we saw at the start of the previous section of this chapter, it was the arrival of these people that provided us with the first reliable record of life in this part of ancient India - the 'Rig Veda'. This and the other 'Vedas' are the Hindus' oldest and most sacred scriptures, providing instructions, prayers and hymns created for the purpose of performing rituals, and also information about their deepest religious beliefs. They are **extremely** important documents in the history of religion.

The Indo-Aryans had a well-established 'caste' system, with 'Brahmins' (priests and professionals) at the top and the so-called 'untouchables' at the very bottom. They believed that this rigid stratification was 'intended' by the gods, and was a fundamental part of the nature of reality. To challenge the system would thus be to challenge the gods themselves, with what could be dire consequences. They performed many different rituals for many different reasons, the most important being the 'shrauta rites', which were intended to help people to prosper in everyday life. Only suitable members of the Brahmin caste could conduct these rituals, because only they had the knowledge and skill to do so. Setting up and performing each ritual (which usually involved a sacrifice of some sort) could take several days or weeks. The most important aspect of the ritual, however, was the singing of prayers and hymns, using verses from the Vedas, by the Brahmin priests. The sacred words had to be correctly uttered, or the ritual might be ineffective, or even dangerous. Eventually, uttering sacred words during rituals became akin to 'tapping into' the 'creative power' of the sacrifice. The Brahmins regarded themselves as the 'sole custodians' of this power, becoming increasingly important and influential as a result.

Following the 'Vedic' period (1500 - 800 BCE), the period of 'classical Hinduism' began with the onset of the 'Axial Age'. During this period, the complex traditions that characterised the Hindu religion began to be established. The development of classical Hinduism involved adapting and reinterpreting many of the Vedic notions, traditions and practices, but adding many totally- new ideas and practices to the 'mix'. The eventual result was the religion that we now call 'Hinduism', which gradually spread throughout India, evolving and maturing as it did so. One of the most important changes was a growing doubt in the value of ritual, which, as we saw earlier, had completely dominated religious practice during the 'Vedic' era. This coincided with an important 'change of priorities' among some practitioners of Indian religion, for whom 'earthly riches' began to count for less and less. What was **really** important was the 'spiritual development' of the individual, and this eventually became the main focus of Hinduism - and, as we will see, Buddhism and Jainism. These changes were reflected in the appearance of an important new set of spiritual writings - the 'Upanishads' - during this transition period - probably sometime between 800 and 400 BCE. These provided detailed information about the new ideas.

Central to the 'new Hinduism' that developed during the Axial Age were the ideas of 'rebirth' ('reincarnation') and 'karma'. Hindus came to believe that we all go through a seemingly-endless succession of births, deaths and rebirths, a process known as 'samsara'. This is governed by the moral principle known as 'karma', in which how we behave in one life affects what happens to us in later lives, or even the very **nature** of these lives. If we accumulated too much 'bad karma', for example, we might be reincarnated as an animal rather than a human being! Hindus increasingly came to regard samsara as an essentially undesirable process from which they wished to be released - by eventually attaining the ultimate goal of life - liberation from samsara altogether. Hindus call this liberation 'moksha'. They developed a variety of processes and practices for helping them along the road to such release. One was 'meditation', which could be carried out by everyone while still remaining an integral part of normal society. The other was to withdraw from normal society, and to concentrate exclusively on your spiritual development.

In addition to an ever-increasing wish to understand the nature of the 'self' and how we could eventually achieve 'moksha', Hindu thinkers wanted to gain a deeper understanding of the nature of 'ultimate reality' itself. They regarded this as the 'fundamental power or principle supporting all that there is', and eventually gave it a special name - 'Brahman'. Hindus also developed a huge pantheon of gods, which they believed were all different manifestations or aspects of Brahman. This enabled ordinary, practising Hindus to relate closely with particular members of this pantheon, as they had traditionally always done, making them their own 'personal' gods and goddesses. Contemplating the 'deeper' aspects of Hindu theology and philosophy could thus be safely left to the Brahmins, and to people who decided to withdraw from normal life. As Hinduism continued to develop and mature during and after the Axial Age, more and more Indians decided to go down this route - either on their own as 'ascetics' or as part of a religious community of some sort. As a result, India eventually became the most intensely religious country on earth, a status that it still largely holds today.

In the course of its evolution and development during the 600 years of the Axial Age, more perspectives and practices were regularly added to Hinduism in order to accommodate individual beliefs and tastes. It thus effectively became a 'family' of religions, without a core creed or universally-agreed set of beliefs. Hinduism also recognised that different people were at different stages of their spiritual development, and that beliefs and practices that were suitable for some might not be equally-suitable for others. The composition of the 'Bhagavad Gita', probably the most popular and widely-read of all the Hindu scriptures, encouraged this 'personalisation' of Hinduism, and provided detailed guidance on how to do so. I have a (translated) copy in my personal library (reading a document in Sanskrit is **not** one of my skills!)

Let me now end this introduction to Axial-Age developments in South Asia by briefly discussing two of the most important 'offshoots' of the 'new Hinduism' that developed during this period - 'Buddhism' and 'Jainism'.

One of the most important of all the 'Axial sages' in India was Siddhartha Gautama, a northern-Indian allegedly of 'noble descent' who subsequently became known as the 'Buddha' (the 'Enlightened One'). According to tradition, he was born in 563 BCE, although most contemporary scholars believe that his birth took place considerably later - around 490 BCE. Very little is known for certain about his early life, but he is believed to have left his home and family at around the age of 30 in order to become a 'samona' - a wandering ascetic seeking to find the secrets of life and a way of obtaining release from all its suffering. According to legend, he ultimately achieved 'enlightenment' while sitting under a 'Bodhi tree' near the village of Gaya roughly 5 years later, and found how to enter 'nirvana' - a state of utter bliss in which he became totally-immersed in and united with ultimate reality. In Hindu terminology, he effectively became 'one' with 'Brahman'. He could have decided to leave this world there and then and remain in 'nirvana' permanently, but decided not to do so, in order to help others along the path to enlightenment that **he** had just taken. He then began a 45-year ministry of teaching, which only ended with his death at the age of about 80, according to legend. He collected many followers, who gave him the title by which he is known today - the 'Buddha'. He also became the founder of a new religion - 'Buddhism'. This is still one of the most important of our world religions, although it now takes several different forms.

I will describe the Buddhist religion and the different forms that it eventually took in some detail in Chapter 5, but will try to summarize some of its key features here.

First, Buddhism recognises no conventional god of any type - only the deep, underlying ultimate reality that Hindus refer to as 'Brahman'. It is probably unique in that its adherents do not worship a 'Supreme Being' of the type worshipped by Jews, Christians and Muslims, or a pantheon of gods of the type worshipped by Hindus. Buddhism also recognises reincarnation and karma-based 'samsara' of roughly the same types as in Hinduism.

Second, Buddhism teaches that the ultimate purpose of life is to find a way of obtaining release from the unavoidable suffering that living in the world entails. The Buddha analysed the nature and origins of this suffering in meticulous detail, expressing them in what he called his four 'Noble Truths' - now one of the foundations of Buddhist doctrine.

Third, Buddhism shows its followers how they can escape from this suffering by putting its teachings on how to live into practice. Different forms of Buddhism now advocate different ways in which this can be achieved, but, in its original form, it involved following the Buddha's clearly-described 'Eightfold Way', which, if properly practised, could eventually enable **anyone** to enter nirvana - and remain there permanently if they wished. This might take a very long time, however - possibly many lifetimes.

Another of the most important of the 'Axial sages' in India was Vardhamana Mahavira, who is generally acknowledged as the founder of the third important religion to be founded in that country during the Axial Age - 'Jainism'. It is believed that he was a near-contemporary of the Buddha, with 'tradition' giving his date of birth as 599 BCE. It is also believed by some scholars that the doctrines that he embodied in his new religion had been around for a long time before he appeared on the scene. Like the Buddha, Mahavira attracted a community of followers, and taught them for a long period of time, until his death aged 72 according to tradition. Although it never attracted anything like the number of followers that Hinduism and Buddhism achieved, Jainism has had a tremendous influence on the history of India and on its other religions. They have also influenced many other subsequent thinkers, including Mahatma Gandhi, whose various non-violent movements were greatly influenced by Jainism.

Jainism teaches a strict moral code based on 'ahimsa' (avoidance of injury to any living creature), and a path of spiritual training through austerity (eventually leading to 'nirvana' if correctly followed). Devout Jains believe that Jainism is an 'eternal' religion, whose truths had no 'beginning in time'. They believe that the world is subject to a 'universal life cycle', wherein Jainism's various 'truths' have to be re-introduced to humanity periodically because they have been forgotten or lost. Jainism's teachers are known as 'Tirthankaras' (or 'bridge-builders'), and show the way to 'salvation' (liberation from 'samsara') through their words and example. They believe that there have been 24 Tirthankaras so far, the latest of which was Mahavira, and that there will be 24 more in the current universal cycle; the next is expected in 81,500 years!

Axial developments in East Asia

The land that eventually became the country we now call China had a long history prior to the Axial Age. The Chinese trace their history back 5000 years, to roughly 3000 BCE - the same time that the first major civilisation (ancient Egypt) was founded in the West. Though there is no written or archaeological evidence to support them, Chinese legends speak of the 'Era of Three Sovereigns' and the 'Era of Three Sages' several millennia before our current era. During these very early times, the basic features of Chinese civilization were established - hunting and fishing, agriculture, use of boats and carts, use of silk, religious rituals, development of centralised governments, and writing. Whether based on fact or myth, these ancient eras have great symbolic value for the Chinese, explaining why the culture exists as it does (or at least **did**, before communism took over in the middle of the last century), and providing standards by which later people could judge their values and behaviour.

The 'Shang Dynasty' is the earliest Chinese period for which there is firm historical evidence. This arose in the northeastern region of China during the 15th or 14th century BCE, and, thanks largely to an important archeological discovery made during the 19th century of the Common Era, we now know quite a lot about its religious beliefs and practices. The discovery involved the detailed study of inscriptions on the shoulder blades of cattle and the shells of tortoises, which had been used by Shang kings to communicate with the gods, and with their ancestors. Bones were also used for the purpose of 'divination', which has always played an important role in Chinese culture. The bone inscriptions also revealed that there was a close connection between the 'spirit realm' ('heaven', or 'tian') and the 'human realm' ('earth', or 'di'). In early Chinese thought, heaven and earth were continuous, overlapping realms, in which gods and spirits were readily accessible to humans. The concept of 'virtue' ('de') also played a key role in early Chinese culture, leading to such things as strong family obligations, and reverence for their ancestors.

The 'Zhou Dynasty' supplanted the 'Shang Dynasty' around 1045 BCE according to Chinese records, and lasted until it was, in turn, replaced by the 'Qin Dynasty' in 221 BCE, the time when China effectively became a single united nation. The Zhou Dynasty thus ruled throughout the entire period of the Axial Age (800 to 200 BCE). The Zhou family justified its overthrow of the Shangs through the 'Mandate of Heaven', which claimed that the divine world bestowed favour on 'just' rulers, and withdrew favour from 'corrupt' ones. This concept had a profound influence on subsequent Chinese politics and religion, although the Zhou's claim to possess 'heaven's mandate' did not always translate into a just and peaceful reign. As we saw earlier, the start of the Axial Age overlapped with the end of the 'Period of Warring States' - one of the most violent epochs in Chinese history. It was against this backdrop that China produced the towering figure of 'Confucius', one of the 'learned men' who were trying to find solutions to the pressing political and moral issues of the day. He was later widely recognised as 'the most influential figure in Chinese history' - at least until the emergence of 'Chairman Mao' over two millennia later. (I suspect that Confucius would not have approved of Chairman Mao.)

It is believed that 'Confucius' (of 'Kung Fu Tzu', to give him his Chinese name) was born around 551 BCE and died around 479 BCE, although there is considerable uncertainty about the accuracy of these dates. He was the founder of one of the two main religions that developed in China during the Axial Age - what became known as 'Confucianism'. At around the same time, the second major figure in China's 'Axial Age' ('Lao Tzu') is believed to have founded a rival religion that became known as 'Taoism', or 'Daoism' as some scholars prefer. Both 'religions' were in fact closer to 'philosophical schools' than 'true' religions such as Hinduism, Buddhism, Christianity and Islam, but I will continue to refer to them as 'religions' because that is what most people do. They represented two radically-different sides of Chinese philosophy, but, in China, they were always seen as 'poles' of one and the same 'human nature', and thus as 'complementary' rather than as 'irreconcilable opposites'. Both had tremendous influence on the subsequent development of Chinese civilisation and culture.

Confucianism embodied the philosophy of 'common sense' and 'practical knowledge'. It provided Chinese society with an extremely-advanced system of education (probably the best in the world at the time), and also with strict conventions of social etiquette. One of its main purposes was to provide an 'ethical basis' for the traditional Chinese family system, with its complex structure, 'filial piety', and its rituals of 'ancestor worship'. The most historically-reliable information about Confucius and his teachings comes from a book called 'the Analects' ('Lunyu'), a collection of his sayings, conversations and anecdotes compiled posthumously by his disciples. No-one knows to what extent the 'Analects' is historically reliable, but most scholars agree that much of it reflects the perspectives and words of his many followers, some of whom may have lived generations after Confucius himself.

Taoism, on the other hand, was primarily concerned with the observation of nature, and with the discovery of its 'Way' (or 'Tao'). Human happiness, according to the Taoists, is achieved when people follow the 'natural order', acting 'spontaneously' and trusting their 'intuitive knowledge'. Modern sinologists distinguish between 'philosophical Taoism', or 'daojia', which means the 'School of the Way', and 'religious Taoism', or 'daojiao', which means the 'Teaching of the Way'. The former is associated with the literate and intellectual class, and has two key classic texts - the 'Daodejing' and the 'Zhuangzi'. The latter appeared much later - after the end of the Axial Age', in fact, and was intended for the 'common people'. During the 'Han Dynasty' which eventually replaced the 'Qin Dynasty', it developed into a formal 'Taoist Church', complete with priests, temples and rituals.

I will provide more detailed information about Confucianism and Taoism in Chapter 5 of my book, so will say no more about them here.

Axial developments in the Eastern Mediterranean area

The fourth part of the civilised world in which major intellectual developments took place during the 'Axial Age' was the Eastern Mediterranean area, particularly the parts in which Greek civilisation developed and flourished, and the areas where the Jews made their home between Egypt and Syria. The rise and spread of Greek culture effectively laid the foundations for the development of western philosophy and science, while religious advances made by the Jews were the triggers for the subsequent development of two of the world's most important religions - Christianity and Islam. In this chapter, I will provide a broad introduction to each of these key 'Axial Age' developments, following these up by more detailed examination in Chapters 3, 4 and 6.

The origins of Greek civilisation and culture can be traced back to the latter part of the Neolithic Era, with the so-called 'Minoan' civilisation on Crete reaching its height in the early 15th century BCE. Despite the discovery of extensive ruins and intriguing artefacts, its religious culture is almost impossible to reconstruct. The cause of the decline and subsequent disappearance of the once-flourishing Minoan civilisation is still a subject of much debate among scholars. Many link it with the catastrophic explosion that took place on the nearby volcanic island of 'Thera' (what is left of it is now called 'Santorini') sometime between 1600 and 1500 BCE. What **is** clear is that within a few generations of the Theran explosion, Minoan civilisation went into terminal decline. The subsequent 'Mycenaean' civilisation developed on the Greek mainland during the 'Bronze Age', as incursions of Indo-Aryans settled in geographically-distinct areas of the Achaean peninsula. Mycenaean civilisation is the historical setting for the events described in the 'Iliad' and the 'Odyssey', centred on the 'Trojan War'. We now know that Troy (an important city in North-Western Asia Minor, a few miles inland from the Aegean Sea) actually existed, since its ruins were discovered by, and systematically excavated by, the German archaeologist Heinrich Schliemann in the late 19th century. These and subsequent excavations have revealed ten periods of occupation of the city, (which was destroyed and rebuilt each time). The Mycenaean civilisation declined rapidly around 1200 BCE, as much of the Eastern Mediterranean sank into a 'dark age'. Classical Greek civilisation eventually arose from the ashes of this. This took the form of independent 'city-states', which were founded throughout the region - on the Greek mainland, in the islands of the Aegean, on the shores of Asia Minor, and also in Italy and Sicily. Several hundred of these 'poleis' (singular 'polis') were founded from the 8th-century BCE onwards. Most were fairly small, but two of the largest ones (Sparta and Athens) eventually became the dominant powers in the Hellenic world. They fought a major war (the 'Peloponnesian War') between 431 and 404 BCE, which ended in the defeat of Athens, and the effective end of its hegemony in the Hellenic world. (This is described in detail by the Athenian historian Thucydides.)

The 600 years of the 'Axial Age' between 800 and 200 BCE coincide almost exactly with the rise of classical Greek civilisation, the spread of its influence and culture throughout the region, the conquest of much of the known world by Alexander the Great, and the subsequent spread of Greek influence and culture throughout the three main empires into which his 'world empire' was divided after his death. These developments were so important in the intellectual history of the world and the on-going investigation of the nature of reality that I have devoted two entire chapters of this book to a detailed discussion of two of them. Chapter 3 shows how the ground-breaking work of one particular group of early Greek thinkers (the 'Presocratics') during the early part of the Axial Age effectively laid the foundations for the whole of western philosophy and science. Chapter 4 shows how their work led to the so-called 'golden age' of classical philosophy and science, which lasted from the rise of Athenian civilisation, influence and power during the 6th-century BCE till the capture of Alexandria by the all-conquering Muslim army in 641. Because of the highly-detailed descriptions of these important developments that are given in these two chapters, I will again say no more about them here.

Let me now end the section on the 'Axial Age' developments that took place in the Eastern Mediterranean area by saying a few words about the highly-important and influential work that was carried out by the Jewish people during and immediately after this era. The Jewish account of their very early history is given in the first five books of the Old Testament, known to them as the 'Pentateuch' (Genesis, Exodus, Leviticus, Numbers and Deuteronomy). It is now widely accepted by religious scholars that these early accounts have little or no genuine historical or archaeological support, and are probably a mixture of 'myths' circulated orally within a largely-illiterate culture and 'deliberate fiction'. There is even some doubt over whether many of the early Jewish patriarchs, including Abraham and Moses, actually existed! The same is true to a lesser extent of many of the later chapters of the Old Testament, particularly those that deal with the events before the conquest of Jerusalem by the Babylonians in in 597 BCE , and the subsequent deportation of a large part of the Jewish population to Babylon, where they lived in 'exile' until the defeat of the Babylonian Empire by the Persian Empire in 539 BCE, One year later, the Persian King, Cyrus the Great, gave them permission to return home if they wished. (Very few of them actually did.) Our knowledge of Jewish history became progressively more accurate in the centuries after the exile.

It is now acknowledged that the greatest Jewish contribution to the development of religious thought during the Axial Age was their change from what was in effect a largely 'polytheistic' religious culture to a purely 'monotheistic' one. The man thought to be largely responsible for this was a prophet known as 'Second Isaiah', or 'Deutero-Isaiah'. He is believed to have lived around the time of the Babylonian 'exile', and is thought to be the author of a key section of the 'Book of Isaiah' - the longest book in the Old Testament apart from 'Psalms'. He is now widely acknowledged as one of the great 'sages' of the Axial Age, although we know next to nothing about him.

As I said earlier, the history of the Jewish people and the development of the Jewish religion will be described in much more detail in a later chapter of this book (Chapter 6). I will therefore say no more about them here.

The legacy of the Axial Age

As I explained in the 'foreword' to this chapter and in the opening part of its first main section, the 'Axial Age' was one of the most important eras in the religious and intellectual development of the human race - arguably **the** most important. First of all, it raised religious thinking to a whole new level, and saw the appearance (or radical transformation) of most of the great world religions - Zoroastrianism, Hinduism, Buddhism, Jainism, Confucianism, Taoism and Judaism. Not only that, one of the religions that matured during the Axial Age (Judaism) subsequently triggered the development of the two 'western' religions that have probably had the greatest impact on the world since the advent of what we now call the 'Common Era' - Christianity and Islam. The 'Axial Age' also saw the birth of western rational philosophy and western science, the second of which completely transformed the world during the latter part of the second millennium of the Common Era. Modern civilisation is now totally dependent on the fruits of western science, which has made agriculture progressively more productive, and has transformed the way we live, through the original 'Industrial Revolution' that began in Britain in the second half of the 18th century, and by ushering in the new 'Information Age', through which we are currently moving at ever-greater pace. Thanks largely to these developments , the population that the world could support has increased massively since prehistoric times. In 15,000 BCE,it amounted to 10 million people at most - all primitive 'hunter-gatherers'. By the year 1500 of the Common Era, it had risen to roughly 350 million, of whom only 3 or 4 million were still hunter-gatherers. By 1960, it had risen to roughly 3 billion, with only around 30,000 of these still being hunter-gatherers. Now, it is well over 7 billion, and hunter-gatherer communities have practically disappeared - and seem likely to disappear completely in the not-too-distant future. Modern human beings have only been around for roughly a quarter of a million years. Let us hope that we are still here after another quarter of a million years!

Some of the sources of information on material covered in Chapter 2

As in Chapter 1, I drew this information from several of the books and courses in my personal library, but by far the largest part came from the following two sources.

- 'Religions of the Axial Age', a 'Teaching Company' course written and presented by Professor Mark W. Muesse.
- 'Religions in the Ancient Mediterranean World', a 'Teaching Company' course written and presented by Professor Glen S. Holland.

Chapter 3: Pre-Socratic Greek philosophy and science

'The problems that the Presocratics tried to answer were primarily cosmological ones, but there were also questions of the theory of knowledge.'

- Karl Popper ('Back to the Presocratics' - Chapter 5 of 'Conjectures and Refutations')

In the previous chapter ('The 'Axial Age' of religious and intellectual development'), I argued that the six centuries between 800 and 200 BCE were probably **the** most important era in the development of the modern world. I also showed how the revolutionary ideas of the so-called 'Pre-Socratic' Greek thinkers played a key role in this development. In this chapter, I will take a much-more-detailed look at the work of the Presocratics, which, according to Popper, concentrated primarily on 'cosmological questions' (Popper believed that **all** science was cosmology' in its broadest sense, ie questions about the **nature** of reality), but also on 'epistemological' questions (i.e., questions about how we **acquire** such knowledge). I hope it will encourage readers to move on to even-more-detailed study of these fascinating people.

How the Presocratics gave birth to western philosophy and science

In October 1958, the Austrian-born British philosopher Karl Popper delivered the 'Presidential Address' at a meeting of the Aristotelian Society in London. During this lecture ('Back to the Presocratics') Popper introduced his audience to his revolutionary views on the nature of science and the scientific method. These had been published in German in 1934 in his seminal book, 'Logik der Forschung', but an English translation of this ('The Logic of Scientific Discovery') only became available in 1959. Thus, practically no-one in the English-speaking world was familiar with his ideas on science. Many people knew about his ground-breaking books on politics and sociology, 'The Open Society and its Enemies' (published in English in 1945) and 'The Poverty of Historicism' (also published in English, in 1957). But it was not until his 1958 Presidential Address to the Aristotelian Society that most people outside the German-speaking world were made aware of his views on science - views that would change the way in which science was conducted throughout the world. I will discuss this 'Popperian Revolution' in some detail in Chapter 11, but will outline its central ideas here, since a basic understanding of these is essential if we are to understand the pivotal role of the 'Presocratics' in the development of the modern scientific 'world picture'.

The full text of Popper's 1958 talk was eventually published in 1963, as one of the chapters in 'Conjectures and Refutations', his first new book on science since 1934. This presented his ideas on the scientific method in great detail. Its main contention was that the only practicable way of expanding human knowledge, including scientific knowledge, was by an on-going feedback process based on 'constructive criticism'. He believed that the way we add to our knowledge was by thinking up plausible explanations of hitherto unexplained phenomena, or possible solutions to problems ('conjectures'), and then 'testing' them to see if they 'fit' or 'work'. Furthermore, he contended that the only way to carry out rigorous testing of such conjectures was to try to prove them **wrong** rather than by trying to prove them **right** (Hume had shown that the latter was logically impossible roughly 200 years earlier).Popper described this second stage of his methodology as 'refutation'. Thus, the title of his 1963 book ('Conjectures and Refutations') encapsulated a whole new epistemology - one that was to change the world of science utterly and completely.

Let me now continue the story by quoting an entire paragraph from Bryan Magee's intellectual autobiography, 'Confessions of a Philosopher', which was published in 1997. This explains the importance of the 'Presocratics' in the development of western philosophy and science better than I ever could.

'How the Pre-Socratics come into the picture is this. Popper claims it was they who inaugurated the tradition of critical discussion as a consciously used way of expanding human knowledge. Before them, he says, all societies regarded knowledge as something to be handed down inviolate and uncontaminated from each generation to the next. For this purpose institutions came into being - mysteries, churches, and at a more advanced stage schools. Great teachers and their writings were treated as authorities that it was impossible to dispute: indeed, merely to show that something had been said by them was to prove its truth. Dissent, in primitive societies, was normally punishable by death. The upshot of this was that a society's core body of knowledge and doctrine tended to remain almost static, especially if inscribed in writings that were regarded as holy. It was against this historical background that the pre-Socratic philosophers of ancient Greece introduced something wholly new and revolutionary: they institutionalised criticism. From Thales onwards each of them encouraged his pupils to discuss, debate, **criticise** - and to produce a better argument or theory if he could. Such, according to Popper, were the historical beginnings of rationality and scientific method, and they were directly responsible for that galloping growth of human knowledge that characterises not only ancient Greece but the whole of western culture that has seen itself, from the Renaissance, as the legatee of the ancient world'.

I hope that I have now made my case. Let me therefore move on to examining the work of some of the most important and influential of the 'Presocratics', starting with the very first of them, - 'Thales of Miletus'.

The 'Milesian School' (Thales, Anaximander and Anaximenes)

As we saw in the previous chapter, the ancient Greeks spread throughout the Northeastern Mediterranean area during the early stages of the 'Axial Age', forming 'colonies' as they did so. These took the form of independent 'city-states' known as 'polies' (single, 'polis'), most of which remained fairly small, but some of which went on to become large, and, in some cases, extremely rich, important, and influential. One of the earliest colonies was 'Miletus', which was founded on the western coast of 'Ionia' (what is now Turkey) by a group of migrants who came from the vicinity of Athens, on the Greek mainland. It eventually became a rich and successful city, largely on the basis of the wool that it exported throughout the eastern half of the Mediterranean. It eventually became rich enough to found colonies of its own. Miletus was fairly far south in Ionia, and some scholars believe that Thales and the other Milesian thinkers got some of their ideas from Eastern or Egyptian traditions. For example, Thales was famous for having predicted a solar eclipse in 585 BCE, and, if he really did that, he may have made use of Babylonian astronomical tables. There is also some evidence that he actually visited Egypt at some time during his life.

Thales is credited as being the very first of the Pre-Socratic Greek philosophers. He was born and brought up in Miletus, probably sometime during the first half of the sixth century BCE, and later founded what became known as the 'Milesian School' of philosophy. We know very little about his life and work except for the aspects of the latter that were subsequently described by Aristotle roughly 100 years after he is thought to have lived. Apparently, Thales thought that 'water' played a key role in the world. Aristotle tells us that he believed that the world floated upon water like a piece of wood. This was fully in keeping with earlier cosmological ideas, which envisaged a 'three-layered' universe in which 'heaven' was located somewhere above the earth, and the 'underworld' was located somewhere beneath it. Aristotle tells us that Thales also believed that water was a basic 'cosmic principle', and that, in some sense, everything was 'made of', or 'emerged from' water. Another philosophical belief ascribed to Thales is that a magnet has a 'soul' of some sort, and so has amber, primarily because both could give rise to 'motion' by attracting or repelling things, something that they could not do unless they had some 'soul-like' features. One of the sayings most commonly ascribed to Thales is that 'all things are full of gods', although we are not sure what exactly he meant by this.

We know a bit more about two of the Milesian philosophers who followed on from Thales - 'Anaximander' and 'Anaximenes', although **reliable** knowledge about them is still 'pretty thin'. As with Thales, much of it comes from Aristotle, who studied many of his important Pre-Socratic predecessors in some detail. According to tradition, Anaximander was one of Thales' students, and Anaximenes was then one of Anaximander's. There is no real firm evidence for this, because ancient authors loved to construct teacher-student relationships whether they existed or not. What we **do** know with some degree of certainty is that Anaximander was a bit younger than Thales, and that Anaximenes belonged to the generation after that. Let me now say a few words about what we know about ideas that each of them produced.

Anaximander is best known for saying that the underlying principle of all things is what he called 'the infinite', for which the Greek word was 'apeiron', which means, literally, 'that which has no limits'. Anaximander apparently believed that the 'apeiron' was infinitely big, in that it stretched out indefinitely far 'in space', and also that it 'surrounded' the cosmos in which we live. We also know that he believed it to be 'eternal', so that it was effectively infinite in 'time' as well as in 'space'. These were exciting new ideas, showing that Anaximander thought deeply about cosmological questions. He also thought deeply about how the world around us was formed, and, in particular, how the sky and heavenly bodies came into being. He was also extremely interested in the various 'opposing forces' that we see in nature - things like 'mist' and 'flame', for example. This theme of 'constant and dynamic opposition', taking place against a background of 'underlying unity', is one of the most enduring themes of Pre-Socratic philosophy. Anaximander was also one of the first Greek philosophers to think about possible 'cosmic cycles' operating within the universe, an idea that was also developed by Hindu philosophers. All in all, he was clearly one of the 'deepest thinkers' among the Presocratics. He certainly made philosophy more 'abstract' and 'conceptual'.

His immediate successor, Anaximenes, took philosophy in the opposite direction. While agreeing with Anaximander that the basic principle of everything is 'infinite', he was happy to identify it with a particular concrete substance - not 'water', as Thales had believed, but 'air'. He also built on Anaximander's cosmological ideas in one important respect - by explaining how the different 'stuffs' that make up the cosmos are generated out of one another. If you start with air, Anaximenes postulated, you can change it by making it 'thinner' or 'thicker'. When it gets 'thinner', more diffuse, it gets hotter, and eventually becomes fire. But when it gets 'thicker', it gets colder and becomes wind, then cloud, then water, and finally earth and rocks. Like Thales and Anaximander, Anaximenes wanted to explain the entire cosmos in terms of basic components. He also had ideas about the possible nature of the 'soul', which he believed to be made of his favourite 'stuff' - air, which, in this case, took the form of 'breath'. This connection of the 'soul' with 'breath' would be highly influential in later ancient philosophy, and also in 'Eastern' religious culture.

The 'Pythagorean School' and the importance of mathematics

The one Pre-Socratic philosopher that virtually everyone in the Western World has heard of is 'Pythagoras', mainly because we all had to learn the proof of the famous geometrical theorem that bears his name at school. (I hate to disillusion readers, but there is no reliable evidence that he himself **discovered** this theorem, although we do know that he and his followers were **familiar** with it.) Be that as it may, Pythagoras is now widely recognised as one of the most important and influential figures in the entire history of Western thought. At the start of the chapter on 'Pythagoras' in his massive 'History of Western Philosophy', for example, Bertrand Russell claims that he was, intellectually, 'one of the most important men that ever lived'. In 'The Story of Philosophy' (one of my favourite books on the subject), Bryan Magee describes him as 'a many-sided genius', and claims that he 'originated more of the fundamental ideas of Western philosophy than any thinker before Plato'. Powerful claims, indeed!

Let me begin by telling you about what little we know of the life of this remarkable man. He was a native of Samos, an island off the west coast of Ionia, where a large and flourishing city was built, being born in the early part of the 6th- century BCE. Samos was a commercial rival of Miletus, trading throughout virtually all parts of the Mediterranean, including Italy. We know that Pythagoras eventually moved from Samos to Croton, one of the largest and most important cities in the southern part of that country. It was there that he founded a 'society of disciples', which, for some time, was highly influential in that city. Later, it appears that the citizens of Croton turned against him, so he and his followers moved to Metapontion, another important city in Southern Italy. It was there that he died, but, by this time, the

'Pythagorean School' was well-established, and continued to have influence for a long time after the death of its founder.

In the society that Pythagoras founded and initially led, men and women were admitted on equal terms (highly unusual in those days), property was held in common, and there was a communal way of life. Indeed it had much in common with a modern Israeli 'Kibbutz'. (I spent a night in one in 1979, as part of a three-day tour of Israel prior to an educational conference, and was very impressed by what I learned about this way of life.) Even scientific and mathematical discoveries were deemed to be 'collective', and the members of the community took great pains to preserve the secrecy of some of the most important of these. They were very different from the 'open' school that Thales had founded in Miletus.

One of the key features of the 'Pythagorean School' was the great importance it attached to **mathematics** and **mathematical ways of thinking.** Mathematics impressed them because it appeared to be 'certain', 'exact', and 'applicable to the real world' (fast-forward to Chapter 17, where the last of these is discussed in great detail.) Moreover, mathematical knowledge was obtained by mere 'thinking', without the need of observation, and thus represented a more reliable route to 'certain knowledge' than a more 'empirical' approach. (This was a feature of mathematics that greatly impressed Einstein when he was developing his 'General Theory of Relativity' at the start of the 20th-century; he regarded this as a product of 'pure thought.')

Pythagoras, as almost everyone knows, said that 'all things are numbers'. This statement, interpreted in a modern way, is logically nonsensical, but what Pythagoras was saying was anything but nonsensical. He discovered the importance of numbers in music, and laid the foundations for many subsequent developments in the theory and practice of music, especially in the western world. He also thought of numbers as 'shapes', as they appear on dice or playing cards; we still speak of 'squares' and 'cubes' of numbers, which are terms we owe to him. He also spoke of 'oblong numbers', 'triangular numbers', 'pyramidal numbers' and so on. He and his followers also carried out pioneering work on what we now call 'irrational numbers'. One number that was particularly important to them was 'ten', which they called the 'tetraktys'. (The amazing properties of this number were one of the things that they tried to keep secret.) Pythagoras was the first great thinker to bring mathematical thinking methods into philosophy, where it has had considerable influence ever since. He is also believed to be the person who **invented** the term 'philosophy' (which is derived from the Greek term 'love of wisdom'). He was also the first person to apply the word 'cosmos' to the universe, as far as we are aware. Some man!

The work of Pythagoras and his followers had a tremendous influence on the subsequent development of philosophy in the Hellenic world, particularly on the ground-breaking work of Plato and Aristotle in Athens, and on the work of their immediate successors. After this, their influence became less important for some time, but made a big comeback in the last century BCE, when the tradition we now refer to as 'Neoplatonism' started to take hold, as we will see in the next chapter.

I cannot end this section on Pythagoras without mentioning the ridiculous set of rules that he required the members of his community to follow. These included 'to abstain from beans', 'not to pick up what has fallen', 'not to stir the fire with iron', and 'not to look into a mirror beside a light'. I can understand the first of these, since he was obviously anxious to enforce a 'clean air' policy within the community's buildings, but most of the rest simply beggar belief. They show how highly-intelligent people can sometimes have 'daft' ideas as well as good ones.

Two different approaches to metaphysics (Heraclitus and Parmenides)

Apart from Pythagoras, Heraclitus is probably the best-known of the Pre-Socratic Greek philosophers. One of his greatest contributions to the field was undoubtedly the idea that formed the basis of his metaphysics - that 'everything is always changing', and that there is 'no stability' and 'no unity'. Parmenides, who lived somewhat later, took exactly the opposite view of metaphysics, claiming that 'change was impossible'. For change to happen 'one thing would have to become something else', and, since Parmenides believed that everything was essentially the same 'basic substance' (a doctrine that later came to be known as 'monism') this simply could not happen. These were clearly two radically different metaphysical points of view, and we will now examine them in detail, along with the other main ideas of the two men.

Heraclitus was born in the Ionian city of Ephesus, and reached the peak of his powers around 500 BCE. Unlike Pythagoras, he did not move to the west, since he was quite happy to live and work in the region in which he grew up. There, he became famous for his 'philosophical aphorisms'. Two of the best-known of these were 'you can't step into the same river twice', and 'the road up and down is one and the same'. Often, his sayings involved 'wordplay' of some sort, and took people some time to 'figure out'. It is with good reason, then, that his contemporaries referred to him as 'the riddler', or 'Heraclitus the obscure'. This sort of behaviour did not make him particularly popular with his fellow-Ephesians, but they fell short of condemning him to death, as the Athenians later did with **their** 'annoying philosopher', Socrates!

Most of the Pre-Socratic philosophers we have discussed so far tried to reduce the whole cosmos to one fundamental substance or principle. Thales chose 'water'. Anaximenes chose 'air'. Anaximander had his own, somewhat more abstract principle - the 'infinite'. Heraclitus also had his own basic element, namely, 'fire'. As we have seen, he also believed that the basic metaphysical principle that underpinned empirical reality was 'change'. Some scholars believe that this is a gross oversimplification, if not a downright misrepresentation, of his core doctrine, and is one that is largely due to Plato. In his dialogue the 'Theaetetus', Plato set out clearly the idea that the 'flux' interpretation of Heraclitus's metaphysics was diametrically opposed to the 'underlying unity' metaphysics that was later developed by Parmenides. Heraclitus's doctrine of 'change' was in fact much more subtle than the version presented by Plato, but, because it was the mighty Plato who had highlighted the fundamental differences between the two metaphysical theories, it was his views that were subsequently accepted by practically everyone. (Interested readers can find more information about the matter in the book by Peter Adamson that is cited as one of my main sources of material for this chapter.)

Heraclitus had several other interesting philosophical ideas, but the ones I have outlined here were probably the most important. I will therefore now move on to a more detailed examination of the work of Parmenides.

Parmenides was a native of Elea, a city in the south of Italy, and carried out his most important work in the first half of the fifth century before the Common Era. According to Plato, the young Socrates actually **met** Parmenides in around 450 BCE, when the latter was an old man, and 'learned a lot from him'. Whether or not this meeting actually happened, it is fairly clear that **Plato** was strongly influenced by Parmenides's ideas - particularly his ideas about metaphysics, the study of 'basic reality'. Parmenides appears to have been the first philosopher to study this in a really systematic way. He came to believe that **reality itself** is 'one', that nothing ever changes or moves. According to Parmenides, multiplicity of every sort is an illusion, whether it is the multiplicity of different objects, different colours, or different events happening at different times. He presented these ideas in a highly-ponderous poem written in hexameter lines, the first half of which consisted of a relentless chain of arguments that proceeded on the basis of 'pure reason' rather than from observations about the world around us - what later became known as the 'empirical world'. In this first part of his poem, Parmenides was the first 'armchair philosopher', thinking that he could discover the true 'nature of reality' using purely abstract arguments; he called this his 'way of truth'. In the second part of his poem, he turned his attention to the mere **opinions** of mortal men, calling this his 'way of opinion'. Thus, Parmenides was effectively devoting half his poem to 'knowledge', and half to 'belief'. As we have seen, his main conclusion was that change was impossible. Not many people now agree with this, however.

The arguments presented by Parmenides are long and complicated, and rather difficult to follow, so I will not attempt to explain them in any more detail here. (Interested readers can again find much more detailed information about them in the book by Peter Adamson that is cited as one of my main sources of material for this chapter.)

The birth of modern physical science (Empedocles and the 'Atomists')

Empedocles is one of the most 'interesting' of the early-Greek philosophers, not only because of the extremely wide range of his ideas, but also because of his highly-eccentric lifestyle, and the extremely high opinion that he had of himself and of his own importance (he apparently used to boast about his own 'divinity'!) Bertrand Russell described him as 'a mixture of philosopher, prophet, man of science and charlatan' (characteristics that he had also identified in Pythagoras). Somewhat later, Peter Adamson observed that he combines 'the religious experience of Pythagoras, the pithy inscrutability of Heraclitus, and the cosmic vision of Anaxagoras' (of whom you will hear more later in this chapter). Empedocles was a native of Acragos, a city on the south coast of Sicily, and apparently drew a lot of his ideas from Heraclitus and Parmenides (of whom he was a younger contemporary). He reached the peak of his powers around 440 BCE, so it would seem.

Like many other Presocratics, Empedocles tried to marry 'religious trappings' with a 'rational account of the cosmos', but his fascination with the 'physical world' seems to outstrip that of any of the rest of these. Indeed, in some ways, he can be regarded as the 'father of modern physical science'. He was extremely interested in biology, making several important discoveries, in medicine (where his work greatly influenced that of Hippocrates, as we will see later), in astronomy, and also in what later became known as the 'physical sciences', Here, one of his most important discoveries was that 'air' is a 'separate substance'; he proved this by showing that when a bucket is put into water upside down, the water does not enter the bucket. He was also the very first person to suggest that the entire cosmos was constructed from a few basic 'building blocks' - earth, water, air and fire. He called these 'roots', but they were subsequently re-named as 'elements' by Aristotle and his successors. He also believed that the universe is dominated by 'cosmic cycles, marked by the waxing and waning of the power of two opposing forces - 'love' and 'strife'.

The pioneering work of Empedocles in the physical sciences was followed by the even-more-impressive work of what we now call the 'Atomists'. Here, the 'founding figures' were two near contemporaries of Empedocles - Leucippus and Democritus. Leucippus is believed to have originated in Miletus, and was later greatly influenced by

Parmenides - as were so many subsequent Greek philosophers. It is believed that his most important work was carried out around 440 BCE. We know a little more about Democritus, who was a native of Abdera, in Thrace, and is believed to have carried out **his** most important work around 420 BCE. According to Bertrand Russell, is it 'difficult to disentangle' the two men, because they are 'generally mentioned together'; indeed, it appears that 'some of the works of Leucippus were subsequently attributed to Democritus'. According to Russell, Leucippus was originally led to 'atomism' in an attempt to mediate between the 'monism' of Parmenides and the 'pluralism' of Empedocles. He and Democritus subsequently developed a model of the physical world that was remarkably similar to that developed by modern scientists **very** much later - during the last four centuries of the second millennium of the 'Common Era', in fact. They believed that everything is composed of tiny, indivisible particles known as 'atoms', which had different geometrical shapes, and were in continuous motion within an otherwise empty space known as the 'void'. This picture of 'atoms moving in the void' later became a key feature of the 'Newtonian' world picture and the completely-deterministic world picture subsequently developed by Laplace, as we will see in later chapters. It was, however, only in the early years of the 20th-century that the **existence** of atoms was finally proven experimentally; up till then, several prominent scientists (including Mach) refused to believe in them because of this lack of definitive physical evidence. Now, of course, **everybody** believes that the physical world is primarily composed of atoms, together with other things such as radiation and (possibly) 'dark energy'. Much more about this later!

What really impresses me about the pioneering work of the Greek atomists is that they came to their conclusions **through purely rational arguments**, without relying on **observational evidence** at all - because there was none at the time. In my opinion, this anticipation of what is now the central paradigm of modern physical science must be regarded as one of the most incredible feats in the whole of intellectual history - if not **the** most incredible. Truly, the Greek Presocratics were remarkable people, as I hope I have made clear by now.

Hippocrates: the 'father of modern medicine'

'First of all, do no harm'. This fundamental precept of medical ethics goes right back to the man widely recognised as the 'father of medicine' - Hippocrates. He hailed from Kos - an island off the west coast of Ionia, not far from the city of Miletus where the Greeks developed their first philosophical thoughts. We are not sure exactly when he lived, but it seems to have been in the latter part of the 5th-century BCE. We know it must have been around the time of Plato and Aristotle, because both refer to him in their writings, describing him as a 'pre-eminent doctor'. Plato also reports that he 'accepted students for a fee', and 'taught them medicine'. It seems likely that he was younger than Socrates, and was perhaps a near-contemporary of Plato. This would date him around the end of the fifth-century BCE.

Greek medicine had clearly become well established long before Hippocrates appeared on the scene. In its early days, it was closely related to religion, and there were elaborate cults which involved asking the gods to help in healing the sick and injured. An even bigger influence came from the philosophical and scientific ideas that developed in Pre-Socratic times. Here, the most important figure was undoubtedly Empedocles, whose work was described in the previous section of the chapter. Not only did he boast about his powers of healing and knowledge of drugs, but his medical interests are borne out by details of his 'theory of nature', particularly his belief that everything is made of four basic kinds of 'stuff' - earth, water, air and fire'. If you were ill, it was because these elements were 'out of balance'. Hippocrates took many of Empedocles's ideas on board when he was developing his own all-embracing medical system, which became known as the 'Hippocratic corpus'. More than 60 medical works within this corpus are ascribed to him, but many of these were probably written by his colleagues. Even today, we talk about doctors taking their 'Hippocratic oath', which apparently originated in one of his works, appropriately titled 'The Oath'.

The various authors of the 'Hippocratic corpus' covered virtually all aspects of the theory and practice of contemporary medicine in their writings, including medical ethics, the use of drugs in healing, and numerous specialist areas such as gynaecology. They also moved on from the often-simplistic ideas developed by some earlier Greek practitioners of medicine, claiming that medical practice should be firmly based on the teachings of the firmly-established 'medical tradition', which were 'gleaned from long and careful experience'. Certainly, many of the teachings incorporated in the 'Hippocratic corpus' have stood the test of time. Although things have now moved on considerably from a scientific and technical point of view, many of the general medical principles that were developed by Hippocrates and his colleagues still form the basis of modern medicine, particularly in the west. The modern world owes a great debt of gratitude to them.

Other key figures (Xenophanes; Anaxagoras; Zeno; the 'Sophists')

Let me now end this chapter on the Presocratics by taking a brief look at three more of the key philosophical figures from this era - Xenophanes, Anaxagoras and Zeno, and also at a highly-influential group of people who became collectively known as the 'Sophists'. These were not really 'philosophers' in the true sense, but nevertheless made a major contribution to the development of Greek philosophy, mainly through the influence they had on Socrates, and, especially, Plato.

First, Xenophanes. We know very little about the man himself, except that he came from Colophon, a bit up the Western Ionian coast from Miletus, and that he lived most of his long life during the sixth-century BCE. Xenophanes is most famous for his criticism of the 'poetic tradition' in Greek culture, and, in particular, the undue influence of poets such as Homer and Hesiod. His basic complaint was that the gods depicted by these poets were far too human, indulging in scandalous behavior such as adultery, theft and mutual deception. Such gods, claims Xenophon, were not really worthy of human worship, and should be replaced by 'something better'. The type of god he believed should be worshipped would be much more morally attractive than the gods on Mount Olympus, and thus much more worthy of human respect. In saying this, he was actually trying to move the Greeks away from their traditional 'polytheistic' beliefs towards something approaching the 'monotheism' that was eventually adopted by Jews, Christians and Muslims. In this, he was clearly well ahead of his time.

Second Anaxagoras. He was born in Clazomenae, in Ionia, around the year 500 BCE, but later spent roughly 30 years of his life in Athens, between 462 BCE and 432 BCE or thereabout. Although not the equal of Pythagoras, Heraclitus or Parmenides, Bertrand Russell believed that he played an important role in the development of Athenian philosophy. Russell reports that he was probably persuaded to come to Athens by Pericles, 'Tyrant' of Athens at the time, who was 'bent on civilising his fellow-townsmen'. Pericles certainly succeeded in this, leading Athens into a period of high culture and intellectual achievement that would become one of the 'crowning glories' of the ancient world. Virtually nothing like it has been seen since. Being an Ionian, Anaxagorias carried on the rational, scientific tradition of that part of the Hellenic world. He was the first to introduce philosophy to the Athenians, and the first to suggest 'mind' as the primary cause of physical change. In this, he had a tremendous influence of the subsequent work of Socrates, and, following him, Plato.

Third, Zeno. He was born in Elea in the early part of the 5th-century BCE, where he became an associate and student of Parmenides. Zeno is renowned for the 'paradoxes' he invented in support of Parmenides' theory that 'being' cannot change or be more than 'one thing'. The word 'paradox' is another English word that derived from Greek roots, 'para' meaning 'against' and 'doxa' meaning 'belief'. Two of his most famous 'paradoxes - the 'arrow' paradox, and 'Achilles and the tortoise' - seem to show that 'movement' is impossible, and that it is also impossible for a 'fast' runner like Achilles to catch up with a 'slow' mover like a tortoise if the latter is given a head start of any sort. Some of Zeno's paradoxes (including the second one that I have just described) have been explained by subsequent developments in mathematics, but others (such as the 'arrow' paradox) have not. Indeed, this particular paradox lies at the very heart of modern thinking about the underlying nature of space and time.

Finally, the Sophists. These flourished in Athens at around the time of Socrates and Plato, and had a tremendous influence on both of these. It was not that they introduced these two great men to any new **philosophical** ideas; they simply showed them how it was possible to use rhetorical techniques to win an argument without regard to truth, or to use argumentative tricks to embarrass an opponent. The sophists thus gained a reputation for duplicity and underhandedness. Thus, the term 'sophist' came to denote the very opposite of a 'wise person' - someone who was out to **undermine** the 'search for wisdom' that was the mark of a true 'philosopher' (a 'lover of wisdom'). They made their reputation even worse by charging people large sums of money to learn how to use their dubious methods when arguing with other people, as in a court of law or a public meeting. Nevertheless, Plato learned a great deal from the sophists, even naming four of his 'dialogues' after four of the most prominent of them - Protagoras, Gorgias, Hippias and Euthydemus. In short, Plato was obsessed with the sophists, treating them with a mixture of humour, fascination, dismay and disdain. He also found it very difficult to get the better of one in an argument!

Some of the sources of information on material covered in Chapter 3

I referred to several of the books in my personal library when writing this chapter, including the books by Karl Popper and Bryan Magee quoted from or mentioned in the text. Practically all of the information that I used came from the following two sources, however.

- 'History of Western Philosophy', by Bertrand Russell, the first ten chapters of which are entirely devoted to the 'Presocratics'.
- 'Classical Philosophy', by Peter Adamson, the first twelve chapters of which are entirely devoted to the 'Presocratics'.

Chapter 4: The 'Golden Age' of classical philosophy and science

'The whole of western philosophy consists of footnotes to Plato'

- comment allegedly made by Alfred North Whitehead (1861-1947)

Like Chapter 3, the present chapter is a follow-on from, and amplification of, Chapter 2 (The 'Axial Age' of religious and intellectual development). It begins by looking at the amazing philosophical developments that took place in Athens during the 5th - and 4th centuries before the 'Common Era', when three of the greatest of all practitioners of western philosophy (Socrates, his pupil Plato, and **his** pupil Aristotle) effectively founded the subject. Indeed, Plato is widely regarded as the very greatest of **all** western philosophers, (see the above quote from Whitehead), his only rivals for this title being his pupil Aristotle and the towering figure of Immanuel Kant, who worked in Germany roughly 2000 years later. It goes on to review the developments that took place during the following nine centuries, after which scholars in the rapidly-expanding Islamic empire took over responsibility for the continuation of the philosophical and scientific traditions established during the classical era. Indeed, had it not been for these muslim scholars, the entire corpus of classical knowledge might well have been lost forever. The modern world owes them a very real debt of gratitude.

Socrates - the philosopher who never wrote anything

There is a very old academic joke that is told about Socrates. It involves two of the people present at his death in 399 BCE, at the order of his fellow Athenians. The first of these observed that 'They tell me he was a great teacher'. To which the second replied: 'Yes, but he never

published anything!' While some people may feel that this joke is in rather poor taste, I find it extremely funny, and highly relevant - as anyone who has experienced the 'publish-or-perish' rat-race of modern academe will testify. But be that as it may, we probably know more about his work, ideas and teachings that we know of any other Greek philosopher before Plato and Aristotle. This is because Plato became his pupil, and clearly came to revere the man. Indeed, it was he who immortalised the work of Socrates in his own writings. As Peter Adamson observes, 'it is mostly through the dialogues of Plato that Socrates lives on today'. I would go further, and replace 'mostly' with 'almost entirely', and I am sure that many people would agree with me.

Let me begin by telling you what we know about the life of this remarkable man, who was such an important and influential figure that all earlier Greek philosophy came to be classified as 'PreSocratic', as we have seen. We believe that he was born in Athens around 469 BCE, and that he lived and worked there for all his life. We know that he became interested in philosophy, probably because of the influence of Anaxagoras, who, as we saw in the last chapter, lived in Athens between 462 and 432 BCE - exactly the time when Socrates was growing up and maturing. We believe he came from a reasonably-well-off family, was rather an 'ugly man', having a 'snub nose' and a 'paunch', and that he had a rather 'shrewish' wife - Xanthippe (who allegedly emptied a chamber pot over his head on one occasion!). At any rate, Socrates established a considerable reputation as a philosopher, becoming particularly skilled at disputing points with his fellow citizens, and always coming off best, Indeed he often succeeded in humiliating them during such arguments, something that annoyed them greatly, so despite his reputation as the 'wisest man in Athens', he was not particularly popular - quite the opposite, in fact. When the Peloponnesian War between Athens and Sparta began in 431 BCE, he did his civic duty and joined the army. He took part in three campaigns during the first nine years of the war - at Potidaea, Delium and Amphipolis - and distinguished himself by his bravery, remarkable physical endurance and indifference to the weather. He otherwise remained aloof from politics, confining himself to challenging and criticising the views that prevailed in Athens at the time. This again did not make him particularly popular, and was no doubt a major factor in the decision to put him on trial for 'impiety' and 'corrupting the young' at the age of 70. He was found guilty by his fellow citizens, declined the option of merely paying fine, and later turned down a chance to escape from prison. As everyone knows, he was sentenced to die by drinking hemlock; Plato later gave an extremely-moving account of his death in 399 BCE in the 'Phaedo', one of the greatest and most important of his 'dialogues'.

So much for the life of Socrates. Let me now take a look at the influence he had on the development of Greek philosophy, and explain why he was such a key figure. According to Bryan Magee, one of the reasons why the 'PreSocratics' were so named was that Socrates 'consciously rebelled against them'. It was not that he disagreed with their actual doctrines - simply with their choice of the questions to be raised, addressed and discussed. He maintained that the most important things that we as human beings really needed to know were not 'impersonal truths about the world' (interesting though they might be), but 'how we ought to live'. So for Socrates, the vital questions were not 'scientific' but 'moral'. He went around Athens asking people questions such as 'What is justice?', 'What is courage?', 'What is piety?', 'What is friendship?', and many, many more. As far as we know, he never wrote anything down, all his 'teaching' being by 'word of mouth'. It took a form that subsequently became known as 'Socratic dialogue'. He used to claim (somewhat ingenuously) that he had 'no wisdom to impart', but only 'questions to ask'. He usually began by asking his selected 'victim' to state what he thought was the meaning of an important concept such as 'justice', and then, whatever the person said, Socrates would go on relentlessly questioning him in such a way that it became obvious that there were self-contradictions in the offered definition, so that 'justice' could not possibly be what the other person said it was, and that person clearly did not **know** what justice really was, even though he had **supposed** that he did. By the end of this ruthless and systematic 'demolition' of his original views, the 'victim' would be left 'profoundly troubled', the 'ruins of his previous assumptions littered around his feet', no longer knowing what was meant by some concept 'fundamental to his life'. Needless to say, this procedure disturbed and annoyed many of his victims, and was regarded as 'socially subversive' by some. As we saw earlier, it all ended with Socrates being put on trial and condemned to death. But by that time, he had 'launched a mode of philosophical enquiry that has continued to the day', and is now 'inextricably associated with the very concept of Western civilisation', as Bryan Magee so succinctly and clearly puts it.

Although he never accepted money for his teaching, Socrates did take on 'pupils', by far the most gifted of these being Plato. He was roughly 31 when Socrates died, and was actually present at his execution. He subsequently made it his business not only to 'clear his master's name', but also to 'continue his work'. Plato therefore wrote and circulated a series of 'dialogues' in which Socrates was always the 'star performer' who 'came out on top' at the end. In these early dialogues, it is virtually certain that Plato was simply reviving and reiterating the questions that had actually been asked and addressed by Socrates. As his own philosophical ideas progressively matured, however, he gradually replaced the ideas of Socrates with those of himself, and it was these, very-much-more-advanced ideas that formed the basis of virtually all of his later dialogues, which included most of his greatest works. He still published these in the form of 'dialogues', however, and still tended to use Socrates as the successful protagonist. This explains the fact that in Plato's 'early' dialogues, the 'Socrates' character largely expresses one philosophical viewpoint, whereas in the 'middle' and 'later' dialogues, he usually puts forward another. They are, in fact, the two different philosophies of two very different philosophers: in the first case the 'historical Socrates', and in the second case, the 'developing Plato', as we will see in the next section of this chapter.

Plato: the greatest of all western philosophers?

Before I describe Plato's key philosophical ideas, let me again tell you what we know of his life. He was probably born in Athens in around 428 BCE, to a 'distinguished aristocratic family', but little is known of his early life. We believe that he was a 'pupil' of Socrates, or at least a 'close associate', but never paid Socrates for his services, since Socrates never founded an official 'school' of any sort. At any rate, Plato grew to 'revere' his mentor, and was absolutely 'shattered' when he was condemned to death and executed in 399 BCE. Plato later immortalized the story of Socrates' trial and last days in three of his 'dialogues' - the 'Apology', the 'Crito' and the 'Phaedo', where his profound affection and respect for Socrates came through vividly. After the execution, Plato and some other 'disciples' of Socrates took temporary refuge in Megara, and then travelled widely in Greece, Egypt, the Greek cities in southern Italy, and Sicily. It is believed that he returned to Athens in 387 BCE in order to found the 'Academy', which became a famous centre for philosophical, mathematical and scientific research, and over which he presided until his death in 348 BCE. Plato's 'Academy' outlived all the other Greek philosophical 'schools', remaining the 'centre' for pagan Greek philosophy until the 529th year of the of the 'Common Era', when it was closed down by Justinian, the Christian Eastern Roman Emperor, because of his 'religious bigotry'. This was a sad day for civilisation, and was one of the events that ushered in the subsequent 'Dark Ages' in Europe.

Let me now turn to Plato's philosophy, and explain why he was such a pivotal figure in the development of western philosophy - arguably the most important and influential figure in its entire history (see the quotation from Whitehead at the start of this chapter).

As we saw at the end of the previous section of this chapter, Plato's philosophical development went through two distinct stages. In the first (represented in his 'early' dialogues) he effectively revived and improved on the previous work of Socrates, with practically all the major ideas originating from him. In the second (represented in his 'middle' and 'late' dialogues) he 'moved on' from the influence of Socrates, and started to present his own, revolutionary ideas. The 'early' dialogues were almost totally concerned with 'moral' and 'personal' questions, the issues that had interested Socrates to the exclusion of virtually anything else. The 'middle' and 'late' dialogues, on the other hand, ranged over 'the whole of human experience': cosmology and science, mathematics, the arts, political and social life, personal mortality, and much, much more. It was because Plato came so close to mapping out the terrain with which western philosophers have concerned themselves ever since that the 20th-century English philosopher Alfred North Whitehead was prompted to make his famous observation that 'the whole of western philosophy consists of footnotes to Plato'. Although this is probably going a bit too far, it certainly has a great deal of truth in it.

In 'Confessions of a Philosopher', Bryan Magee made another highly-perceptive comment on Plato's philosophy. Not only did Plato embrace the 'cosmological concerns' which Socrates completely ignored and rejected, he put 'mathematical physics' at the very heart of his account of the empirical 'physical world' that we 'believe' we see around us, and in which we 'believe' that we live out our lives. However, Plato did not believe that the empirical world is all that there is. On the contrary, it is, in his view, a world of 'appearances only', of 'fleeting phenomena' that have no abiding reality. Lying behind and beyond this 'phenomenal' world is, according to Plato, a world of timeless, non-material entities that constitute the only 'permanent reality' there is. This is his famous doctrine of 'Forms', a doctrine that is described in vivid terms in what is probably the most famous passage in all Plato's writings - the 'cave' metaphor in his 'Republic'. He had a great deal to say about the relationship between his world of 'Forms' and the world of our everyday experience, and also about the way in which human beings can hope to gain knowledge of the 'eternal'. Plato's ideas on the world of 'eternal forms' had a great influence on the early development of Christianity. Indeed, Bryan Magee believes that some of the ideas that we now think of as 'Christian' are in fact essentially 'Platonic' in origin. As we will see later in the book, some of his ideas about a transcendental 'Platonic realm' are still highly influential today.

Let me end this section on Plato by outlining yet another very telling and perceptive series of comments that Bryan Magee made in 'Confessions of a Philosopher'. First, he pointed out that the works of Plato were the 'first written works of any Western philosopher to survive in the form in which he wrote them'. Socrates, as we have seen, wrote nothing, with practically all of our knowledge of him, and of what he said, being derived from Plato's 'dialogues'. And as for the 'PreSocratics', **not a single one** of their complete works has survived, our knowledge of them consisting **entirely** of quotations, summarized and referenced in the work of others, although some of these are 'quite long'. Magee also points out that we believe we are in possession of **all** Plato's written works, something that he regards as near-miraculous. As he said, there is 'something uniquely awe-inspiring' about Plato's achievement, in that he 'produced work of genius across the entire range of philosophical thought' at a time when 'no-one else had ever come remotely close to doing any such thing'.

Not only that, but 'a great many of his ideas have remained at, or very near, the centre of western thinking ever since'.

Magee also points out that Plato was 'a wonderful literary artist as well as a great philosopher'. It has long been agreed among classical scholars that his is 'the most beautiful Greek prose ever to have been written'. His dialogues display 'mastery of literary form', 'economic yet effective characterisation', 'cunning use of dramatic irony' and many other admirable characteristics. There are roughly two dozen of them, varying in length between 20 and 300 printed pages, and good English translations of nearly all of them are now easily available. As Bryan Magee concludes, 'nearly all are well worth reading'.

Aristotle: the father of empiricism

We now turn our attention to the third of the great Athenian philosophers who completely transformed the subject during the 5th - and 4th-centuries before the Common Era - Aristotle. As I did with Socrates and Plato, let me begin by telling you what we know about his life - quite a lot, as it happens. He was born in Stagira, a Greek colony on the Chalcidice Peninsula, in 384 BCE, where he was the son of the Court Physician to the King of Macedon (the father of Philip II and the grandfather of Alexander the Great). In 367, he moved to Athens, where he became a pupil at Plato's 'Academy', and later, a teacher, remaining at the Academy until Plato's death in 347 BCE. Speusippus succeeded Plato as Head of the Academy, and Aristotle left Athens for 12 years. He spent some time at Atarneus in Asia Minor (where he married) and then at Mitylene, and, in about 342 BCE, was appointed by King Philip of Macedon to act as a tutor to his son Alexander, then aged 13. He finally returned to Athens in 335 BCE to found his own School (which was named the 'Lyceum' because of its proximity to the Temple of Apollo Lyceius), where he taught for the next twelve years. When Alexander the Great died in 323 BCE, there was a strong 'anti-Macedonian' reaction in Athens, and Aristotle was accused of 'impiety'. Remembering what had happened to Socrates 76 years earlier, he took refuge at Calcis in Euboia, where he died in the following year - 322 BCE. With him died the last of the three 'Athenian Immortals' in the field of philosophy, the like of which it would never see again. Nor would anywhere else, as it turned out.

'The School of Athens', by Raphael, is one of my very favourite paintings. I have a print of it in my front hall, opposite the bottom of the stairs, so I see it every time I come down them. At the very centre are two figures, walking towards us. One is a clearly-aging Plato, and the other is a much-younger Aristotle. The index finger of Plato's right hand is pointing 'upwards', indicating that this is where the 'secrets of the universe' can be found. Aristotle's right arm is extended, with the palm of his hand moving 'downwards', indicating that **this** is where these secrets can be found. In these two gestures, the incomparable genius of Raphael succeeded in capturing the key difference between the contrasting philosophical beliefs and approaches of the two men, which, in various forms, were to confront each other down through the ages, right up to the present time, in fact. On the one hand, there are philosophers who believe that the world of actual and possible human experience (what we now call the 'empirical' or 'phenomenal' world) is not what is permanent, or permanently important, so that we should try to 'transcend it with our minds'. If that proves impossible, we should try to 'think' our way towards the boundary between the 'empirical' and 'transcendental' worlds, so that even if we cannot **cross** the frontier we can at least 'pin it down' and 'see where it runs'. On the other hand, there are philosophers who think that, **whether or not the empirical world is all that there is,** it is all that we can **experience** or **know**, and if we try to 'soar towards it on the wings of unsupported thought' (to quote Bryan Magee yet again), 'we shall talk nonsense during the flight and inevitably crash'. Furthermore, there is no need to 'pass beyond this world of experience' in our search for something worth philosophising about, for it is **in itself** an inexhaustible source of curiosity, wonder, richness and beauty; trying to understand it will engross us, and reward us, for a lifetime if we really want it to. During the 20th century, Karl Popper did exactly that, and enriched philosophy as a result.

The difference between these two approaches relates strongly to most of the 'great bifurcations' in the history of Western philosophy - 'rationalism' versus 'empiricism', 'idealism' versus 'realism' or 'naturalism', and so on. The 'temperament' of individual philosophers tends to draw them towards one side or another, with most of them eventually becoming either 'Plato persons' or 'Aristotle persons' by some sort of 'natural inclination'. According to Bryan Magee, it was the 'unique greatness' of Immanuel Kant that showed how the two approaches could be integrated, and, in so doing, showed philosophy its 'true path'. I will describe how he did this, with later help from Schopenhauer, in Chapter 8.

Aristotle was the first and the greatest philosopher of the 'second kind', the greatest of the 'natural empiricists', although the British produced some 'pretty good ones' too, as we will again see in Chapter 8. He was 'in love with experience', and he devoted his life to 'deepening and enriching his understanding of it', always working from **inside** experience, and never trying to impose abstract explanations of it from the **outside.** In the course of a hard-working lifetime of doing this, he became a sort of 'one-man encyclopaedia'. He not only 'marked off' the subject areas of the basic sciences for the first time, he actually gave some of them the names by which they are still known today. He also did some of the earliest worthwhile work in several of them. Not only did he seek 'scientific explanations', he actually had the insight to ask fundamental questions about what a 'scientific explanation' **is,** and how we should go about formulating one. He also codified all known logic into principles that formed the basis of the subject for the next 2000 years. He studied plants, animals, human beings and their many different forms of political organisation, and made significant contributions to ethics and aesthetics. He explored some of the most fundamental metaphysical problems, covering areas such as the respective natures of 'mind', 'identity', 'form', 'substance, 'continuity', 'change', and 'causal connection', saying permanently-important things about each. There was a period of several hundred years, much later, when his work constituted 'the largest organised body of knowledge that Western man possessed'. Indeed, when universities came into existence in Medieval Europe, they invariably made the works of Aristotle the 'foundation of the curriculum'.

The numerous works that Aristotle prepared for publication during his own lifetime were praised throughout antiquity for their 'superlative beauty of style'. Cicero, for example (no mean judge!) described his writing as a 'river of gold'. Tragically none of it survives, and all we have today is material written up from 'lecture notes', mostly by his pupils, but some probably by himself. References in ancient literature to him and his published writings are so numerous that we have a pretty good idea about what has been lost, and the general consensus is that what we now possess represents something like a fifth of his total output. It fills twelve volumes, and ranges over the whole of what was then 'human knowledge'. The fact that it consists of 'written-up lecture notes' also makes it rather 'stodgy reading', so that it tends to be read only by students and scholars. This is a 'great tragedy', according to Bryan Magee, since it means that his work is seldom read for pleasure by 'intelligent people' - unlike, the wonderful 'dialogues' that Plato has left behind for us. These could well have been lost in the same way, which does not bear thinking about.

Classical developments after Plato and Aristotle

After discussing the work of Aristotle and Plato at great length in the first volume of his 'History of Philosophy Without Any Gaps', Peter Adamson made the (to me, somewhat-surprising) observation that the work of these two great philosophers played 'a relatively small role' in subsequent Hellenistic philosophy for a long time after their deaths, and that 'it took a few hundred years for their influence to become dominant'. It is true that both had founded 'Schools' to teach their successors about their ideas, but it is also true that Hellenistic philosophy went off in a number of completely-different directions until the work of Plotinus and the so-called 'Neoplatonists' during the later stages of the western part of the Roman Empire brought their work back into the 'mainstream' once again. I will now describe four of the most important of these 'philosophical diversions' before discussing the work of Plotinus and his followers at some length in the next section of the chapter.

Let me begin by looking at the work of the 'Cynics', the first of the new branches of philosophy to make an appearance. It is now believed that one of Socrates's 'disciples', Antisthenes, was the first of that order, but it was Diogenes (who Plato described as 'Socrates run mad') who really brought it into prominence. He and his fellow Cynics (so called because they 'lived like dogs') launched a major assault on the 'civilised values' of the ancient world. They did this both by their 'unconventional lifestyles', in which they eschewed all the comforts of civilised life, and by their 'anarchistic doctrines'. There are many stories about Diogenes, the most famous being his alleged encounter with Alexander the Great, who came to visit him in the 'tub' in which he lived. When Alexander enquired what he could do to help him, he simply asked him to 'get out of my light' since he was standing between Diogenes and the sun. (Some of the other stories about him are far too scurrilous to include in a respectable book like this.) One of the best-known of his followers was Crates, who had abandoned a rich inheritance in order to live the possessionless life of a cynic. He left his fortune 'in trust', with instructions that if his sons were 'ordinary men', they should have the money, but if they were 'philosophers', it should be 'given to the people' since his sons would have 'no need of it'. Crates also wrote popular verse extolling the natural life, 'devoid of luxury, pride or malice'. Although they despised and denigrated the 'intellectual and political currency of their day', Diogenes and his fellow cynics were actually 'dedicated moralists', not 'nihilists', as has sometimes been claimed. They must have been very interesting people to meet!

Let me now turn to the 'Epicureans', whose views on how to live could not have been more different from those of the cynics. The movement was founded by Epicurus, who was born in Athens around 341 BCE, and founded a school of philosophy in 306 BCE. He purchased a large house with an extensive garden just outside the walls of Athens for this purpose; the house provided accommodation, with the actual teaching taking place in the garden - hence the name by which his school became known: 'The Garden'. Epicureanism was founded on two basic principles. The first was metaphysical, with its followers being expected to embrace a purely 'materialistic' view of reality, based on the teachings of the 'atomists'. The second defined the way of life that they were encouraged to adopt, and it is for this aspect of their philosophy that they are best known. Its central purpose was to produce 'happiness', through having 'a mind free of disturbance' and 'a body free from pain'. As a consequence, it gained a reputation for attracting 'voluptuaries' who were only interested in living a life of luxury and indulgence. But Epicurus' own words make it abundantly clear that his 'hedonism', although 'theoretically permissive', was in reality 'very austere'. Seneca was probably just about right when he observed that Epicureanism 'has a bad name, is of ill repute, and yet undeservedly'. Epicurus was the leader of the 'Garden' community until his death in about 270 BCE, when he was succeeded by Hermarchus, and, in about 250 BCE, by Polystratus. 'The Garden' was still in existence 450 years later, and Epicureanism had considerable influence in the Hellenistic and Roman worlds throughout this time. After going out of fashion for some time due to Christian opposition, it was 'rediscovered' during the sixteenth and seventeenth centuries of the 'Common Era', and became highly influential in modern science and modern humanism.

The other philosophical school to exert a major influence on the way Greeks and Romans lived at the time when Epicureanism was flourishing was 'Stoicism'. This was founded by 'Zeno of Citium' (334-262 BCE) and developed by Cleanthes and Chrysippus, being named after the 'Painted Porch' (Stoa poikilē) in Athens where they taught. The last major figure in antiquity to have stoicism as his primary allegiance was the Roman Emperor Marcus Aurelius in the second century of the Common Era, but the influence of the school's ideas lived on, and the term 'stoical' has become a common expression to indicate acceptance of misfortune without complaint. Stoicism placed ethics in the context of an understanding of 'the world as a whole', with 'reason' being paramount both in 'human behaviour' and in the 'divinely-ordered cosmos'. The highly-systematic nature of Stoic philosophy reflected the school's view of the 'systematic nature of the world' itself, which it sought to explain without recourse to 'Platonic other-worldliness'. Much of earlier Greek philosophy had placed considerable importance on 'material achievement' and the acquisition of 'worldly goods', despite the arguments against these by Socrates. The Stoics agreed with Socrates, arguing that the only thing that **really** mattered was trying to do what is 'right'. They accepted that health and wealth were clearly **preferable** to sickness and poverty, and that it was perfectly acceptable to **pursue** them provided that we did no harm to others by doing so, but that **achieving** them was effectively beyond our control. Thus, we should accept whatever fate has in store for us with 'stoical' good grace. From a religious point of view, the stoics were essentially 'pantheists', believing that God not only orders 'everything for the best', but is also **present** in everything as some sort of 'spirit'. (They were clearly well ahead of their time here, since the term 'pantheism' did not come into common usage until 1705, when it was first used by John Toland.)

Before moving on to Plotinus and the 'Neoplatonists', let me end this section of the chapter by taking a brief look at the work of the 'Sceptics'. Their name comes from the Greek word 'skeptikoi', and denotes those philosophers who refuse to adopt 'dogmatic' positions, preferring to remain in 'investigation', or 'consideration' ('skepsis') of questions. The roots of the movement can be found in several early Greek philosophers, including Xenophanes, Parmenides and Democritus, but the man who is credited with turning the movement into a philosophical 'school' was Pyrrho of Elis, who was born around 360 BCE and died roughly 90 years later. He attracted one important 'disciple', Timon of Phlius, who travelled to Elis as a young man and later moved to Athens in order to 'challenge the prevailing dogmatisms in the spirit of his master'. The most important development for scepticism during the 3rd-century BCE was its introduction into the curriculum of Plato's 'Academy' by Arcesilaus. Here, Arcesilaus and the other members of the Academy who adopted his views directed their 'increasingly refined destructive arguments' against stoic ideas in theology and ethics. The academy must have been a very 'lively place' at the time! Our best source of information on Pyrrhonist sceptical thinking are the writings of Sextus Empiricus, a later member of the school. During the 16th century of the Common Era, the writings of Empiricus and other early sceptics became widely known in Europe, and triggered the modern 'revival' of interest in scepticism, eventually leading to the ground-breaking work of Descartes, as we will see in Chapter 8.

Plotinus: the most influential of the later classical philosophers

It is generally agreed that Plotinus, the founder of the philosophical school that came to be known as 'Neoplatonism', was by far the greatest and most influential of the philosophers who worked in the later part of the classical period. Indeed, Peter Adamson says that 'a good case can be made for seeing Plotinus as the most influential Western philosopher of all time, apart from Plato and Aristotle themselves'. Before we examine this claim in greater detail, let me again begin by giving a short account of his life. We believe that he was born in Egypt, of Roman parentage, around the 205th year of the Common Era, but that his education and intellectual background were Greek. We know that he studied in Alexandria under Ammonius Saccas for over 11 years, after which he joined a Roman military expedition to the East so that he could 'learn from Persian and Indian philosophers' according to his editor and biographer Porphyry. When the expedition was subsequently aborted, he moved to Rome at the age of 40 or thereabout. There, he acquired important 'court patronage', and spent the rest of his life teaching. From the age of 50, he wrote in Greek, producing a series of essays and shorter articles which were 'chatty in style' but at the same time 'difficult and earnest', and were also 'enriched with superb similes'. After his death in 270, Porphyry 'chopped them up', and 'gathered them into six groups of nine', which became known as the 'Enneads'. At the age of 60, he tried to found a utopian community in Campania based on Plato's 'ideal republic', but the Emperor Gallienus 'put a stop to the project' before it really got going'. Knowing what we now know about the blatantly-totalitarian nature of Plato's 'ideal republic' thanks to the ruthless and systematic attack on it made by Popper in Volume 1 of 'The Open Society and its Enemies', this was probably just as well!

So much for his life; let us now turn to his philosophical ideas, which became the foundations of what eventually became known as

'Neoplatonism'. In this, he re-visited the key ideas of Plato and Aristotle, incorporating many of these into his new 'philosophy/ religion', along with a 'healthy dose of stoicism'. The resulting 'mixture' proved 'highly appealing' (to put it mildly). It would be embraced by 'pagans' throughout the now-totally-dominant Roman Empire, by Christians in Byzantium and Western Europe, and, later, by Christians, Jews and Muslims who lived in the vast Islamic Empire that swallowed up large parts of the Eastern and Western worlds during the seventh century. Within decades of Plotinus' death, Augustine (the greatest of all the early Christian philosophers) 'drank deeply from the Neoplatonic stream', and a thousand years later, Thomas Aquinas (the greatest of the Medieval Christian philosophers) would do the same. Neoplatonism would become, if anything, even more dominant during the 'Renaissance', before it was finally 'chased away from centre-stage' in the early-modern period. As we have seen, Western philosophy began roughly two-and-a-half thousand years ago, with the 'PreSocratics'. And for roughly half that time, from the 3rd to the 15th centuries of the Common Era, philosophy was, to a significant extent, dominated by Neoplatonism. I think that this more than justifies Peter Adamson's views on his importance in the history of philosophy and religion.

Let me now try to outline the ideas themselves. This will be difficult, since they are fairly complicated and, in many ways, highly abstruse, but I will try. Although he was not a Christian, Plotinus shared with his Christian contemporaries a preoccupation with religion. Central to his philosophy was his metaphysical doctrine of the 'Trinity', which he developed around the time when Origen was developing the idea of the Christian 'Trinity'. The three elements of Plotinus' Trinity were the 'One', 'Nous' (or 'Spirit'), and the 'Soul'. The 'One', which Plotinus sometimes called 'God', sometimes the 'Good', was derived from the ideas of Socrates and Plato, and Plotinus believed that it could never be 'explained' or even 'described' without causing confusion. 'Nous', or 'Spirit', which came next in his scheme, could be regarded as 'rational intelligence', and was believed to 'emanate' from the 'One'. Finally the 'Nous' gives rise to the 'Soul', and this, in turn, gives rise to the visible, phenomenal world, which we, as humans, are able to perceive because each of us partakes of the 'Soul'. Details of his highly-complicated doctrine of the 'Soul' drew on the ideas of both Plato and Aristotle, and, as we have seen, from some aspects of Stoic philosophy. Although he 'took no notice of Christianity' in formulating his doctrines, Christianity certainly 'took notice' of **his** in formulating **theirs**, as we have seen.

There are many other important ideas embedded in Neoplatonism, but I have no space to deal with them here. Peter Adamson devotes four chapters of the second volume of his 'History of Philosophy without any Gaps' to Plotinus and his philosophy. These are clear, highly-perceptive, and very easy to read, and I again commend them to readers who wish to study his ideas in greater detail.

The key role played by Alexandria in philosophy and science

Before discussing Alexandria's 900-year history as the greatest centre for philosophy and science that the world has ever seen, let me set the background for this by outlining the world-changing career of its founder - Alexander the Great. It was actually his father, Philip II of Macedon, who devised the unbeatable military tactics that enabled Alexander to conquer most of the known world between 336 BCE, when he succeeded to the Macedonian throne following his father's assassination, and 323 BCE, when he himself died during the return from his campaigns in India. These were built round the virtually-invincible 'Macedonian phalanx', which was supported by superb 'shock cavalry' that were used to encircle and destroy the enemy. Phillip had shown the Greeks what his army could do at the Battle of Chaeronea in 338 BCE, and his son subsequently completed the conquest of Greece, making all their hitherto-independent 'city states' part of the burgeoning Macedonian Empire. He then won the first two of his three major victories against the Persian Empire (Granicus in 334, and Issus in 333), after which he turned his attention southwards for a while, taking and destroying Tyre, annexing the whole of Palestine, and then moving to Egypt, where he was welcomed as a 'liberator' from the Persians. Indeed, the Egyptians hailed Alexander, then aged 24, as the 'living god Horus', and declared him their new 'Pharaoh'. He remained in Egypt for roughly 18 months, winning the loyalty of his subjects by endowing and restoring temples and shrines. He also founded Alexandria on the western edge of the Nile delta; this had a superb harbour, thus ensuring the supply of Egyptian grain to the Hellenic world. As we saw in Chapter 1, Egypt came under the rule of one of Alexander's leading generals (Ptolemy) after his death, and it was he who turned Alexandria, now his capital, into a centre for commerce, and for the cultivation and promotion of Greek culture. Indeed it became **the** cultural, philosophical and scientific centre for the entire 'Hellenic world', which, thanks to Alexander's eastern conquests after he left Egypt in 331, now extended far further than it had ever done before.

In around 300 BCE, Ptolemy I chose his new capital, Alexandria, as the site for a highly-ambitious project. This would involve setting up a huge 'Library', which would gather together **all** the writings that could be found on **all** topics, together with a so-called 'Museum', dedicated to the 'Muses', in whose honour and with whose guidance activities in the Museum would be conducted. Scholars and scientists would receive free lodgings in the Museum, along with a place where they could carry out research, investigate and collaborate. It was here that 'scientific activities' ran alongside 'literary activities' for the first time, and where scholars began to 'specialise' much more than earlier Greek thinkers.

Euclid, arguably the most famous of all the Greek mathematicians, was the first great scientific figure to work in Alexandria, where he is believed to have founded a mathematical school. He was followed by Archimedes (287-212 BCE) who moved from Syracuse in Sicily in order to study there, and, at about the same time, by Appollonius, about whom we will hear much more later. Astronomy had always fascinated Greek philosophers, and this tradition was continued and greatly expanded by a string of famous astronomers who worked in Alexandria. Aristarchus (who anticipated Copernicus by suggesting that the Earth revolves around the Sun rather than the other way around) was one of them, as was Ptolemy, who produced the most refined version of the earth-centred cosmology in the second century of the Common Era. This was to dominate astronomical thinking for over 1400 years, especially after it was adopted as the 'official Christian cosmology' during the 13th century (again, more of that later). Another prominent late Alexandrian scientist was Hero, who worked there during the first century of the Common Era. In addition to being a mathematician. He invented many mechanical devices, including an early precursor of the steam engine. From the outset, Alexandria also became the seat of a famous school of medicine, where the theories of earlier thinkers were supplemented by a systematic study of the human body; it is known that the first anatomical dissections of the deceased were carried out here.

The scientific dominance of Alexandria continued throughout most of the 'Roman' period, but was gradually weakened by the rise of Christianity and the decline of Alexandria's political importance after it became part of the Byzantine Empire in the fourth century of the Common Era. Since Greek science was thought of as 'heathen' or 'pagan' learning by the early Christians, it was regarded with 'suspicion' by the early Church, especially after Christianity became the 'official religion' of the Roman Empire. So-called 'pagan' thinkers were often given a very hard time by the early Christian Church.

Perhaps the most disgraceful episode was the death of Hypatia (375-415), the first notable female astronomer and mathematician, who taught at Alexandria, and later became Head of the Neoplatonist School there. Cyril, the Archbishop of Alexandria, came to resent her influence, and she was subsequently brutally murdered by a Christian mob he may have incited to riot. The details of Hypatia's 'lynching' are too gruesome to repeat here, but can be found on page 365 of the '2000' paperback edition of Bertrand Russell's 'History of Western Philosophy' if you want to know what happened to her. In the end, the ancient scientific and philosophical tradition in Alexandria outlived the closing of Plato's 'Academy' in Athens by just over a hundred years until 640, when the city was captured by the Arabs and its famous 'library' was destroyed. This is generally regarded as the greatest loss of knowledge in the entire history of humanity.

Some of the sources of information on material covered in Chapter 4

I have drawn this information from an extremely wide range of sources in my personal library, but by far the most of this came from the following:

- 'Confessions of a Philosopher', by Bryan Magee, perhaps the most perceptive commentator on the history of philosophy that I have ever read.
- 'The History of Western Philosophy', by Bertrand Russell, a mammoth tome that is an endless source of useful information in the same area.
- 'Classical Philosophy' and 'Philosophy in the Hellenistic and Roman Worlds', the first two volumes in Peter Adamson's 'History of Philosophy without any Gaps' series; he is a perceptive and amusing writer who is well worth reading.

- 'The Oxford Companion to Philosophy', edited by Ted Honderich, of which I own the 2005 edition; a key reference source of information on all aspects of philosophy.
- 'Chambers Biographical Dictionary'; I picked up the 1990 edition, edited by Magnus Magnusson, at a library clearance sale, and have found it to be a veritable mine of detailed information about practically everybody of any importance, including philosophers.

Chapter 5: Eastern religion and philosophy

'A person must understand the approach and the answers offered by Eastern thought to be a truly educated citizen of the world'.

- Grant Hardy (Great Minds of the Eastern Intellectual Tradition)

Today, everyone takes this statement as 'accepted truth', but it took a **very** long time for eastern religious and philosophical ideas to become widely known in the western world, and the same was true for other parts of the world outside Asia. (As late as the early 19th century, for example, one of the greatest of our Western philosophers, Schopenhauer, was able to write his masterwork 'Die Welt als Wille und Vorstellung' ('The World as Will and Representation') without knowing **anything** about Eastern philosophy, mainly because few translations of the major texts were available at the time. He later discovered that one of the key doctrines proposed in his book, that Kant's 'noumenal world' was intrinsically undifferentiated, had been anticipated by Hindu and Buddhist thinkers over 2000 years earlier, and, for the rest of his life, became an avid reader of some of their key texts.) In the 'small', highly-connected world of today, people who want to know about the 'human condition' and the 'nature of reality' can no longer hope to do so merely by studying 'Western thought' on these matters. As I hope I have demonstrated in this book, it is now necessary to have much 'broader horizons'. Beside which, the variety and richness of the Eastern intellectual tradition is 'truly breathtaking', so that it is a fascinating field of study in its own right. I have certainly found it so. In this chapter, I will take a much-closer look at the four most important Eastern religions to emerge from the 'Axial Age' – **Hinduism, Buddhism** and Chinese religion in the form of **Confucianism** and **Taoism**. In each case, I will provide a review of their origins and subsequent history, but will concentrate on their core ideas and on the way in which they are now practised by their many followers.

A closer look at Hinduism

As we saw in Chapter 2, Hinduism was born in the Indus Valley in North-Western India near the start of the 'Axial Age' in around 800 BCE. It had its roots in the ritual-based 'Vedic' religion that was practised in this part of India between 1500 and 800 BCE, a religion that was based on India's oldest and most sacred scriptures, the 'Vedas'. Between 800 BCE and around 400 BCE, the period of 'classical Hinduism' began with a progressive move away from a 'ritual-based' religion to one based on the 'spiritual development' of the individual. It was during this 'transitional' period that an important new set of spiritual writings, the 'Upanishads', were written, and came to define Hindu doctrine and practice. Hinduism continued to develop, evolve and mature during the final stages of the Axial Age, which also saw the composition of the 'Bhagavad Gita' (the 'Song of God'), which took Hinduism into new areas and became the most frequently-read Hindu scripture; it still is. By the end of the Axial Age, Hinduism had spread throughout most of India. It continued to evolve and develop during the following thousand years or so, with its underlying doctrines undergoing a significant change during the 8th-century of the Common Era as a result of the influence of Hinduism's greatest-ever religious thinker – Shankara. He was born in Kaladi, a village in the Kerala region in Southern India, in 788, to a 'Brahmin' family 'known for its learning'. He died in 820 at the early age of 32, but, during his short life, moved Hinduism in a radically new direction. He held that the conventional distinction between ourselves and 'Brahman' (the 'fundamental power or principle supporting all that there is') rested upon 'ignorance and illusion', and that we are all actually 'one' with Brahman. Some Hindu teachers later tended to react against Shankara's 'monism'. They stressed the 'devotional life', which presupposes a 'personal God' who is distinct both from the worshiper and from the world. Of these later teachers, Ramanuja was by far the most important and influential. He was born near Madras in Southern

India early in the 11th century, although the exact date of his birth and death 100 years later are not known. He prepared the way for the 'bhakti, or 'devotional', branch of Hinduism (see below). Hinduism remained the dominant religion in India during the ensuing centuries, and still is today.

In Chapter 2, I attempted to introduce readers to some of the key concepts that underpin the vast and complicated entity to which we give the name 'Hinduism'. Let me now try to explain some the most important of these in more detail.

First let us look at its basic metaphysics. As we have seen, this centred on a belief that there is a single, underlying power or principle that underpins and supports the universe and everything that it contains. Hindus call this 'Brahman'. Some Hindu philosophers, such as Shankara, believed that this was really all that there was, and that everything else, including ourselves, is some sort 'manifestation' of Brahman. This 'monistic', highly-abstract view of reality appealed to some Hindu thinkers, but others found it far too 'impersonal', and felt that most 'ordinary' Hindus would find it difficult to relate to such an entity, let alone worship it. It was for this reason that Hindu thinkers had developed their vast 'pantheon', thus enabling individual Hindus, individual families, or individual communities or regions to worship their own, highly 'personal' gods and goddesses. At the 'top' of this pantheon were three 'gods', who represented different but complementary aspects of life: Brahma the 'creator' (the 'personification' of Brahman), Vishnu the 'sustainer', and Shiva the 'destroyer'. The fundamental aspects of the process of constant change that they saw in the world around us were each acknowledged and portrayed as 'embodied' in the image of their respective god. They also believed that this 'phenomenal' world was essentially an 'illusion', although it appeared very real to us. Quite a metaphysics!

Second, let us look at their concept of the 'self'. Whereas **ultimate** reality is called 'Brahman', the individual 'self' is called 'Atman', which is sometimes translated as 'soul'. One of the central subjects of discussion, debate and disagreement among Hindu scholars throughout the ages is the 'relationship' between Atman and Brahman. Some, like Sankara, followed the teachings of the Upanishads and maintained that they were, literally, one and the same thing. In other words they believed that the 'self' was 'one' with the 'absolute'. Others, like Ramanuja, believed that there **was** a distinction between the two, a distinction that enabled 'devotion to' and 'worship of' personal gods and goddesses to take place. All Hindus also believed in 'reincarnation', and in 'samsara', a seemingly-endless succession of births, deaths and rebirths which was governed by the moral principle of 'karma', whereby what we do in each life affects what happens to us in subsequent lives. At the very heart of Hinduism is the belief that the ultimate goal of life is to escape from the bounds of 'samsara' altogether by achieving 'moksha'.

Third, let us look at the way in which Hinduism is practised. As we also saw in Chapter 2, Hinduism has always been a very 'broad church', in which the different natures and different needs of individual human beings were recognised and catered for. Over a long period of time, Hinduism came to recognise that there were really only four different types of person. Some are basically 'reflective'. Others are primarily 'emotional'. Still others are essentially 'active'. Finally, some are most accurately characterised as 'empirical', or 'experimental'. For each of these four personality types, a different 'path', or 'yoga' is recommended. The word 'yoga' comes from the same root as the English word 'yoke', which carries a double connotation: to 'unite' (to 'yoke together'), and to place under 'discipline' or 'training' (to 'bring under the yoke'). Both connotations are present in the Sanskrit word. Defined generally, then, a 'yoga' is a method of training designed to lead to 'integration', or 'union'. But integration of 'what' with 'what', you might ask. The Hindu answer is this: to unite each human being's individual spirit with whatever lies at the heart of ultimate reality, whether it is the abstract concept of 'Brahman' or the more personal concept of 'God'. In what follows, I will use the latter term, since this is the term that is used in most descriptions of the four Hindu 'yogas'. I will now spend some time trying to explain what each of these involves, since they are absolutely central to understanding what modern Hinduism is all about. The four 'yogas' can be succinctly described as 'the way to God through **knowledge**' ('jnana yoga'), 'the way to God through **love**' ('bhakti yoga'), 'the way to God through **work**' ('karma yoga'), and 'the way to God through **psychological exercises**' ('raja yoga'). Let us now look at each of these in turn.

Jnana yoga is intended for spiritual aspirants who have a strong intellectual bent. These are, by nature, 'philosophical', and 'ideas' and 'concepts are of primary importance to them. When such people become convinced of something, it makes a real difference to the way they behave, since their lives 'follow where their minds lead'. Socrates and the Buddha are typical examples. For such people, Hinduism advocates a systematic programme of meditation and logical demonstrations designed to convince the thinker that there is more to them than their 'finite self'; once this kind of person really 'sees this', they will shift their central concern to the 'deeper reaches of their being', and if they persist with the programme for long enough, will eventually attain the 'unity with God' that they seek. This effectively involves moving **beyond** the confines of their individual 'personality'. This word comes from the Latin 'persona', which originally denoted the mask an actor donned before stepping onto the stage to play their role, the mask 'through which' ('per') he 'sounded' ('sonat') his part. The mask carried the make-up for the role, while the actor behind it remained hidden and anonymous, aloof from the emotions enacted. This, say the Hindus, is precisely what our 'personalities' are - the roles in which we have been cast in this greatest drama of all - the tragicomedy of life itself. We have, however, lost sight of the distinction between our 'true self' and the 'veil of personality' that is its present, temporary 'costume'. The purpose of this form of yoga is to correct this false identification, and thus enable the 'yogi' to attain the 'union with God' that they seek. It is said to be the shortest path to such union, but is also the steepest, requiring as it does a rare combination of rationality and spirituality. Thus, it is suited only for the 'select few'.

Bhakti yoga is much more suited to the personalities and needs of many more people. For most of us, life tends to be controlled not so much by **reason** as by **emotion**, and, of all the many emotions that crowd our lives, by far the most powerful and persuasive is 'love'. The aim of bhakti yoga is to direct towards God the 'geyser of love that lies at the base of every heart'. All the basic principles of bhakti yoga are richly expressed in Christianity, which we will examine in detail in Chapter 6. Indeed, from the Hindu point of view, Christianity represents one of the most brilliantly-lit 'bhakti' highways towards God. When following this path, God must be conceived in a totally different way from that of a jnana yogi, where the guiding image is 'an infinite sea of being underlying the tiny waves of our finite selves', their task being to try to 'identify' with this. For a person who elects to go down the 'bhakti' route, and for whom 'love' means **much** more than 'mind', 'God' must be a totally different type of entity. First, since 'healthy' love is essentially an 'out-turning' emotion, the 'bhakti yogi' will reject all suggestions that the God they love is themselves, even their deepest self, and insist on his 'otherness'. Second, because of their sense of God's 'otherness', the bhakti's aim will not be to perceive their **identity** with God, but to 'adore him with every element of their being'. It is here that Hinduism's numerous 'myths' and magnificent 'symbols' help the bhakti yogi down their chosen path, as anyone who has been in a Hindu temple will appreciate. They make a European 'baroque' church look positively bare and austere! It is therefore not surprising that 'bhakti yoga' has countless followers, and is by far the most popular of the four 'paths to God'.

Karma yoga, the way to God through work, is intended for people of a more active bent. Work is the staple of human life. The point is not simply that all but the few of us who are born into the true 'leisure class' **have** to work. Ultimately, the impulse to work is **psychologically**, not **economically**, motivated. If we are forced to be idle through unemployment or illness, most people become irritable, and, if forced to retire before they really want to, many people go into decline, or even die. Hinduism has a message for all working people: you don't have to 'retire to a cloister' to realise God. You can find him in the world of 'everyday affairs' as readily as anywhere. Throw yourself into your work with everything you have, only do it wisely, in a way that will bring the 'highest rewards', not just 'trivia'. Learn the secret of work by which every movement can carry you 'Godward' even while other things are being accomplished. The Hindus also tell us that this can be done in different ways, depending on other aspects of the worker's nature. By electing to go down the 'karma yoga' route, they have already indicated their 'predominantly active' propensities, but there remains the question of whether they wish to seek God 'philosophically' or with an 'attitude of love'. In other words, do they wish to build some elements of 'jnana yoga' or 'bhakti yoga' into their 'karma yoga' programme. Their Hindu advisers will be able to guide them down either route, showing them how to progress towards their ultimate goal in the most efficient and effective way. Virtually anyone can decide to go down the 'karma yoga' route, but some will be more suited to it than others.

Raja yoga has long been known in India as the 'royal road to re-integration' because of the 'dazzling heights' to which it can lead if practised by a person who is best suited to such a route. Designed primarily for people who are basically 'scientific' in bent, it is the 'way to God through psychological experiment'. Traditionally, the West has honoured the 'empiricist' in the laboratory, but has often distrusted their approach in 'things of the spirit', typically accusing them of 'prideful deification of personal experience as the final test of truth'. India has never had any such fear, believing that 'affairs of the spirit' can be approached just as 'empirically' as can the phenomenal world around us. Thus, people who have the inclination and self-discipline to approach God in this way have always been given full encouragement. Theirs is the fourth path to the ultimate goal, the 'royal way' of 'raja yoga'. All that is required is a strong suspicion that our 'true selves' are vastly more wonderful than we now realise, and a passionate desire to gain 'direct experience' of their full reach. **Without** these dispositions, the empiricist will either lack the patience to 'see the thing through', or will turn their experiments 'outwards' and become a 'research student' in the conventional sense. **With** these dispositions, on the other hand, all that is asked is that the 'yogi' should carry out a series of inner, 'mental' experiments with the same patience and rigour as a 'frontier experiment' in physics, and carefully observe the outcome of each. If these outcomes prove to be progressively more positive, the 'raja yogi' will be well on the road to personal 'enlightenment'. Over the centuries, the Hindu 'spiritual masters' have developed powerful and highly-effective methods for helping them do so.

I will now conclude this 'closer look at Hinduism' by discussing one aspect that 'Westerners' often find difficult to understand – its close connection with the Indian 'caste system'. As I showed in Chapter 2, this had its origins in the 'Vedic' society that immediately preceded the 'Axial Age', becoming progressively more embedded in Indian life during the long transition to 'classical Hinduism'. The caste system was based on the traditional 'stratification' of Vedic society, and was regarded as something that was 'imposed on society by the gods' rather than being a purely 'human invention'. It assumed that not all people are created equal, but are born with 'innate differences' derived from 'how they acted in previous lives' through the 'law of karma'.

Structurally, the Indian caste system reflected the four main components of Aryan society. At the top, were the 'Brahmins', comprising the 'priests' and 'intellectuals', who were regarded as having the greatest 'spiritual purity', and were therefore most worthy of respect. Just below them were the 'Ksatriyas', the 'warriors' and 'administrators', followed by the 'Vaisyas', the 'merchants', 'farmers' and 'artisans'. Finally, at the bottom of the four-caste hierarchy, were the 'Sudras', the 'peasants', or 'common folk'. The first three castes were known as the 'twice-born', because, as children, their members underwent a ritual 'second-birth'. The 'Sudras', on the other hand, had no such ritual initiation, and were known as the 'once-born'. Outside the caste system, below its fourth layer, were those who had no 'official caste', known variously as 'outcastes', 'untouchables' and 'Harijans'. This comprised all the people who carried out jobs that were regarded as 'highly polluting' – 'handlers of leather', 'handlers of the dead', 'toilet cleaners', 'scavengers', and so on. Despite carrying out crucial functions in Indian society, they were made to live outside of towns and villages, and could not use the same 'public facilities' as full caste members. Today, they prefer to call themselves 'dalits', meaning the 'oppressed ones', or 'those ground down'. Although technically outlawed by the Indian constitution, the practice of 'untouchability' remains an integral part of daily Hindu life. Despite its somewhat dubious moral status in most modern eyes, the Indian caste system has resulted in a highly-stable society for more than 2,500 years, mainly because of its religious foundations. Far be it for us in the west to be so arrogant as to criticise it; we have done **far** worse things (think slavery and racist colonialism, for example, not to mention the more-recent horrors of fascism and communism).

A closer look at Buddhism

As we saw in Chapter 2, Buddhism was effectively 'born' when Siddhartha Gautama, who had left his home and family behind at the age of 30 in order to become a 'samona' (a wandering ascetic trying to find how to obtain release from the sufferings of life) finally achieved 'enlightenment' at around the age of 35. He had found how to enter 'nirvana', a state of 'utter bliss' in which he became 'totally immersed in' and 'united with' ultimate reality. He could have decided to leave this world there and then, but decided **not** to do so yet, so that he could help other people to follow the path to enlightenment that he had just taken. He then began a 45-year 'ministry of teaching' which only ended with his death at around the age of 80. During this time, he attracted many followers, who gave him the name by which is known today – the 'Buddha' ('Enlightened One'). He and his 'disciples' also founded the religion that is now known as 'Buddhism'. Shortly after the Buddha had moved permanently into nirvana (a process known as 'parinibbana' when it happens to an already-enlightened person), his followers gathered in order to consider how to preserve his 'Dhamma', as his teachings had come to be known, and spread their message even further. Early Buddhist 'councils' led to the eventual creation of authoritative texts ('Suttas'), and to the discussion of important 'doctrinal issues' that eventually split the community into different factions. The spread of Buddhism throughout India and beyond was greatly aided by the patronage it received from King Ashoka, one of India's greatest rulers, who reigned more than a century after the Buddha's death. After converting to Buddhism, he sent missionaries throughout India, Southeast Asia and the Greek Kingdoms in Afghanistan and Central Asia, in order to spread the Buddha's 'Dhamma'. It is now a genuine 'world religion', being practised in some form in virtually every major country. There are currently three main 'schools' of Buddhism. The oldest is 'Theravada' Buddhism (the 'way of the elders'), which is probably closest to the way Buddhism was practised around the time of the Buddha himself. Shortly after the start of the 'Common Era', a radically-different form of the religion ('Mahayana' Buddhism) began to take shape in North-West India. This introduced new 'mythologies', giving the Buddha a more divine, god-like status, and also developing the idea of the 'bodhisattva', an 'enlightened being' who (like the Buddha himself) remains in the 'samsaric realm' for a time in order to help others to gain enlightenment. Mahayana Buddhism was 'exported' to China and other parts of East Asia, and eventually became the most popular form of the religion. It still is. The third main 'school' is 'Vajrayana' Buddhism, an 'off-shoot' of the 'Mahayana' form. This was practised for centuries in Tibet and Mongolia, its spiritual leader being the 'Dalai Lama', who at the time of writing (June 2020) is in exile in India.

I have already provided an outline summary of the key features of the Buddhist religion in Chapter 2, so will not repeat this here. You might find it helpful to re-read it before moving on to the fairly detailed description of Buddhist doctrine and practice that I am about to give.

Buddhist philosophy is based on a highly-complicated metaphysical picture of the 'conditioned world' in which we live, and our place within it, known as 'pratitya samutpada'. This recognises three universal features of this 'conditioned world'. The first, 'Anicca', states that nothing is fixed, since **everything** is in a constant process of change, being dependent on the 'conditions' that maintain it in existence. The second 'Anatta', states that not only is everything changing, but nothing exists in and of itself, because everything is 'interconnected'. This implies that there is no such thing as an inherent 'self' such as the Hindu 'Atman', the Buddhist view seeing each individual as a bundle of five 'skandhas' – 'body', 'feelings', 'perceptions', 'volitions' and 'consciousness'. These come together when we are born, and, when we die, cease to operate together, so that this particular conventional 'self' ceases to exist. The third,

'Dukkha', states that if we do not have a permanent 'self', and if everything is changing and dependent on 'conditions', then life will **inevitably** involve frustration, unhappiness and suffering. To pretend that life does **not** involve dukkha is seen by Buddhists as a deliberate refusal to 'face the facts'.

Buddhism does offer a way out of this unfortunate situation, however, namely, by following the path set out so clearly by the Buddha in his 'Dhamma'. This is based on what he calls the 'Four Noble Truths', and the 'Noble Eightfold Path', otherwise called 'Magga' - the Middle Way. Let me now try to explain what these are, and how they constitute a logical, systematic process that **anyone** can find their way through with the help of appropriate instruction and guidance.

The 'Four Noble Truths' can be very simply stated, taking the form of four 'propositions', each following from the previous one.
1. All life involves 'dukkha' (suffering, or unsatisfactoriness).
2. The cause of suffering is 'tanha' (craving; longing for things to be other than they are).
3. If this craving ceases ('nirodha'), suffering too will cease.
4. The way to eliminate craving is to follow the 'Noble Eightfold Path' (called 'magga', the 'middle way').

The 'Noble Eightfold Path' is generally referred to as 'steps on a path', but these eight key features of a proper Buddhist life are **not** intended to be taken 'in sequence', but 'simultaneously'. They represent features of attitude, lifestyle and spiritual practice which have been found to be helpful in setting up the conditions under which a person will be able to move progressively towards the **goal** of the Buddhist path, namely, seeing things as they 'really are', and thus eventually achieving 'enlightenment' - as the Buddha himself did. The eight 'components' of the Buddhist path are the following.

1. **Right (or perfect) view.** (This refers back to 'interconnectedness' and the fundamental features of the Buddhist 'view of life'; **without** such a view, the path simply does not make sense.)
2. **Right intention.** (This introduces the element of personal, existential **commitment**, since the Buddhist path requires **complete engagement** rather than 'detached reflection'.)
3. **Right speech.** (This specifies various forms of speech that are to be avoided: 'false speech'; 'harsh speech'; 'speech liable to cause dissension'; 'idle chatter', and so on. The opposite - 'truthful', 'gentle', constructive' and 'purposeful' speech - is to be 'cultivated'.)
4. **Right action.** (This sets out the various 'moral precepts' on which a 'good' Buddhist life should be based: 'not to take life' (but to cultivate compassion and goodwill towards all living things); 'not to steal' (but to cultivate generosity); 'not to indulge the senses harmfully' (but to cultivate stillness, simplicity and contentment); 'not to practise **wrong** speech' (but to cultivate **right** speech); 'not to cloud the mind with intoxicants' (but to practise 'mindfulness').
5. **Right livelihood.** (Clearly, Buddhists are encouraged to follow a livelihood that is in line with the fundamental 'Buddhist vision', and, in particular, follows the 'five precepts' given in 'step four' above.)
6. **Right effort.** (Buddhism identifies four 'right efforts': eliminating harmful thoughts or desires that already exist; preventing these from arising in the future; encouraging the arising of 'positive' thoughts and desires; maintaining those positive thoughts that have already arisen.)
7. **Right mindfulness.** (Basically, the Buddhist path requires a person to cultivate awareness of the body, feelings, mental processes, and the objects of thought. This follows from the basic Buddhist view that lack of awareness leads to suffering, and that the goal of the 'spiritual path' is to become 'fully awake' or 'aware' - in other words, to achieve 'buddha nature'.)

8. **Right contemplation.** (As in Hinduism, 'meditation' of various kinds plays a crucial role in the Buddhist path. In general, one might say that the taming and gentle controlling of the mind, calming it, and harmonising the various 'conscious and unconscious urges that determine its activity' is the means by which the path can best be followed.)

I hope that I have managed to give you some idea of the basic features of Buddhism, but am fully aware that it is impossible to do it justice in a few pages. Let me therefore end this section of Chapter 5 with another lengthy quotation from Bryan Magee's 'Confessions of a Philosopher', which has taught me more about philosophy than any other book in my library. Bryan was **not** a religious man, but spent part of his life making a serious study of all the main religions, to see if he could 'get anything out of them'. He concluded his reflections on these investigations with the following words.

'The religion I found most attractive was Buddhism. There are many different varieties of it, and I know too little about any of them to say much, but it did seem to me that some of them were genuinely insightful and genuinely profound. These did not assert the existence of a God, or of a soul, or of immortality, and yet they confidently dismissed the claims of commonsense realism as trivial and wrong. If I may so put it, Buddhism came across to me as an agnostic religion, one that often did justice to the difficulty and complexity of fundamental questions facing human beings (which common sense realism hopelessly fails to do) without attempting to impose dogmatic answers. It occurs often in philosophy that there is more insight in the formulation of a problem than in any of the proposed solutions to it; and it seemed to me that recognition of this was a distinctive characteristic of Buddhism.'

I wish I had written that! It sums up my own views on Buddhism better than I ever could, because Bryan was a 'wordsmith' of the first rank. He will be greatly missed.

A closer look at Chinese religion

We saw in Chapter 2 how the two main Chinese religions, 'Confucianism' and 'Taoism', emerged during the sixth-century BCE, partly in response to the chaos that had prevailed during the 'Period of Warring States' that had ushered in the 'Axial Age' in China. These represented two radically-different sides of Chinese philosophy, but were always seen as 'complementary' rather than as 'irreconcilable opposites'. Both had considerable influence on the subsequent development of Chinese society, an influence that became even greater after the unification of China in 221 BCE, when the 'Qin Dynasty' came to power. During the first century of the 'Common Era', however, both Confucianism and Taoism were seriously challenged by the arrival of Mahayana Buddhism in China, and its spread throughout the country. During the following 900 years or so, China was effectively a 'three religion' country, with the 'Confucianist', 'Taoist' and 'Buddhist' traditions becoming increasingly intermingled among the people. For their 'personal religion', they tended to turn to Buddhism; for help with 'material problems', to Taoism; and for 'social teachings', to Confucius. Starting in the eleventh century, however, a 'new' form of Confucianism, known as 'Neo-Confucianism' became increasingly dominant throughout China, and was eventually adopted as the official 'state cult'. This became much 'broader' than traditional Confucianism, taking into itself a number of new ideas and attitudes that probably originated within the Taoist and Buddhist traditions. It became much more 'metaphysical', for example, teaching that the 'life of the cosmos' involves a constant interplay between two 'principles', one 'spiritual', the other 'corporeal'. Out of this interplay emerged the 'yang' and the 'yin', 'male' and 'female' forces that were identified respectively with 'heaven' and 'earth'. Neo-Confucianism remained the dominant Chinese religion until the first half of the 20th-century, when an influx of western ideas, particularly those associated with 'Marxism', presented a serious challenge to traditional Chinese thought. This culminated in the Communist take-over of China in 1949. China has never been the same since.

Before taking a detailed look at Confucianism and Taoism, let me say something about how the nature of the Chinese written language has had considerable influence on the development of its philosophical and religious traditions. In Chinese, a word gains its meaning largely from the **context** within which it is used. What is more, Chinese written characters are 'ideograms' depicting **whole concepts**, and those characters change as further ideas are added to them. As a consequence, Chinese is an excellent written language in which to set a number of complex ideas next to one another, hinting at their relationship. It is, however, not so easy to weld concepts into a logical argument in Chinese. It is also important to recognise the very conservative nature of Chinese writing, which has changed very little since it was 'standardised' around 200 BCE. Contrast this with the continuous process of change that a Western reader has to deal with, not only **between** languages, but also **within** individual languages. Take the development of English, for example. I recently worked my way through a 'Teaching Company' course on 'The History of the English Language', which described how it had evolved and changed over a 1500-year timespan. It went through three main stages of development, known as 'Old English', 'Middle English' and 'Modern English', and it was only the last of these that I was able to understand without help!

Let me now try to describe some of the main features of Confucianism. As we saw in the brief outline that I gave in Chapter 2, this was primarily designed in order to show how a 'good society' should operate, and thus help the Chinese people to escape from the barbarism and chaos of the 'Period of Warring States'. It was based on the following five concepts.

1. **'Jen'** (or **'Ren'**). This involves simultaneously showing 'humanity' towards others, and 'respect' for oneself, thus demonstrating recognition and acceptance of the 'dignity of human life' wherever it appears. Once this basic ethical principle has been adopted, subsidiary attitudes follow automatically, the most important being 'magnanimity', 'good faith', and 'charity'. By adopting 'Jen' as the basis of your life, you effectively separate yourself from the 'beasts', and show what it means to be 'human'.

2. **'Chun-tzu'**. If 'Jen' is the ideal **relationship** between human beings, 'Chun-tzu' specifies the ideal 'terms' of such relations. What it means is always trying to behave as a true 'gentleman' or true 'lady', in the traditional sense of these words. The 'Chun-tzu' is the opposite of the 'petty' person, the 'mean' person, the 'little' person. Such a person has been compared with the 'perfect host', one who is so relaxed and 'at home' in their surroundings that they can concentrate fully on putting others at their ease and meeting their needs.

3. **Li.** This has two meaning. The first meaning is 'propriety', doing things in the way they **should** be done. This covers a wide range, but Confucius identified five main areas in which 'Li' should be practised, what he called 'Rectification of Names', the 'Mean', the 'Five Key Relationships', the 'Family', and 'Age'. The second meaning of 'Li' is 'ritual'. By this, Confucius means trying to run your entire life in a pre-planned, highly-ordered way, leaving no room for impulsive improvisation.

4. **Te.** Literally, this word meant 'power', specifically the power by which people are ruled. But **how** should this 'power' manifest itself? Confucius disagreed with the 'Realist' thesis that the only effective rule is by 'brute force', backed up by 'physical might'.

This had been tried, and had failed. He maintained that a 'good state' should try to rule with the 'full consent of its people' in so far as this was possible. This required the people to have 'faith' in its 'overall character', and to 'trust' its leaders.

5. **Wen.** The final concept in the Confucian 'gestalt' refers to the 'arts of peace' as contrasted with the 'arts of war' - to music, art, poetry and all the other manifestations of a 'cultured society'. Unlike Plato, who would have banned art in his 'ideal republic' because it was 'imitative' and thus distracted people from recognising and appreciating his 'Forms', Confucius loved the 'arts', regarding them primarily as an 'instrument for moral education'. I know whose 'ideal state' I would have preferred to live in!

So much for Confucianism. Let me now turn to the other main Chinese religion - Taosim. On opening Taoism's 'bible', the 'Tao Te Ching', we see at once that everything revolves round the pivotal concept of the 'Tao' itself. Literally, this means 'path' or 'way', but there are three senses in which this 'way' can be understood. First, 'Tao' is the 'way of ultimate reality'. This 'Tao' cannot be perceived, because it transcends the 'reach of the senses'. Second, although 'Tao' is ultimately 'transcendent', it is also 'immanent'. In this secondary sense, it is 'the way of the universe', the 'norm', the 'rhythm', the 'driving power in all nature'. In the third sense, 'Tao' refers to the way people should 'order their lives' in order to 'fit in with the way the universe operates'.

The Taoists saw all changes in nature as manifestations of the dynamic interplay between the 'polar opposites' **yin** and **yang**, and thus came to believe that **any** pair of opposites constitutes a 'polar relationship' where each of the two poles is dynamically linked to the other, and that the two should be 'kept in balance'. From this concept, Taoists deduced two basic rules for human conduct. First, whenever you want to **achieve** anything, you should start from its 'opposite'. Second, whenever you want to **retain** anything, you should recognise that it contains **something** of its opposite. This is the way of life for a 'sage' who has reached a 'higher' point of view.

When we talk of the Taoist concept of 'change', it is important to realise that this change is not seen as occurring as a consequence of some 'force', but rather as a tendency which is innate in all things and all situations. The movements of the 'Tao' occur naturally and spontaneously, and, since all human conduct should be modelled on the 'Tao', spontaneity should also be characteristic of **all** human actions. The actions of the Taoist 'sage' thus arise out of their 'intuitive wisdom', spontaneously and in harmony with their environment. They do not need to 'force' themselves, nor anything around them, but merely adapt their actions to the natural movements of the 'Tao'; in other words, they should always try to 'go with the flow'.

One of the key 'tools' that is available to Taoists (and also to Confucianists) in deciding which action to take is the 'Book of Changes' ('I Ching', in Chinese). This is one of **the** most important books in world literature, its origins going back to 'mythical antiquity'. The starting point of the book is a collection of 64 figures, or 'hexagrams', each consisting of six horizontal lines which may either be broken' ('yin') or 'unbroken' ('yang'), the set of 64 representing all possible combinations of these. These hexagrams were considered to be 'cosmic archetypes', representing the patterns of the 'Tao' in nature and in human situations. Each of them was given a 'Title', which was supplemented by a brief text, called the 'Judgement', to indicate the course of action appropriate to the 'cosmic pattern' associated with that particular hexagram. The so-called 'Image' was another brief text, added later, which elaborated on the meaning of the hexagram in a few poetic lines. A third text interpreted each of the hexagram's six lines in language charged with poetic images which were often difficult to understand. Those three basic texts formed the key parts of the book, which was used for 'divination' with the aid of an elaborate 'ritual' involving 50 'yarrow stalks'. The object was to make the 'cosmic pattern' of the moment 'visible' in the hexagram that the ritual produced, and to learn which course of action was appropriate to it. The purpose of consulting the 'I Ching' was thus not merely to 'know the future', but rather to discover the disposition of the 'present situation', so that 'proper action' could be taken. This lifted the 'I Ching' above the level of an ordinary 'book of soothsaying', and made is a 'book of wisdom'.

Let me end this introduction to Confucianism and Taoism by asking whether they are actually 'religions' or 'schools of philosophy'. The answer is that they are 'both', and, for this reason, are often referred to simply as 'chiao' ('teachings'). They both developed 'religious' and 'cultic' elements, but it is clear that they both **originated** as 'philosophical systems' that were followed both by 'schools' of teachers and by individuals.

Some of the sources of information on material covered in Chapter 5

Once again, I drew this information from several of the books and courses in my personal library, but most came from the following:

- 'Teach Yourself Eastern Philosophy', by Mel Thompson, a highly-informative book that is also clear and easy to read.
- 'The Religions of Man', by Huston Smith, an excellent review of these that I bought while at University almost 60 years ago, but is still highly relevant (it cost me 'five shillings' - 25p today).
- 'Religions of the Axial Age', a 'Teaching Company' course written and presented by Professor Mark W. Muesse.
- 'Great World Religions: Hinduism', a 'Teaching Company' course written and presented by Professor Mark W. Muesse.
- 'Great World Religions: Buddhism', a 'Teaching Company' course written and presented by Professor Malcolm D. Eckel.

- 'The Tao of Physics', by Fritjof Capra, a ground-breaking book that had a tremendous impact when it was first published in the 1970s.

Chapter 6: The three 'Religions of the Book'

'There is no God but Allah, and Mohammed is his prophet'

- the 'Kalima' (the basic Muslim statement of belief)

I have already given you a brief introduction to the early history of the Jewish people and the religion that they founded ('Judaism') in Chapter 2, where I showed that they made a very significant contribution to the development of religious thought during the 'Axial Age'. Their most important idea during this period was the 'invention' of 'monotheism', which meant abandoning their largely-'polytheistic' culture and worshipping a single God, which they claimed was the **only** god. Early in what is now called the 'Common Era', a hitherto-unknown Jewish Rabbi called Jesus suddenly appeared in the Roman province of Palestine, and spent three years teaching people about his highly-revolutionary ideas on how people should live. At the very end of his life, he travelled to Jerusalem at the time of the most-sacred of all Jewish traditions — the 'Festival of Passover', and caused so much trouble that he was arrested, brought before the Roman Governor of Palestine, and sentenced to death. After his death, his followers founded the sect that eventually became known as 'Christianity', which subsequently became one of the great world religions. Roughly 600 years later, an Arab businessman called Mohammed living in Mecca (in what is now Saudi Arabia) received a 'visitation' from the Christian Archangel Gabriel, in which part of the contents of what later became known as the 'Koran' were revealed to him. Two years later, he began to preach the 'message' of this, and eventually founded the religion that is now known throughout the world as 'Islam'. Muslims (as they called themselves) recognised the founders of the Jewish religion, Abraham and Moses, as 'prophets', and also recognised Jesus as a 'prophet', but claimed that these had merely been preparing the way for the appearance of God's ('Allah's') 'final prophet' —

Mohammed. This was incorporated in the basic Muslim 'statement of faith' that is given above. Since Judaism, Christianity and Islam all worshipped the same God (although they gave him different names), and all traced their origins back to the same early Jewish 'Book', they subsequently became known as the 'Religions of the Book'. In this chapter, I will take a detailed look at each of them.

A closer look at Judaism

During the first half of the second millennium BCE, it is believed that a small group of Semitic tribes (the 'Hebrews') left Mesopotamia for the 'Land of the Philistines' ('Palestine'). According to Jewish tradition, their first 'patriarch' was Abraham, who was not only the 'progenitor' of the Israelite people, but the 'father of their faith'. Again according to Jewish tradition, a group of Abraham's descendants later travelled on to Egypt, where they were held in 'bondage' until the 13th-century BCE. They were eventually led out of Egypt by Moses, who also gave the ancient religion of the Hebrews - Judaism - its first real shape. He is alleged to have had a 'profound spiritual experience' on Mt. Sinai, in which he 'met God', and was given the 'Ten Commandments'. This led him to insist that 'Jahweh' ('Jehovah') should be the only 'God' to be worshipped by the twelve Hebrew tribes - the 'Children of Israel', who came to be known as the 'Jews'. (The Jews did not completely abandon their worship of 'old gods' for a long time, however, and it was not until the time of 'Second Isaiah' sometime during the 6th-century BCE that they finally became truly 'monotheistic', at least in principle.) The early books of the 'Hebrew Bible' describe the above events in great detail, and also their entry into, and initial conquest of, their 'Promised Land' in Palestine, although it must be said that there is little firm **historical** or **archaeological** evidence for any of these accounts. They are, however, all firmly lodged in Jewish 'tradition'.

The subsequent portions of the Hebrew Bible describe the various stages in the establishment of 'Israel' as a nation in its promised land. Following further conquest and a period of political consolidation under a series of 'Judges', a monarchy finally emerged. David, their second King, whose reign is commonly dated in the 10th-century BCE, was the founder of a monarchical dynasty that would last for roughly 400 years. He moved its capital to Jerusalem, where his son Solomon built a magnificent 'Temple' that became the focal-point of Jewish worship. After Solomon's death, the kingdom was divided into two parts - 'Israel' in the North, and 'Judah' in the South, which retained Jerusalem as its capital. In 722 BCE, the 'northern kingdom' was invaded and destroyed by the Assyrians, and the ten 'lost tribes' that comprised it 'vanished from history'. The Assyrians also captured the 'southern kingdom', including Jerusalem. Nevertheless, the period from the 8th-century BCE to the capture of Jerusalem by the new Babylonian Empire in 586 BCE turned out to be the richest in the religious history of the ancient Jews. It was the era of the 'Prophets, who, more than any others, helped to establish a religious faith that was truly 'monotheistic', as we saw in Chapter 2. The utterances of the Prophets were strongly ethical, and also highly critical of established views and customs. Their teachings had tremendous influence on the subsequent development of Judaism, and also served as a cornerstone of Christianity five hundred years later.

The capture of Jerusalem by the Babylonians in 586 BCE was one of the pivotal events in Jewish history. Not only was their Temple destroyed, but a large number of Jews were deported to Babylon, where they remained until Babylon was captured by the Persians during the growth of **their** 'World Empire'. Their time in Babylon, known as the 'Exile', did have a strong influence on the development of Judaism, however; their account of the 'creation' in the first chapter of 'Genesis', for example, is clearly based on the Babylonian 'creation myth'. As we saw in Chapter 2, Cyrus the Great, the Persian King, decided to allow the exiled Jews to return home in 538 BCE, a year after he had captured Babylon, although very few of them actually did. Like the rest of the southern kingdom, Jerusalem was now part of the Persian Empire, and the Persians allowed the Jews to re-build their Temple. This 'Second Temple' was completed in 516 BCE, and remained the focal point of Jewish worship until it was destroyed by the Romans after the end of the 'Jewish Revolt' in the 70th year of the Common Era.

Between the end of the 'Exile' and the time of Christ, the Jews had to struggle to retain their culture and religion, mostly under various 'occupying powers'. First, there were the Persians. Then, with the conquest of the Persian Empire by Alexander the Great between 334 and 331 BCE, came over 150 years of 'Hellenistic' rule - first by the Egyptian 'Ptolemies' and then by the 'Seleucid' monarchs of Syria. This was followed by a comparatively brief period of independence under the 'Maccabees', which ended with the conquest of Palestine by Pompey in 63 BCE, after which it became one of the 'Provinces' in the rapidly-expanding Roman Empire. In the 66th year of the Common Era, the Jews revolted against their Roman occupiers, and, after a long and bitter war (brilliantly described by Josephus in 'The Jewish War') were totally defeated in 70 CE. The victorious Romans destroyed the Jewish Temple, and also drove many Jews out of Palestine. Thus began what became known as the 'Jewish Diaspora', when the Jewish people gradually spread throughout the world.

With the destruction of the Second Temple, Judaism faced a major challenge to its very existence. Without a recognised and unifying 'cultic centre', and without access to 'sacrificial worship' as the prime mode of religious expression, new systems and contexts for Jewish religious life began to emerge. Until then, religious activities had been the primary responsibility of a hierarchy of 'Priests'. Now this responsibility passed to the 'Rabbis' ('Teachers'), ushering in the emergence of the 'Rabbinic Judaism' that has lasted to the present day. Jews also had to find new places to worship, and did so in the 'Synagogues' that were located wherever there were sufficient numbers of Jews to warrant their establishment. The principal mode of worship also became private prayer, supported by public worship in in the Synagogues, with the Rabbis taking a leading role in the various standard rituals held there. These rituals no longer included sacrifice in any form, however.

In the 'Middle Ages' of the Common Era, new challenges to the Jewish way of life and worship began to appear. By now, the vast majority of Jews no longer lived in their traditional homeland in Palestine, but were dispersed throughout lands controlled by either Muslim or Christian rulers. No less important were the 'intellectual challenges' to Judaism from the theologians of both religions. These challenges stimulated an enormous literary output, including philosophical treatises, a growing corpus of 'mystical literature', 'polemical' works, and the expansion and application of the existing legal system of Judaism to meet 'new realities'. Throughout this period, the vast majority of Jews throughout the world still adhered to the 'major guidelines' and 'practical strictures' of Judaism, however.

The advent of the 'European Enlightenment' in the 18th Century and the major political upheavals throughout Europe during the 19th Century following the 'French Revolution' and the 'Napoleonic Wars' introduced further, totally-new challenges. For the first time, Christian society in Western Europe 'opened its doors' to Jews, conditional on their willingness to forgo some of the 'norms of behaviour' that tended to mark them as a 'race apart'. 'Assimilation' thus became an ever-growing challenge to the Jewish world. Deriving from the 'Enlightenment' movement, Jews also began to raise serious questions about the nature of their religious beliefs. These various developments eventually resulted in Judaism splitting into two parts - 'Orthodox

Judaism' (which adhered strictly to 'traditional' teachings and practices) and 'Reform Judaism' (which was willing to accept change).

Moving on to the 20th Century, there were clearly two key events that dominated Jewish history. The first was obviously the 'Holocaust', in which German Nazis systematically murdered roughly 6 million European Jews during the 1940's. I still find it hard to believe that such an atrocity could happen in the country that produced Bach, Kant, Schiller, Beethoven, Goethe and Gauss, during an exceptional 'flowering of European civilisation' that rivalled that of Periclean Athens and the Italian Renaissance. The second was the establishment of the State of Israel in 1948, when the British Mandate in Palestine ended. This provided the Jews with their own country for the first time since the days of the Maccabees, over 2000 years earlier. Its creation was bitterly opposed by the Palestinian Arabs (many of whom were expelled from their homes), and by Syria, Lebanon, Jordan and Egypt, and the Israelis had to fight no fewer than five bitter wars in order to preserve their independence - indeed, their very existence. They survived, thanks to the skill and tenacity of their fighting forces.

By the start of the new millennium, it was estimated that there were roughly 15 million Jews worldwide, with about 40% in the USA, 20% in Israel, 12% in the Republics of the former Soviet Union, and significant numbers in Argentina, Brazil, Canada, France, South Africa and the UK. Despite being a very 'small' racial group in terms of 'pure numbers', they have made a **tremendous** contribution to the development of the modern world. Look at the list of Nobel Prize winners, for example and you will find **many** Jewish names.

Let me now try to outline some of the most important features of Judaism. Before doing so, however, I have to point out that there is no formal body or organisation that represents all of Judaism today. Nor is there any authoritative body or person whose decisions are binding on all adherents to Judaism. Despite this, all practising Jews share a common heritage, and a common set of core beliefs and practices. As I see it, these fall into three broad areas.

First, all practising Jews base their beliefs, religious practices and lives on the same corpus of key documents. The first, and by far the most important, is the 'Hebrew Bible', which corresponds roughly to the 'Old Testament' in the 'Christian Bible'. The origins of this date back to the very earliest days of Judaism, but what eventually became the standard, 'authorised version' was only finalised during the early part of the Common Era. It consists of the following three parts. First, and most important, is the 'Torah', or 'Pentateuch', which contains the five books that were believed to have been written by Moses. We now know that they were actually written by four different authors, generally referred to by the initials 'J', 'D', 'E' and 'P'. The second part is 'Nevi'im' (Hebrew for 'Prophets'), and covers the period from the first settlement in the 'Promised Land' after the death of Moses until the destruction of the 'First Temple' in 586 BCE. The third part is called 'Ketuvim' (Hebrew for 'Scriptures'), and consists of a mixture of 'wisdom literature', poetry, and historical accounts. The second major corpus of Jewish literature was produced by the formulators of 'Rabbinic Judaism' after the destruction of the 'Second Temple' in 70 CE. This consists of two main collections of texts - the 'Books of Midrash' (detailed commentaries on the contents of the 'Hebrew Bible') and the 'Mishna' (which became the basis for all subsequent Rabbinic legislation). The third was the vast collection of religious literature that was written in 'Medieval' times, literature that had a profound influence on all subsequent students of the 'Torah'. The fourth was the 'Jewish Prayer Book', which probably had its origins in the last two centuries of the 'First Millennium', and again had a tremendous influence on all subsequent generations of Jews.

Second, all practising Jews share essentially the same set of core religious beliefs. Probably the most famous attempt at formulating a list of Judaism's basic 'principles' was made by the renowned 12th-century Jewish philosopher Maimonides. This comprised a list of 13 things that all Jews were expected to believe. 1. The existence of God. 2. God's 'unity'. 3. That God has no 'corporeal aspect'. 4. That God is 'eternal'. 5. That God alone (and no 'intermediaries') should be worshipped. 6. That 'prophesy' should be believed. 7. That Moses was the 'greatest of prophets'. 8. That all of the 'Torah' in our possession is 'divine', and was given through Moses. 9. That the 'Torah' will not be changed or suspended. 10. That God knows the actions of man. 11. That God rewards those who 'keep' the 'Torah' and punishes those who transgress against it. 12. That the 'Messiah' will come. 13. That the dead will be resurrected. Some of these 'principles' were clearly aimed at refuting what Maimonides believed were major challenges posed by Christianity and Islam. Although Maimonides' list of 'principles' was eventually embraced by broad segments of the traditional Jewish community, this took some time, since there were several attempts to shorten it, revise it, or add aspects they felt had been overlooked. More recently, progressive Jewish thinkers have tried to inject new ideas regarding the relationship between the 'communal' and 'religious' aspects of Judaism, particularly within 'Reform Judaism'.

Third, all practising Jews base their modes of worship, communal life, and individual life on Judaic principles. As we have seen, 'prayer' effectively replaced 'ritual sacrifice' as the main Jewish form of worship after the loss of their 'Second Temple' in 70 CE. This took place both 'in public' (mainly in the new Synagogues that were established to serve Jewish communities) and 'in private'. A standard program of public worship in these Synagogues also evolved over the following centuries, with some 'Holy Days' being regarded as particularly important. These included the 'Day of Atonement' and the 'Festival of

Passover'. Practising Jews were also expected to follow all the 'dietary', 'hygienic' and other 'laws' that were spelt out in detail in the 'Torah'. Jews were also given detailed guidance on how to bring up their children, including the mandatory requirement of having all male children 'circumcised' roughly 8 days after birth. The next important 'rite of passage' for all Jewish children was the 'coming of age', that is, assuming all the obligations of an adult. Girls were formally considered to be 'of age', and required to keep all the religious laws incumbent on women, at 12; for boys, the age was 13. All in all, there is hardly an aspect of communal or individual life that is **not** affected by some aspects of Judaic law or Judaic 'custom and practice'.

To conclude this 'closer look at Judaism', let me once again turn to Bryan Magee, and end with the comments that he made in 'Confessions of a Philosopher', following his wide-ranging examination of all the main religions. They are, I am afraid, rather negative:

'Of all the religions I studied, the one I found least worthy of intellectual respect was Judaism. I have no desire to offend any of my readers, but the truth is that while reading foundational Jewish texts, I often found myself thinking: "How can anyone possibly believe this?" When I put that question to Jewish friends they often said that no intelligent Jew did. To quote the precise words of one: "There's not a single intelligent Jew in the country who believes the religion". What they do believe, they tell me, that it is desirable that traditional observances should be kept by at least some Jews because it is these observances more than anything else that give the Jewish people its identity, and therefore its cohesion; but that the doctrinal content or implications of the observances are not expected to be taken with full intellectual seriousness by 'intelligent people'.'

The rise and spread of Christianity

Christianity is one of religion's great 'success stories'. It began as a sect of Judaism in an 'obscure province' of the Roman Empire in the first century of the Common Era, expanded and spread during the following centuries, and, in the 4th century, became the 'official religion' of the Roman Empire. It went on to dominate the religious, political and cultural life of Europe throughout most of its history, and is now believed to have roughly 2 billion followers in all parts of the world, making it by far the largest of the main 'world religions'. Christianity is also one of the most 'paradoxical' of religions. While spreading a message of 'peace' and 'unity', it has often been a source of conflict and division. While proclaiming a 'heavenly kingdom', it has often been deeply involved in 'earthly politics'. And while rejecting 'worldly wisdom', it has always claimed the intellectual allegiance of 'great minds'. These apparent contradictions arise from the complex nature of Christianity's claim about God, the world, and, above all, Jesus of Nazareth, whose death and alleged resurrection form the heart of the 'good news' proclaimed by this religious tradition.

We know very little about Jesus's early life, and practically all that we know about his three-year 'ministry' comes from 'insider' Christian writings, particularly the four 'Gospels' in the 'New Testament' of the Christian Bible that are attributed to Matthew, Mark, Luke and John. It is now accepted by scholars that these were actually written by highly-educated Greek-speaking Christians long after the death of Jesus, and are largely based on an earlier 'oral tradition'. It is generally believed that Jesus was a Jewish Rabbi ('Teacher'), who suddenly 'appeared out of nowhere' at the age of 30, and began spreading his revolutionary social and ethical ideas in the general vicinity of the Sea of Galilee, in the North of Palestine. He also gathered a core group of followers, his '12 disciples', all but one of whom were to play key roles in founding the Christian religion after his death (the missing one was, of course, Judas, who hanged himself after betraying Jesus). The essence of Jesus's 'message' was that God was not at all happy with the way people were currently behaving, and would soon intervene in the course of history, and establish his 'kingdom on earth'. At the end of his ministry in the North, he and his disciples travelled to Jerusalem at the time of the 'Festival of Passover', and caused so much trouble among the local Jewish 'establishment' that they brought him before the Roman 'Governor' of Palestine, 'Pontius Pilate', who, with some reluctance, sentenced him to death by crucifixion. He was placed in a tomb provided by a local sympathiser, and his body was later found to have 'disappeared'. He then made several appearances to his disciples and other followers, thus establishing the legend of his 'resurrection', which became the 'core belief' upon which Christianity was subsequently founded.

The early Christian movement was largely confined to the Jewish community in Palestine, but soon began to spread throughout the eastern part of the Roman Empire. Next to Jesus himself, the key figure in the early phases of this expansion was the apostle Paul. He was a Jewish Pharisee who spent the early part of his career persecuting the growing Christian Church, but, as the result of a traumatic 'visionary experience' on the 'road to Damascus', became an 'instant convert' to Christianity. He then spent the rest of his life spreading the 'Christian message' among the 'Gentiles' (that is, 'non-Jews'), and establishing Christian communities in major urban areas around the Mediterranean. He also wrote them long letters, some of which became 'Books' of the 'New Testament'. Without Paul, Christianity might well never have 'got off the ground'; his 'missionary work' marked the beginning of Christianity as a non-Jewish 'world religion'.

Christianity had started off as a small 'cult' of Jesus's immediate followers in Jerusalem, probably numbering no more than 100 people or so. Over the course of the next 300 years, it spread throughout the

Roman Empire, with its total number of adherents rising to roughly 3 million. It also developed a progressively-larger 'hierarchical structure', with the appointment of 'bishops' and then 'archbishops'. During this period, it was subject to regular bouts of 'persecution' by the Roman authorities, who resented the growing power and influence of the Christian Church. This only ended with the arrival of Constantine as Emperor. In 313 CE, he decreed that persecution of Christians should cease throughout the Roman Empire. He also became highly active in Church affairs, calling the 'Council of Nicea' in 325 in order to establish a consensus on major points of faith and practice. The Council also devised a 'Creed', which became the heart of what we now call the 'Nicene Creed'. Towards the end of the 4th century, one of Constantine's successors as Emperor, Theodosius I, made Christianity the 'official state religion', with the 'Bishop of Rome' (the 'Pope') having ultimate religious authority. Christianity never looked back, eventually becoming **the** religion to be handed down to the 'Dark Ages', the 'Middle Ages' and onwards.

Despite it's ideal of 'unity', Christianity has always experienced divisions from within, some of which persist to this day. This has led to two major moments of division, the 'schism' between the 'Orthodox' and 'Roman Catholic' branches of the Christian Church in the 11th century, and the 'Protestant Reformation' in the 16th century. The Roman Catholic Church simply claims to be 'catholic' (ie. 'universal'), but the designation 'Roman' signifies what distinguishes it from Orthodoxy and Protestantism. It claims a continuous tradition reaching back to the Apostle Peter, the 'Rock' upon which Jesus wanted to 'build his Church'. The Orthodox Church also claims continuity with the earliest Church, and shares many of its doctrines and traditions with the Roman Catholic Church. The 1054 'schism' was the climax of centuries of growing tension between the 'Old Rome' in Italy and the 'New Rome' in Constantinople, particularly between their respective 'Patriarchates'. The Protestant Reformation began as an attempt to 'reform' what was regarded as the 'corrupt Catholicism' of the late-Medieval period. Its most important early figure was Martin Luther, who wanted a return to 'Scripture' as the norm for Christian life, and a concentration on 'faith' as the means of being in the right relationship with God. 'Protestantism' subsequently split into many different 'branches', three of the most important being 'Anglicanism', 'Calvinism' and 'Methodism'.

Let us now look at some of the most important things in which Christians believe, and which constitute the 'foundational doctrines' of their faith. It must be stressed, however, that there are many differences between the 'detailed doctrines and practices' of the three main 'branches' of Christianity, and also between their various 'sub-branches'.

At the very heart of Christianity is their belief in the resurrection of Jesus. There are certain historical 'facts' about this event, if we are to believe the detailed accounts that are given in the four 'Gospels' with which the 'New Testament' of the Christian Bible begins: his 'death on the cross', his subsequent 'entombment', the discovery by a group of women that his body had 'disappeared', and his later 'appearance' to various people. But there are other aspects of the 'resurrection legend' that are problematic to historians, the main one being that the New Testament accounts are hopelessly contradictory in their details. Also, the 'resurrection' is a 'supernatural' event that is beyond the purview of the historian. What **is** certain is that some of Jesus's followers came to **believe** that he had been raised from the dead, and that made all the difference in the world. Jesus had talked about a coming resurrection of the dead at the 'end of the age'; his followers came to believe that he was the first to be raised and therefore that the 'end' had begun. He had also talked about the imminent arrival of the 'Son of Man' from heaven, after which people would be 'judged', and his followers came to believe that **he** had been 'exalted to heaven', and was himself the 'Son of Man'. Jesus has also talked about the future 'Kingdom of God' that would be ruled by his 'Messiah', and his followers also came to believe that **he** was the predicted Messiah. Jesus had also talked about God as the 'father of all', and of himself as having a 'special relationship' with God. As a result, they came to believe that **he** was the 'Son of God', and eventually, came to maintain that he was himself 'divine'.

As we have seen, Christianity began as a small sect of Judaism, and, until the time of Paul, only Jews could 'join' the sect. They continued to believe in the monotheistic 'Jewish God', but, with the increasing belief that Jesus was himself 'divine', this posed several theological problems. The solution that early-Christian thinkers eventually came up with was the development of the doctrine of the 'Trinity', the early work on which was carried out by Origen of Alexandria, one of the very greatest of the early Christian thinkers, during the first half of the third century CE. This maintained that 'God' is in fact manifested in 'three persons' – 'God the Father' (the original Jewish God), 'God the Son' (Jesus), and 'God the Holy Spirit' (the invisible 'holy presence' that permeates and sustains the whole of creation). The exact nature of this 'Triune God' was the subject of considerable debate and disagreement until the 'Council of Nicea' in 325 CE, which agreed on what became known as the 'Nicene Creed'. This established the doctrine that the 'Father', 'Son' and 'Holy Spirit' (or 'Holy Ghost') were all 'equal partners' in the Trinity. Although the doctrine was 'fine-tuned' during the following centuries, it has remained one of the 'foundations' of Christian belief ever since.

Another subject that 'exercised the minds' of the early Christian thinkers was the 'exact nature' of Jesus. The 'New Testament' ascribes both 'divine' and 'human' attributes to Jesus, and both have been considered essential to a full understanding of him. After considerable discussion and disagreement, the 'Council of Chalcedon' in 451 CE finally decreed that he is 'two natures in one person', that is, he is both 'true God' and 'true man'. Because this 'orthodox' position was clearly highly paradoxical, subsequent groups of Christians have tended to focus either on the 'humanity' or on the 'divinity' of Jesus. All are agreed, however, that the main 'social' and 'ethical' teachings of Jesus should form the basis of a 'good' Christian life. These are centred on his two basic 'commandments' – 'love God unconditionally and with all your heart and soul', and 'love your neighbour as yourself'. His revolutionary (and somewhat disturbing) pronouncement that God loves **everybody** equally, whether they deserve it or not, has also had a profound influence on subsequent Christian thinking. Like Socrates, Jesus confined his teaching to questions of morality, and had absolutely nothing to say about the 'nature of the world'. But within the confines of morality, Bryan Magee believes that he went 'as deep as anyone was to penetrate for the better part of two thousand years', and was probably 'the most remarkable moralist there has ever been'.

One of the least-attractive features of Christianity, in my opinion, is its claim that Jesus, the 'Son of God', was 'sent down to Earth' by his 'Father' in order to offer human beings an opportunity to escape from the dire consequences of 'original sin' - the 'disobedience' of Adam and Eve in the garden of Eden. Only by accepting Jesus as 'Lord', and following his teachings, could we avoid 'eternal damnation'. This idea of 'original sin', from which the only way out was to become a Christian, was developed very early on, but its most 'severe' form dates from Saint Augustine of Hippo, a brilliant Christian philosopher who worked in the early part of the 5th century and had a tremendous influence on the subsequent development of Christianity. To the 'modern mind', the doctrine seems somewhat ridiculous. Not only is it based on an event that is now believed by most intelligent people to be 'pure myth', but it automatically rules out all non-Christians from having any chance of achieving 'salvation' – as well as everyone who lived before the time of Jesus. Christianity would be far more worthy of respect if it dropped this arrogant claim of its supreme importance. I am glad that another of its arrogant actions – dating the entire history of humanity as either 'BC' ('Before Christ') or 'AD' ('Anno Domini' – the 'Year of our Lord') is now falling into disuse. I do not know how Christians 'got away' with this for so long, but I now refuse to use the terms 'BC' and 'AD' at all, preferring the terms 'BCE' (Before the Common Era') and 'CE' (Common Era). I hope that this convention soon becomes universal. As readers will no doubt have noticed, I am using it throughout this book.

The rise and spread of Islam

Islam is another of religion's great 'success stories'. Following its foundation by Mohammed early in the 7th century, it soon started to spread out of Arabia, and, during the next hundred years or so, established a vast Muslim Empire occupying most of North Africa and large parts of Eastern and Southern Asia. After this initial explosive expansion, it gradually spread throughout the rest of the world, and now has over a billion followers in 56 different countries, making it the second largest 'world religion' after Christianity – and by far the fastest growing. Let us now take a detailed look at the history of Islam, before examining its core beliefs and practices.

It is believed that Mohammed was born around the year 570 in Mecca, one of the most important towns in the Southern part of Arabia. It was a traditional centre for pilgrims who came to worship at the 'Kaaba' (a shrine regarded as the 'home' for many of the gods who were worshipped in Arabia at the time), and was also a cosmopolitan 'trading town'. Orphaned at an early age, Mohammed was brought up by his uncle, who found him a place in the 'caravan business'. He subsequently married his employer, a rich widow named Khadijah, by whom he had several children. He was known for his integrity, trustworthiness and 'reflective nature', regularly retreating to a hilltop in the desert in order to ponder the 'meaning of life'. One night in 610, he was called to be a 'prophet of God', hearing a voice commanding him to 'recite' what had just been revealed to him. This was to be the first of many revelations from God ('Allah'), communicated by an 'intermediary' – the Archangel Gabriel. He continued to receive these for 22 years, until his death in 632; they would later be collected and compiled into the 'Koran' – the Islamic equivalent of the Hebrew and Christian 'Bibles'.

Mohammed's initial reaction to his 'visitations' was 'fear', and it took him roughly two years to tell other people what was happening to him. Although he gathered a small group of convinced 'disciples', including Khadijah and several members of his family, his progress in Mecca was slow. It was also hampered by 'persecution', since his repeated attacks on the 'idolatry' associated with the Kaaba was seen as a 'threat' to the highly-lucrative 'pilgrimage trade'. However, the unending flow of 'pilgrims' always provided new 'audiences', and one such group, from Medina (a town 280 miles north-east of Mecca), was so impressed that they formed a 'colony of believers' in their home town. In 622, Mohammed decided to move from Mecca to Medina. This event, the 'Hegira' ('Flight'), marked the true beginning of the 'Mohammedan Era'. In Medina, he found that mere 'preaching' was not converting the large numbers he had hoped for, so he and his followers decided to go down another route – 'forced conversion' by violence and war. This was to prove **much** more successful! Mecca was captured in 630, and, before his death in 632, all the tribes in Arabia had been united under Mohammed's rule and beliefs.

As we saw at the start of this chapter, the basic 'message' of Islam was very simple – accept that 'Allah' was the one true god and submit to his will, and accept that Mohammed was his 'final prophet', and follow the way of life that he prescribed. Since the 'moral' requirements of Islam were not particularly severe, and devout Muslims could also look forward to 'eternal life' in 'Paradise' after their deaths, most of the people in the areas subsequently conquered by the Muslim armies were very happy to convert to Islam. And those who refused to do so were left pretty well alone, so long as they accepted Muslim rule and paid their taxes to the 'Caliphate'. As a result, Islam spread from the Himalayas to the Pyrenees in the first century following the Prophet's death. Their attempts to conquer France were stopped by the Frankish leader Charles Martel in 732, so they never managed to move into northern Europe. But by then, they had established the largest empire the world had ever seen, and were content to end their wars of conquest. Thereafter, they would rely on **voluntary** conversion to increase the number of Muslims throughout the rest of the world. This is a policy that is still proving highly successful today.

Let me end this description of the birth and spread of Islam by saying something about the only major split that has ever taken place within the Muslim community – its division into 'Sunnis' and 'Shi'ites'. This took place shortly after the death of Mohammed, and arose from a disagreement over who should succeed him as 'leader' of the Muslims. The majority of Muslims believed that the leadership should pass to the 'most qualified person', and not through automatic 'hereditary' succession. They therefore chose Abu Bakr, Mohammed's close companion and trusted advisor, as well as his father-in-law, to be the 'Caliph'. In this role, he became the political and military leader of the community. A minority of Muslims opposed the selection of Abu Bakr as Caliph, however, believing that succession should be hereditary, within the Prophet's family. Since Mohammed's first cousin Ali was his closest living male relative, they felt that **he** should become Caliph. To cut a long story short, this division of the Muslim community into 'Sunnis' – followers of the 'Sunnah' ('example') of the Prophet, and 'Shiis', or 'Shi'ites' – the 'Party of Ali', has persisted to the present day. 'Sunni' Muslims now make up roughly 85% of the world's Muslims, with the other 15% being 'Shi'ite' Muslims. They are **still** fighting each other after nearly 1400 years!

Let us now take a look at the 'Five Pillars of Islam', the five simple required 'observances' that are prescribed in the Koran. Despite enormous religious, cultural and political differences and divisions, **all** practising Muslims accept and follow these without question.

The first 'Pillar' is the 'Kalima', the 'declaration of faith' which I used as the 'introductory quotation' for this chapter. A 'Muslim' is one who testifies that there is 'no God but Allah', and that Mohammed is the final 'messenger of God' (his 'Prophet'). ('Allah' is the Arabic word for 'God', just as 'Yahweh' is the Hebrew name for God that is used in the Hebrew Bible). To become a 'Muslim', all you have to do is make this simple confession of faith before witnesses. This proclamation affirms Islam's 'absolute monotheism', the uncompromising belief in the 'oneness' or 'unity' of God; association of anything else with God is 'idolatry', and is the main 'unforgivable sin' for a Muslim. It also confirms the key role that Mohammed plays within Islam. Not only was he the 'messenger' through which God gave Muslims their 'sacred book' (the 'Koran'); he also provides Muslims with the perfect 'role model' through his own 'life example', just as Jesus does for Christians.

The second 'Pillar' of Islam is 'prayer' ('salat'). All practising Muslims are required to 'pray' (or, perhaps more correctly, 'worship') at five set times during the day – at 'daybreak', 'noon', 'mid-afternoon', 'sunset', and 'evening'. The prayers consist of 'recitations' from the Koran in Arabic, and 'glorification of God', accompanied by standing, bowing, kneeling, touching the ground with one's forehead, and sitting. Muslims can pray in any 'clean environment', alone or together, in a Mosque or at home, at work or 'on the road', indoors or out. When they pray, Muslims face Mecca, the 'holy city' that houses the 'Kabba'. It is also considered preferable and more 'meritorious' to pray with others, demonstrating 'brotherhood', 'equality' and 'solidarity'. Once a week, on a Friday (the Muslim equivalent of the Jewish 'Sabbath') the noon prayer is a 'congregational prayer' at a Mosque or Islamic centre.

The third 'Pillar' of Islam is called the 'zakat' or 'tithe', which means 'purification'. 'Zakat' is both an 'individual' and a 'communal' responsibility, expressing 'worship of' and 'thanksgiving to' God by supporting the 'poor'. It requires an annual contribution of 2.5 percent of an individual's 'wealth' and 'assets', not merely a percentage of 'annual income'. 'Zakat' is **not** viewed as 'charity', but as an obligation to respond to the needs of the 'less fortunate' members of the community; it thus functions as a form of 'social security' in a Muslim society.

The fourth 'Pillar' of Islam, the 'Fast of Ramadan', occurs once each year during the month of Ramadan – the ninth month of the Islamic calendar, in which the first 'revelation of the Koran' is believed to have been given to Mohammed. During this month-long fast, Muslims whose health permits them to do so must abstain from food, drink and sexual activity during the period from dawn to sunset. For Muslims, fasting is not simply an act of 'self denial'; it is a discipline intended to stimulate religious reflection on 'human frailty' and 'dependence on God'. The month of Ramadan ends with one of the main Islamic celebrations – the 'Feast of the Breaking of the Fast', called 'Eid al-Fitr'.

The fifth and final 'Pillar' of Islam is the 'pilgrimage', or 'hajj' to Mecca. At least once in his or her lifetime, every adult Muslim who is physically and financially able is required to make this pilgrimage. Every year, more than 2 million people, representing a tremendous diversity of cultures and languages, travel from all over the world to the 'holy city' of Mecca, to form one community 'living their faith'. Those who participate wear simple garments that symbolise 'purity', as well as 'unity' and 'equality' of all believers. One of the most important 'rituals' during their time in Mecca involves 'mass marches' round the 'Kabba', an event that most people will have seen on television.

Like Judaism, Islam requires its adherents to observe various 'dietary laws', all of which are spelled out quite clearly in the 'Koran' (just as the corresponding Jewish laws are spelled out in the 'Torah'). These include total abstention from drinking alcohol, a ban on eating pork or any other meat from the pig, and only eating 'halal' food that has been prepared in accordance with Islamic law. Adult Muslim women are also required to observe prescribed 'dress codes', and to comply with 'social rules' that govern their allowed interaction with men. These vary considerably between different Muslim communities, however, with some being much 'stricter' than others. Anyone visiting a predominantly Muslim country should try to find out what the local 'ground rules' are, and try to comply with them at all times. **Not** to do so can cause offence, and even lead to arrest. I have worked in several Muslim countries during my long academic career, including Saudi Arabia, and know how seriously they can take such things. Complying with 'local customs' is, after all, only 'good manners'. Having said that, I have developed a deep respect for Muslim culture, and a genuine liking for their people. They welcome and look after 'foreign guests' like me in a way that is seldom now seen in 'Western' countries, and I am sure that this is largely due to their 'religious upbringing'. In my opinion, there is a great deal to be admired in Islam, despite the recent abhorrent behaviour of some of their more extreme 'militant elements'. The great majority of 'true Muslims' deplore their activities just as much as non-Muslims do.

Some of the sources of information on material covered in Chapter 6

Once again, I drew this information from several of the books and courses in my personal library, but by far the largest part came from the following seven sources.

- 'Confessions of a Philosopher', by Bryan Magee, whose comments on the three religions covered by the chapter were, as always, highly penetrating and insightful.
- 'A History of the Bible', by John Barton, a mine of basic information and deeply-insightful comments that has only just been published; it covers many aspects of early Judaism and early Christianity.
- 'Great World Religions: Judaism', a 'Teaching Company' course written and presented by Professor Isaiah M. Gafni.
- 'Great World Religions: Christianity', a 'Teaching Company' course written and presented by Professor Luke T. Johnson.
- 'From Jesus to Constantine: A History of Early Christianity', a 'Teaching Company' course written and presented by Professor Bart D. Ehrman.
- 'Islam – A Short History', by Karen Armstrong, a highly-informative and insightful book written by my 'favourite theologian' (I have five of her books in my personal library).
- 'Great World Religions: Islam', a 'Teaching Company' course written and presented by Professor John L. Esposito.

Chapter 7: The development of the 'Newtonian' world picture

'Nature and nature's laws lay hid in night.
God said 'Let Newton Be!' and all was light'

- Alexander Pope.

This is the famous epitaph that was intended for Sir Isaac Newton, and was written by the great 'Augustan' poet, Alexander Pope, in 1730. Pope realised that Newton had revolutionised our picture of the physical world, as indeed he had. What came to be known as the 'Newtonian world picture' dominated science until the end of the 19th century, after which it was almost completely overthrown by what became known as the 'Einsteinian Revolution' - the subject of Chapter 11. After this was well underway, and had left the world of physics in a state of confusion that had yet to be fully resolved, J.G. Squire wrote a very apt continuation of Pope's epitaph in 1926:

'It did not last: the Devil howling "Ho!
Let Einstein be!" restored the status quo.'

Let us now take a close look at what the 'Newtonian Revolution' achieved, but, before we do so, we need to look at the series of events that 'prepared the ground' for it - the so-called 'Copernican Revolution' in astronomy, and the work of Francis Bacon on the development of what became known as the 'scientific method'.

The 'Copernican Revolution'

To fully understand the importance of the 'Copernican Revolution', we need to go back to the times of the ancient Egyptian and Assyrian civilisations that I described in Chapter 1, and the 'cosmologies' (models of the universe) that they developed. Both developed 'three-layered' cosmologies, that of the Assyrians picturing a flat 'Earth' covered by an inverted 'bowl' to which the stars were fixed, and across which the Sun, Moon, and planets moved. Beyond this was the 'abode of the gods', while beneath it was the 'abode of the dead'. This cosmology was adopted by the authors of the early books of the Hebrew Bible, who pictured a flat Earth lying between the two places where the dead could finish up - a place of 'reward' ('heaven') beyond the stars, and a place of 'punishment' ('hell') beneath the Earth.

In the fifth century BCE, Aristotle developed a somewhat-more-sophisticated cosmology. This pictured a spherical Earth at the centre of the universe, with the 'abode of the dead' ('Hades') lying deep beneath its surface. He believed that the Earth was surrounded by a series of seven transparent rotating spheres, respectively carrying the Moon, the Sun, and the five known planets (Mercury, Venus, Mars, Jupiter and Saturn) on their different paths round the Earth. Beyond this was a further opaque sphere which carried the 'fixed stars' and rotated once a day, and beyond this was the 'abode of the gods'. It was eventually realized that this simple Aristotelian model could not explain the so-called 'retrograde' movements of the planets, whereby they sometimes appear to 'double back' in their orbits before moving on once again, so a more and more complicated system of 'cycles' and 'epicycles' was developed over the following centuries. The final version of this was produced by Ptolemy, working in Alexandria, during the second century of the Common Era, and was able to describe the movements of the planets with great accuracy. It became known as the 'Ptolemaic System', and remained in use for over 1400 years. In the 13th century, the Earth-centered Aristotelian/Ptolemaic cosmology was officially adopted by the Roman Catholic Church as a result of the work of St. Thomas Aquinas, the greatest Christian philosopher since St. Augustine. As a result, it became universally accepted throughout Western Europe, and also became part of

'Church doctrine', so that no Roman Catholic was **allowed** to challenge its truth.

During the early part of the 16th century, the Polish monk Nicolaus Copernicus realised that the Ptolemaic System of cycles and epicycles could be greatly simplified by supposing that the Earth orbited the Sun along with all the other planets. Although he had fully worked out his revolutionary theory by 1533, and had set it all out in a book which he called 'De Revolutionibus Orbium Coelestium' ('Concerning the Revolutions of the Celestial Bodies'), he did not dare to have it published during his lifetime. Since his theory deposed the Earth from its God-given position at the centre of the universe, he knew that it would get him into 'deep-trouble' with the Roman Catholic Church. It was finally published in 1543, by which time Copernicus was extremely ill; it is said that the first printed copies of his great work only reached him a few hours before his death. At first, only a few astronomers dared to come out in open support of the new theory. The Roman Catholic authorities were strongly against it, although the real storm did not break out until over half a century after Copernicus's death. As late as 1600, one of the supporters of the theory, Giordano Bruno, was publicly burnt at the stake in Rome after a seven-year trial by the Inquisition.

Because of the on-going opposition of the Roman Catholic Church, Copernicus's revolutionary 'heliocentric cosmology' was not fully accepted until roughly 150 years after his death. Four other people, Tycho Brahe, Johannes Kepler, Galileo Galilei (known as 'Galileo') and Isaac Newton all played key roles in bringing this acceptance about, so let us now look at each of their contributions.

Tycho Brahe was quite simply the greatest observational astronomer who worked before the invention of the telescope. Born into a noble family at Knudstrup in South Sweden in 1546, he went on to receive an excellent education in Copenhagen, Leipzig, Wittenberg, Rostok and Augsburg. A political career was planned for him, but, from the age of 14 when he witnessed the partial solar eclipse of 1560, he was obsessed by astronomy. In 1563, he discovered serious errors in the existing astronomical tables, and, in 1572 carefully observed an extremely bright 'new star' in the Constellation of Cassiopeia, a 'supernova' now known as 'Tycho's star'. This was a highly-important discovery which 'made his name' as a leading astronomer. As a result, he received an extremely-generous offer from King Frederick II of Denmark to set up a large astronomical observatory on the little island of Hven in the Baltic, between Elsinore and Copenhagen, and to pay all its running expenses for an indefinite period. Tycho was quick to accept, and, in 1576, began the construction of his observatory - 'Uraniborg', the 'Castle of the Heavens'. During the next 20 years, he built a succession of extremely-sensitive 'open sight' astronomical instruments, and carried out the most accurate measurements of the positions of stars and the movements of the planets that had ever been carried out. The vast amount of data that he accumulated on the latter proved to be of immense assistance to later astronomers, particularly Johannes Kepler. Tycho's 'sponsor', King Frederick, died in 1588, and his successor was less inclined to continue financial support for Uraniborg. Tycho eventually left Denmark in 1596, and, three years later, the Holy Roman Emperor, Rudolph II invited him to Bohemia, placing at his disposal the Castle of Benatek, roughly 20 miles from Prague. He worked there for a short period, but later moved to Prague itself. In 1600, he took on Johannes Kepler as an assistant, and, in 1601, Kepler succeeded him as Court Astronomer to Rudolph II after his death. As we will now see, Kepler proved to be just as brilliant as a 'theorist' as Tycho had been as an 'observer'.

Johannes Kepler was born at Weil der Stadt in Wurttemberg in 1571. He studied at Tubingen, and, in 1593, was appointed Professor of Mathematics at Graz. As we have seen, he later moved to Prague as

Tycho's assistant, and a year later, became his successor as Court Astronomer to Emperor Rudolph II. There, he had access to all Tycho's data on the motions of the planets, data that he subsequently put to very good use when developing his famous 'Three Laws of Planetary Motion'. In 1612, he became a mathematics teacher in Linz, and, in 1628, became 'astrologer' to Albrecht Wallenstein, at Sagan in Silesia. He died in 1630, but, by then, had made many discoveries in optics, general physics and geometry. But by far his most important work was his theoretical work on the movements of the planets - his 'First Law' was published in 1609, and stated that the planets move round the Sun in **ellipses** rather than combinations of circular 'cycles' and 'epicycles', the centre of the Sun being placed at one 'focus' of the ellipse, while the other focus is empty. By this radical change, he was able fit elliptical orbits to Tycho's data on planetary movement with perfect accuracy, something that Copernicus's simplified systems of cycles and epicycles had never managed to do. His 'Second Law' was published in the same year. It stated that the 'radius vector' of each planet (an imaginary line joining the centre of the Sun to the centre of the planet) sweeps out **equal areas** in **equal times**. It took him a further ten years of work to develop his 'Third Law', but this was eventually published in 1619. It states that for any planet, the square of the 'sidereal period' (the time taken to complete one journey round the Sun) is proportional to the cube of the planet's 'mean distance' from the Sun. This explained the long-established observation that planets move more slowly the further they are from the Sun, and thus take longer to complete each orbit. The importance of Kepler's three laws in astronomical theory cannot be over-stressed. As we will see later, they enabled Newton to establish the truth of the 'heliocentric theory' beyond all reasonable doubt by 'deriving' all three of Kepler's laws from his own three 'laws of motion' and his 'theory of universal gravitation'. But before we discuss this work, we need to look at the crucial part played by Galileo in establishing the truth of the heliocentric theory that had been first suggested by Copernicus in 1543.

Galileo Galilei was born in the Italian city of Pisa (famous for its 'leaning tower') in 1564, and was to go on to become one of the most important figures in the entire history of science as a result of his work in astronomy, mathematics and physics. After entering Pisa University in 1581, he discovered that the 'period' of a pendulum (the time required for a complete oscillation) is independent of the 'range' of these oscillations (the 'size' of the swings). He was subsequently appointed as Professor of Mathematics at the University, but had to resign his 'chair' in 1591 due to the hostility of his 'Aristotelian' colleagues, whose work he had criticized. Before then, however, he had carried out ground-breaking work on the theory of 'falling bodies'. He was subsequently appointed Professor of Mathematics at Padua University, a post that he held from 1592 till 1610. During this time, he made many more important discoveries, and also perfected the 'refracting telescope' (a Dutch invention of 1608). With this, he was able to make a whole series of amazing discoveries, and it was his work during the years from 1609 until 1619 which marked the start of 'telescopic astronomy'; astronomy would never be the same again. The first thing he looked at was the Moon, and found that its surface was rough and mountainous. Next, he looked at the stars, and found that 'clusters' like the Pleiades contained far more stars than had previously been supposed. Galileo then turned his attention to the 'Milky Way', and found that it was made up of a 'mass of stars', apparently crowded close together. In 1610, he turned his attention to the planets, and soon discovered that Jupiter was in fact a 'miniature solar system', with four moons (now called the 'Galilean moons') orbiting around it. This discovery excited Galileo greatly, and made him more convinced than ever that Copernicus had been right. He found an even more positive proof of this when he saw that Venus shows 'phases', or changes of shape, similar to those of the Moon; sometimes it was a 'crescent', sometimes a 'half disk', and sometimes even a 'full disk'. By carrying out detailed study of these phases, Galileo was able to show that they could **only** be explained by assuming that the Earth orbits the Sun rather than the other way round. This was decisive, and was the key piece of **observational** evidence that eventually led to the 'heliocentric' theory being generally accepted. There still was a long way to go before this happened, however.

In 1610, Galileo was 'recalled' to Florence (where he had spent some time before moving to Padua) by the Duke of Tuscany, and, a year later, was received 'with great distinction' in Rome. His on-going support for the banned 'heliocentric theory' resulted in him receiving a 'formal censure' from the ecclesiastical authorities, and, in 1616, he promised to 'abstain from all future advocacy' of the condemned doctrines. He was now living a relatively quiet life in Florence as Mathematician to the Duke of Padua, and the Church authorities left him more or less in peace. Then, in 1632, he published his great book 'Dialogue Concerning the Two Chief World Systems - Ptolemaic and Copernican'. This took the form of a conversation between two imaginary philosophers, and Galileo made his support for 'Copernicanism' so clear that the Church decided to take action. In 1633, he was summoned to Rome and put on trial by the 'Inquisition'. Under threat of torture, he was forced to 'abjure his scientific creed' and agree that the Church's doctrine that the Sun revolved around the Earth was correct. He was also sentenced to 'indefinite imprisonment', a sentence later commuted to 'indefinite house arrest' after intervention by the Duke of Tuscany. For the remainder of his life, he was carefully watched by the Church authorities, and expressly forbidden to carry on with his astronomical work. He died in 1642, by which time he had become completely blind.

The 'Copernican Revolution' was eventually completed by Isaac Newton, who, as we have seen, succeeded in deriving Kepler's 'Three

Laws of Planetary Motion' from first principles. This work will be discussed in greater detail in the third section of this chapter, after I have described the work of Francis Bacon on the development of the 'scientific method'.

Bacon and the birth of modern science

Galileo is widely recognised as the first 'modern' physical scientist, and, as we have seen, spent his entire life making important discoveries in astronomy, mathematics and physics. Francis Bacon, on the other hand, who lived and worked at almost exactly the same time as Galileo, made no actual scientific discoveries at all, but is widely regarded as the man who gave modern science its 'method', and gave scientists their 'inspiration'. Such was his influence that he was once described as 'buccinator novi temporis', the 'herald of new times'. All this happened very late in his life, however, most of which was spent as a lawyer, politician and statesman. He was born in 1561, the son of Sir Nicolas Bacon, Lord Keeper to Queen Elizabeth I. He entered Trinity College, Cambridge at the age of 13, and, while there, developed a strong antipathy towards Aristotelian philosophy and methodology, which was still highly influential at the time. He subsequently studied law at Gray's Inn, and was admitted to the Bar in 1586. Bacon made numerous attempts to secure a Government appointment from the Queen, but, although his Uncle William Cecil, later Lord Burghley, was Elizabeth's most important minister, this was not forthcoming. (This was probably due to Bacon's defence of the 'Rights of Commons' against certain proposals being urged by the Queen's ministers.) Following the accession of James I in 1603, Bacon's fortunes soared. He was knighted almost immediately, and subsequently became Attorney General in 1613, Lord Keeper in 1617, Lord Chancellor in 1618, Baron Verulam in the same year, and Viscount St. Albans in 1621. Shortly afterwards, he pleaded guilty of taking 'gifts' from persons with cases before him in his capacity as Lord Chancellor. Bacon insisted that he had never allowed the receipt of gifts to influence his judgment in these cases, but offered no defence against the charge that he had accepted the gifts. He was fined, jailed, and banished from public life by his fellow peers in the House of Lords, but the King remitted the fine and terminated his imprisonment after a few days. Bacon spent much of his time during the last five years of his life working on his 'Great Instauration', a proposed 'reformulation' of the sciences. His most important contribution towards this 'Instauration' was the 'Novum Organum' which he had published in 1620. In this work, he outlined a 'new' scientific method to replace that of Aristotle. He also created a highly-influential image of 'co-operative scientific inquiry' in his 'New Atlantis', which was published in 1627.

So much for his highly-eventful life; let us now turn to his main ideas on how science should be carried out.

Bacon's argument was typically 'English' in its approach. The 'new science', he held, was not just an 'intellectual enterprise' to give people **knowledge** of nature, but a 'practical project' to give them **mastery** over nature. Once people knew how nature 'worked', they could 'exploit it to their own advantage'. Bacon foresaw, as no-one before him had foreseen, how science could improve the 'condition of human life on earth'. Bacon was a true 'Renaissance Man' in his optimism and his great faith in humanity and the future. He pointed to such practical achievements as the geographical discoveries of Marco Polo, the scientific discoveries of Copernicus and Galileo, and the invention of printing, gunpowder and the magnetic compass. All these, he claimed, were 'changing the world', so the world thus changed must have a 'new philosophy'. He once suggested that the 'bees' provided the ideal model for scientific inquiry. His 'new science' required that people should work together as a fully co-operative 'team', systematically 'learning from experience' by 'ordered observation', 'amassing data', 'storing it', and 'interpreting it judiciously'. Science also required people to 'break with their traditional prejudices', with 'magic', and with 'superstition'. Bacon also warned people of the dangers presented by their favourite 'Idols'. First, 'Idols of the Tribe', the tendency to believe what they **wanted** to believe. Second, 'Idols of the Den', the problems that arise from individual 'crankiness' and 'idiosyncrasies'. Third, 'Idols of the Marketplace', arising from 'corruption of language'. Fourth, 'Idols of the Theatre', caused by people's veneration of 'traditional systems of philosophy'. The 'dragon' of 'Aristotelian thinking', he said, had to be 'decisively slain'.

But how was all this to be done? Quite simply by adopting and practising the 'new scientific method' that he was proposing. The essence of this 'Baconian method' was that scientific studies in a particular area should start with the 'open-minded accumulation of relevant data'. This should be followed by the development of a 'hypothesis' (a 'theory' or 'model') aimed at 'explaining' or 'collating' the data thus gathered. Finally, the resulting hypothesis should be 'tested' by devising and carrying out 'key experiments'. If, as a result of this process, the hypothesis is verified, it then acquires the status of a 'scientific law', and becomes a 'permanent addition' to the body of 'certain' (or 'scientific') knowledge.

Let me illustrate this methodology with a simple example. Suppose that a scientist wished to investigate the 'dynamics of colliding bodies'. As a starting point, they might carry out an extended series of experiments with trollies of different masses, noting down the changes in velocity produced when such trollies collided under different experimental conditions. When it was felt that sufficient data had been collected, the scientist would then look for some 'common feature' of the various collisions studied, and attempt to formulate a 'general law' capable of describing what happens in **all** such collisions. By this means, our scientist might (according to the Baconian 'view of science'), discover the 'principle of conservation of momentum'. Having done so, the hypothetical 'principle' would be used to make specific predictions about what would happen in collisions carried out under as-yet-unstudied conditions, followed by carrying out further experiments in order to 'test' these predictions. If, after a sufficiently-long series of such experiments, the predictions all proved to be correct, the hypothetical 'principle', would have been 'verified', and would then become a 'scientific law' - a permanent addition to the body of 'scientific knowledge'.

The key step in the above process is that by which a 'general statement' (the 'hypothesis') is derived from 'individual observations' (the 'original data') - the so-called process of 'scientific induction'. Indeed, followers of the 'Baconian method' believed that this 'inductive process' was the thing that distinguished 'science' from 'non-science'. Only statements of 'observable fact', or statements 'derived from' such facts by a process of 'induction' were 'scientific', and only such statements could be regarded as 'certain knowledge'. Although the logical validity of 'scientific induction' was challenged by the Scottish philosopher, David Hume, in the mid-18th-century, it remained at the 'heart' of the 'scientific method' for well over 300 years, even though the 'problem of induction' raised by Hume was never properly resolved until it was eventually **dis**solved by the work of Karl Popper during the 1930's. I will tell you all about this in Chapter 11.

The Newtonian 'mathematical universe'

Isaac Newton was born at Woolsthorpe, near Grantham in Lincolnshire, in 1642 - the year Galileo died. His father had died before he was born, and his mother was left in charge of the family farm. Isaac went to the local village school, but showed no signs of 'unusual intelligence'. When he was 12, he went to King's School, Grantham, where he remained 'near the bottom of the class' for his first few terms. According to legend, all this changed after he 'got into a fight' with a 'bigger boy' who had 'jeered at him,' and 'kicked him'; Isaac eventually 'got the better of him', and 'rubbed his nose against the wall'. The world has reason to be grateful to that 'bigger boy', because the incident stimulated Isaac into 'working harder', and he eventually reached the 'top position in the school'. He never looked back! In 1661, he enrolled as a student at Trinity College, Cambridge, where he met Professor Isaac Barrow, the Lucasian Professor of Mathematics, who tutored him in the subject, and clearly became very impressed by his 'outstanding promise'. In 1665, all the colleges in Cambridge had to close down because of the arrival of the bubonic plague in England, and Newton had to return to Woolsthorpe, taking with him 'the many insights in mathematics and natural philosophy that had been rapidly unfolding in his mind'. These matured and developed during his two-year 'lockdown' at Woolsthorpe, which he later described as 'the most creative of his life'. During these 'miracle years', as they were later called, he began to think about 'the method of fluxions' (his version of 'calculus', of which he was co-inventor with the German philosopher/mathematician Leibziz), the 'theory of colours', and 'gravity'. Newton later told people that his very greatest idea, 'universal gravitation', came to him when he saw an apple fall from a tree in the garden at Woolsthorpe; if gravity brought the apple down here on Earth, he thought, why wouldn't it reach much higher - as high as the Moon perhaps? After he eventually returned to Cambridge to complete his degree, he held various junior posts at Trinity before being appointed Lucasian Professor of Mathematics at the early age of 27. His patron for this surprising promotion was the retiring holder of the 'chair', Isaac Barrow, who had seen enough of Newton's work to recognise his brilliance.

Newton's subsequent career was an increasingly 'glittering' one. In addition to all his ground-breaking work in 'natural philosophy' and mathematics, none of which he published until much later, he invented the 'reflecting telescope', an instrument that would eventually replace the 'refracting telescope' as the main telescope used in front-line astronomy during the early 20th century. (This produced much sharper images than the early refracting telescopes because of a problem known as 'chromatic aberration', which was only solved with the invention of 'achromatic doublet' lenses in 1758.) In 1671, Newton's invention came to the attention of the 'Royal Society of London', a scientific body that had been founded in 1662, early in the reign of Charles II. It caused a 'major sensation', and he was elected as a 'Fellow of the Royal Society' in 1672. Thus began a 'love-hate' relationship with the Society that lasted for many years, mainly due to an on-going dispute with Robert Hooke, its highly-influential 'Curator of Experiments', over Newton's ideas about the nature of light. It was, however another prominent Fellow of the Royal Society, the astronomer Edmond Halley, who persuaded Newton to write what was to become one of the greatest masterpieces in scientific literature - his 'Philosophiae Naturalis Principia Mathematica' ('Mathematical Principles of Natural Philosophy'), usually shortened to the 'Principia'. (I will have much more to say about its contents later.) Halley even paid to have the book published and 'read the proofs' for Newton, as well as 'preparing the geometrical figures' that it contains. His other major scientific book ('Opticks') was published in 1703, after the death of Robert Hooke; Newton knew that Hooke would 'cause trouble' if it was published while he was still alive.

One unfortunate after-effect of the 18-month effort of 'hammering out' the 'Principia' was that Newton's health deteriorated, eventually leading to a complete nervous breakdown. Once he had recovered, his friends got to work to try and find him a 'new position' that would 'give him a change from Cambridge', and, at the same time, enable him to 'earn a bit more money' (professors' salaries were not all that large). Newton's interest in metals was well known, and he had been consulted more than once about alloys used in the English 'coinage', which was 'in a mess' and 'needed reform'. It was clearly a job for a mathematician and metallurgist, so, in 1696, Newton was appointed 'Warden of the Royal Mint' at a 'handsome salary'; he moved to London, taking a house in fashionable Jermyn Street, just south of Piccadilly. Although his really great, original scientific work was over, he still 'kept his hand in', trying to explain all the irregularities in the Moon's motion, and being consulted on 'all sorts of problems'. Now in his 'mid-fifties', he was also 'enjoying social life' for the first time! By the turn of the century, he had successfully completed the reform and recasting of the country's coinage; a grateful nation duly promoted him to 'Master of the Mint'. In 1701, he became a Member of Parliament for his University, a post that he would hold almost until his death. In 1703, the Royal Society elected him President, and, two years later, he was knighted by Queen Anne for his 'services to science'. During the last few years of his life, his health began to deteriorate, although he would not give up presiding at meetings of the Royal Society. In March 1727, he took to his bed, lapsed into a coma, and, on March 20th, died in his sleep. The following week, he was buried in Westminster Abbey, the first English scientist to be so honoured. He is now widely recognised as the 'greatest scientist of all time', an accolade with which I completely agree.

Let me now list some of the most important of Newton's many achievements before taking a detailed look at the greatest of them all - the development of the 'Newtonian world picture' that turned natural philosophy and astronomy into highly-mathematical disciplines, and dominated these subjects for over 300 years.

First, he was (along with Leibniz, who worked completely independently of him at more or less the same time) the inventor of both 'differential calculus' and 'integral calculus', arguably the most important single development in the entire history of mathematics.

Modern theoretical astronomy and modern physical science simply could not happen without them.

Second, he invented the 'reflecting telescope', which brought early 'telescopic astronomy' into whole new areas, and, without which, the great discoveries of the 20th-century could simply not have been made (although it is almost certain that it would have been invented by someone else long before then).

Third, he carried out ground-breaking experimental and theoretical world on the nature of light, and, although his 'corpuscular theory' went 'out of fashion' for a long time with the appearance of the rival 'wave theory', it came right back 'into fashion' during the early 20th-century, with the discovery of 'wave-particle duality' (see Chapter 14).

Fourth, he wrote 'Principia', arguably 'the most important and most influential scientific book ever. Let me try to explain **what** it said, and **why** it is regarded as so important in the development of our understanding of physical reality.

Newton's 'Principia' was written in three 'parts': 'Book 1', 'Book 2' and 'Book 3'. The first dealt with the dynamics of bodies moving through empty space, without resistance, and included his three 'laws of motion', his 'law of universal gravitation', and his derivations of Kepler's 'three laws of planetary motion' from these. The second dealt with the dynamics of bodies moving through fluids that offer some resistance to such motion, and also discussed sound waves. The third, and most important part, described his 'System of the World', showing how the material covered earlier (mainly in Book 1) could be combined with empirical astronomical observations to explain the dynamics of the solar system and the stars that existed beyond it (this was **long** before the discovery of the structure of our 'Galaxy', and the discovery that 'spiral nebulae' were 'island universes' similar to our own Galaxy).

It was also written using the scientific terminology of his time rather than modern terminology (using the term 'motion' for what we now call 'momentum', for example), and its arguments were also presented 'geometrically' rather than in modern mathematical terms. This made it a very difficult book to 'get to grips with' at the time of its publication, let alone today. For this reason, I have decided to provide my own outline of the 'Newtonian world picture' rather than attempt to guide readers through the 'Principia' itself - which I would have great difficulty in doing anyway!

First, let me outline some of the basic assumptions on which his mathematical 'world picture' was based. Newton believed that the 'basic framework' within which his system operated consisted of fixed 'Euclidean' space and 'linear' time that flowed uniformly from the past, through the present, into the future. He also assumed that the universe consisted of 'particles' (or 'atoms') moving in an 'empty void', and that all larger bodies (such as planets) were composed of 'aggregations' of such particles. Finally, he believed that we live in a 'deterministic universe', whose evolution depended on what had gone on before. He often compared it to a 'clock', which, once it had been created and started up by God, would continue to run smoothly forever, following the 'laws' that Newton had discovered.

Next, let me describe his three 'laws of motion'. Newton's 'First Law' states that 'Every body continues in a state of rest or uniform motion in a straight line unless it is compelled to change that state by forces impressed upon it'. This was derived from the earlier work of Galileo on the dynamics of moving bodies. 'Newton's Second Law' states that 'The rate of change of momentum of a moving body is proportional to the strength of the force acting upon it, and takes place along the line of action of the force'. This was again largely built on earlier work by Galileo. 'Newton's Third Law states that 'For every action there is an equal and opposite reaction'. This was entirely Newton's own work, and, stated very simply, tells us that if you 'push' something, it 'pushes back'. Newton believed that these three basic 'laws', combined with his 'Law of Universal Gravitation', control virtually everything that happens in the 'dynamic universe' that he envisaged.

Let me now turn to this 'Law of Universal Gravitation', which was undoubtedly Newton's greatest contribution to science. It states that 'Any two bodies exert an attractive gravitational force on each other that is proportional to the product of their respective masses and inversely proportionally to the square of the distance between them'. He also maintained that the 'intrinsic strength' of this gravitational force is determined by the value of the 'Universal Gravitational Constant' G, which constitutes the 'constant of proportionality' in the resulting mathematical equation, and is one of the basic 'universal constants' in physics. Because the strength of the gravitational force falls by a factor of four when the distance between the two bodies doubles, the Law is sometimes called the 'Inverse Square Law of Gravitation'. It is one of the most important 'laws of physics' that anyone has ever discovered, arguably **the** most important.

I hope I have now convinced you of the world-changing significance of Newton's work, but, in case I have not done so, here are three further points for you to consider. 1. He provided the final, irrefutable proof of the truth of the Copernican 'heliocentric' cosmology, thus totally-discrediting the out-dated doctrines on cosmology that had been imposed by the Church for over 400 years. 2. He drove the final nail in the coffin of 'Aristotelian science', which had dominated 'Western thinking' for far too long. Aristotle was one of the greatest philosophers and scientists in the history of humanity, but his ideas were now well past their 'sell-by date'. 3. He showed how a few 'simple' ideas, generated by one outstanding man, could totally change our view of the physical world. The next person to do this would be Einstein, as we will see in Chapter 11.

The many subsequent achievements of Newtonian science

As I have already told you, the 'Newtonian world picture', or 'Newtonian paradigm' (to use modern terminology) totally dominated physics and astronomy until the very end of the 19th century. During this time, it not only transformed astronomy from an essentially-observational activity backed up by a succession of relatively crude theories into a complete marriage of increasingly-accurate observations and highly-mathematical theories which could explain them with perfect accuracy. Indeed, astronomy became the most 'exact science' that the world had ever seen. I will discuss these developments in much greater detail in Chapter 12, so will say nothing more about them here. What I **will** tell you about now is how two totally-new major branches of physics - 'thermodynamics' and 'electromagnetism' - were gradually 'brought into' the 'Newtonian paradigm'. Both were developed during the 19th century, and, by the end of the century, both had been virtually completely absorbed by the Newtonian 'world picture', so that **all** the physics that was known at the time had effectively been 'unified' within that world picture. This led one of the most eminent scientists alive at the time (Lord Kelvin) to make the famous remark that I use as my 'opening quotation' in Chapter 11, and say that 'there was nothing new to be discovered in physics'. As we will see in Chapter 11, he could not have been more wrong!

Thermodynamics was in fact a 'child' of the 'Industrial Revolution' that began in Britain in the second half of the 18th-century, and spread throughout Europe and beyond during the 19th. This became increasingly-dependent on the steam engine, which engineers were trying to make more and more efficient - and safer. The new science of 'thermodynamics' (the study of 'heat' and its movement) was developed in order to help them to do so, and soon became one of the most important branches of physics. Its early pioneers included Sadi

Carnot and his colleague Emile Clapeyron, followed by Rudolf Clausius, Willard Gibbs and William Thomson (who later became the 'Lord Kelvin' that I mentioned earlier). For a long time, thermodynamics was regarded as a completely-free-standing branch of physics, whose basic concepts were unrelated to those of other branches. All this changed with the development of 'statistical mechanics', or 'statistical thermodynamics' from the middle of the 19th-century onwards. Its two 'founding fathers' were James Clerk Maxwell (who also played a major role in the development of electromagnetic theory, as we will see below) and Ludwig Boltzmann. Both based their work on Newton's picture of 'particles moving in the void', and showed how the behaviour of such particles could be explained with great accuracy by employing **statistical** methods rather than trying to deal with them individually. The latter approach was completely impracticable, since there were far too many 'particles' for it to work (A single cubic centimeter of gas for example, is now known to contain several million million **million** molecules; just try **counting** them, let alone trying to calculate their paths through space!) Maxwell carried out the initial mathematical work, which Boltzmann subsequently built upon. Together, they developed the theory of what became known as the 'Maxwell-Boltzmann distribution', the basis of so-called 'classical' statistical mechanics. This showed how the number of molecules in a gas with a given speed at first increased from zero as the speed rose, reached a peak, and then decreased to zero once again. Using this basic distribution as a starting point, they were able to describe all the key parameters used in thermodynamics ('temperature', 'entropy' and so on) in terms of the motion of molecules. I learned all about statistical mechanics in the latter part of my honours degree in natural philosophy at Aberdeen University, and later taught it to 'honours level' at Robert Gordon's Institute of Technology. I found it to be one of the most 'beautiful' subjects in the whole of physics and could only marvel at the way in which its creators had effectively 'unified' thermodynamics and the 'classical dynamics' that had been developed by Newton and his successors.

Electromagnetism was another 'late arrival' in physics. It had its roots in the study of 'magnetism' and 'static electricity', both of which had been known about for thousands of years. Following pioneering work by people like André Marie Ampere (after whom the 'amp' is named) and Alessandro Volta (after whom the 'volt' is named), and Hans Christian Oersted (who discovered that a wire carrying an electric current slightly disturbed the magnetic needle of a nearby compass), the links between 'electricity' and 'magnetism' were studied in detail by Michael Faraday, working at the Royal Institution in London in the middle of the 19th century. Although he knew virtually no mathematics, he was a brilliant experimentalist, and discovered the principles by which 'electric motors' and 'generators' could be built. He is recognised as the 'father' of the modern electricity industry. He also produced the revolutionary theory that magnetic, electric and electromagnetic effects were transmitted through space along 'lines of force', which effectively defined a 'field'. Faraday's associates admired and believed in his 'experimental work', but not his 'field theory', which at the time, did not seem to fit into the 'Newtonian paradigm', which pictured gravity as 'acting at a distance', without the need for any intervening 'field'. But Faraday was eventually joined by two brilliant young scientists - William Thomson and James Clerk Maxwell - both of whom you have heard of earlier. Thomson fashioned a limited mathematical theory of Faraday's electric lines of force, and Maxwell went **very** much further. Over a period of almost two decades he developed a 'great theoretical edifice' based on Faraday's 'field concept'. This consisted of four mathematical 'equations', now known as 'Maxwell's equations', which condensed into a few lines the theory of **all** electric, magnetic and electromagnetic phenomena, including Faraday's idea that light consisted of 'electromagnetic waves'. The scope and utility of 'Maxwell's equations' were vast, and they are now regarded as just as important and 'universal' as the four laws produced by Newton. Indeed, Maxwell is now generally regarded as Britain's second-ever greatest physical scientist, after Newton himself. Since all 'waves' were thought at the time to require a medium through which to propagate, scientists came up with the concept of the 'luminiferous ether', a 'substance' that permeated the whole of space. They also came to believe that Newton's 'gravitational force' was propagated by 'gravitational waves' similar to the 'electromagnetic waves' that were such a key feature of Maxwell's magnificent theory. From then on, physics became increasingly concerned with the study of the 'ether', and it was realised that electricity and magnetism had now joined thermodynamics as integral parts of the 'Newtonian' paradigm. As we will see in Chapter 11, the failure of physicists to detect the motion of the Earth through the supposedly-fixed ether was one of the key pieces of evidence that led to the 'Einsteinian Revolution' at the start of the 20th-century.

Some of the sources of information on material covered in Chapter 7

For the first time in writing this book, I was on 'home territory', since I studied natural philosophy (physics) to honours level, and then spent ten years as a professional physicist until I moved into educational development in 1973. I have kept fully up to date with developments in physics, astronomy and other branches of science ever since, however, and have retained my membership of the Institute of Physics, which made me a 'Fellow' in 1980. They send me their excellent monthly magazine, 'Physics World', which covers **all** the latest developments in physics and astronomy. I therefore had to do very little 'deep background research' when writing this chapter, although I did have to refer to many of the books and other materials in my personal library for some details. I found the following particularly useful:

- 'The Story of Astronomy'. By Patrick Moore, which provided highly-detailed information about the 'Copernican Revolution' and about Newton himself.
- 'Great Scientific Ideas that Changed the World', a 'Teaching Company' course written and presented by Professor Stephen L. Goldman.
- 'Great Physicists', by William H. Cropper, a highly-detailed book that provided me with a large amount of useful information on all the physicists covered in this chapter.
- 'Chambers Biographical Dictionary' (1990 edition, edited by Magnus Magnusson), an invaluable reference source that I used more and more as I worked my way through the 20 chapters of my book - and to think that I only paid 50p for it at a library clearance sale! We Aberdonians certainly recognise a bargain when we see one!

Chapter 8: The development of 'modern' western philosophy

'In most of its essentials our metaphysical understanding of the human condition is where Kant and Schopenhauer left it'.

- Bryan Magee ('Confessions of a Philosopher')

As readers will have already gathered, I am a great admirer of the late Bryan Magee, who died in 2019. Although he was never an 'active practising philosopher' himself, he was by far the most brilliant 'writer on philosophy' that I have ever known. I have now read his intellectual autobiography, 'Confessions of a Philosopher', nine times, and, every time, I get something 'new' out of it. Through the ground-breaking radio and television programmes that he made on philosophy from the end of the 1960s onwards, he was also largely responsible for introducing the 'thinking public' to the subject, which had always been considered 'too difficult' for them to understand. So when he came out with highly-penetrating observations like the one quoted above, I took them very seriously indeed. So much so, in fact, that I have modelled this entire chapter on Bryan's general overview of how 'modern' western philosophy has evolved since the time of Descartes, whose work is generally regarded as the real 'starting point' of such philosophy. It will show how the early work of two radically-different 'schools' of philosophy, the 'continental rationalists' (who were essentially 'Plato' people) and the 'British empiricists' (who were essentially 'Aristotle' people) were effectively 'unified' by the revolutionary work of Kant and Schopenhauer on either side of the start of the 19th century. Bryan regarded Kant as one of the 'three greatest western philosophers of all time', right up there with Plato and Aristotle. Indeed, he makes a strong case for Kant being the 'best of the lot', and believed that the 'greatest single advance in the entire history of western philosophy' was the distinction made by Kant between the 'empirical, phenomenal world' that we observe around us and the unobservable 'noumenal world' that he believed to lie beneath and beyond it. He also believed that western philosophy has not really made much significant progress since the time of Kant and Schopenhauer. I hope that the broad review of the history of modern western philosophy that I have given in this chapter will help readers to make up their own minds on these matters, or at least stimulate you into reading more widely about them, if you have not already done so.

Continental rationalism

'Continental rationalism' is based on the 'Platonic' view that we can gain a deep understanding about the nature of reality simply by 'thinking' about it in a systematic, 'rational' way. The three leading philosophers who worked in this manner were René Descartes, Benedict Spinoza, and Gottfried Wilhelm Leibniz, each of which I will now examine in turn.

By far the most important and influential of these three philosophers was Descartes, who has often been described as the 'father of modern western philosophy'. He did for philosophy what Bacon did for science, giving it a 'new method' – the method of 'systematic doubt'. He was born in Tours, a small town in France, in 1596, and received an excellent education at the Jesuit College at La Flèche. He subsequently studied law at Poitiers, graduating in 1616. In 1618, he enlisted for 'private military service', mainly in order to 'travel' and to have the leisure to 'think'. While he was serving in Germany in the army of the Duke of Bavaria, he had the famous 'intellectual vision' that transformed his life. He conceived a reconstruction of 'the whole of philosophy', and, indeed, the 'whole of knowledge', into a unified system of 'certain truth', modelled on 'mathematics', and supported by 'rigorous rationalism'. From 1618 to 1628, he travelled widely in Holland, France and Italy, eventually returning to Holland, where he remained, living quietly and writing, until 1649. During this time, he produced his three 'key works' – 'Discourse on Method' in 1637, 'Meditations' in 1641, and 'Principles of Philosophy' in 1644. In 1649, he left Holland for Sweden at the invitation of Queen Kristina, who wanted him to give her 'tuition in philosophy'. These 'lessons' took place three times a week at **5am**, and were particularly taxing for Descartes, whose lifetime habit was to stay in bed, thinking and reading, until about 11am. As a result, he contracted pneumonia, and died in 1650. He was buried in Stockholm, but his body was later removed to Paris, and eventually transferred to Saint-Germain-des-Pres. He is now recognised as the greatest philosopher that France has ever produced, and as one of the greatest and most influential of all modern western philosophers.

Descartes was a mathematician of genius, and invented a completely new branch of the subject known as 'analytic geometry', or 'co-ordinate geometry'. He also invented the 'graph', the two familiar co-ordinates of which are now known as 'Cartesian co-ordinates'. The transparent and utterly-reliable 'certainties' of mathematics thrilled him, and he wondered whether what gave mathematics **its** 'certainty' could be applied in other areas of study such as philosophy. He eventually developed an entire 'philosophical system' based on this idea, presenting this to the world in his 'Discourse on Method' in 1637. His 'method' was based on the following four 'rules of logic'. 1. Accept nothing as true which he could not clearly recognise to be so, so that he could have 'no possible reason to doubt it'. 2. Divide each 'problem' or 'difficulty' into as many component parts as seemed possible or necessary. 3. Start any subsequent 'reflections' with 'concepts' which were the 'simplest and easiest to understand', and proceed from these to 'more complex' concepts. 4. Make the development of ideas so complete, and reviews of them so general, that he could be 'certain' that he had omitted nothing. Descartes' greatest innovation was to make the 'starting point' of his philosophical system a decision to 'doubt everything' – to doubt that a 'material world' existed; to doubt that 'God' existed; to doubt that 'other people' existed; to doubt that even his 'own body' existed. Nothing was to be believed until it could be **proved**. By 'proof', he meant not mere 'empirical evidence' or 'commonsense assurance', but **rational** and **incontrovertible** demonstration. By means of his new 'method', Descartes was able to build up, to his own satisfaction at any rate, an elaborate 'metaphysical structure' to explain the 'nature of the universe'. He took as his 'starting point' his realisation that his own 'doubting' could not rationally be denied, so that his own 'existence' as a 'thinking entity' could not also be denied. In his own famous words, 'Cogito ergo sum' ('I am thinking, therefore I exist'). Thus, Descartes gained **certainty** of the existence of at least one 'thinking entity' – his 'own mind'. From this, he passed directly to a realisation that a 'perfect mind', that of 'God', must also exist, as a matter of 'necessity'. From here, he proceeded to 'prove' the existence of the 'material world', including his 'own body'. As a result of all this, Descartes was able to recognise the existence of three completely different 'kinds of substance' – 'created spirit' (or 'human mind'), 'uncreated spirit' (or 'God') and the 'material world' (or 'body'). From this, Descartes was able to develop his concepts of 'mind-body dualism' and the related 'mind-body problem', concepts that have continued to haunt European philosophy until the present day, as we will see in Chapter 10, which is entirely devoted to them.

The greatest of Descartes' immediate successors in Continental philosophy were both mathematicians, like himself. Both shared Descartes' passion for 'rational certainty', and each developed a metaphysical system that was intended to be better than Descartes' own. The first, Benedict (originally 'Baruch') Spinoza was born in Amsterdam in 1632, a member of a distinguished Jewish family that had fled from Portugal to escape Catholic persecution. He had an 'orthodox' Jewish upbringing and education, but, because of his 'heterodox opinions', was expelled from the Jewish community in Amsterdam at the age of 24; it was then that he changed his first name from the 'Hebrew' to the 'Latin' form. He proceeded to live a solitary life, earning his living by grinding and polishing lenses for spectacles, microscopes and telescopes – at that time, a 'new profession'. Despite this, his writings made him increasingly famous, but when he was offered a Professorship of Philosophy at Heidelberg University in 1673, he turned it down because he wanted to be left alone to do his philosophising 'in accordance with his own mind', as he put it. Spinoza, like so many of the great philosophers, was a genuine 'polymath', speaking Spanish and Portuguese as well as Dutch and Hebrew, and using Latin for nearly all of his serious writing. In addition to being an accomplished mathematician, he was a distinguished biblical scholar, took an intense interest in the 'new science', and, through his work on microscopes and telescopes, was fully aware of the great potential of the 'new technologies' that were being 'opened up' by this new science. His philosophy, it might be said, attempted to bring all these things, and their implications, together into an 'integrated and orderly whole'.

Before his early death in 1677, almost certainly because of a chronic lung complaint brought about by regular inhalation of powdered glass during his lens-grinding work, Spinoza developed a highly-personal philosophical system which he believed to be a 'great improvement' on that produced by Descartes. He agreed with Descartes that the right way to build up an accurate 'world picture' was to start from 'indubitable premises', and deduce the consequences of these by 'logical reasoning', and also agreed with Descartes that the existence of God as a 'perfect being' could be demonstrated by 'purely rational arguments'. But Spinoza denied that this 'perfect being' was the God of Descartes' Catholic Church, or even the God of Spinoza's own Jewish faith, views that proved 'highly offensive' to followers of both religious traditions. God, for Spinoza, was not a 'Heavenly Father' with attributes like those of men; he was, quite literally, the 'perfect being'. Therefore, his 'attributes' must also be 'infinite', even though the human mind, in its imperfection, can 'know' only two of them – 'thought' and 'extension'. But whereas Descartes supposed that 'thought' was the attribute of 'mind', and 'extension' was the attribute of 'body', Spinoza saw 'thought' and 'extension' as attributes of **one and the same substance,** which in turn, is simply a **manifestation of God.** And, since God is 'infinite', there can be **nothing** in the universe that is **not God.** Among other things, this means that **the Universe is perfect,** precisely because **God is perfect.** We can see that Spinoza's philosophical system was in fact a form of 'pantheism' – seeing God as a 'perfect being' who was not only **involved** in 'all things', but actually **was** 'all things'. These ideas, and various other aspects of his philosophy that I have not dealt with here, were described in detail in Spinoza's most important work, 'Ethics', which was published posthumously in 1677. It addresses not only ethics, but the whole range of philosophy, proceeding from the premise that 'everything could be demonstrated logically'. An earlier work, 'Tractatus Theologico-Politicus' (the 'Theological-Political Treatise') was published anonymously in 1670, but was banned in 1674 because of its 'controversial views on the Bible and Christian theology'. Spinoza certainly knew how to offend people!

Although his work was largely ignored for roughly 100 years after his death, it was eventually 'revived' and treated with 'near-veneration' by the 'Romantics'. Also, his robust repudiation of 'Cartesian dualism' was to become the 'orthodox' philosophical and scientific position in the 20th-century, but not until then. He was also the first great western philosopher to set out the basic case for 'freedom of speech', thus anticipating the work of Locke in this area by roughly a generation. Subsequent philosophers who admired him, and learned from him, including Hegel, Schopenhauer, Nietzsche and Bertrand Russell – not a bad list! And it was not only philosophers who 'came under his spell', with 'giant thinkers' in other fields such as Einstein and Freud, and 'creative artists' such as Goethe and George Eliot acknowledging their debt to him. Thus, Spinoza is now recognised as a 'major figure' in 'western culture' generally, as well as in 'western philosophy'.

Gottfried Wilhelm Leibniz, the second of Decartes' brilliant successors, was a man of unusually wide genius, even for a great philosopher. He was born in Leipzig in 1646, the son of a professor of moral philosophy, studying there and at Altdorf. He showed 'great precocity of learning', and, in 1667, obtained a position at the court of the Elector of Mainz, on the strength of an essay on legal education. There, he codified laws, drafted schemes for the unification of the churches, and was variously required to act as a courtier, civil servant and international lawyer, while, at the same time, absorbing the philosophy, science and mathematics of the day. He travelled widely, meeting many of the key figures in these fields, and, in 1676, moved to Hanover to take up what turned out to be his last post – as librarian to the Duke of Brunswick. Here, he continued to develop, without publishing them, his mathematical and philosophical theories. He never wrote a major book, only two short 'treatises' – 'Theodicy' (1710), which expressed his faith in 'enlightenment' and 'reason', and 'Monadology' (1714), which argued that everything consisted of 'basic units' called 'monads'. By the time of his death in 1716, he had invented 'calculus' independently of (and unknown to) Newton, and actually developed the notation that all mathematicians subsequently used once they found out about his work. He also invented 'mathematical logic', although he never published his work on this; had he done so, the subject would have 'got going' one and a half centuries before it did. And, as well as being one of the greatest mathematicians of all time, he was one of the greatest, and most influential of all philosophers. Let me now outline some of the most important contributions that he made in this discipline.

First, he was the first philosopher to draw a distinction between two basically-different types of 'statements' – what later came to be known as 'analytic statements' and 'synthetic statements'. The first are statements whose truth or falsehood can be determined 'internally', simply by examining **the statements themselves**, without having to look **outside** them. The second are statements which **might** be either true or false, but require external, empirical evidence to determine which is the case. This distinction was developed with increasing sophistication and depth over roughly 300 years, culminating in the work of the 'logical positivists' during the 20th-century.

Second, he was the first to introduce the idea of 'alternative possible worlds' into modern philosophy. This was based on his doctrine of 'compossibilities' – possibilities which are 'compatible' with one another, as against possibilities which are not. According to Leibniz, the sum total of any set of 'compossibilities' makes up a 'possible world', and there are an infinite number of them. Leibniz believed that God could have chosen any 'possible world' that he wished, but, being a 'perfect being', chose to create the 'best of all possible worlds' – one that contained 'free-will' and 'evil'. In this way, he provided a possible rational solution to the 'problem of evil' – why a 'perfect God' created a world with so much evil in it. This is a problem to which theologians have yet to produce a satisfactory answer.

Third, he developed a key concept that has played an important role in philosophy and science ever since – his 'principle of sufficient reason'. For everything that **is** the case, he said, there must be a reason **why** it is the case. If the 'truth' in question is what is now called an 'analytic' one, its 'sufficient reason' can be found internally. If it is what is now called 'synthetic', on the other hand, involving a 'factual' state of affairs, its 'sufficient reason' should be sought by examining the 'physical causes' that brought it about. The 'principle of sufficient reason' is possibly Leibniz's greatest single contribution to our understanding of the world, and is now regarded as one of the few 'self-evident truths' in philosophy.

Fourth, Leibniz developed an extremely interesting alternative 'world model' to that produced by Newton. Newton regarded the 'particles' or 'atoms' that make up his world as essentially 'lifeless' and 'inert'. Leibniz, on the other hand, regarded the 'world' as being made up of 'dots of consciousness' occupying 'points in space'. He called these 'monads', and believed that **everything** was made up of them. Although he saw all monads as intrinsically 'spaceless', he also saw them as differing widely in 'intensity', from those that make up 'inorganic matter' at the lower end of the scale, to 'human minds', each of which is a monad, and then on to God, who is also a monad. Although Newton's purely-mechanistic world picture dominated western thinking for over 300 years, as we saw in the previous chapter, Leibniz's ideas underwent something of a 'revival' during the 20th century, as we will see later.

Bryan Magee once described Leibniz as a 'philosopher's philosopher'; while the best of his work is 'too technical' for untrained readers to follow, its influence on other philosophers has been 'enormous'.

British empiricism

'British empiricism' is based on the 'Aristotelian' view that our knowledge of the world is best obtained by actually 'observing', 'studying' and 'investigating' it rather than merely 'thinking' about it. It is generally associated with the names of three men – the Englishman John Locke, the Irishman George Berkeley, and the Scotsman David Hume, although the modern British tradition could be said to have got seriously underway with the work of Bacon. I have already looked at his work in Chapter 7, so will move straight on to Locke.

John Locke was born in 1632, the son of a West-of-England lawyer who fought with the Parliamentarians against the King in the English Civil War. In 1646, he was enrolled at Westminster School, possibly the finest school in England at the time, where he studied the 'classics', as well as Hebrew and Arabic. He then moved on to Oxford University, where he discovered the 'new philosophy' and the 'new science', eventually qualifying in medicine. In 1667, he joined the household of the Earl of Shaftsbury as his 'personal physician', and also serving him in more 'political' capacities. He spent four years in France between 1675 and 1679, where he studied Descartes, and came into contact with some of the 'greatest minds of the age'. In 1681, the Earl of Shaftsbury was tried for treason, and acquitted, but fled the country out of fear for his safety, settling in Holland. Things became dangerous for his associates in England, so, in 1683, Locke also moved to Holland. It was there that he wrote the bulk of his main philosophical 'masterwork', 'Essay Concerning Human Understanding'; it was eventually published in 1689. While in Holland, Locke became part of a 'conspiratorial world' of English political exiles. In the plot to set the Dutch Prince, William of Orange, on the English throne, he was one of those giving advice directly to William. After the 'Glorious Revolution of 1688', when the Catholic King James II fled abroad, Locke personally escorted Mary, the Princess of Orange, from Holland to England, where she and William became 'joint monarchs'. In the same year, Locke published the first of his important books on political philosophy, 'A Letter Concerning Toleration'. In 1690, this was followed by 'Two Treatises of Government', and, in 1693, by 'Some Thoughts Concerning Education'. Thus, although he lived for a further 11 years and wrote other things, all of his most influential writings came out in a period of less than five years. After his triumphant return to England in 1689, he declined an ambassadorship, serving as

'Commissioner of Appeals' until 1704, when he died after a period of declining health, at the age of 72.

Locke was a thinker of the first rank in two different areas of philosophy – the 'theory of knowledge' ('epistemology') and 'political philosophy'. In the former, he launched what many to this day regard as its most important project, namely, an enquiry into what is 'intelligible to humans'. In other words, 'what can we know?', and 'how can we know that we know it?'. He himself laid the foundations for this project in his 'Essay Concerning Human Understanding', and his work was continued by some of the outstanding figures in modern western philosophy – Hume and Kant in the 18th century, Schopenhauer in the 19th, then Russell, Wittgenstein and Popper in the 20th. Locke's epistemological ideas were extremely complicated, but can be summarised as follows. He began by attacking the then-prevailing notion that we are all born with a certain amount of knowledge in the form of 'innate ideas'. Locke maintained that we are born knowing nothing. The mind, to begin with, is a 'tabula rasa' (an 'empty tablet'). Everything we subsequently learn ultimately comes from our 'sensory experience' – 'seeing', 'hearing', 'touching', 'smelling' and 'tasting'. These 'forms of perception' give us 'simple ideas', out of which our minds then construct 'complex ideas'. For Locke, the 'ideas of perception' were 'representations', or 'copies' of things in the 'external world'. His central problem was therefore to determine how far the ideas that come from the senses really correspond to things that exist in the external world. Locke concluded that material objects have two sorts of 'properties', or 'qualities'. They have 'primary qualities', such as 'extension in space'; 'figure' or 'shape'; 'number'; and 'impenetrability' or 'solidity', which belong entirely to them. And they also have 'secondary qualities', such as 'colour', 'scent', or 'taste', which are primarily dependant on the 'sensory apparatus' and 'mind' of the observer. 'Primary qualities' are 'rooted in substance', a mysterious 'something' that 'underlies' or 'supports' them, whereas 'secondary qualities' are not. An essential element in Locke's 'theory of knowledge' is the view that because we are able to 'observe' only an object's 'observable characteristics and behaviour', we have no way of apprehending it **independently of these characteristics.**

Let us now turn to his equally-ground-breaking work on political philosophy, in which he effectively 'invented' the concept of a 'liberal democracy'. This was based on two key ideas. Firstly, he believed that when people originally emerged from a 'state of nature' to form 'organised societies', they did so 'voluntarily' and 'knowingly', since God had given them 'reason' and 'conscience'. Like his predecessor Hobbes, he regarded the resulting 'social contract' being not between 'government' and 'governed', but between 'free men'. Unlike Hobbes, however, he believed that 'ultimate sovereignty' within a state should 'remain with the people' after its 'government' had been set up. Indeed, he believed that the protection of the 'life, liberty and property' of its citizens was the 'sole legitimate purpose of government'. Second, he believed firmly in 'tolerance', seeing it as 'mistaken' and 'morally wrong' for political and religious authorities to 'impose their beliefs and doctrines' on the people. He was also a passionate believer in 'free speech', whereby every member of the type of 'liberal society' that he advocated would have the right to express their ideas openly, without fear of persecution. He was far ahead of his time here, but, as we will see in the next chapter, his ideas effectively triggered off the 'European Enlightenment' that would so transform society during the 18th, 19th and 20th centuries. Locke's ideas were also taken up by the men who drew up the American Constitution at the end of the 18th century, after America had won independence from British rule. These 'Founding Fathers' drew heavily on Locke's work when they were doing so, and referred to him by name in their correspondence with one another. As Bryan Magee observed, it is doubtful whether any political philosopher between

Aristotle and Karl Marx has had a greater influence on 'practical politics' than Locke.

The next great figure in British empiricism was George Berkeley, an Irish Anglican Bishop. He was born in 1685 at Dysert Castle, in Kilkenny, and was educated at Kilkenny College and at Trinity College, Dublin, where he remained as a 'Fellow' and a 'Tutor' until 1713. His three most important books were all published during these early years – 'Essay towards a New Theory of Vision' in 1709, 'A Treatise concerning the Principles of Human Knowledge' in 1710, and 'Three Dialogues between Hylas and Philonous' in 1713. After leaving Trinity College, he visited London, and then travelled in Italy and France for several years. He returned to Ireland in 1721, with a new-found concern about 'social corruption' and 'national decadence', expressed in his anonymous 'Essay towards preventing the Ruin of Great Britain'. In 1724, he became Dean of Derry, but became increasingly obsessed with a romantic scheme to found a college in the Bermudas to promote 'the propagation of the gospel among the American savages'. After years of intense lobbying in London for financial support, he sailed for America in 1728 with his new wife, and made a temporary home in Rhode Island, where he spent three years waiting for the promised 'grants' to materialise. They never did, so he never actually reached Bermuda, and his college was never built. He returned to London, and then moved back home to Ireland, becoming Bishop of Cloyne in 1734. Here, his remaining literary work was divided between questions of 'social reform' and 'religious reflection'. In 1752, he resigned his episcopate and moved to Oxford, where he died in 1753.

Most of the famous philosophers of the past have produced a body of work that addressed a wide range of problems, but Berkeley is remembered for a single brilliant 'insight', which no-one since has been wholly able to 'ignore' or 'explain away'. Locke was entirely correct, said Berkeley, in believing that all we can ever **directly** apprehend are the 'contents of our own consciousness'. But in that case, he asked, what possible warrant can we have for asserting that the existence of these 'mental contents' is 'caused' by 'things' of an 'entirely' and 'fundamentally different' character from them, to which we can never have **direct access**, namely, 'material objects'? If, as people said, we have **indirect** access to such objects via the 'sensory images' we receive of them, in what sense could that be true? People explained it by saying that our 'sensory images' are 'copies' of the objects, but what could this so much as even **mean**? How could an experience like a 'colour' or a 'sound' be a 'copy' of something that is not an experience, or be in any way 'like' it. The whole thing is 'conceptual nonsense', said Berkeley. Locke was postulating the existence of a whole realm of independently-existing, non-sensory, non-mental 'reality', which we cannot even 'conceptualise', which we could never have 'evidence for', and whose existence could make 'no possible difference to us'. What 'conceivable grounds', he claimed, are there for doing this? We know, said Berkeley, that 'experiences inhere in a subject', because each of us has 'immediate awareness' of **being** such a subject, and a subject **having experiences**, to boot. But we could never possess corresponding grounds for believing that these experiences are 'attached' to objects that are 'not us'. Therefore, said Berkeley, a 'consistent empiricism' leads us to the conclusion that what exists are 'minds' and their 'contents', or 'subjects' and their 'experiences'. There are no grounds for believing in the existence of anything else. In asserting the existence of 'things' that are 'beyond the bounds of all possible experience', Locke was 'breaking the fundamental principle of empiricism'. This is formidable philosophical argument, and one that thinkers ever since have found difficulty in dealing with. Being a Christian, Berkeley fitted it into a view of 'total reality' as 'existing in the mind of God', an 'infinite spirit' who has created us 'finite spirits', and who is 'communicating with us via our experiences'. In this view, everything that exists does so **either** in 'our minds', **or** in 'God's mind', or else, of course **is** either 'us' or 'God'.

Thinkers who are not religious have dispensed with this 'religious framework', postulating that Berkeley has 'insufficient grounds' for postulating the existence of a 'God', or even of a 'continuous self'. But the rest of his 'philosophical challenge' remains disconcertingly difficult to answer to this day.

The last of the three great British empiricists was the Scotsman David Hume, one of the 'most attractive' as well as one of the 'most important' figures in the history of philosophy. In France, where he lived for several years, he was known as 'le bon David', and, in his native Edinburgh, he was known as 'Saint David'. Born in Edinburgh in 1711, his early years were 'unsettled'. He studied at, but did not graduate at, Edinburgh University. He took up law, but suffered from 'bouts of depression', and tried his hand in commerce, working as a 'counting-house clerk' in Bristol. In 1734, he moved to La Flèche in Anjou, where he stayed for three years, studying, and working on his first and most important book, 'A Treatise of Human Nature'. This was eventually published in London in two volumes in 1739-40, when he was still only 28; to his great disappointment, no-one 'took any notice' of it. In his thirties, he developed his ideas further, in what he hoped would be a 'more popular form'. The results were published in two smaller volumes: 'An Enquiry concerning Human Understanding' (1748), and 'An Enquiry concerning the Principles of Morals' (1751); still no-one 'took very much notice'. He then turned away from philosophy for some time, or at least **appeared** to, and, in his forties, wrote a six-volume 'History of England' (1754-62) which was to remain the standard work on the subject for the next hundred years. He also acquired a reputation as an economist, producing some original 'monetarist theories', and being a close friend of Adam Smith, a fellow-Scot who is generally regarded as the 'founder of modern economics'. His chief fame as a philosopher, however, was not to come until after his death in 1776. In 1779, his 'Dialogues concerning Natural Religion', which some consider to be his best work, was published posthumously. He had been working on this in secret, but did not dare to publish it while he was still alive because of the 'trouble' it might give rise to, since it effectively 'demolished' all the then-most-attractive arguments for the existence of God.

Let me now turn to Hume's philosophical work, and outline some of the most important contributions that he made in the field.

First, he took the earlier work of Locke and Berkeley in epistemology into completely new areas. He shared with Locke the basic empiricist premise that it is only from 'experience' that our knowledge of anything outside ourselves can be ultimately derived, and shared with Berkeley the principle that this premise needs to be employed 'with consistency', and that we can never know, with 'absolute certainty', that an external world exists externally to, and independently of ourselves. However, he took this not to be primarily a 'point about the world', but a 'point about knowledge'; 'certainty', in matters of fact, is not available to us, since we deal only in 'hopeful probabilities'.

Second, he turned Berkeley's own basic principle against Berkeley, using it to undermine the idea of the existence of an independent, continuing, experiencing 'self'. Hume claimed that we can never actually 'observe' our own self, simply experience a series of 'sensations' and 'thoughts' that we (incorrectly) identify with such a 'self'. The 'experiencing self', the 'subject of knowledge', is a fiction, says Hume. If you ask, in that case, who, or what 'I' am, the only answer that can be sustained by experience is that 'I' am a 'bundle of sensations'.

Third, Hume used a similar argument to show that you cannot 'prove' the existence of God, as both Descartes and Berkeley had claimed that you could. His existence is a 'question of fact' – either he 'exists', or he 'does not exist', and 'questions of fact' can be settled only by 'observation'. Who has 'observed' God, said Hume, who claimed that there is 'no serious observational evidence for his existence'. Hume had little difficulty showing that what people **claim** as 'observational evidence' is 'inferential', 'indirect', 'vague', and invariably 'highly personal'.

Fourth, Hume threw whole new lights on the basic empirical concept of 'causality', one of the 'foundations' of science. He pointed out that 'causal connections' between two successive events cannot be 'observed', only 'inferred' from the fact that one follows the other. The 'actual mechanism' that brings this about is simply 'not accessible' to us, says Hume. Although many people disagree with Hume's 'ideas' about causality, they have found it very difficult to refute his arguments.

Finally, Hume came up with a devastating attack on the process of 'scientific induction', which, as we saw in the last chapter, lies at the very heart of Bacon's 'scientific method'. What he claimed is that no number of 'individual observations' can **prove** the truth of a 'general law', based on these observations, only demonstrate that it is **probably** true, provided that no subsequent evidence is found to contradict it. The example usually quoted is the general statement that 'all swans are white', a 'self-evident truth' that Europeans had believed for thousands of years - until they travelled to Australia and discovered 'black swans'. As I will show you in Chapter 11, Hume's criticism of the logical validity of 'scientific induction' remained unchallenged until Popper developed a 'new' picture of the 'scientific method' roughly 300 years later.

If we could stop at this point, we might think that Hume was an 'unmitigated sceptic', a man who denied that we could be sure of **anything.** He did, indeed, believe that this was the correct position **in theory**, but not **in practice**, since we **have** to assume the truth of many things in order to 'survive' in a potentially-dangerous world. We should therefore think of him as a 'modified sceptic', probably the greatest who has ever lived. He was also a 'lovely man', to use the delightful Irish expression.

The Kantian/Schopenhauerean unification

The two main streams in European philosophy - the 'Continental rationalism' of Descartes, Spinoza and Leibniz, and the 'British empiricism' of Locke, Berkeley and Hume - were effectively 'brought together' in the 'epistemological and ontological revolution' that was initiated by Immanuel Kant and completed by Arthur Schopenhauer. This set modern western philosophy on the whole new path, a path that has dominated the field ever since, and has still to be completed. Let me now try to explain how they did this in as simple a way as I can.

Immanuel Kant is generally regarded as the 'outstanding figure to have emerged in Western philosophy since Plato and Aristotle', and is thought by some to be the 'greatest of the three'. The son of a saddler, he was born in Konigsberg in Prussia in 1724, and stayed there all his life. He studied and then taught at the local university, becoming Professor of Logic and Metaphysics in 1770. Unlike the other great philosophers I have discussed in this chapter, he led a 'quiet, orderly life', and local people were said to have 'set their watches' by the time of his daily walk. His early publications were in the 'natural sciences', particularly geophysics and astronomy. In the latter field, he anticipated many future discoveries on the origin of the Solar System and the true nature of the 'spiral nebulae', and might well have become one of the great figures in astronomy had he not turned his attention to philosophy relatively late in his life, producing the three books that were to revolutionise the subject. The first, and greatest of these, was his 'Critique of Pure Reason', which was published in 1781. The second, his 'Critique of Practical Reason' followed in 1788, and his third, 'Critique of Judgement' in 1790. The first of his three 'Critiques' was probably the most important and influential book in the history of modern Western philosophy. Let me now try to explain why.

What Kant did in his first 'Critique' was to devise a totally-new philosophical system that addressed the 'rationalist' objections to 'empiricism', and the 'empiricist' objections to 'rationalism', and, in his opinion, 'answered the problems posed by both'. This Kant achieved by what he described as his 'Copernican Revolution' in philosophy. All previous philosophers had assumed that for knowledge to be 'true', it must 'conform to the objects' in the 'external world'. Kant put the matter the other way round, saying, in effect that the 'external world' must 'conform to our knowledge of it'. This, he contended, produced a much 'simpler' view of the nature of reality, just as Copernicus's 'heliocentric theory' had produced a much 'simpler' view of the nature of the Solar System. Kant went on to say that if the 'external world' is to be an 'object of understanding', it must satisfy certain 'conditions' that the 'mind' lays down. Nothing can be known unless it corresponds to certain 'a priori' **categories**, categories that are intrinsically 'known' to the mind prior to any 'external experience' of the world, and, without which, no real understanding of the world would be possible. These included the assumption that we live in a world located in 'space' and 'time', in which events are 'causally interrelated', and can be 'accurately predicted' if we apply 'scientific laws' to the 'facts of observation'. But Hume had shown that it was impossible for us to have 'derived' this knowledge from any possible combination of observation and logic. Therefore, it **must have been there all the time**, as part of our 'mental apparatus'. At the end of his argument, he pronounced that the whole 'nature of the world' **as we experience it** is dependent on the nature of our **apparatus for experiencing**, with the inevitable consequence that 'things as they appear to us' are not the same as 'things as they are in themselves'. From this, it followed that 'reality' consists of two different 'levels', the 'phenomenal world' of 'appearances' in which we believe we live, and the 'noumenal world' that lies 'beneath and beyond it'. Kant postulated that the boundaries between these two 'worlds' were determined by the nature of our 'perceptual apparatus' - the 'physical senses' which gather 'raw information' about the 'phenomenal, empirical world' and the 'mental faculties' that 'interpret', 'structure' and 'integrate' it. All that **can** be 'caught' or 'captured' by this 'apparatus', and can thus be 'known' to us, belongs to the 'phenomenal world'. All that **cannot** be so caught belongs to the underlying 'noumenal world', and is **completely** and **permanently inaccessible** to us, and is, indeed 'beyond our apprehension'. This, then, is Kant's basic model of the 'nature of reality', a model that Bryan Magee described as 'the greatest single advance in the history of Western philosophy'. The outline that I have given above is a grossly-simplified version of Kant's full epistemological and ontological system, the 'full version' being described in detail in his philosophical 'masterpiece', his 'Critique of Pure Reason'. This is a notoriously difficult book to 'get to grips with', however, and interested readers are referred to the clear, easily-understandable explanations of Kant's basic ideas that are given by Bryan Magee in 'Confessions of a Philosopher'. That is where I first learned about them, during a memorable two weeks working in Saudi Arabia in 2002.

In the second of his 'Critiques', Kant discussed the place of his postulated 'a priori' knowledge in 'ethics' and 'religion'. In the third, he turned his attention to the 'arts'. Since the contents of both are less **directly** relevant to the investigation of the nature of reality than those of his first 'Critique', I leave it to readers to explore these for themselves, if they are interested. Once again, Bryan Magee's 'Confessions of a Philosopher' is a good 'starting point'.

The man who effectively completed the initial stages of Kant's 'philosophical revolution' was Arthur Schopenhauer, another German.

He was born in Danzig in 1788, where his father was a wealthy banker, and his mother was a novelist. His family moved to Hamburg in 1793, and he was (reluctantly) preparing for a career in business. But after his father's sudden death in 1805, he became 'financially independent', inheriting enough money to enable him to live in great comfort for the rest of his life without the need for 'paid employment'. He embarked on an extended academic education at Gotha, Weimar, Göttingen, Berlin and Jena, where he completed his 'dissertation in philosophy' in 1813. He completed his philosophical 'masterwork', 'The World as Will and Representation', in 1819, but this was largely ignored for most of his life. He did finally gain widespread recognition, largely due to the publication of a diverse collection of essays and 'aphoristic writings' under the title 'Parerga und Paralipomena' (which might be idiomatically translated as 'Additions and Omissions') in 1851. He is now regarded as one of our greatest and most-influential philosophers, as was acknowledged by major 'cultural figures' such as Wagner, Tolstoy, Proust and Mann. He died in 1860.

The main task that Schopenhauer set himself when writing 'The World as Will and Representation' was to 'correct' the main 'errors' that he believed to have been committed by Kant, and to develop and extend his ideas into a 'cohesive and comprehensive world picture'. He therefore regarded himself as 'Kant's natural successor', and is, indeed, widely regarded as such. Probably his most important 'correction' of Kant was his recognition that the basic concept of noumenal 'things in themselves' underlying and 'causing' phenomenal 'things as they appear to us' was 'logically inconsistent', since it implied that the 'noumenal world' was itself 'multiply-differentiated'. By detailed analysis of Kant's formulations of the concepts of 'space', 'time' and 'causality', Schopenhauer showed that the noumenal world cannot possibly consist of 'things' in the plural, but must be 'intrinsically undifferentiated'. As we saw earlier in the book, this concept of an undifferentiated 'ultimate reality' underlying an essentially-illusory 'physical world' was developed by Hindu and Buddhist thinkers over 2000 years earlier, but Schopenhauer was not aware of this when he developed his own 'world picture'. He did learn about the consistency of his views with the Eastern philosophical tradition later, however, much to his delight. Schopenhauer regarded 'ultimate reality' as consisting of an un-self-aware, undifferentiated, unknowable 'something' to which he gave the name 'will' – a choice that was to cause endless later confusion. He regarded the 'phenomenal world' as having developed through the progressive 'manifestation' and 'objectification' of this 'metaphysical will', first as 'pure energy', then as 'inanimate objects', then as 'living things' of greater and greater complexity, and finally as creatures with 'conscious minds' (us). In doing so, he not only anticipated many of the subsequent 'discoveries' of modern science, but also had a profound influence on 'cultural development' throughout Europe. Interested readers can again find clear, easily-understandable explanations of his work in Bryan Magee's 'Confessions of a Philosopher', and also in his excellent monograph on 'The Philosophy of Schopenhauer'.

Subsequent 19th-century developments

I knew that this would be a long chapter, because it had a great deal of ground to cover. Since I have almost reached the notional 'word count' that I set myself for each of the seven earlier chapters, I will now 'speed up', and 'limit the space' that I devote to all the philosophers and philosophical schools that I still have to describe. I will do this by omitting the detailed descriptions of the lives of the people involved that I have given for each of the eight philosophers that I have dealt with so far, and by providing only very brief outlines of their work. I hope that these succeed in letting readers know what their most important ideas were. If you want to learn more about any of them, their lives and work are all described in much greater detail in Bryan Magee's 'Story of Western Philosophy', which was actually my main 'source of information', when writing this chapter. It is by far the best general introduction to the history of philosophy that I have ever come across, being well-written, comprehensive, and beautifully illustrated. Something to ask for as a birthday or Christmas present, perhaps?

I will begin by looking at the work of three German philosophers who, like Schopenhauer, regarded themselves as the 'intellectual successors' to Kant – Hegel, Fichte and Schelling.

George William Frederick Hegel (1770-1831) was by far the most important and influential philosopher who worked in the 19th-century, apart from Schopenhauer. He founded a 'school of philosophy' that became known as 'Hegelian Idealism', and made two major contributions to the development of the subject. The first was the novel 'method' that he employed, which he called the 'dialectical process', or simply the 'dialectic'. This involves three main stages. It starts with the 'thesis', a description of the 'initial state of affairs' in respect of whatever problem or situation is to be examined. The opposing reactions that this always provokes are described by him as the 'antithesis' of the 'thesis'. The conflict between the two eventually resolves itself into a new situation which 'sheds' elements of both and also 'retains' elements of both, and is called the 'synthesis'. This then becomes the 'starting point' of the next 'round' of the dialectical process, and so on indefinitely. This, said Hegel, is why nothing ever remains the same in **any** particular field. After Hegel's time, the 'dialectic' was often referred to as the 'law of change'. Hegel's second important contribution was the use of his 'dialectic' to construct an all-embracing 'world picture' based on the historical evolution of the 'Zeitgeist', the non-material 'Spirit of the Time'. He believed that 'change' was the product of 'historical forces' over which individual human beings have no real influence; they are simply 'swept along' by them. Hegel was later fiercely criticised by Popper for his 'strongly totalitarian views' on how states should be run.

Johann Gottleib Fichte (1762-1814) was an even more extreme 'idealist' than Hegel. Far from 'human knowledge' being derived from 'empirical reality', he claimed, the 'empirical world' is actually the 'creation of the knowing mind'. He also believed that 'the primary and fundamental nature of **all** reality consists in its moral character', and that, in our capacity as 'moral agents', we have 'direct experience' of the existence of our 'selves'. And, because we bear moral responsibility for our actions, we know that our 'selves' persist over time. His views on the 'nature of the self' were thus radically different from those of Hume.

Friedrich Schelling (1775-1854) became known as the 'philosopher of nature', and, as such, his ideas strongly influenced the development of the 'Romantic Movement', during the first half of the 19th-century. He believed that 'man is part of nature', from which it followed that 'human creativity' is part of 'Nature's productivity', so that 'in man', Nature has arrived at 'self-awareness'. His philosophy was, in many ways, a reaction against the 'extreme idealism' of Fichte.

The next great German philosopher was Karl Marx (1818-1883), who turned Hegel's 'dialectical idealism' on its head, and converted it into 'dialectical materialism', which he used to develop the all-embracing theory of historical development that became known as 'Marxism'. This was based on an in-depth study of economics and contemporary 'capitalism', and 'proved' that the inevitable end of historical social development would be the appearance of a 'classless society', in which the 'proletariat' would be in complete control. It can seriously be claimed for Marx that his ideas had a greater influence, in a shorter time, than any other thinker in history. During his lifetime, he was a 'little-known, impoverished intellectual', living on the 'charity of friends', and 'spending his days reading and writing', often in the British Museum. Yet, within 70 years of his death, something like a third of the entire human race was living under governments that described themselves as 'Marxist'. This included all the countries of Eastern Europe, the whole of Russia and the former Tsarist land empire, and the whole of China, apart from one 'rebel' offshore island. Nothing like this had ever happened before, nor is likely to happen again. Most 'thinking people' now believe that Popper's devastating attack on Marxism in 1945 totally destroyed its 'intellectual credibility', however.

The last great 19th-century German philosopher was Friedrich Nietzsche (1844-1900). He was a brilliant thinker and writer who worked in several different areas of philosophy, but is best known for his sustained and vehement attack on religion – and, in particular, on Christianity, and the 'ethical code' that was associated with it. Since he believed that 'God is dead' (to quote his most famous saying), we had no justification in basing our entire moral system on 'Christian teachings' on the subject. In any case, he regarded these as the 'morality of the slave', and felt that they were preventing 'natural leaders' – the confident, the courageous, the innovators – from 'flourishing', held back and 'shackled' by value systems that set them on equal terms with the 'mediocre mass of mankind' (what the Roman poet Horace once disparagingly referred to as the 'profanum vulgus'). Nietzsche regarded this as the 'worst possible decadence', a 'denial of everything that had produced culture and civilisation'. His idea of a talented and courageous human becoming a 'super-human-being' (or 'superman') by fulfilling his maximum potential has now entered into most European languages, including English.

During the first half of the 19th-century, philosophy in the English-speaking world proceeded without any knowledge of the revolutionary work of Kant and Schopenhauer, since no English translations of Kant's 'masterwork', 'Critique of Pure Reason', became available until 1854, a full half-century after his death, and very few 'educated people' could read German at the time. For this reason, no serious further work on metaphysics or epistemology was carried out in the British Isles during this period. Their philosophers therefore turned their attention to another important area – moral and political philosophy – since many social and political reforms were now starting to take place. The resulting philosophical 'school' became known as 'Utilitarianism', in which the leading figures were Jeremy Bentham and John Stuart Mill.

Jeremy Bentham (1748-1832) was the first major philosopher to write in English since David Hume. As a guiding principle for public policy, he adopted the following maxim: 'That action is best which brings about the greatest happiness for the greatest numbers'. In other words, the 'rightness' or 'wrongness' of an action was to be judged solely on its 'consequences', with underlying 'motives' being 'totally irrelevant'. Its proponents, led by Bentham, applied these principles to private morality as well as to political, legal and social policy, and it had a lasting influence on the way Britain was governed. Utilitarian principles were also applied to the punishment of criminals, where the policy was that these should be harsh enough to deter, but no harsher, since that would create 'useless suffering'. As a result, punishments became progressively less severe during the 19th-century, and prisons started to be reformed.

John Stuart Mill (1806-1873) was the son of James Mill, who had been highly-influential in persuading politicians to adopt Bentham's utilitarian policies. He went on to become, and, indeed remains, the greatest and best-known of all English-speaking philosophers of the 19th-century. He was a champion of 'women's rights', and wrote what many now believe to be the most important book on the rights of the individual in a liberal society that has ever been published anywhere –

'On Liberty' (1859). His ground-breaking book on 'The Subjugation of Women' (1869) proved equally influential, and continues to be held in esteem by feminists everywhere. I will have more to say about him in Chapter 19.

American philosophy was a 'late developer', and it was only in the latter part of the 19th-century that it had advanced to the point where it commanded international recognition and respect. Three outstanding American philosophers who worked during that period have since acquired 'classic status', and became known as the 'American Pragmatists'. Of these, Bryan Magee considered Charles Sanders Peirce (1838-1910) to have been the 'most original', William James (1842-1910) to have been the 'most enjoyable to read', and John Dewey (1859-1952) to have been the 'most widely influential'. They all took the view that 'knowing' is something we 'do', and is best seen as a 'practical activity', and that questions of 'meaning' and 'truth' were also best considered in this 'pragmatic' context. Once again, interested readers can find more detailed descriptions of their work in Bryan Magee's 'Story of Western Philosophy'.

20th-century western philosophy

Summarising 20th-century philosophy in a few pages will be even more difficult than summarising 19th-century philosophy, because there were many more philosophers around – mostly employed as 'academics' in the rapidly-increasing number of universities that were being set up in all parts of the civilised world. To give you an idea of the scale of this expansion, Britain had only six universities until the middle of the 19th century – Oxford, Cambridge and the four 'ancient' Scottish Universities (St. Andrews, Glasgow, Aberdeen and Edinburgh). The establishment of the so-called 'civic' universities (Durham, London, Birmingham, Manchester, Liverpool and so on) during the 19th and early 20th centuries eventually increased the total number of

British universities to 23. The next major expansion took place during the 1960's, with all the 'Colleges of Advanced Technology' gaining university status, and several completely new ones (such as Stirling and Keele) being established; this increased the total number of universities in Britain to 44, and also led to the foundation of the 'polytechnics'. The latest phase of expansion, which was initiated in 1991, would eventually increase the number of universities in Britain to over 140. Many of these had 'Philosophy Departments', so many more 'academic philosophers' were required. Not all of these were 'practising' philosophers, of course, but many of them were, particularly in the 'older' universities. The same sort of thing was happening in every other part of the developed world.

In the early years of the 20th-century, a number of 'breakthroughs' took place in 'logic', which had remained largely unchanged since the time of Aristotle. These affected the whole of the rest of philosophy, which became increasingly 'logic based'. These 'breakthroughs' had actually began during the latter part of the 19th-century, as a result of the work of the German mathematician and philosopher Gottlob Frege (1848-1925), but only really 'took off' during the 20th-century, with the work of an English mathematician and philosopher, Bertrand Russell (1872-1970). He 'discovered' Frege, and made his name known to the world, but not before Russell had done a great deal of hard work re-discovering and re-inventing things that Frege had already done.

Bertrand Russell was also largely responsible for initiating the next phase of 20th-century philosophy, when it began to turn its spotlight on 'language', and on an 'analytic approach' to the subject. Russell used the 'new logic' that had been developed by Frege and his successors to analyse statements in 'ordinary language', inaugurating a whole new way of 'doing' philosophy. Russell's approach was subsequently taken up by one of his 'pupils', the Austrian-born Ludwig Wittgenstein (1889-1951), who subsequently became one of the best-known and most-influential figures in the history of modern western philosophy.

Wittgenstein was actually responsible for initiating two major changes in direction for European philosophy. In 1921, he published his most-important and most-influential book, 'Tractatus Logico-Philosophicus', which readers with a good memory will recognise as being based on the title of Spinoza's 'Tractatus Theologico-Politicus'. This amazing book, in which he claimed to have solved 'all the outstanding problems in philosophy', became the 'ur-document' of the 'logical positivists' – a highly-influential group of German-speaking philosophers and scientists whose work dominated scientific thinking until their basic ideas were totally discredited by the work of (guess who?) Karl Popper. Wittgenstein was also largely responsible for inaugurating the 'real-language' school of English philosophy, which took it 'down the wrong track' for many years, and led to it 'losing the respect' of most of the rest of the world's philosophical community, according to Bryan Magee.

The most 'fashionable' philosophy in Continental Europe during the period immediately following the Second World War was 'Existentialism'. This 'flourished' not only in universities, but also in the worlds of 'quality journalism' and 'café intellectuals', in 'poems, novels, plays and films', and even in 'night clubs' and 'cabarets'. It was undoubtedly one of the 'dominant intellectual movements' of the 20th-century, and remains a significant element in contemporary thinking, as well as leaving behind it a number of long-lasting plays and novels. One curious thing about all this is that the 'fashion' came a long time after the 'philosophy' on which is was based. The leading existentialist philosopher of the 20th-century, Martin Heidegger (1889-1976) had produced his most important work ('Being and Time') in 1927, and the basis for **his** work went very much further back – to the 19th-century philosophers Soren Kierkegaard (1813-1855) and

Friedrich Nietzsche (1844-1900), in fact. Kierkegaard laid the foundations of what was later to become 'Existentialism', claiming that it is the 'individual himself' who is the 'supreme moral entity', and, therefore, it is the 'personal, subjective aspects of human life' that are the most important. Heidegger's subsequent masterpiece, 'Being and Time', is one of the most 'inaccessible' books in the whole of philosophical literature, and its ideas are far too abstruse and complicated for me to even begin to explain them here. They did, however, form the basis of modern existentialism, in which the best-known figure is probably the novelist and playwright, Jean-Paul Sartre (1905-1980).

Let me now end this all-too-brief survey of the most important features of 20th-century philosophy by looking at the work of the man who is widely regarded as the greatest and most-influential of its figures – Karl Popper (1902-1994). He has already been mentioned several times in this book, and will be mentioned several times more in later chapters, so I will simply list his main achievements here. First, he was undoubtedly one of the greatest 'philosophers of science' who ever lived, arguably **the** greatest. As we will see in Chapter 11, he completely revolutionised the way we think about science and the status of 'scientific knowledge', developing a model for the 'scientific method' that has now completely replaced the 'Baconian' model that had dominated science for 400 years. He was also an ontologist and epistemologist of genius, developing a three-part model of the world around us that has greatly influenced many people, myself included. Finally, he was one of the greatest of all political philosophers, not only destroying the intellectual credibility of the totalitarian doctrines of the 'right' and the 'left' in his 1945 masterpiece 'The Open Society and its Enemies', but also replacing the age-old question 'Who shall rule?' (which is effectively un-answerable) with the completely-answerable question 'How can we organise society in order to minimise **mis-rule**'. His answer to the latter was to ensure that its members could 'kick out' a government they did not like, and replace it with one they thought they **would** like – a so-called 'open society'. All the truly 'liberal democracies' in the world are now based on this principle, and, as a result, are generally the most 'stable' and 'prosperous' countries. The modern world has many good reasons to be very grateful to Popper, and much of it is.

Note that I have not described 'Post-Modernist Philosophy' in this chapter, because I will deal with it fully at the end of the next one. As you will see, I do not hold it in very high regard, to put it mildly.

Some of the sources of information on material covered in Chapter 8

I have been studying philosophy in a serious manner since I retired from full-time employment in 2001, and, as a result, the 'philosophy' section of my personal library now contains over 150 items, with many items in other parts also dealing with 'philosophical topics'. So, by the time I started to write this book, I already had all the 'deep background' knowledge of the subject that I needed. I still required a lot of 'detailed' information, of course, and obtained practically all of this from the following sources.

- 'The Story of Philosophy', by Bryan Magee, which I regard as by far the best general introduction to the subject that is currently available.
- 'Confessions of a Philosopher', by Bryan Magee, which has provided me with more 'in-depth understanding' of philosophy than any other book in my library. That is why I have now read it nine times, and will continue to do so periodically for as long as I live, and can still think rationally.
- 'History of Western Philosophy', by Bertrand Russell, a massive tome that runs to over 800 pages in my 'paperback' version; I have

read this twice from cover to cover, and always refer to it when I need detailed information on some aspect of the subject.

- 'Great Minds of the Western Philosophical Tradition', a massive 'Teaching Company' course written and presented by 12 eminent American academics. This consists of 84 half-hour lectures delivered on 14 DVDs, backed up by a 450-page 'Course Guidebook'. I worked my way through the entire course when I purchased it roughly 15 years ago, and, as with Bertrand Russell's book, always refer to the 'Course Guidebook' when I need detailed information on some aspect of philosophy.
- 'Chambers Biographical Dictionary' (1990 edition, edited by Magnus Magnusson), which, as I have already told you, I always refer to if I require detailed biographical information about any one, or wish to check the accuracy of information from other sources.

Chapter 9: The 'European Enlightenment' and its aftermath

'Si Dieu n'existait pas, il faudrait l'inventir'
(If God did not exist, it would be necessary to invent him)

- Voltaire (François Marie Arouet)

Such a statement would simply not have been possible before the series of developments that we now describe as the 'European Enlightenment'; it would have been regarded as highly disrespectful at best, and, at worst, heretical or even blasphemous, and the Church or secular authorities would have taken 'appropriate action'. Remember what happened to Giordano Bruno in 1600 for daring to challenge the official Roman Catholic 'doctrine' on cosmology'! All this changed during the 17th and 18th centuries, when, for the very first time, people began to **challenge** the teachings of the Church, and also began to ask serious questions about the validity of the established 'social structure'. The 'Enlightenment' was, in the words of Edward O. Wilson, 'a vision of secular knowledge in the service of human rights and human progress', and was 'the West's greatest contribution to civilisation'. In his opinion, 'it launched the modern era for the whole world, and we are its legatees'. Powerful claims! Let us now examine the early history of the 'Enlightenment Project', look at three of the major changes that it brought about, and see where its ideas stand today.

The origins of the 'Enlightenment' in Britain and France

People sometimes describe the 'European Enlightenment' as the 'French Enlightenment', because it was in France that it eventually came to full fruition, but it actually had its roots in Britain during the

17th Century, largely as a result of the influence of two men – Francis Bacon and John Locke, both of whose lives and work were examined in some detail in earlier chapters. As we saw in Chapter 7, Bacon believed strongly in 'human progress', forecasting that this could best be achieved by 'harnessing science and its technological products' in the 'service of man'. His ideas 'raised the sights' of a small but influential group of people, helping to 'prime' the 'scientific revolution' that was to blossom so spectacularly in the decades ahead. To this day, his 'vision' remains at the very heart of the 'scientific-technological ethic', and he can, with some justification, be described as the 'father of the European Enlightenment'.

The contribution of John Locke was at least equally important to that of Bacon, arguably more important, because it was his radical work on political philosophy that had the greatest influence on later French thinkers. As we saw in Chapter 8, he was a fervent believer in the 'rights of man', and virtually 'invented' the concept of a free, liberal society based on these rights. He had seen how these rights were being violated during the reign of the last of the 'Stuart' Kings, James II, and played a major role in the bringing about the 'Glorious Revolution' of 1688, which many people believe was the true beginning of 'modern Britain'. After Locke, the 'centre of gravity' of the Enlightenment movement transferred to France, where the 'baton' was taken up, and moved forward, largely because of two men – Voltaire and Denis Diderot – although many others were also involved. Important developments still continued in Britain, however, with the 'Scottish Enlightenment' being one of that wee country's 'finest hours'. Indeed, Edinburgh came to be described as the 'Athens of the North', because it contained so many prominent Enlightenment figures. Let us now take a closer look at the part played by the two main French figures in the early history of the Enlightenment project.

François Marie Arouet (1694 – 1778), who later adopted the 'nom-deplume' Voltaire, is widely regarded as 'one of the cleverest men who ever lived'. When he wrote his ground-breaking book on 'Civilisation' during the 1970's, the English art historian, Kenneth Clark, entitled the chapter that dealt with the Enlightenment 'The Smile of Reason', and placed a full-page photograph of Houdon's famous sculpture of Voltaire opposite its opening page. I have a 'head and shoulders' version of that same sculpture in my living room, since I admire and revere Voltaire and everything that he stood for; his was, indeed, 'the smile of reason'. He was born in Paris, and received an excellent education from the Jesuits, after which he took to 'satirical writing', which led him to be banished from France several times, and also to be imprisoned in the Bastille on two occasions. While still young, he also established himself as the 'best playwright in France', and went on to dominate the French stage for 50 years. After being released from his second spell of imprisonment in 1726, he was forced into exile in England, where he lived for over two years. This experience turned out to be the 'intellectual turning point of his life'. The 'high level of freedom' that he found there, and the 'respect that was shown for the individual and the law' gave him the yardstick with which he was to 'beat the French for the rest of his life'. He mastered the English language, and immersed himself in serious study of the 'new science' (as represented by Newton) and the 'new liberal philosophy' (as represented by Locke). He was never able to contribute any new ideas of any great significance in these two areas, but the ideas 'took him over', and, during the remainder of his uncommonly-long writing career, they provided him with the 'staple intellectual content' of his work. He propagated them through every medium available to him (plays, novels, biographies, historical works, pamphlets, open letters, critical reviews), and did so with such wit and brilliance that they became known to every serious reader in Western Europe. Seldom, anywhere, has there been so 'gifted a populariser', or one who had such a substantial impact on the society around him. His work continued right up to his death in 1778, and played a vitally-important role in the development of the Enlightenment movement.

Denis Diderot (1713 – 1784) was another 'all-round genius', working as a philosopher, satirist, novelist, playwright and art critic, as well as being the leading editor of the 'French Encyclopaedia', whose impact was truly 'international'. Like Descartes and Voltaire before him, he received an excellent education from the Jesuits before 'turning against them'. He refused to settle down in any profession, even after his family's allowance to him had long been cut off, preferring to spend his time absorbing 'fundamental knowledge' in one field after another, ranging from mathematics and science to ancient and modern languages. For many years, he lived in 'poverty and obscurity' while doing this, but eventually became well known – and started to 'make money' – by translating intellectually-important books from English into French. His first important book, 'Philosophical Thoughts', was published in 1746, and, in the same year, he became involved in the 'Encyclopaedia project'. This had begun 'in a modest way' as a straightforward 'commercial undertaking' to translate the Chambers 'Cyclopaedia' of 1728 from English into French, but the project subsequently grew and grew, until it lost all connection with its humble beginnings. Diderot became its 'editor', and it provided his chief occupation and source of income until 1772. Volume after volume appeared under him, until the complete work eventually comprised no fewer than 55 of them, making it by far the largest 'publishing venture' that had appeared in any language up to that time. What made it intellectually and historically important was that it embodied the 'new attitude to knowledge' that Voltaire had imported from England – a 'scientific approach' based on the ideas of Francis Bacon and Isaac Newton, married to a 'philosophical approach' based on the ideas of John Locke. Diderot admitted that, as its editor, his aim was to 'change the common way of thinking', and, to a very considerable extent, this is exactly what he did. The negative side of this was of crucial importance, and was to bring the 'Encyclopaedia project' into serious trouble with the French authorities. The whole huge work implicitly denied that 'religious teaching' was a 'valid source of factual information' about the world, and thus denied any 'intellectual authority' to the Bible or the Church. It also refused to recognise the 'political establishment' as a 'valid source of authority' in intellectual or artistic questions. Thus, it subverted nearly all the basic social, political and religious 'orthodoxies' of the day, and did so on a 'massive scale'. Its influence was enormous, and, both in the 'sciences' and in the 'arts', it presented a new conception of 'knowledge' and 'learning' that was to become 'one of the leading characteristics of the modern age'. The 'Encyclopaedia' got into more and more trouble with 'official censorship' as successive volumes appeared, and, in 1759, it was 'suppressed by royal decree'. Diderot, his numerous 'authors', and, of course, his 'publishers' continued to 'work in secret', however and made 'underground preparations' for the remaining volumes, which all eventually 'saw the light of day'. The importance of Diderot's 'Encyclopaedia' in the inexorable advance of the 'Enlightenment project' cannot be over-exaggerated; it was truly 'enormous'.

A third French-speaker, Jean-Jacques Rousseau (1712 – 1778) also played an important part in the 'Enlightenment project' and its aftermath, not because he **supported** its aims, but because he **opposed everything it stood for.** He was actually not 'French' but 'Swiss', because he was born in Geneva while it was an 'independent state'. This was an important fact about him, since, despite the fact that he **wrote** in French, he was never an admirer of 'French culture' – or, indeed, of **any** culture. Unlike most eminent philosophers, he received very little in the way of 'formal education', and this was also an important factor in his subsequent development, in that it reinforced his espousal of 'spontaneous feeling' as against 'conceptual thinking'. His mother died a few days after he was born, so he was brought up by an aunt and an 'erratic father', who at least taught him to read. He was then 'parcelled out', first to a 'country minister' and then to an uncle, and undertook two 'apprenticeships', to a 'notary' and then to an 'engraver', who treated him brutally, and from whom he eventually 'ran away'. His life was to continue like this, often full of 'violent emotions', always 'rootless', always 'wandering' – from one job to another, from one woman to another, from one country to another. But he eventually met Diderot and other 'philosophes' (the name still used to denote contributors to the 'Encyclopaedia'). He actually wrote some articles (on music) for this, after which he began to write the materials that were to bring him 'lasting fame'. He began with two essays, then, in 1761 and 1762, wrote three of his four most famous books – 'La Nouvelle Héloise', 'Emile', and 'The Social Contract', the fourth being his autobiography, 'Confessions', which was not published until after his death. In the mid-1760's, he decided to move to England in response to an invitation by David Hume, who was 'loved and revered' by many of the leading 'philosophes'. But in England he had some sort of 'paranoid mental breakdown', denounced Hume for 'seeking his undoing', and fled in panic back to France, where he eventually died in 1778.

During his active life as a philosopher, Rousseau introduced three revolutionary ideas into the 'mainstream of Western thought', all of which have had 'tremendous influence' ever since. The first is that 'civilisation' is not a 'good thing', as everyone had always assumed, and not even a 'value-neutral' thing, but positively a 'bad thing'. He believed that human beings were 'born good' as 'noble savages', as he so memorably put it, but were then 'corrupted' by being brought up in a society where their 'natural instincts' were curbed and frustrated. The second is that we should ask of everything in our lives, both 'private' and 'public', that it meet the requirements not of 'reason', but of 'feeling', and the 'natural instincts' that living in society tended to supress. In other words, 'feeling' should replace 'reason' as the ultimate 'guide' to living. The third is that a human society is a 'collective being' with a 'will of its own' that is different from the 'sum of the wills' of its individual members, and that the citizen should be 'totally subordinate' to this 'general will'. This was by far his most important – and most 'dangerous' – new idea.

All three of Rousseau's 'revolutionary ideas' have had what can only be described as 'highly negative effects' on the development of human society. As we will see later on in this chapter, his doctrine of a 'general will' that **has** to be obeyed by everyone without question had a disastrous effect on the development of the French Revolution, which had shown so much 'early promise' during the early 1990's, leading to the period known as the 'Terror'. It also sowed the seeds for the appearance of the dreadful fascist and communist totalitarian states that caused so much death and misery during the 20th-century. His hostility to civilisation as such also encouraged the appearance of the various 'anarchist groups' that caused so much mayhem during the 19th-century and beyond. On balance, it would probably have been better for humanity if he had never lived, in my opinion.

Let me now end this review of the early history of the "Enlightenment project' on a happier note, showing how it was supported by two of the world's greatest literary figures – the German dramatist, poet and historian, Johann Christoph Friedrich von Schiller (1759 – 1805) and the Scottish 'national bard', Robert Burns (1759 – 1796). Schiller is best known for his great poem 'An di Freude' ('Ode to Joy'), later magnificently set to music by Beethoven in his 9th symphony. This includes the lines:

'Alle Menshen werden Brüder
Wo dein sanfter Flügel weilt'

('All men will become brothers under your tender wing'), perfectly capturing one of the key aims of the 'Enlightenment' in a few apt words. Burns was one of the most notable figures in the 'Scottish

Enlightenment' that I briefly mentioned earlier. I am a great admirer of Burns's 'work', if not of his 'morality', and have a large print of the famous 'Nasmyth' portrait of him in a prominent position in my hall. I have also turned myself into something of a 'Burns scholar', and, in this capacity, am regularly invited to speak at the annual 'Burns Suppers' that are held to celebrate his date of birth (January, 25th). The main speech at such events is the 'Immortal Memory', in which a local or invited 'expert' talks about some aspect(s) of his life and work. I have given many of these over the years, my favourite topic being a detailed examination of why he is regarded as a 'great poet'. The end of this talk always takes the following form, which, I think, perfectly summarises Burns's importance in the Enlightenment Project. Let me quote it in full here.

'Finally, Burns was a 'poet of the people' – indeed a poet for 'all men and women', and 'all races'. No poet is more widely-known and lauded throughout the world, and not only in the English-speaking world. Take, for example, his song 'Auld Lang Syne', which is probably sung more often than any other song ever written – with the possible exception of 'Happy Birthday to you!'

Burns was also a strong supporter of the 'European Enlightenment', particularly as it related to the injustices and hypocrisy in contemporary society, to the 'rights of man', and to the creation of a true 'world brotherhood'. The sentiments expressed in the final verse of 'A Man's a Man for a' that' are surely as relevant and inspiring today as they were in Burns's time:

> 'Then let us pray that come it may –
> As come it will, for a' that –
> That sense and worth, o'er a' the earth,
> May bear the gree, an' a' that.
> For a' that, an' a' that,

It's comin' yet, for a' that,
That Man tae Man, the warld o'er,
Shall brithers be, for a' that!'

Ladies and gentlemen, I will not attempt to follow that, but will simply ask you to rise and drink to the 'Immortal Memory of Robert Burns'.

'The immortal Memory!'

How it led to the 'French Revolution'

For some time now, historians have been able to explain the origins of many major wars by applying the techniques of 'situational analysis', in which they draw a distinction between the 'underlying cause' and the 'proximate cause' of the war. This is based on the work of the Athenian historian Thucydides, who applied such an analysis to the 'underlying cause' of the Peloponnesian War that was fought between Athens and Sparta between 431 and 404 BCE: 'What made war inevitable was the growth of Athenian power, and the fear this caused in Sparta'. The 'proximate cause' of the war was a comparatively minor dispute between two other Greek city states, Corcyra and Corinth, which the leaders of Athens and Sparta allowed to get 'out of control'. A similar analysis has been applied to the origins of the 'Great War' of 1914 to 1918, which later came to be known as the 'First World War'. Here, historians now agree that the 'underlying cause' was the growing fear in **Germany** of the steady rise in **Russian** power, and that the 'proximate cause' was the dispute between Austria-Hungary and Serbia, which was brought to a head by the assassination of Archduke Franz Ferdinand of Austria in June, 1914. Somewhat worryingly, informed commentators are now talking about America and China being drawn into a similar 'Thucydides trap', which could well lead to all- out war if any of the current disputes in South-East Asia are allowed to get out of control.

A similar type of 'situational analysis' can be applied to the events that led up to the 'French Revolution'. Here, it is generally agreed that the main 'underlying cause' was the steadily- growing unhappiness of the 'Third Estate' (the 'Common People') with the 'First and Second Estates' (the Nobility, led by the King, and the Roman Catholic Church). This resentment had been steadily 'stoked up' and 'encouraged' by the work of Voltaire and Diderot in promoting the 'Enlightenment project'. (This was described in detail in the previous section). One of the greatest grounds for this unhappiness was the fact that the members of the 'First' and 'Second' Estates paid virtually no taxes, with practically the entire fiscal burden falling on the members of the 'Third Estate', who were extremely heavily taxed. France had been at war almost continuously for more than a century, with military expenses consuming roughly three-quarters of the national budget. Things had become even worse when they entered the 'American War of Independence' on America's side, which had virtually bankrupted France. By the end of the 1780's, France was rather like a 'powder keg', waiting for someone to 'strike a match' to make it explode.

That match was struck by the French Monarch, Louis XVI, in the early summer of 1789, when he summoned all 1100 'Deputies' of the 'States General' to his palace at Versailles, in order to 'try to find a solution' to all France's problems, particularly their desperate financial problems, something that had not been done since 1614. The 'Deputies' of the 'States General' had been elected by the three 'Orders', the First, Second and Third Estates that then made up French society, with roughly half of these now representing the huge 'Third Estate', which comprised the vast majority of France's population of roughly 25 million, as against the three or four hundred thousand nobles and clergy represented by the other two 'privileged' Orders. Summoning the 'States General' to Versailles is now recognised as the 'proximate cause' of the French Revolution. It spent nearly two months arguing over how it should vote, and failed to agree. Finally, on June 17th, the

'Third Estate' (estimating that it represented 96% of the population) proclaimed itself the 'National Assembly', and took on the power to run the country, with the King's role effectively becoming that of a 'Constitutional Monarch' rather than an 'Absolute Monarch', as had previously been the case. King Louis XVI was terrified at these developments, as were the 'nobles' and 'clergy', who saw that all their privileges were about to disappear. He concentrated troops at Versailles, and the 'Third Estate', fearing a royal or aristocratic 'counter-attack', took to the streets, thus instigating a period of utter chaos which eventually led to the 'storming of the Bastille' on July, 14th. By now, the 'Third Estate' had won, and their self-proclaimed 'National Assembly' began to run the country – and to change it utterly, basing their rule of the 'rationalist principles' that had been the driving force behind the 'Enlightenment project'. At first, things seemed to go well, with the new 'National Assembly' removing all traces of what they called the 'Old Regime', and replacing them with what they now called 'the Revolution'. The new state became the 'French Republic', with King Louis XVI and his family being kept under virtual 'house arrest' at Versailles and being stripped of all real power. The Assembly completely centralised the Government in Paris, declared France to be a 'secular country', abolished all ranks and titles (everyone was now simply addressed as 'citizen'), and even changed the calendar. But, very soon, things started to go wrong. Badly wrong.

In one of the most perceptive passages in 'Confessions of a Philosopher', Bryan Magee points out that 'violent revolutions **never** achieve their aims', partly because much of the 'old society' still continues in the 'new' one, and partly because they contain the 'seeds of their own eventual demise'. As he says, there is a 'situational logic' to such revolutions. Disparate groups unite to overthrow the existing regime, but, once they have succeeded in doing so, the 'cause' that brought them together has gone, and they then fight one another to fill the 'power vacuum' that they themselves have created. These 'internecine struggles' among 'erstwhile allies', which are usually extremely savage, perpetuate the revolutionary breakdown of society far beyond the overthrow of the 'old regime' and delay the full establishment of a 'new order'. The population-at-large then begins to feel itself 'threatened' by unending 'social chaos', and, eventually, a 'strong man' who can bring the 'warring factious' to heel and impose order comes forward, and meets with widespread support, or, at least 'acquiescence'. Thus, a revolution carried out in the name of 'civil liberties' or 'equality', or to 'bring tyranny to an end', will itself end by putting into power an 'authoritarian dictator'. In the case of the 'French Revolution', this turned out to be Napoleon, who kept the French 'Nation' (later the French 'Empire') more or less permanently at war for over 15 years, and was responsible for the deaths of millions of its own citizens, and even larger numbers of the citizens of other European counties. All revolutions, claims Magee, are 'uncontrollable', and all revolutions are eventually 'betrayed', for it is 'in their nature' that things should be so. This fact, he claims, makes belief in 'violent revolution' as a method of changing society not only 'irrational' and 'delusory', but also 'profoundly immoral'. The 'French Revolution' and its aftermath provides a 'paradigm case study' of this process in action.

As we have seen, the new 'National Assembly' that had assumed supreme power in 1789 made a very promising start, and appeared to be realising its highly-idealistic aims of turning France into a completely-egalitarian, secular society where everything was based on 'reason'. Two events were to threaten this happy state of affairs, however, events that would lead to the rise of Robespierre, to the 'Terror', and to the eventual rise of Napoleon. The first was the attempted 'escape' of the Royal Family, who tried to flee to Austria, and were 'caught' at Varennes on June 20th, 1791. The already-existing 'paranoia' about Louis XVI and his Austrian wife, Marie Antoinette, was confirmed in the minds of the 'ordinary people', and eventually led to their trial and execution in 1793. The second was the outbreak of war in April, 1792, when several other European countries, worried about the 'subversive' influence of the Revolution, declared war on the new French Republic, whose very existence was now under threat. Partly in response to the war, a 'Constitutional Convention' was organised. This first met on September 21st, 1792 and did in fact draw up a 'new constitution', but this was never put into effect. Instead, the 'Convention' become, in effect, a new 'revolutionary parliament' which assumed 'total power'.

This marked the beginning of the rise to power of Maximilien Robespierre (1758 – 1794). Born in Arras to a 'poor family', he won scholarships to study law in Paris, and returned to set up a small law practice in his native town. He was elected to the 'States General' of 1789, and soon found his new role in the 'Jacobin Club', where his extreme radical oratory won him a following. He was elected to the radical 'Commune of Paris' in August, 1792, and, in July, 1793, to the 'Committee of Public Safety'; he was made its 'Chairman' because of his 'moral and intellectual authority', in effect, because of his 'purity'. He was the 'spiritual leader' of the 'Jacobin' faction of the revolutionaries, and was 'severe' in his 'personal dedication'. His 'fundamental faith', and that of the Jacobins, was that the 'general will' was, by definition, 'right', and **had** to be obeyed. The object of the Revolution was to make people 'virtuous', said Robespierre, and anyone who defied the 'general will' must therefore be an 'enemy of the people', and **had** to be 'eradicated'. This Robespierre proceeded to do on an 'industrial scale' during what became known as the 'Terror'. Between March, 1793 and June 10th, 1794, 1251 people became victims of the 'guillotine' in Paris alone, and, between June 10th and July, a further 1376 people were executed. When no-one felt safe anymore, the more-moderate members of the Convention eventually rebelled, arrested Robespierre and two of his close colleagues, and seized control of the Commune of Paris. On July 28th, 1794, Robespierre and 21 of his fellow-Jacobins were executed, without trial, by guillotine. The next day, 71 more Jacobin supporters of Robespierre were guillotined in the largest mass execution of the 'Terror'. The 'Revolutionary War' continued, however, and eventually led to the rise of Napoleon, and to the start of what became known as the 'Napoleonic Wars'. These only ended in 1815, with his final defeat at Waterloo.

How it changed much of Europe from a religious to a secular society

One of the most significant and far-reaching long-term effects of the 'European Enlightenment' has been the gradual conversion of much of Western Europe from a 'highly-religious' to a 'largely-secular' society. This took a very long time to come to full fruition, but we are all seeing its effects now, with church attendances progressively falling, and more and more churches being closed, and their buildings converted into flats or offices. When I was a teenager living in a Council flat near the centre of Aberdeen, I could see two churches from our third-floor living room window, directly opposite one another. Indeed, our family had joined one of them soon after moving into our flat from another Council apartment in one of Aberdeen's suburbs, so that my dad could be nearer to his work. There were at least 12 other churches within easy walking distance of our flat. Now, all but two of these have closed, and one of the two remaining churches is about to join them. Very few people now attend church regularly, and many of those who retain their membership of a particular church only do so in order to make use of them for weddings, christenings and funerals and for other 'social reasons'. Not only that, but many church members openly admit that they no longer believe in the basic doctrinal teachings of Christianity. I joined the Church of Scotland while I was at University, and even transferred my membership to a small Scottish Church in a nearby village when I moved to Harwell in rural Berkshire in order to take up my first job after graduating in 1963. As far as I am aware, my 'papers' are still with this Church (if it is still open), since I never joined another Church after I moved back to Aberdeen in the summer of 1965. I had 'tried Christianity', and found that it 'did not work for me', and now describe myself as a 'pagan', although I still make regular financial contributions to the local Church that my wife attended regularly before she had to go into a nursing home in 2015, since I know that she would have liked this. I also get on very well with the Minister, as I did with his predecessor, and we have 'mutual respect' for one other's views and beliefs. In 2008, I even invited him to join me in co-presenting a major public lecture on the (alleged) conflict between science and religion that I had been asked to give at our annual local 'Science Festival'; we worked together very well, and did not disagree about anything!

The seeds of this progressive move away from almost-universal Christian belief and Church attendance were all laid down during the 'European Enlightenment'. First, people were able to openly challenge the teachings of the Church without fear of persecution, or even prosecution. Take, for example, the traditional philosophical 'proofs' for the 'existence of God'. Kant had shown that these were of three main types:

- arguments based on 'reason alone' (**ontological** arguments)
- arguments based on the 'general fact' of the 'existence' of the world (**cosmological** arguments)
- arguments based on 'particular features' of the world (**teleological** arguments)

'Ontological' arguments were based on the 'definition' of God, proponents of this argument maintaining that this definition contains **within itself** clear proof that God exists, as a matter of 'logical necessity'. Two versions of such arguments were developed, one by St. Anselm during the 12th century, and one by Descartes in the early 17th century. The first was strongly criticised by one of St. Anselm's fellow monks, and the second was largely discredited by Kant towards the end of the 18th century. It is now generally agreed that **all** ontological arguments are 'logically flawed' in some way, and do **not** provide convincing proof of the existence of God.

'Cosmological' arguments are based on the obvious fact that the world 'actually exists', so that there is 'something rather than nothing'. This obviously requires explanation, unless we follow Bertrand Russell and simply accept it as a 'brute fact'. The best-known form of the argument was presented by the 13th-century theologian St. Thomas Aquinas in his 'Summa Theologiae', and is based on the claim that God is the 'first cause', or 'uncaused cause' of everything in the world. This form of the argument was strongly criticised by, and largely discredited by, David Hume, during the 18th century. After Hume, discussion of the cosmological argument was centred on the self-evident philosophical truth that no one 'thing' **in** the observable universe can account for the **entire universe**. As Wittgenstein so memorably expressed it in his 'Tractatus', 'the sense of the world must lie **outside** the world'; indeed it must!

'Teleological' arguments are based on the observation that the world in which we live has a number of features which suggest that it has a 'definite purpose', and was 'deliberately designed' by an intelligent designer (God) in order to fulfil this purpose. The 'teleological' argument was attacked by Hume in 1779, in his 'Dialogues Concerning Natural Religion'. He claimed that we have **no justification** in inferring the existence of a 'designer God' simply by observing that the world contains 'evidence of order'. The argument was further undermined by successive scientific developments during the 19th and 20th centuries, which appear to show that the 'order in the world' could be explained by 'purely natural' factors such as Darwin's 'theory of evolution'.

While fully accepting that it was impossible to 'prove' the existence of God, practically all Enlightenment philosophers firmly believed that there **was** a God, since they found the concept of atheism 'intellectually unacceptable' at the time (see the quotation from Voltaire at the beginning of this chapter). They **needed** a God to explain the fact that the 'world existed', but envisaged a **very different** god from the traditional 'Christian' God. They found such a God far too 'anthropomorphic', as was wittily expressed in another of Voltaire's maxims: 'If God created us in his own image, we have certainly returned the compliment'. They also disliked the idea of a God who was constantly 'tampering with the world' that he had created, and constantly interacting with individual human beings. They therefore replaced the 'theist' God of traditional Christianity with their own 'deist' God. Such a God, they believed, was responsible for 'creating the world', but, once he had done so, left it strictly alone to 'get on with its business'. This fitted well with their concept of a 'transcendental God' who kept himself completely separate from 'human affairs'.

It was entirely due to the influence of the 'European Enlightenment' that people were able to start talking openly about such matters, and, in due course, were also able to challenge the truth of the religious doctrines that they had previously accepted 'without question'. As I showed earlier, this eventually led to the development of the largely 'secular societies' that we find in many Western European countries today. Religion still has a role to play in such societies, but it is not the 'totally dominant' and 'controlling' role that it once had. And that, in my opinion, is all for the better. Let those who wish to practise religion do so, but please leave the rest of us to get on with our lives in the way **we** wish.

How it led to the 'Darwinian Revolution'

The so-called 'Darwinian Revolution' in biology was **the** most important 'paradigm change' that has ever taken place in that area, and was also the most important revolution in the whole of science since the world-changing 'Copernican Revolution' that began roughly 400 years earlier. The 'Copernican Revolution' totally **changed** the relationship between religion and science; the 'Darwinian Revolution' was only possible **because of that change**, and because of the subsequent changes in the relationship that were brought about by the 'European Enlightenment'. Indeed, I do not think that the 'Darwinian Revolution' could have taken place **without** the 'European Enlightenment'. Let us now take a detailed look at it.

Until the late 18th century, virtually all Christians believed that God had created all the species that we observe today **in their present forms**, as described in the first chapter of 'Genesis'. They also believed that the Earth was **comparatively young** – a few thousand years old at most. In 1785, however, James Hutton's book, 'Theory of Earth', was published. This presented strong evidence that the Earth must be many **millions** of years old. In the first half of the 19th century, the idea that current species **might** have evolved from earlier species started to be looked at seriously by some biologists. The idea was strongly opposed by the Church, since it **directly contradicted** what the Bible said about the matter. Before the 'European Enlightenment', the Church would probably have been able to prevent further discussion of the matter, but things were **very** different now. In 1858, Charles Darwin and Alfred Russell Wallace, two English 'naturalists', simultaneously published papers suggesting a possible mechanism for evolution. This held that species evolved **gradually**, by means of 'natural selection' among randomly-changing individuals. The main problem with their theory was that nobody had any idea of how parents passed on characteristics to their offspring, i.e. **of how**

heredity worked. Geologists had also failed to find any fossils that represented creatures that lived during the long, gradual **transition** from one species to another. Their ideas were also strongly attacked by the Church, since they again **directly contradicted** what was said in the Bible.

In 1857, Gregor Mendel, an Austrian monk who was also interested in how plants passed on 'inherited characteristics' during the 'breeding' process, began a detailed study of the matter, based on pea plants. He published a key paper on his work in 1866, but this was completely ignored for over 30 years. In 1900, Hugo de Vries, a Dutch botanist working in Harlem and two other botanists independently carried out similar studies. They also re-discovered Mendel's earlier work, and subsequently founded the new science of **genetics**. This led to the development of what became known as the **Neo-Darwinian Synthesis**. This explained the handing-on of heritable characteristics via **genes**, although nobody knew what these were. By the early 1950's, it was believed that the chemical **deoxyribonucleic acid (DNA)** played a key role in heredity. In 1953, the English physicist, Francis Crick, and the American biologist, James Watson, working together at Cambridge University, discovered the 'structure' of DNA, for which they subsequently won the Nobel Prize for Medicine and Physiology. This founded the new science of **molecular biology**, and led to the unravelling of the genetic code. This completed the Neo-Darwinian Synthesis, and led to the general acceptance of the view that evolution could now be completely explained. This view was strongly promoted by the English biologist Richard Dawkins, who used it to make a strong case for atheism in books like 'The Blind Watchmaker' and 'The God Delusion', which we will hear much more about in Chapter 19.

In the latter part of the 20th century, a number of biologists began to challenge the view that the Neo-Darwinian model could explain **all** features of evolution. In 1968, Motoo Kimura showed that most evolution at molecular level simply **eludes** the effects of 'natural selection', because the mutations involved neither **help** nor **harm** the host organisms. Soon afterwards, it was found that the individual organisms that make up a species have a much greater variation in their genes than is compatible with natural selection. It was subsequently found that only a **fraction** of an organism's genes are actually 'expressed', the others remaining 'dormant' until they are 'switched on' by some environmental or other change. And in 1972, Niles Eldredge and Stephen Jay Gould showed that evolution did not take place **gradually**, but in **jumps**. In their **punctuated equilibrium** model, species remained more or less the same for long periods before they suddenly disappeared, and were replaced by new ones. This cannot be explained by the accumulation of 'gradual changes' brought about by Darwinian 'natural selection'. Other subsequent discoveries that are incompatible with the 'Neo-Darwinian paradigm' include: the transfer of genes between different species, especially bacteria (so-called 'jumping' genes); strong evidence that 'inheritance' of acquired characteristics **does** sometimes occur (this was long thought to be 'impossible'); the discovery that several unseen genetic variations can reveal themselves **simultaneously** when an organism comes under environmental stress.

So what is the **current** situation in evolutionary theory? The first thing to stress is that 'evolution' is now an 'established fact', since the scientific evidence in its favour appears to be 'overwhelming'. Nevertheless, evolution is **still** not accepted by many 'religious fundamentalists', and also by over 50% of the population of the United States, if recent surveys are to be believed. But it is also now becoming gradually accepted that the 'Neo-Darwinian' model does **not** give a satisfactory model of **all features** of evolution. The model is very good at explaining **minor evolutionary changes within a species**, e.g. the development of different shapes of beaks in Darwin's 'Galapagos finches', and changes in the colour of moths in response to changing amounts of soot in the air. What it does **not** do is explain the actual **origin** of species – the sudden, wholesale changes that lead to one species being replaced by another. It is now clear that the characteristics of a given species depend not only on the **types** of genes that its members possess, but also on how these genes are **controlled** and **expressed**. All species share many, (if not most) of their genes, with closely-related species (such as chimpanzees and human beings) having the most in common. Thus, **much more research** needs to be carried out before we have a **full understanding** of how evolution has taken place.

How it is still highly influential today, despite opposing 'dark forces'

The ideas that inspired the European Enlightenment have now been around for over 400 years, and are just as inspiring and influential today as they were in the time of Bacon, Locke, Newton, Voltaire and Diderot – despite two 'nasty scares' along the way. The first, of course, was the near collapse of the Enlightenment dream during the early stages of the French Revolution, when the baleful influence of Rousseau took over for a time – with disastrous results for France. France eventually recovered, however, and regained its place as the 'cultural centre of Europe', and the country where 'reason' ruled. The second nasty scare was much more recent, and we are still emerging from its effects. I am, of course, referring to the full-frontal attack on Enlightenment principles in general, and science in particular, that led to the so-called 'Science Wars' on either side of the start of the new Millennium. Let us now end this chapter by taking a detailed look at these events, which could well have dealt the 'Enlightenment project' a serious blow from which it would have been very difficult to recover, at least in the immediate future.

The origins of the 'Science Wars' can be traced back to the publication of Thomas Kuhn's ground-breaking book, 'The Structure of Scientific

Revolutions', in 1962. This not only brought several completely-new terms into common use, including 'normal science', 'paradigm' and 'paradigm shift', it also presented serious challenges to the general assumption that science was a purely-'objective' activity that was not influenced by 'subjective' or 'social' factors. Popper's highly-influential book on the nature of the scientific method ('The Logic of Scientific Discovery') strongly defended the 'traditional' view of science, but had only been available in English since 1959. Thus, during the 1960's and 1970's there was considerable discussion over who was right. (I became personally involved in the debate during the late 1970's, when I wrote articles on the ideas of Popper and Kuhn, for inclusion on a new national course for fifth- and sixth-form students entitled 'Science in Society'. I took the view that they were **both** right, with Popper's picture of science being valid in some situations and Kuhn's in others. This matter was subsequently the subject of an 'exchange of letters' in 'School Science Review' in the early 1980's, which I greatly enjoyed!).

The debate over the 'objectivity' of science continued through the 1980's and beyond, becoming increasingly centred on the claim that so-called 'scientific knowledge' was in fact a 'social construct'. This, in turn, led to the claim by 'post-modernist' philosophers that so-called 'reality' was actually 'a state constructed by the mind', rather than something that was 'perceived by it'. In the most extreme version of this 'constructivist' theory, it was claimed that there **is** no 'real' reality, nor are there any 'objective truths external to mental activity', only 'prevailing versions disseminated by ruling social groups'. They also denied that **ethics** could be 'firmly grounded', given that 'each society creates its own codes for the benefit of the same oppressive forces'. If these premises are correct, it follows that 'one culture is as good as any other' in the expression of truth and mortality, 'each in its own special way'. Thus, 'political multiculturalism' is fully justified, with each 'ethnic group' and 'sexual preference' in the community having 'equal validity'. And, more than mere 'tolerance', each deserves 'communal support', and 'mandated representation in educational agendas', not because it has 'general importance' to society, but because it **exists**. To **disagree** with these conclusions, say the extreme post-modernists, is 'bigotry', which, to them, is a 'cardinal sin'. 'Cardinal', that is, if we agree to waive, in this one instance, the post-modernist denial of the existence of 'universal truth', and all agree 'for the common good', in compliance with 'the general will'. Shades of Rousseau; shades of Robespierre!

By the end of the 1980's what had begun as a 'scholarly assessment of the status of scientific knowledge' had transmogrified into an open assault on science and everything it stood for. 'Universality', 'objectivity', and 'value-neutrality' were, it was claimed, 'powerfully-entrenched cultural myths', as were 'knowledge' and 'rationality'. Initially, the natural-science community largely ignored these attacks, or dismissed them as 'too irrational to be worth commenting on'. Once they realised the threat that the extreme post-modernists represented to modern society, however, they began to fight back. High points of the 'Science Wars' that followed were the publication in 1994 of 'Higher Superstition', by Paul Gross and Norman Leavitt, and the brilliant hoax perpetuated by the eminent American physicist, Alan Sokal, in 1996. Let us now look at each of these in more detail.

In 'Higher Superstition', Gross and Leavitt focussed on the 'left-wing' humanist' and 'social- scientific' critics of science. They cited numerous instances of the 'manifest ignorance of science' of these 'critics', and, what was even worse, their 'blatantly nonsensical misappropriation of science' to support antiscientific claims. Their attacks were particularly concentrated on 'post-modernist cultural constructivism', the 'social construction of knowledge' theory, 'feminist science criticism', and the radical environmental movement called 'deep ecology'. They were particularly appalled at the 'irrationality of the writings' of these critics of science, at the 'venom of their hostility to science', and at their potential for doing 'serious damage to western social institutions', particularly the science upon which is so strongly depended.

The second 'high point' in the 'Science Wars' was inspired by 'Higher Superstition' and the favourable response to it. What Sokal did was submit a paper to the left-wing, cultural-studies journal 'Social Text' with the following title:

'Transgressing the Boundaries; towards a Transformative Hermeneutics of Quantum Gravity'.

This purported to expose the socially-constructed, ideology-based character of 'quantum gravity theory' (one of the key current interests of contemporary physics). In fact, the 'paper' was a tissue of 'physics nonsense', clearly 'lashed together' with terminology that Sokal had extracted from a 'brief but intensive immersion' in post-modernist literature. The paper was duly published, and aroused considerable interest among the post-modernist community. Sokal later revealed that his paper was in fact a hoax – a cunningly-worded 'parody' designed to ridicule the 'meaningless jargon' of the 'extreme post-modernist' critique of science that was in vogue at the time'. Sokal completely fooled the journal's editors and readers, who were too ignorant of science to realise what he was doing. The many opponents of post-modernism (myself included) are still laughing about it!

I myself have two major objections to the anti-science views of the extreme postmodernists. First, I, strongly disagree with the views themselves. The great physicist Wolfgang Pauli, one of the founders of modern quantum mechanics, was renowned for his acerbic criticisms of ideas he 'found wanting'. He had three levels of criticism of such ideas: 'wrong', 'completely wrong' and 'not even wrong' (meaning that the ideas were not worthy of serious discussion). Had he still been around during the recent 'Science Wars', I am in no doubt about the category to which he would have assigned the post-modernist attacks on science. Second, I am appalled at the way in which the post-modernists try to suppress the ideas of their opponents, using such anti-democratic techniques as 'no-platforming' a speaker, or, if this fails, organising 'spontaneous' mass protests designed to disrupt the speech. Voltaire passionately believed in 'free speech', as evidenced by what is perhaps the most famous and most important maxim that is attributed to him: 'I disapprove of what you say, but will defend to the death your right to say it'. The extreme post-modernists would find that their ideas attracted much greater respect if they made even a token attempt to comply with this maxim.

In his outstanding book 'Consilience', which was published in 1998 when the 'Science Wars' were about to enter their closing stages, the eminent American biologist, Edwards O. Wilson, presented the most powerful case for the ideas of the 'European Enlightenment' that I have ever read. After totally-demolishing the anti-science views of the extreme postmodernists, he concluded the chapter in which he did so with the following words, which I have decided to quote in full. As you will see, Wilson is a **brilliant** writer; read, and enjoy!

'Nevertheless, here is a salute to the postmodernists. As today's celebrants of corybantic romanticism, they enrich culture. They say to the rest of us: Maybe, just maybe, you are wrong. Their ideas are like sparks from firework explosions that travel away in all directions, devoid of following energy, soon to wink out in the dimensionless dark. Yet a few will endure long enough to cast light on unexpected subjects. That is one reason to think well of postmodernism, even as it menaces rational thought. Another is the relief it affords those who have chosen not to encumber themselves with a scientific education. Another is the small industry it has created within philosophy and literary studies. Still another, the one that counts the most, is the unyielding critique of traditional scholarship it provides. We will always need postmodernists or their rebellious equivalents. For what better way to strengthen organised knowledge than continually defend it from hostile forces? John Stuart Mill correctly noted that teacher and learner alike fall asleep at their posts when there is no enemy in the field. And if somehow, against all the evidence, against all reason, the linchpin falls out and everything is reduced to epistemological confusion, we will find the courage to admit that the postmodernists were right, and in the best spirit of the Enlightenment, we will start over again. Because, as the great mathematician David Hilbert once said, capturing so well that part of the human spirit expressed through the Enlightenment, 'wir müssen wissen. Wir werden wissen'. We must know, we will know'.

I wish I could write like that!

Some of the sources of information on material covered in Chapter 9

Once again, I drew material from several of the books and other material in my personal library when writing this chapter, but by far the greatest amount came from the following sources:

- 'The Story of Philosophy', by Bryan Magee, once again, an invaluable source of detailed information on the main philosophers covered in the chapter.
- 'Confessions of a Philosopher', by Bryan Magee, yet again, a key source of information and ideas.
- 'European History and European Lives: 1715 to 1914', a 'Teaching Company' course written and presented by Professor Jonathan Steinberg, a key source of detailed information on the French Revolution.
- 'Philosophical Arguments for the Existence of God', by Henry Ellington, a handout that I produced to support work in schools.

- 'Does the Neo-Darwinian Synthesis still give a Satisfactory Explanation of Evolution, as we Currently Understand it', by Henry Ellington, another handout produced to support work in schools.
- 'Consilience – The Unity of Knowledge', by Edward O. Wilson.
- 'Science Wars: What Scientists Know and How they Know It', a 'Teaching Company' course written and presented by Professor Steven L. Goldman.
- 'Chambers Biographical Dictionary' (1990 edition, edited by Magnus Magnussen).

Chapter 10: Dualism and the 'mind-body' problem

'Behind the veil of monistic protestations there still lurks the dualism of body and mind'

- Karl Popper ('Objective Knowledge, Chapter 4)

The idea that 'body' and 'mind' are completely different types of entity can be traced back to Plato (428-328BCE) and Augustine (354-430CE), but was given its most famous expression by Descartes (1591-1650), whose work we have already met in Chapter 8. As we saw, Descartes is widely regarded as the 'father of modern western philosophy', being the first of a series of philosophical 'system builders' who worked in Europe from the 17th century onwards. It was Descartes who introduced the concepts of 'mind-body dualism' and the related 'mind-body problem' into modern philosophical thinking, and philosophers and scientists have been arguing about them ever since. They have generally tried to resolve the matter by denying that one or other of Descartes' two basic entities ('mind' and 'body') does in fact exist. 'Idealists', who believe that the 'mental world' is the only 'real' world, hold that the 'body' is a purely mental construct. 'Materialists', on the other hand, who believe that the 'physical world' is the only 'real world', hold that the 'mind' is simply a 'secondary characteristic' (what we would now call an 'emergent feature') of that world. During the next 350 years or so, neither of these two approaches to 'explaining away' the mind-body problem achieved general acceptance, however, as was memorably stated by Karl Popper in 1972: 'Western philosophy consists very largely of world pictures which are variations of the theme of body-mind dualism, and of problems of method related to these. The main departures from this western dualistic theme were attempts to replace it by some kind of monism. It seems to me that these attempts were unsuccessful, and that behind the veil of monistic protestations there still lurks the dualism of body and mind.' When he wrote these words, Popper was very much in the minority regarding the matter, since the great majority of western thinkers had come to accept the conventional 'scientific' position – that the 'mind' is simply an 'emergent feature' of the 'brain'. Let us now examine the history of 'dualism' and the 'mind-body problem' in greater detail, and see how things stand today.

Cartesian dualism and the 'mind-body problem'

As we saw in Chapter 8, the starting point of Descartes' philosophical 'system building' was his famous 'cogito', his realisation that he was able to know **with certainty** that he himself actually existed, because he was a **'thinking being'**. As he himself expressed it, 'cogito, ergo sum' (I am thinking, therefore I exist). Building upon this apparently-unshakable foundation, he was able to deduce, by purely rational methods, that the **body** ('res extensa' – the 'extended thing') and the **mind** ('res cogitans' – the 'thinking thing') were completely different types of ontological entity. This then led him to the idea of the **mind-body problem**, the problem of how two such radically-different 'things' could possibly interact with one another. Descartes fully appreciated that the two **did** interact, as the following quotation shows:

'I am not just lodged in my body like a pilot in his ship, but I am intimately united with it, and so confused and intermingled with it that I and my body compose, as it were, a single whole'.

Nonetheless, he found it difficult to see how they **could** interact. He eventually came up with the idea that they did so through the 'pineal gland' – a tiny, cone-shaped structure located deep within the brain, below the rear part of the 'corpus callosum'. We now know that this theory is incorrect, since the sole function of the pineal gland appears to be the secretion of the hormone 'melatonin', which helps the body to synchronise its 'circadian body rhythms' with the day-night cycle. Descartes was not to know this at the time, however, since the physiological function of the pineal gland was discovered **very** much later.

For Descartes, this idea of the interaction of 'mind' and 'body' (or 'soul' and 'body') was as basic and certain as the clear and distinct idea of 'self' and of 'body'. On such 'certainties', he based his ideas about ethics, metaphysics, physiology, physics and theology. Such a mixture of 'materialism' and 'spiritualism' did not satisfy some of his near-contemporaries and successors, however. It was strongly criticised by Spinoza (1632-1677) and by Leibniz (1646-1716), for example, and also by Nicolas de Malebranche (1638-1715), who proposed the theory called 'occasionalism'. This avoided the idea of direct interaction between such incompatible things as 'mind' and 'body' by stating that God 'intervenes directly':

'Our sensations are occasions on which God exerts ideas in our minds; our will to act is an occasion on which God moves our bodies.'

Thus, according to Malebranche, the 'mind' and the 'world' are 'brought together' **in** and **by** God.

John Locke (1632-1704), on the other hand, accepted Descartes' 'dualism' – the 'two parts of nature', 'active immaterial substance' (soul) and 'passive material substance' (body), neither of which could be turned into the other. Nevertheless, Locke questioned why 'mind' should not be material, and why God should not have endowed matter, in the case of man, with the mysterious power of 'thinking' and 'knowing'. In making this suggestion, Locke was admitting the possibility of Hobbes's 'materialist concept' of 'the thinking body', but was not fully convinced by it. His reasoning eventually led him to the problem of 'personal identity': the unity of the 'self that thinks', and the unity of 'one person as he appears to another'. He also re-formulated, but could not answer, the old 'dualistic problem': if the essence of the 'mind' (as Descartes had claimed) was 'thinking', what happened when it stopped 'thinking', or 'feeling' or 'willing'?

These were only some of the early questions that were raised by Descartes' work on 'dualism' and the 'mind-body problem'. Let us now 'fast forward', however, and examine some of the objections to 'Cartesian Dualism' that were raised during the 20th-century, when it came under really serious and prolonged attack for the very first time.

As I showed you in Chapter 8, Ludwig Wittgenstein (1889-1951) was responsible for initiating two major changes in the development of European philosophy during the first half of the 20th-century, the second being the inauguration of the 'real-language' school of analytical philosophy. This had its centre in Oxford University, with Wittgenstein being one of its leading figures until his death in 1951. Their members believed that the main (indeed, the **only**) role of philosophy was to subject 'philosophical problems' to rigorous 'linguistic analysis', and, by so doing, show that most of them were only 'pseudo-problems' that had arisen through 'mis-use of language'. In other words, they thought that they could 'resolve' philosophical problems by making them 'go away'.

This is what one of the leading members of the School, Gilbert Ryle (1900-1976) attempted to do to 'Cartesian Dualism' and the related 'mind-body problem' when he published his ground-breaking book, 'The Concept of Mind', in 1949. This was 'brilliantly written', and had a tremendous impact on contemporary philosophy, especially in England. Ryle's central thesis was that 'dualism' was in fact an 'error', because there is in fact **no such entity as a 'mind'**, which he memorably described as 'the ghost in the machine'. On the basis of extensive and highly-detailed linguistic analysis, he argued that what we humans do is 'categorise' certain aspects of our own behaviour and experience as 'mental', attribute them to a different 'subject' from the rest, and then 'reify' that subject as a 'mind'. He claimed that careful investigation of our use of 'mental concepts' showed that we had no rational justification for doing this, and that the 'human being' is a 'single entity', 'one subject of behaviour and experience' with a 'single identity' and a 'single history' – not 'two entities mysteriously laced together', as Descartes and his followers had claimed. In believing this, he claimed that they had made what he called a 'category mistake' (a term which subsequently gained wide currency in philosophy). Dualists believed that our so called 'mind' is a separately-existing entity that 'does things' and 'has experiences', when all the time it is merely an 'umbrella term' for a particular sub-group of our various 'modes of behaviour' – 'performance', 'disposition', 'experience', and so on – all of which should be correctly attributed to a 'single subject'. According to Ryle, this 'category mistake' gave rise to a whole range of other 'mistakes' in our assumptions about ourselves, and in our various ways of 'thinking' and 'talking' about ourselves. It was a prime example of a 'philosophical error' of the type that he and his colleagues were attempting to 'put right'. In writing his book, he had provided a 'paradigm case study' on how this could be done.

Although it made a great impression at the time, and made Ryle's reputation in philosophy, it has to be said that his ideas have not stood the test of time. Indeed, the 2005 edition of 'The Oxford Companion to Philosophy' (of which I own a well-thumbed copy), describes 'The Concept of Mind' as 'an impressive but perhaps not wholly coherent book'. I purchased a copy a few years ago, and read it with great interest. I am afraid that I disagreed with practically everything it said, and found it difficult to believe that it once had so much influence. It was, however, typical of the type of philosophy practised and taught at Oxford at the time (see 'Confessions of a Philosopher').

As I indicated in the 'preface' to this chapter, 'Cartesian dualism' was subsequently subjected to a much stronger, and much more sustained, attack than the one that had been made by Gilbert Ryle. This was the development of the modern 'scientific' model of the 'brain-mind system', which appeared to be capable of explaining many (if not all) of the features of the 'mental world', without the need for an ontologically-separate 'mind'. I will examine this in detail in the next section, but, before I do so, I would like to introduce you to the work that Karl Popper carried out in this area during the 1970's.

As we saw earlier, Popper was not convinced by any of the attempts that had been made to 'explain away' dualism since the time of Descartes, and remained a firm believer in the existence of an ontologically-distinct 'mental world' for the rest of his life. Indeed, he went even further, and postulated the existence of a **third** ontological world that he believed to be **distinct from**, but **connected to**, the other two. Descartes and his successors had believed in a 'dualistic ontology', with two interacting components, the 'objective physical world' ('body') and the 'subjective mental world' ('mind'). Popper believed that this should be replaced by a three-part 'pluralistic ontology' in which the three 'components' were the 'objective physical world' (which he re-named as 'World 1'), the 'subjective mental world' (which he re-named as World 2') and the 'world of objective ideas and structures created by living things' (which he called 'World 3'). He produced a 'schematic diagram' of this pluralistic ontology, in which the three components, contained in three circles, were arranged in a horizontal row, with 'World 1' on the left, 'World 2' in the middle, and 'World 3' on the right. In this revised ontology, 'World 1' only interacted directly with 'World 2' (shown by two-way arrows), as did 'World 3', so that World 2 (the subjective mental world) effectively formed an 'indirect link' between World 1 and World 3, which could **not** interact with each other **directly**, without the intervention of World 2. Popper first presented his revolutionary new ontology in Chapter 4 of 'Objective Knowledge', which was published in 1972. This was the source of the quotation at the very start of this chapter, and of the longer version of this given later on in the 'preface' to the chapter.

Popper also made a highly-detailed and highly-convincing case for the existence of 'World 3', which he believed contained **all** 'intelligibles', or 'ideas in the objective sense'. These included all 'scientific or other theories' that had been written down or stored in some way, all 'physical products' of human or animal thought, all 'products of art and human culture', and so on. Developing the concept of 'World 3' was one of Popper's most important contributions to philosophy – and, as we saw in Chapter 8, he made **many** such contributions. Four years after publishing 'Objective Knowledge', Popper wrote a book dealing specifically with the relationship between our 'minds' and our 'bodies', which was entitled 'The Self and Its Brain'. This was co-authored with the eminent Nobel-prize-winning Australian physiologist Sir John Eccles. It spelt out the 'dualistic' picture of the 'mind-brain' relationship that both men strongly held, and had considerable influence throughout the scientific and philosophical community, despite being, by then, very much a 'minority position' as we will now show.

The modern 'neurophysiological model' of the brain-mind system

During the last 60 years or so, most western philosophers and scientists have moved away from Cartesian dualism, maintaining that 'minds' and 'mental events' are **caused by** and **realised in** physiological, neural and electrical activities that take place **within** the brain. Furthermore, many of them believe that we will eventually succeed in explaining **all mental phenomena** by detailed scientific investigation of its physiology and neurology. According to this 'materialist' view, mental activities have **no separate ontological status**, being analogous to the execution of a **computer program** within the hardware of a **computer**. In 1984, the American philosopher, John Searle, gave one of the clearest, and most convincing, statements of this modern 'neurophysiological' position in the first of his six 'Reith Lectures' on 'Minds, Brains and Science', in which he tackled the 'mind-body problem' head on. All six lectures were subsequently published in a slim paperback book with the same title, now one of the most-read, most-thumbed and most-worn books in my personal library. In view of its importance, let me now describe this model in some detail.

Searle bases his 'neurophysiological model' of the 'brain-mind system' on two basic theses, which he explains, justifies and elaborates on in some detail. His first thesis goes as follows:

'Mental phenomena, **all** mental phenomena whether conscious or unconscious, visual or auditory, pains, tickles, itches, thoughts, indeed, all of our 'mental life' are **caused by processes going on in the brain**.'

To give people an idea of how this 'works', he goes on to describe the causal processes for one particular kind of 'mental state' – pain. According to the state of knowledge of the subject in 1984, pain signals are transmitted from sensory nerve endings to the spinal chord by at least two types of fibres – 'Delta A fibres' (which carry 'prickling' sensations), and 'C fibres' (which carry 'burning' and 'aching' sensations). When they enter the spinal chord, they terminate on the neurons of the chord, and then send further signals up the chord to the brain, which they enter by two separate pathways – the 'prickling pain' pathway and the 'burning pain' pathway. Both go through the thalamus, but the 'prickling pain' signals are then 'localised' in the somato-sensory cortex, whereas the 'burning pain' signals are more spread out, travelling not only upwards into the cortex, but also laterally into the hypothalamus and other regions at the base of the brain. Because of these differences, it is much easier for us to locate a 'prickling' sensation (we can all tell fairly accurately where someone is sticking a pin into us, for example), whereas 'burning' and 'aching' pains can be more distressing, because they activate more of the central nervous system. The actual sensation of pain appears to be caused both by the stimulation of the basal regions of the brain, especially the thalamus, and by the stimulation of the somato-sensory cortex.

So what does all this tell us? It tells us that our 'sensations' of pains are **caused by** a series of events that begin at free nerve endings and **end up** in the thalamus and other regions of the brain. Indeed, as far as the actual **sensations** are concerned, the events **inside the central nervous system** are quite sufficient to cause pains (we know this from 'phantom limb' pains felt by amputees, and from pains caused by stimulating appropriate parts of the brain itself). Searle goes on to say that what is true for pain is also true for mental phenomena generally, and that everything that matters for our 'mental life', all our 'thoughts' and 'feelings', are **caused by processes happening inside the brain.** As far as 'causing' mental states is concerned, the crucial step is the one that goes on 'inside the head', **not** the external or peripheral stimulus. If the events outside the central nervous system occurred, but nothing happened **in the brain**, there would be **no mental events**. But, if the right things happened **in the brain**, the mental events would happen **even if there was no outside stimulus**. But if pain and other mental phenomena are 'caused by' processes in the brain, what **are** pains? What **are** they **really**? The obvious answer is that they are 'unpleasant sensations', but that answer leaves us unsatisfied, because it doesn't tell us how 'pains' fit into our 'overall conception' of the world. To answer the question 'properly', Searle says that he needs to add a second thesis to the first:

'Pains and other mental phenomena are just **features of the brain** (and perhaps the rest of the central nervous system).

But how, Searle goes on, can **both** these theses **be true at the same time**? How can it **both** be the case that 'brains cause minds', and yet minds are just 'features of the brain'. Searle maintains that it was the failure to see how **both** these propositions could be true together that prevented us from solving the 'mind-body problem' for so long. He claims that the 'puzzlement' arises from a misunderstanding of the basic nature of 'causation'. It is tempting to think that whenever A 'causes' B, there must be two discrete events — one identified as the 'cause', and the other as the 'effect'. Searle maintains that it is this crude model of 'causation' that leads us to adopt some sort of 'dualism', and to think that events in one 'material realm' (the 'physical') cause events in another 'insubstantial realm' (the 'mental'). Searle believes that this is a mistake, and that the way to 'remove' the mistake from our thinking is to adopt a more sophisticated view of causation. To help us do this, he turns away from the relationship between 'minds' and 'brains' for a few minutes, and asks us to look at some other sorts of 'causal relationships' in nature. In particular, he asks us to look at the relationship between the 'macroscopic' (large-scale) properties, and the 'microscopic' (small-scale) properties, of certain physical systems. Take, for example, 'the chair on which you are sitting', or 'the glass or water in front of you'.

Searle points out that each of these consists of 'microscopic particles' of progressively smaller size (molecules, atoms, and the 'fundamental particles' of which they are composed), and also possess 'macroscopic properties' such as 'solidity' (in the case of the chair) and 'liquidity' (in the case of the water). Furthermore, both of these macroscopic properties can be 'explained' in terms of the behaviour of the microscopic particles – the chair's 'solidity' by the lattice structure occupied by the molecules of which it is composed, and the water's 'liquidity' by the interactions between the water molecules as they move about. Searle suggests that systems such as these provide a simple and easily-understandable model for explaining the apparently-puzzling relationships between the 'mind' and the 'brain'. In the case of 'solidity' and 'liquidity', we have no difficulty at all in accepting that the 'macroscopic' properties are **caused by** the behaviour of elements at the 'microscopic level', and, at the same time, are **realised in** the larger systems that are made up of the micro-elements. There is certainly a 'cause-and-effect' relationship in both cases, but, at the same time, the 'macroscopic' properties of both the chair and the water are just **higher-level features** of the very systems whose behaviour at the 'microscopic' level **causes** these very same features. Physicists and engineers have no difficulty whatsoever in working with such 'double-aspect models' of the systems they deal with every day, and neither should we, when dealing with the 'brain-mind' system, says Searle. If it is any consolation to readers, I would point out that it took me no fewer than three attempts to understand Bryan Magee's explanation of Kant's epistemology when I first encountered it in my hotel room in Saudi Arabia in 2002. So if you have not fully understood Searle's description of the 'neurophysiological model' of the brain-mind system first time round, try again! It is worth the effort! It is a **superb** piece of 'original thinking'.

Some problems with the 'neurophysiological model'

During the last few decades, neurophysiologists have made tremendous advances in explaining mental phenomena and other aspects of human behaviour in terms of physical properties of the brain. Indeed, many workers in the field now believe that they are very close to being able to give a **complete explanation** of **all mental**

activities purely in terms of the various **physical processes** that take place therein. If they succeed in doing so, this will constitute one of the greatest scientific achievements of all time – possibly **the** greatest – and they will also have made the mind-body problem 'go away forever'. If the 'neurophysiological project' is to achieve its highly-ambitious aims, however, it will have to produce satisfactory explanations of the following five basic features of 'minds' and 'mental processes', all of which have puzzled workers in the field for a very long time:

1. The existence of **consciousness** (awareness of the **self**, and its relationship to the world that we perceive to lie around us).
2. The phenomenon of **subjectivity** (the fact that every individual person has their own **private mental world** to which no-one else has direct access).
3. The phenomenon of **intentionality** (the fact that thoughts and mental states are 'about' features of the physical or mental world, i.e. have **semantic content**).
4. The phenomenon of **mental causation** (the generally-held belief that our thoughts and feelings have a real influence on the way we behave, e.g. by controlling the way our bodies move).
5. The existence of **long-term memories** (the fact that we **remember** facts, occurrences, ideas, etc, for a very long time, and can also **recall** these).

Let us now see how the neurophysiological model of the brain-mind system has fared in explaining each of these key features of the mental world.

1. Consciousness

This has been described as the 'hard problem' of the mental sciences, and, despite the claims made by some workers in the field, most western philosophers and scientists agree that the nature and origins of consciousness still remain a complete mystery. In 1991, the American philosopher and scientist, Daniel C. Dennett, published a book on the subject with the highly-ambitious title 'Consciousness Explained'. I bought a copy soon afterwards, and have now read it twice, but on neither occasion did I agree with his claim to have 'explained consciousness' in terms of the 'computer model of the mind' that he proposed therein. In his 1984 book on 'Minds, Brains and Science', John Searle admitted that the 'neurophysiological model' of the brain-mind system had not yet provided a satisfactory explanation of consciousness, and, in a much-longer book published in 1992 ('The Rediscovery of the Mind') admitted that he had not changed his mind on the matter by then. He was not particularly troubled by this, however, and was fairly confident that it would eventually succeed in doing so. At the time of writing this chapter (July, 2020), I have heard no word that this has happened yet.

I have been reading widely on the subject for well over 40 years now, and am slowly coming round to the view that we will **never** succeed in doing so while the majority of western philosophers and scientists remain in a state of denial regarding the possibility that there **may** be more to our minds and mental processes than purely physical processes occurring in the brain, as John Searle so strongly believes. Since being introduced to the work of Popper during the mid-1970's, I have become increasingly drawn towards the 'dualist' position the more I learn about the subject. In 1978, I was introduced to 'transcendental meditation' by a young lad who had been temporarily assigned to my Department at Robert Gordon's Institute of Technology as part of a 'job creation' scheme, went to an introductory talk on the subject, and subsequently enrolled on the full course. I have been practising 'TM' ever since, meditating for 20 minutes every morning and afternoon unless circumstances make this impossible, and have found it **extremely** beneficial, although it has not yet led me down the 'royal road' to 'enlightenment' (it is actually a form of the Hindu 'raja yoga' that I described in Chapter 5). I did, however, study the 'theory' of TM in some detail, and became aware that there was **much** more to consciousness than I had hitherto supposed. My gradual 'conversion' to dualism received a further boost when I was introduced to the ideas of Kant and Schopenhauer during the early 'noughties'. As you will see later in the book, the overall picture of reality that I have now developed has been strongly influenced by such thinking.

2. Subjectivity

It is a firmly-established fact that practically all of us believe that we **do** have our own private 'mental worlds', although we are much less sure as to **why** this should be the case. Study of the matter is largely centred on the study of the 'self', a matter on which there has been considerable discussion and disagreement throughout the ages. As we saw in Chapter 5, Buddhists believe that the 'self' is actually an 'illusion', devoid of 'ultimate reality' or 'continuity'. Their key doctrine of 'Anatta' ('no-self'), pictures individuals as a 'bundle' of five 'skandhas' ('body', 'feelings', 'perceptions', 'volitions', and 'consciousness'). These 'come together' when we are born, and cease to operate together when we die, when this particular 'self' ceases to exist. And as we saw in Chapter 8, Hume has presented a strong case that the 'self' is not an entity that is susceptible to 'epistemological study', so does not really exist as a 'thing' in its own right. We are, according to Hume, simply a 'bundle of sensations' – not a very 'ego-flattering concept', it must be said! Despite these abstruse philosophical considerations, you would find it hard to find any ordinary person who does not 'know' that we have a 'self', and does not 'know' that this 'self' has its own internal 'mental world' to which no-one else has direct access. And they are not particularly bothered about how this happens!

This is basically the position regarding 'subjectivity' that John Searle adopted in 'Minds, Brains and Science'. While accepting that the 'neurophysiological model' of the brain-mind system had yet to give a satisfactory **explanation** of 'subjectivity', he was completely sanguine about the matter, claiming that it would be a 'mistake' to suppose that any definition of 'objective reality' should **exclude** 'subjectivity', since everyone took it for granted that it existed. If a 'scientific account of the world' attempts to describe 'how things are', then one of the features of that account **must** be the 'subjectivity' of mental states. As he put it, 'I have no doubt at all that subjective mental states exist, because I am in one now, and so are you'. If the 'fact' of subjectivity runs counter to a certain definition of 'science' then it is the **definition** and not the **fact** that we will have to abandon! Like Descartes' 'cogito', this is pretty hard to dispute, but it still leaves the basic question of how 'subjectivity' arises unanswered, in my opinion.

3. Intentionality

John Searle again discussed this at great length in 'Minds, Brains and Science', and again, admitted that this was still a mystery. How, he asked, could a 'collection of atoms in the void' have 'intentionality'? How could they be **about** something? And, once again, he was completely sanguine about the fact that the 'neurophysiological model' of the brain-mind system had yet to give a satisfactory **explanation** of the phenomenon. Searle argued that the best way to show that something is 'possible' is to show 'how it actually exists'. As with his detailed justification of his basic model of the 'brain-mind system' that I described in the previous section of this chapter, he claimed that the way to 'master the mystery of intentionality' was to describe, in as much detail as possible, how the phenomenon is 'caused by' biological processes while, at the same time, being 'realised in' biological systems. And this he did with great skill and power, while still leaving the basic question of how 'intentionality' arises unanswered.

In a later chapter of his book, however, he did succeed in delivering a 'killer argument' against the widespread current 'strong AI' belief that we were about to develop digital computers that could actually 'think', in the same way that human beings 'think'. This was based on the indisputable fact that the activities of such machines are purely **syntactical** in nature, involving the manipulation of strings of digital numbers that possess no **semantic** content. His famous 'Chinese room' argument as to why this **must** be the case has yet to elicit a fully-satisfactory rebuttal from the AI community. If Searle's arguments are valid, as I firmly believe to be the case, explaining intentionality in terms of **purely physical processes** (as neurophysiological research workers are currently attempting to do) may simply be impossible. I think that Searle has inadvertently 'hoist himself with his own petard' here!

4. Mental causation

Again, many people believe that this is still a mystery. Almost everyone accepts that 'mental' events **do** cause 'physical' events; when you 'will' your arm to rise, for example, it invariably **does rise**, unless prevented from doing so by intrinsic physiological weakness or mechanical constraint. But we still have **no idea** of the nature of the crucial link between the purely **mental act** of 'willing' and the start of the well-understood **neurophysiological chain** from the innards of the brain to the muscles that **realise** the wishes of the mind. Unless, of course, you believe (like John Searle) that 'thoughts' and other 'mental acts' are **not** 'weightless' and 'ethereal', but **are** the actual electrical and chemical processes that are taking place within the brain. Searle, as we have seen, believes that 'mental states' and 'mental events' are simply 'features of the brain', and have two levels of description – a 'higher level' in 'mental' terms, and a 'lower level' in 'physiological' terms. He contends that the very same 'causal' powers of the system can be described at either level. It has to be said that some recent thinking about the matter does not fully support Searle's position. Possibly on-going work on the so-called **quantum Zeno effect** (a mind-brain phenomenon based on 'quantum decoherence' that appears to occur at a very deep level) will eventually give us some idea about how the crucial link occurs, but there is no guarantee that this will happen in the foreseeable future – if at all.

5. Long-term memory

Surprisingly, this is often overlooked when the mind-body problem is discussed, but, despite the vast amount of research that has been carried out in this area, it still remains a major mystery. Ever since I moved into educational development in 1973, I have been involved in trying to teach tertiary-level lecturers about how students learn, so that they can make sure that their **teaching** is as effective as possible. I have also been heavily involved in writing study guides for students, in order to help them to **learn** in the most effective way. During the latter part of my career, I also became involved in supervising academic staff in education-related Ph.D. projects, all of which involved trying to improve student learning in different ways. I have published extensively in all these areas, producing numerous academic papers, booklets and books related to the teaching/learning process, and I think that I have made a significant contribution to the improvement of the efficiency and effectiveness of this. What I have **not** been able to do is explain to anybody what goes on **in the brain-mind system** when learning actually takes place, because nobody really understands what goes on 'in there'. In particular, nobody knows how information is **stored** in the **long-term memory system**, and how we are able to **access** this information so readily.

Many years ago, the brilliant Hungarian-born American physicist, mathematician and computer pioneer, John von Neumann (1903-1957), calculated that over the course of the average human lifetime, the brain-mind system stores something of the order of 2.8×10^{20} (280 million, million, million) 'bits' of information in its long-term memory. This is a staggering amount of information, and brain researchers have long struggled, without any significant success so far, to come up with a mechanism that explains such a vast capability. Recent efforts to explain long-term memory in terms of neurophysiological activities **within** the brain (e.g., changes in the strength of 'synaptic links', or the development of new 'neural networks') have so far failed to do so, as did earlier attempts to locate 'memory storage systems' analogous to those used in digital computers. What makes matters even more puzzling is the well-established fact that our long-term memories remain largely intact for a very long time while the physical structure of the brain and our short-term memory and cognitive functions are being slowly destroyed by diseases such as vascular dementia. I recently had to go through the harrowing experience of watching my wife, Lindsay, slowly dying of this dreadful disease, over a five-year period. During this time, it was clear that her long-term memory remained **virtually completely intact** until she was approaching the final horrible stages, which she was mercifully spared due to the onset of pneumonia, which our family decided should be allowed 'to take its natural course' on the advice of the hospital medical staff. This experience has strengthened my already-growing belief that long-term memories are not stored **within the physical structure of the brain,** but **somewhere else.**

This may seem a ridiculous suggestion for an experienced scientist to make, but, I believe that I have very sound reasons for doing so, since two very-plausible theories about how this **might** take place have been developed during the last fifty years or so. The first is the theory first suggested by the American neurophysiologist, Karl Pribram, in 1966;

he believes that long-term memories are stored 'holographically' on a 'hidden layer of reality'. I will have much more to say about this 'holographic universe theory' in the final chapter of the book, but, will also refer readers who are interested in the idea to 'The Holographic Universe', by Michael Talbot, which was first published in 1991. This is a truly 'mind-blowing' book, which may change your views about the 'nature of reality' forever. The second is the 'morphic field' theory that was suggested by the maverick biologist, Rupert Sheldrake, in 1981, in 'A New Science of Life'. To say that this caused a 'furore' would be the 'understatement of the century': it was even the subject of an extraordinary attack by the (then) Editor of Nature, who suggested that it was 'A Book For Burning?' (I do not think that Voltaire would have approved of that!). At any rate, Sheldrake continued to develop his theory, which maintains that long-term memories, and indeed many other types of 'information', are 'stored' in all-pervading 'morphic fields'. I have always found his ideas fascinating, and my interest was further enhanced when he published a second major book on the subject in 1988 – 'The Presence of the Past – Morphic Resonance and the Habits of Nature'. As in the case of 'The Holographic Universe', I recommend this book to readers who want to learn more about Sheldrake's ideas; once again, it is a truly 'mind-blowing' book, which may again change your ideas about the 'nature of reality' forever.

Are we any nearer to (dis)solving the mind-body problem?

So, dear readers, where does all this leave us? On the basis of the above analysis, I think that we have to conclude that the modern 'neurophysiological model' of the brain-mind system has, **despite its many spectacular achievements**, so far failed to give a satisfactory explanation of **any** of the five key features of the 'mental world' that I listed at the start of the previous section of this chapter. Thus, we may have to agree with Popper's conclusion that 'behind the veil of monistic protestations there still lurks the dualism of body and mind'. We may also have to agree with Kant that there are some aspects of reality that are, **and will always remain**, completely beyond our understanding, although I hope that this will not prove to be the case. Certainly, the 'mind-body problem' is still very much with us, in my opinion, and is likely to be around for some time yet.

Some of the sources of information on material covered in Chapter 10

This chapter is a greatly-expanded version of an article that I had published electronically in 2016 ('Is There Still a Mind-Body Problem?', by Emeritus Professor Henry Ellington); this is no longer generally available, since the company that published it (Quo Vadis Publications Ltd.) is no longer trading. I also drew on many of the sources in my personal library when writing the chapter, the main ones being the following:

- 'Minds, Brains and Science', by John Searle (the book based on his 1984 Reith Lectures with the same overall title).
- 'Confession of a Philosopher, by Bryan Magee (once again!)
- 'The Story of Philosophy' by Bryan Magee (once again!)
- 'The Concept of Mind', by Gilbert Ryle.
- 'Objective Knowledge', by Karl Popper.
- 'Consciousness Explained', by Daniel Dennett.
- 'The Universe in a Single Atom', by His Holiness, The Dalai Lama.
- 'The Holographic Universe', by Michael Talbot.
- 'The Presence of the Past', by Rupert Sheldrake.

Chapter 11: 'The Einsteinian Revolution' and its aftermath

'There is nothing new to be discovered in physics now. All that remains is more and more precise measurement'.

- Lord Kelvin (1900)

Although this is a lovely quotation, and seems to imply that one of the greatest physicists of the 19th century had a highly-complacent view of the state of contemporary physics, quoting him 'out of context' actually does him a grave injustice. When he gave the speech from which the quotation is taken at the Royal Institution in London on April 27th, 1900, he was actually drawing the attention of the audience to the two most serious outstanding 'puzzles' which then confronted physicists, puzzles which he referred to as 'two clouds' which were currently obscuring 'the beauty and clearness' of the all-embracing Newtonian paradigm. Many physicists hoped that these 'clouds' were 'mere puffs in an otherwise clear blue sky'. As it turned out, they were the 'heralds of storms' that would bring the whole structure tumbling down, to be replaced by what would eventually become the 'two great pillars of 20th century physics'- Einstein's 'theory of relativity' and 'quantum theory'. Let us now see exactly how this happened.

The main achievements of Newtonian science by 1900

I have already described the development of the 'Newtonian world picture' and the subsequent major achievements of 'Newtonian science' in some detail in Chapter 7, so there is no need for me to repeat myself here. I will, however, provide a brief review of what Newton and his successors had achieved by the end of the 19th century in order to remind readers of these, and to prepare the ground for what is to follow.

First, Newton greatly clarified our ideas regarding the nature of the 'basic framework' within which the Universe operated. This consisted of fixed, three-dimensional 'Euclidean' space which extended indefinitely far out in all directions, so that there was no 'edge' or 'boundary' to the Newtonian Universe. Within this framework time flowed 'smoothly' and 'linearly', extending indefinitely far back into the past, and indefinitely far forward into the future. (It was true that Kant had challenged this neat picture in 1781 by highlighting the logical problems raised by his 'antinomies' of space and time, but these had been largely ignored by physicists, probably because most of them were unaware of Kant's ideas at the time.)

Second, he developed a purely-'materialistic' model of the 'world', which he believed to consist of hard, indivisible 'particles' (or 'atoms') moving in an 'empty void', with all larger bodies (such as planets) being composed of 'aggregations' of such particles. The movements of these particles and aggregates were governed by the 'three laws of motion' and 'law of universal gravitation' that he had 'discovered' (with help from his illustrious predecessor, Galileo, of course).

Finally, he believed that we live in a wholly-'deterministic' universe, whose evolution depended entirely on what had gone on before. As we have seen, he often compared it to a 'clock', which, once it had been 'created' and 'started up' by God, would continue to 'run smoothly forever', in accordance with the 'laws' that he had developed, and had presented to an amazed world in his 'masterwork'- 'Principia'.

As I showed in the final section of Chapter 7, the 'Newtonian paradigm' had effectively succeeded in explaining **all** known physical phenomena by the end of the 19th century. First, it turned astronomy into an exact mathematical science, describing, with apparently perfect accuracy, the movements of the planets, and also the movements of the stars. Then, it 'absorbed' the new science of 'thermodynamics' that was developed during the 19th century, and then did the same for the even-newer science of 'electromagnetism' that had been brought to maturity by the work of James Clerk Maxwell. It was these spectacular achievements that led the eminent American physicist, Albert Michelson, to claim, in 1894, that 'the grand underlying principles' of his subject had been 'firmly established', and that 'further truths of physics' were to be 'looked for in the sixth place of decimals'. And, of course, they led the even-more-eminent Lord Kelvin to make his famous 1900 speech to the Royal Institution, and to make the somewhat ill-judged prediction for which he will always be remembered.

Some 'niggling problems' with the Newtonian paradigm

In the 'prefix' to this chapter, I showed how Lord Kevin had identified two annoying 'clouds', which threatened to disturb the otherwise-perfect 'world picture' presented by the all-conquering 'Newtonian paradigm'. Actually, there were three such 'clouds', but the two identified by Lord Kevin in his Royal Institution speech were by far the most worrying. The third had been puzzling astronomers for a very long time, and they were no nearer to solving it at the end of the 19th century than they had been in the 18th century, when it first came to their attention. In order of importance, the three 'niggling problems' were the 'ether problem', the 'ultra-violet catastrophe' and the 'anomalous precession of the perihelion of Mercury'. Let me now try to explain what each of them involved

1. The 'ether problem'

As I showed you in Chapter 7, one of the greatest triumphs of 19th century physics was the development by James Clerk Maxwell of what appeared to be a complete and perfect theory of electromagnetism, as encapsulated in what became known as 'Maxwell's equations'. Among other things, this showed that 'light' was a type of 'electromagnetic wave', and was in fact only a tiny part of a vast 'electromagnetic spectrum'. We now know that this ranges from 'radio waves' with wavelengths up a million metres, through 'microwaves', 'infra-red light', 'visible light', ultra-violet light' and 'x-rays', down to high-energy 'gamma rays' with wavelengths less than a million, million, times smaller than a metre. To use modern 'scientific' notation and nomenclature, this means that the entire electromagnetic spectrum ranges over 20 'orders of magnitude' in wavelength, from over 10^6m to less than 10^{-14}m.

Now scientists had been studying waves for a very long time before Maxwell made this ground-breaking discovery, and knew that all waves require a 'medium' through which to propagate. 'Sound waves', for example, propagate through 'air' (and also through virtually all other media), while 'water waves' propagate along the surface of any open body of water. Thus, physicists assumed that Maxwell's electromagnetic waves would also require a suitable medium through which to propagate, since the idea of them being able to move through empty space (Newton's 'void') seemed ridiculous. They therefore came up with the concept of the 'luminiferous ether', usually shortened to 'ether', a medium that they believed permeated the whole of Newton's fixed, three-dimensional 'Euclidean' space. During the latter stages of the 19th century, much of the work of theoretical physicists involved 'investigating' the 'properties' of this hypothetical 'ether', while experimental physicists tried to prove that it actually existed.

In 1887, Albert Michelson (of whom we have already heard) and his colleague Edward Morley, working at the Case Institute of Technology in Cleveland, carried out one of the key experiments in the history of science – an experiment designed to detect the Earth's motion through the (supposedly fixed) ether. They used an instrument later called the 'Michelson interferometer' for this purpose, now one of the standard pieces of equipment in advanced physics laboratories (I used one in the later stages of my honours degree at Aberdeen University). This uses mirrors to split a beam of monochromatic light into two rays moving at right angles to one another, which are then reflected back and recombined to form 'interference fringes'. The key principle on which the experiment was based was that the resulting 'interference pattern' should gradually change as the Earth moved along its orbit round the Sun, since the two rays would be moving in different directions through the ether, thus allowing the Earth's velocity with respect to the ether to be measured with an extremely high degree of accuracy. It was therefore a considerable shock to Michelson and Morley, and to the world physics community, that no such motion was detected, a 'null result' that was always found when the experiment was repeated in other laboratories – which it was on many occasions. Clearly, something was seriously wrong with one of the key features of the Newtonian paradigm.

2. The 'ultra-violet catastrophe'

This is a highly-technical problem that is difficult to explain to people who lack an advanced education in theoretical physics, but I will do my best. It stems from the ground-breaking work on statistical mechanics that was carried out in the latter part of the 19th century, when physicists were attempting to incorporate all aspects of thermodynamics and electromagnetism within the overall Newtonian paradigm. Most of this work was extremely successful, as I showed in the final section of Chapter 7, but there was one problem that was causing particular difficulties – trying to explain the shape of the 'black body emission spectrum'. To physicists, a 'black body' is one that 'absorbs' all the radiation falling onto its surface, and, as a consequence of one of the basic laws of physics (Kirchoff's Law) is also a 'perfect emitter'. Physicists were able to model such 'black bodies' by coating the inside of a thin hollow sphere with a diffuse layer of black pigment and cutting a small circular hole in its surface; this hole then effectively behaved as a perfect 'black body', and enabled physicists to carry out detailed study of the 'emission spectra' that such bodies produced when heated to different temperatures. When they plotted the amount of energy produced at different wavelengths of the electromagnetic spectrum against the wavelengths themselves, they found that the **basic shape** of the resulting spectrum was the same at all temperatures, with the amount of energy first rising from zero, reaching a peak, and then gradually falling to zero again. (The **total amount of energy emitted** and the **position of the energy peak** were both strongly dependent on the temperature, but there is no need for me to go into this here). Towards the end of the 19th century, two British physicists called Rayleigh and Jeans produced what became known as the 'Rayleigh-Jeans Theory' of the black body emission spectrum. This is far too complicated to explain here, but the essence of the theory was that it gave a fairly-accurate description of the 'high-wavelength' part of the spectrum, but failed catastrophically at the 'low wavelength' ('ultra violet') end of the spectrum, predicting that the amount of energy emitted should 'become infinite' as the wavelength approached zero, instead of falling to zero, as the experimentalists had shown. As in the case of the non-detection of motion through the ether, this so-called 'ultra-violet catastrophe' again suggested that there was something seriously wrong with one of the key features of the Newtonian world-picture.

3.   The anomalous precession of the perihelion of Mercury

As I told you in Chapter 7, one of the greatest triumphs of Newtonian science was its ability to explain the movements of the planets of the solar system with perfect accuracy. There was, however, one planet - Mercury - for which this was not quite the case. This had by far the most 'elliptical' orbit of all the planets known at the time, and astronomers found that it never moved along the same orbit twice, with the line from the Sun to the 'perihelion' of its orbit (its closest approach to the Sun) 'precessing' at a tiny but measurable rate on each successive orbit. Newton's mathematical theory of planetary motion did in fact **predict** such a 'precession', but the value that it 'predicted' was less than the **observed value**. The 'anomalous precession of the perihelion of Mercury' remained one of the most annoying 'unsolved problems' in astronomy as the 19th century drew to a close. One of the most serious attempts to solve it had been made by the French astronomer Urbain le Verrier, co-discoverer along with the English astronomer John Couch Adams of Neptune (see Chapter 17 for details). He postulated the existence of a hitherto– undetected planet, 'Vulcan', **inside** the orbit of Mercury, a planet whose 'gravitational pull' could be 'perturbing' the movement of Mercury by the exact amount required to 'explain' its 'anomalous' movement. Such a planet was never discovered, however, and the 'Vulcan' theory was quietly abandoned.

The scientific revolution inaugurated by Einstein and his colleagues

We are now ready to turn our attention to the 'main business' of this chapter, description of what the so-called 'Einsteinian Revolution' involved. Before we do so, however, let us take a look at the remarkable life of the remarkable man who was largely responsible for bringing it about – Albert Einstein. The entry on Einstein in the 1990 edition of 'Chambers Biographical Dictionary' begins by stating that he 'ranks with Galileo and Newton as one of the great revisers of man's understanding of the Universe', to which I can only add, 'hear, hear!'

He was born in Ulm, in Bavaria, in 1879, to Jewish parents, and was educated in Munich, Arau and Zurich, becoming a Swiss citizen in 1901. In 1902, he became an examiner at the Swiss Patent Office, a not-particularly-onerous job which left him plenty of time to pursue his **real** interest – the theoretical aspects of the current outstanding problems in physics. In 1905, which later became known as his 'annus mirabilis', he published three papers in Volume 17 of the prestigious German journal, 'Annalen der Physik', each dealing with a different subject, and each today acknowledged to be a 'masterpiece'. The first proposed a model that provided a complete explanation of a recently-discovered phenomenon - the 'photoelectric effect' – by suggesting that light consisted of discrete particles called 'photons'. The second, on 'Brownian motion', provided the first unequivocal demonstration of the existence of 'atoms', something that many distinguished physicists had refused to believe in up to then. The third, and by far the most important, was his ground-breaking first paper on 'special relativity', a paper which utterly changed the way in which physicists viewed the world, as we will see later in this section of Chapter 11.

As a result of this work, Einstein achieved international fame, and he soon left his lowly job in the Swiss Patent Office in order to increase his academic qualifications. Until 1909, however, he held no regular academic position, something that was causing considerable embarrassment in view of his increasing fame. In that year, a special junior professorship was created for him in Zurich, after which he took up a more senior post in Prague in 1911, before moving back to Zurich in 1912 and then to Berlin in 1914, where he was appointed Director of the highly-prestigious Kaiser Wilhelm Physical Institute, a post that he held until 1933. It was during this meteoric rise through the academic world that he developed his even-more-revolutionary theory of 'general relativity', publishing this in 1915. (I will again describe this work in more detail later in this section of Chapter 11). In 1922, Einstein was awarded the (delayed 1921) Nobel Prize in Physics, **not** for his work on 'special' and 'general relativity' (which was considered 'too controversial' by the Nobel Committee), but for his work on the 'photoelectric effect'. By 1930, his 'best work' had been completed, and, after Hitler's rise to power, he (very wisely) moved from Germany to the USA. From 1934 onwards, he lectured at Princeton, becoming an American citizen and a professor at Princeton in 1940. In 1939, he wrote to President Roosevelt, warning him of the possibility that Germany might make an atomic bomb, thus playing a major role in initiating the 'Manhattan Project' that enabled America to do so, with considerable help from the British, and from a large number of prominent scientists who had moved to America from Europe during the 1930's. After the end of the Second World War, he became heavily involved in politics, urging the international control of atomic weapons, and protesting against the activities of the 'Un-

American Activities Senate Subcommittee', which had persecuted many prominent scientists because of their (alleged) 'communist sympathies'. As we will see in Chapter 14, he devoted much of the latter part of his life to an unsuccessful attempt to find a 'theory of everything'. He died in America in 1955, by which time he was by far 'the most famous scientist in the world'. What a man!

Between 1905 and 1915, Einstein effectively re-directed the course of modern physics. Although he is best known for his 'special' and 'general theories of relativity', he also played a leading role in the development of 'quantum theory'. In this chapter, I will describe his work on relativity in some detail, but will only provide a brief review of his work on quantum theory, since an entire chapter will be devoted to this topic later in the book (Chapter 14).

As we saw in the previous section of this chapter, the main 'puzzle' that had confronted physicists during the latter years of the 19th century and the start of the 20th century had been the failure to detect the motion of the Earth through the supposedly-fixed 'ether', the 'medium' through which electromagnetic waves were believed to propagate. A number of attempts had been made to 'save' the ether and the concept of 'absolute space', the most ingenious and important of these being the 'Fitzgerald/Lorentz Theory'. This proposed that bodies moving through the ether experienced a 'contraction' in their length along the direction of their motion that was just enough to explain the 'null result' of the Michelson-Morley experiment. In hindsight, the 'Fitzgerald/Lorentz contraction' hypothesis looks like a desperate, 'ad-hoc' attempt to save a threatened theory, but it was later shown to be a key component of Einstein's 'special theory of relativity', but **without** any need for the 'ether' or for 'absolute space'. Let us now see what this theory involved.

At the heart of Einstein's special theory of relativity was a completely new way of thinking about 'location' and 'motion'. In the 'classical physics' that had been developed by Galileo and Newton, these were defined in respect of 'absolute space'. In 'relativity theory', a body's 'location' and 'speed' were defined only in respect of a specific 'frame or reference', or 'state of motion' of an 'observer'. As a consequence, the **lengths** of objects, the **intervals of time** between events, and whether or not two 'events' are **simultaneous** all depend on the 'frame of reference' within which one asks the question. Another key feature of the theory is that **the speed of light, 'c', is the same in all frames of reference**, and is one of the **fundamental constants of nature**. Stranger still, 'space' and 'time' become 'entwined' with one another in a new 'structure' known as **four dimensional space-time**. And strangest of all, **mass** can be converted into **energy** (and vice versa), the relationship between the two being defined by Einstein's 'signature equation', '$E = mc^2$'. It was **this** discovery by Einstein that eventually led to the development of the 'atomic bomb' during the Second World War. Let us now take a closer look at all these key features of the theory.

First of all, Einstein derived new 'transformation rules', showing how the 'lengths' of 'objects' and the 'intervals of time' between 'events' depended on the 'frame of reference' of the chosen 'observer'. These are called the 'Lorentz transformations', and differ from the classical 'Galilean' transformations in the way in which they 'mix' the variables representing 'space' and 'time', and involve the 'speed of light', c. They are too complicated to be included in a non-mathematical book like this one, but can be found in any basic text on special relativity. The essential feature of the 'transformation rules' is that the apparent 'length' of an object **shrinks** along the direction of 'relative motion' with respect to the observer, and that the apparent time interval between events **increases** if the two 'events' are moving relative to one another, a process known as 'time dilation'. Both of these effects have subsequently been 'verified' by countless experiments.

Second, Einstein showed that there was no such thing as 'absolute simultaneity', because there was no such thing as 'absolute time' in his new theory, only 'relative time' that depended on the 'relative motion' of the events involved. Consider two events 'A' and 'B' for example. Depending on the 'relative motions' of these, 'A' can occur **before** 'B', **at the same time as** 'B', or **after** 'B'. Once again, these apparently counter-intuitive effects have subsequently been 'verified' by countless experiments.

Third, Einstein's statement that the speed of light is the same for **all** observers has again been 'verified' by countless subsequent experiments, despite the fact that it 'violates' one of the fundamental principles of classical Newtonian mechanics – the 'velocity addition law'. Consider two 'observers', 'A' and 'B' who are moving towards one another at half the speed of light, and are shining 'torches' at one another. If each observer measures the 'speed' of the 'photons' arriving from the other's torch, each will find that it is **exactly** 'c'. Strange, but true!

Fourth, the combination of 'space' and 'time' into four-dimensional 'space-time'. This idea was first developed by Hermann Minkowski, one of Einstein's old teachers, in 1908. As a result, physicists now regard 'things' that happen in space and time as 'space-time events', and represent what used to be regarded as 'physical objects' in the traditional sense as 'world-lines' in four-dimensional space-time.

Fifth, Einstein's prediction that 'mass' and 'energy' were inter-convertible. Classical physics had developed separate 'conservation laws' for 'mass' and 'energy', but Einstein had shown that they were in fact two different aspects of some more fundamental aspect of nature. As a result of Einstein's work, physicists have now replaced the two original conservation laws by the 'law of conservation of mass/energy', which is now regarded as one of the fundamental laws of physics.

A final prediction of Einstein's theory was that the **mass** of an object depends on the **relative motion** of the object with respect to an observer, **increasing** as the latter increases. Physicists now distinguish between the **rest mass** of such an object and its **relativistic mass**, which **becomes infinitely large** as its speed with respect to the observer approaches the speed of light. It is because of this effect (which has again been 'verified' by countless subsequent experiments) that the 'speed of light' is now regarded as an 'absolute speed limit' in all physical processes. Not much hope of travelling at 'warp speed', then!

So much for 'special relativity'. Let us now look at 'general relativity', which is, in many ways, even stranger, despite the fact that its essential features can be 'summed up' by the following simple words of the eminent American physicist, John Wheeler:

'**Matter** tells **space** how to **curve**; **space** tells **matter** how to **move**'.

Just **how** 'matter tells space how to curve', and **how** 'space tells matter how to move' are rather more complicated however, and the 'field equations' of Einstein's 'general theory of relativity' are just about **the** most complicated and difficult-to-solve ever to be devised by the human mind. Just how complicated they are can be judged from an article that appeared in the May, 2017 issue of 'Physics World', which stated that 'powerful computers are now allowing cosmologists to solve Einstein's frighteningly complex equations in a cosmological setting for the first time'. Despite this, 'general relativity' has been one of the two 'cornerstones' of physics for over 100 years, so I will now try to give you **some** idea of what it involves, as best I can.

Shortly after presenting his 'special theory of relativity' in 1905, Einstein began to worry about the fact that its scope was limited to transformations among 'inertial', frames, frames moving relative to one another with constant velocity in a straight line. He asked himself whether a more 'general theory' could be developed, one valid for transformation among frames moving 'arbitrarily ' with respect to one another. He took a major step towards such a theory in 1907, with what we now call his 'elevator' thought-experiment, through which he discovered a deep connection between 'accelerated frames of reference' and 'gravitation'. From this, he formulated the key insight of his 'equivalence principle', which asserts that 'uniform acceleration' (as in a lift) is equivalent to a 'homogeneous gravitational field'. This cleared up an old problem from Newtonian physics – why the term for 'mass' in Newton's second law of motion ('inertial mass') always has the same numerical value as the term for 'mass' in the law of universal gravitation ('gravitational mass'). Einstein's radical answer was that inertial and gravitational mass were equal because they were **one and the same property of a body**, as a direct consequence of the equivalence principle's demonstration of the indistinguishability of **uniform acceleration** and **gravitation.** Einstein made another important prediction from the same 'equivalence principle', namely, that electromagnetic waves would also be unable to distinguish between acceleration and gravity, so that the paths of **light rays** should be **curved** in the presence of a gravitational field. His predicted bending of light rays in strong gravitational fields like that of the Sun became the basis of the most famous 'confirmation' of his 'theory of general relativity' in 1919, as we will see later.

To cut a long story short, Einstein spent the next eight years trying to convert his **qualitative** ideas into a sound mathematical theory that would be able to make firm **quantitative predictions** that could be tested experimentally. As we will see in Chapter 17, he eventually succeeded in doing this when he was introduced to the mathematical work of Bernhard Riemann on 'differential geometry', which provided him with just the 'tools' that he needed to carry out the work. He completed this in 1915, and presented his 'general theory of relativity' to an astounded world. This showed how the 'curvature' of 'space-time' at a particular point was determined by the 'mass-energy density' at that point, as described by complicated 'mathematical objects' called the 'metric tensor' and the 'stress-energy tensor', whose nature I will not even **begin** to try to describe! Suffice to say that they converted Wheeler's beautifully-simple summary of general relativity into a set of 'field equations' that could be used by physicists and astronomers to make definite predictions – if they were clever enough to do so, and not many people **were**, at the time!

There is a simple 'mental picture' that can help non-mathematicians to understand how space-time curvature determines motion. Try to imagine that 'space' is a two-dimensional 'rubber sheet', stretched on a circular frame, so that it is 'flat'. If a marble is rolled across such a sheet, it will travel in a straight line, **because** the 'space' that it is moving across if 'flat'. Now place a heavy object such as a 'bowling ball' at the centre of the sheet. This will depress the centre of the sheet, causing it to 'curve'. Now roll the marble across the sheet, and you will find that it moves on a 'curved path', just as if it was being deflected by a gravitational field. You would also find that you could, with a little skill, make the marble move in a 'circular path' round the bowling ball, just as the Earth moves in a 'circular path' round the Sun. What Einstein succeeded in doing with his 'general theory of relativity' was to explain 'gravitational forces' in terms of the 'geometry' of 'curved space-time', one of the greatest intellectual achievements in the history of science. As I said earlier, 'what a man!'

Einstein's 'general theory of relativity' had two early successes. First, it solved the outstanding problem of the 'anomalous precession of the perihelion of Mercury', since the rate of precession predicted by application of Einstein's field equations to the movement of Mercury round the Sun turned out to be **exactly** the same as the observed rate. Second, Einstein's key prediction that light rays would be 'bent' when they passed close to a massive object like the Sun turned out to be true. Einstein had proposed that his prediction could be 'tested' during a total eclipse of the Sun, when the Sun's light is blocked by the Moon. In 1919, following the end of the First World War, the British astronomer, Arthur Eddington, organized expeditions to Africa and South America in order to test Einstein's theory. Eddington's announcement in November 1919 that they had **confirmed** the prediction catapulted Einstein from being merely the world's most-respected **scientist** to being, for a time, possibly the world's most famous **person**. Einstein's theory went from strength to strength during the next hundred years, and, at the time of writing this (July, 2020) **every single one** of its predictions has been successfully verified. As I said earlier, it is now one of the two 'central pillars' of physics, the other being 'quantum theory', in whose early development Einstein also played a leading part.

As I explained earlier in this chapter, the failure of 'classical' Newtonian physics to explain the 'shape' of the 'black-body emission spectrum' (the so-called 'ultra-violet catastrophe') had been one of the great 'unsolved problems' of the latter part of the 19th century. The problem was subsequently 'solved' by Max Planck (1848 – 1947) and Einstein. In 1900, Planck made the revolutionary suggestion that electromagnetic radiation is not emitted by a black body as a 'continuous spectrum', as was predicted by 'classical', Newtonian physics, but in discrete 'packets', or 'quanta'.

Neither 'classical mechanics' nor 'classical electrodynamics' allowed for such a discontinuous release of energy, but Planck's new theory for the shape of the black-body spectrum 'worked', so it was assumed that it was pointing physicists towards some deep, new insight into the nature of reality. That 'insight' was provided by Einstein in 1905, with his even-more-revolutionary suggestion that 'light' consisted of 'discrete particles' called 'photons' rather than continuous waves. As we will see in Chapter 14, it was **this** suggestion that provided the basic model on which the whole of the subsequent development of 'quantum theory', the most successful theory in the history of physics, was based. Einstein continued to play a key role in its development until the late – 1920's, by which time the basic principles of quantum theory had been more or less established. For one man to have played such a key role in the development of **both** of the key theories of 20th – century physics is an unprecedented feat that will probably never be repeated.

Subsequent later developments in science

The 'Einsteinian Revolution' influenced virtually everything else that happened in physics and astronomy during the remainder of the 20th century and thereafter, as will be evident from the remaining chapters of this book. It also had a profound and lasting effect on the way **science itself was practised**, and on the perceived **status of scientific knowledge**, as I will now show by looking in some detail at the work of the two men who had the greatest influence on these – Karl Popper and Thomas Kuhn.

Karl Popper (1902 – 1992) was born in Vienna to middle-class parents, and, after studying mathematics and physics, began his career as a secondary school teacher. His first book, 'Logik der Forschung' (later published in English as 'The Logic of Scientific Discovery') appeared in 1934, and presented a completely revolutionary view of the nature and status of scientific knowledge and the way in which it is acquired. These views were greatly influenced by the work of Einstein in overthrowing the long-standing 'Newtonian' world picture, and formed the basis of virtually all his later work. Popper emigrated to New Zealand in 1937 in order to escape persecution and probable murder by the Nazis because of his Jewish ancestry, and throughout the Second World War, lectured in philosophy at Canterbury University College. During this period, he worked on what is probably his best-known book, 'The Open Society and its Enemies', which was published in English in 1945. When the war ended, he moved to England, becoming a Reader at the London School of Economics, and, in 1949, becoming Professor of Logic and Scientific Method, a post that he held until he retired in 1969. He acquired British citizenship, was knighted in 1965, and became widely acclaimed as 'the greatest philosopher of science who has ever lived'. His later books included 'The Poverty of Historicism' (1957), 'Conjectures and Refutations' (1963), 'Objective Knowledge' (1972), and 'The Self and Its Brain' (1977), all of which had considerable influence on contemporary thought. He continued working and publishing until the end of his life in 1992, always producing 'new' and 'exciting' ideas.

As we saw in Chapter 7, the universally-accepted view of science until 1934 was that which had been developed by Francis Bacon early in the 17th century. He pictured scientific study in a particular area as starting with the open-minded 'accumulation of data', followed by the development on an 'explanatory hypothesis' by the process of 'scientific induction'. This was then 'tested' by carrying out key experiments, and, if the hypothesis was 'verified', acquired the status of a 'scientific law', and became a 'permanent addition' to the body of 'certain scientific knowledge'.

In 'Logik der Forschung', Popper showed that the 'Baconian' model of science was flawed in virtually every respect. First, he showed that a 'scientific investigation' does **not** start with the 'open-minded accumulation of data', since **no** experiment can be carried out without having at least a rough idea of the sort of result that is expected. In his view, all scientific investigations should start with the realization that a **problem** of some sort exists, often a significant intellectual achievement in its own right. Next, he argued that scientific theories are **not** arrived at by the process of 'scientific induction', which the 18th – century philosopher, David Hume had shown to be 'logically impossible', as we saw in Chapter 8. Hume's work had cast doubt on the very **status** of scientific knowledge as **certain truth**, an argument that was fully accepted by Popper. Popper maintained that the development of 'scientific theories' was essentially a **creative process** which occurred in ways that were seldom fully understood even by the people involved. Then, he claimed that scientific hypotheses should **not** be tested by attempting to prove them to be **true**, which Hume had shown to be **logically impossible**. Rather they should be tested by trying to think of specific ways in which they might be shown to be **false**, and then carrying out experiments to see if they **are false**. Popper recognized that it is, in principle, possible to prove that a hypothesis is false by carrying out a **single key experiment**, just as the 'ether' hypothesis had been comprehensively falsified by the 'null result' of the Michelson-Morley experiment. Indeed, he regarded such testing by 'attempted falsification' as the 'criterion of demarcation' that distinguished **science** from other, less-rigorous fields of study such as **philosophy** and **religion**, and also from **pseudo-sciences** such as **Marxism** and **Freudian psychoanalysis**. Finally, Popper asserted that a hypothesis that **survives** this process of attempted falsification does **not** automatically acquire the status of **certain truth**, and become a **permanent part** of the growing body of **scientific knowledge**. Rather, is should be regarded as a **provisional working hypothesis** only for as long as it continues to 'fit in with' observations. In other words, **all** 'scientific knowledge' should be regarded as **temporary** and **provisional**, since even the 'best scientific theories' are almost certain to be superseded by 'even better theories' in due course.

Popper went on to propose a **completely new model** of the **scientific method** from that which had been developed by Bacon. The first stage involves realizing that a **problem situation** of some sort exists, which, as we have seen, is often a 'significant intellectual achievement' in its own right. The second stage involves formulation of a **trial solution** to this 'problem situation', usually in the form of a **hypothesis**, **theory** or **model** of some sort. The third (and crucial) stage involves subjecting this 'trial solution' to **empirical testing** by **attempted falsification** of the **most rigorous type**. Once this process has been completed, the 'trial solution' should be **rejected**, **modified**, or **provisionally accepted**, depending on the outcome. Popper also produced a **basic methodological schema**, which he believed could be applied to the resolution of **virtually all problem situations,** not merely those in science.

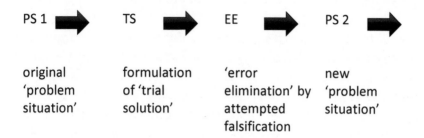

PS 1	TS	EE	PS 2
original 'problem situation'	formulation of 'trial solution'	'error elimination' by attempted falsification	new 'problem situation'

Popper regarded his 'schema' as part of an ongoing, open-ended process, since the solution of one problem usually gives rise to a new one in due course. Once I had been introduced to his ideas during the mid–1970's, I made them the basis of virtually all my work on progressive educational development, particularly in the area of 'educational evaluation'. Practically all the books on 'educational gaming and simulation' and the 'systems approach to instructional design' that I and my colleagues have written are firmly based on 'Popperian principles'. I made Popper 'required reading' for all of them!

The ideas first presented in 'Logik der Forschung' have influenced whole generations of scientists, affecting not only the way in which they carry out their work, but also their entire attitude towards science. Before Popper, the ultimate 'sin' in science was to be proved **wrong** – to publish work that was subsequently discredited. After Popper, it was realized that being shown to have been mistaken was nothing to be ashamed of, since it is only when ideas are subjected to stringent testing **and possible falsification** that science can advance at all. Indeed, a theory that proves to be 'inadequate' (as **all** theories eventually do), can in some cases, play a far more important role in the development of science than one that is corroborated by the various experiments that are carried out in order to test it.

One of the best examples of a theory of this type was the so-called 'steady-state theory' of cosmology that was proposed by Hoyle, Bondi and Gold during the late 1940's. This theory was developed in response to a very real 'problem situation', the fact that the **apparent age of the Universe** as calculated from the observed rate of expansion and the observed mean distance between galaxies (roughly 1800 million years) was considerably less than the **apparent 'geological age' of the Earth** (roughly 4,500 million years). Hoyle, Bondi and Gold attempted to explain this 'discrepancy' by postulating that the Universe has always been, and will always be, basically as it is now, with the space between galaxies that are produced by its observed expansion being filled by 'new galaxies' – formed from hydrogen that is being 'continuously created' throughout space. Subsequent astronomical work showed that the mean distance between galaxies is very much greater than had hitherto been supposed, and that the age of the Universe is in fact significantly greater than the age of the Earth (see Chapter 12). By this time, however, Hoyle and his colleagues had developed the 'steady-state theory', into an extremely powerful 'tool' that was having a profound influence on the development of contemporary astronomy. It was, for example, stimulating astronomers into developing and refining their observational techniques, in an attempt to tell whether the 'steady-state theory' or the rival 'big-bang theory' was correct. The newly-born field of 'radio astronomy' was given a particularly important 'boost' by this work. Equally important, the theory was bringing about major advances in the field of 'astrophysics'. For example, Hoyle and his colleagues were able to discover the mechanism whereby all the heavy elements in the Universe came into being (see Chapters 12 and 16).

As we will see once again in Chapter 12, observational evidence carried out since the 1960's has now totally discredited the 'steady-state theory', and the 'big-bang theory' is (for the time being anyway) the generally-accepted model of how the Universe began and subsequently evolved. It is, however, fair to say that astronomy, astrophysics and cosmology would not have made the same tremendous progress that they have during the last 70 years had it not been for the steady-state theory. The most important thing in science is thus not to be **right**, but to be **stimulating** – to produce ideas that 'encourage' (or provoke'!) one's colleagues into 'fruitful work'. Such an idea would have been 'unthinkable' before Popper.

Thomas S. Kuhn (1922-1996) was born in Cincinnati, Ohio. He studied physics at Harvard, with the intention of pursuing a conventional career in the subject. In the course of his graduate studies, however, he happened to take a course in the history of science, which so interested him that it caused a complete change in his plans. On completing his graduate studies in 1948, he first spent a further three years at Harvard, carrying out studies in the history of science and in a variety of other subjects such as philosophy and psychology. He then started his new career as a lecturer in the history of science, first at the University of California, and then at Princeton, as a Professor of the History of Science. During this time, he gradually developed his ideas on the way in which science evolves, eventually publishing his seminal work, 'The Structure of Scientific Revolutions', in 1962. This had an immediate and profound effect on contemporary thought, and it is no exaggeration to say that it caused an entire generation of scientists to look on their discipline in a completely different way. As we saw in

Chapter 9, his 'revolutionary ideas' also had a strong influence on the subsequent appearance of 'post-modernist' philosophy, and on the 'science wars' of the late 20th- century. He moved from Princeton to Massachusetts Institute of Technology in 1979.

All Kuhn's revolutionary ideas on how science evolves were set out in 'The Structure of Scientific Revolutions'. This introduced three completely new concepts, namely, **paradigms, normal science** and **scientific revolutions**, each of which we will now examine in detail.

1. The 'paradigm' concept

As used by Kuhn, a **paradigm** is the basic, generally-accepted **theoretical model** that underlies a particular branch or sub-branch of science at any given time, together with the generally-accepted set of **procedures, rules**, and **standards** that are used by practitioners in the area covered by it. In **chemistry**, for example, the current paradigm is the idea that matter is composed of basic entities called **atoms** comprising a small, central, positively-charged **nucleus** surrounded by a diffuse, negatively-charged **electron-cloud** whose structure determines how atoms combine with one another to form **molecules**. The people we describe as 'chemists' all accept this paradigm without question, and use it as the basis for all their work, which consists essentially of investigating the different ways in which **atoms** combine to form **molecules**, and the **properties** of these molecules once they have been formed. (I apologize to all chemists, who will probably say that I have grossly- oversimplified this!) Different groups of scientists such as 'nuclear physicists' and 'biologists' have other paradigms.

To summarize, the essential features of a **paradigm**, as envisaged by Kuhn, are as follows:

- It forms the **underlying theoretical model** on which a **branch** or **sub-branch of science**, is based at any given time;
- It is **accepted without question** by **all** (or, at the very least, by the **great majority**) of those working in the field at the time;
- it effectively determines the **sort of problems** that such workers **should** and **should not** investigate.
- It effectively determines the way in which such problems are tackled, by giving rise to set **procedures, rules, and standards.**

Within the context of such paradigms, Kuhn's picture of the way in which science develops is that the development process does not take place in a smooth, cumulative fashion, but in a series of rapid, evolutionary 'spurts', interspersed with longer periods of systematic 'consolidation' and 'expansion'. Kuhn describes the 'spurts' as **scientific revolutions**, or **extraordinary science**, and the periods of consolidation and expansion as **normal science**.

2.   Normal science

According to Kuhn, all branches or major sub-branches of science start their development by going through an 'immature' stage in which there is considerable disagreement among practitioners regarding the nature of the 'basic principles' that underlie the field, the 'sort of problems that should be investigated', and the 'way in which these should be tackled'. This stage is often characterized by the existence of different 'schools', each of which has its own strongly-held ideas regarding these matters. A good example of such an 'immature science' is analytical psychology, which still has its 'Freudian' 'Jungian' and 'Adlerian' schools, as far as I am aware. Kuhn believes that a branch of science makes the transition from 'immaturity' to 'maturity' when the ideas of **one** of these rival 'schools' become generally accepted by other workers in the field, and acquire the status of a **paradigm**. When this happens, the workers involved are able to stop arguing about the fundamental principles, procedures and conventions that underlie and define their field, and can move on to more detailed, more specialized work based on their newly-acquired 'paradigm'. Kuhn points out that the great majority of professional scientists spend most, if not all, of their careers carrying out work of this type, without ever **questioning the validity** of the paradigm on which it is based, and with **no expectation** of making **revolutionary discoveries** that will **radically change the basic principles** on which their discipline is founded. This is what we call **normal science**.

In order to illustrate what 'normal science' entails, let us follow the career of a typical scientist – a **chemist**, say. Such a scientist begins by learning the basic facts, techniques, conventions and standards that constitute the 'paradigm' on which their field is founded – first at school, and then at university. If they show sufficient promise, the aspiring chemist may then be allowed to move on to the next stage of their 'apprenticeship' - postgraduate work – which, in the case of the most able, culminates in the award of their **doctorate**. This is effectively a 'licence to practise' normal science within the scope of their particular paradigm. Our chemist may now decide to pursue an 'academic career', or become a full-time research worker, devoting the rest of their life to what Kuhn calls 'puzzle-solving' – tackling a succession of paradigm-based 'research projects' for their employing organization, or on their own behalf, if they have the freedom to do so.

Kuhn believes that the work carried out during a period of 'normal science' falls into three distinct categories:

- using the paradigm to determine 'interesting facts' about the area that it covers, eg investigating the properties of different chemical compounds;
- finding out how the 'predictions' of the paradigm compare with the actual properties of nature, particularly in new, as-yet-unstudied areas;
- trying to 'extend the scope' of the paradigm (what Kuhn calls 'articulation of the paradigm') by, for example, trying to resolve 'initial ambiguities'.

Such activities, do not, in general, produce **unexpected results**. When they **do** begin to do so, this is a sign that the paradigm may be starting to 'break down', and that **normal science** is about to give way to a **scientific revolution**.

3. Scientific revolutions

According to Kuhn, one of the most important characteristics of paradigms is their **resistance to change**. Once workers in a particular field have adopted a paradigm, they are very reluctant to change to a new paradigm, even if confronted with unquestionable evidence that such a change in necessary. Nevertheless, **paradigm changes** (or **paradigm shifts**) do sometimes occur, and Kuhn believes that they are an inevitable consequence of the nature of 'normal science'. As we have seen, this consists essentially of using a paradigm as a jumping-off point for more-specialized, more-detailed work, employing it as a 'tool' to 'push back' the 'frontiers of knowledge'. If a paradigm is sufficiently open-ended and productive of new ideas, such work can last for a very long time – over 200 years in the case of 'Newtonian physics'. Eventually, however, results that simply **cannot** be accommodated within the paradigm will begin start to appear in ever-greater numbers, and the paradigm will begin to 'break down'. When this happens, some workers in the field will start to question its validity, and suggest possible alternatives. At this point, **normal science** will give way to a period of what Kuhn calls **extraordinary science**, with the fundamental concepts of the field being re-examined to determine which of the rival 'new' paradigms is best suited to explaining the new discoveries. Eventually one such paradigm will prove to be sufficiently superior to its rivals to be accepted as the 'new paradigm' for the field, which will then enter a new period of **normal science** based on this new paradigm.

In some ways, 'extraordinary science' is similar to the immature, pre-paradigm science discussed earlier. The main difference is that it invariably takes place against a background of vehement and sustained opposition from the 'defenders' of the 'old' paradigm, who, for a time, remain the majority. It is thus far easier for the first paradigm in a particular field to become established than for a 'new' to replace an 'old' paradigm. Indeed, in many cases, a new paradigm is **never** accepted by the more 'conservative' members of the field. In the words of Max Planck, writing about his own scientific career:

'A new scientific truth does not triumph by convincing its opponents, and making them see the light, but rather because its opponents eventually die, and a new generation grows up that is familiar with it'.

I have been personally involved in teaching secondary-school pupils and degree students about the revolutionary work of Popper and Kuhn for over 50 years now, and have actually been in correspondence with each of them. During the late – 1970's, I 'persuaded' John Lewis, the charismatic 'mastermind' behind the Association for Science

Education's exciting new 'Science in Society' course for pupils in the top forms of Britain's secondary schools to include 'articles' on the work of Popper and Kuhn in the 'Course Reader' on the 'Nature of Science'. I sent draft copies of my articles to Popper and Kuhn for their approval, and they were both very happy with them. My two articles were also very well received by the teachers that were running the course, and by their pupils. Later, I helped to run a course on the 'History, Philosophy and Social Aspects of Science' for third-year students in one of RGIT's 'Physical Science' degree programmes for over ten years, and taught the students about both Popper and Kuhn. After I retired in 2001, I also gave talks and ran seminars on their work in secondary schools throughout Scotland, all of which was 'completely new' to them, in most cases. In all my work familiarizing pupils and students with their ideas, I have become firmly convinced that **both** their 'models of science' are equally valid, **but are valid in different situations**. Some situations, like the 'Copernican', 'Darwinian' and 'Einsteinian' Revolutions that I have described in detail in this book are perfect examples of Kuhnian 'scientific revolutions'. I also find his concept of 'normal science' to be an extremely-accurate description of the way in which **most** professional scientists carry out their work. There are, however, many situations that are more accurately described by making use of Popper's 'methodological schema', since what is going on is neither 'normal science', nor 'extraordinary science' in the Kuhnian sense. The remarkable advances in 'cosmology' and 'particle physics' that have taken place during the 20th and 21st centuries are good examples of the sort of situations I have in mind. As you will see in the next two chapters, neither of these can really be described as 'normal science', because things have changed so quickly, sometimes in a 'fundamental' way. But neither can they be described as 'extraordinary science', because the scientists involved have adapted to these changes **without** the conflict and rancour that characterize a 'Kuhnian paradigm shift'. I would be interested in hearing what readers think about this matter.

Some of the sources of information on material covered in Chapter 11

As in the case of Chapter 7, I was on 'home-territory' here, since I was thoroughly familiar with most of the material covered, and had, in fact 'taught' quite a lot of it. I did, however, have to refer to many books and other items in my personal library for some details, and found the following particularly useful:

- 'Albert Einstein: Physicist, Philosopher, Humanitarian', a 'Teaching Company' course written and presented by Professor Don Howard (first class!).
- 'Great Physicists', by William H. Cropper, published by Oxford University Press in 2001 (my 'paperback' edition was published in 2004) A **wealth** of useful information.
- 'The Nature of the Scientific Method – An introduction to the ideas of Sir Karl Popper', by Henry Ellington (my article for the 'Nature of Science' Course Reader published by the ASE).
- 'How Science Develops – An introduction to the ideas of Thomas S. Kuhn', by Henry Ellington (my article for the 'Nature of Science' Course Reader published by the ASE).

Chapter 12: The development of modern cosmology

'Space is big, Really big. You just won't believe how vastly hugely mindbogglingly big it is.'

- Douglas Adams (The Hitch Hiker's Guide to the Galaxy)

To any reader who has **not** read this extremely funny book, I would only say that you have missed out on one of the great treats of life. And it is also full of extremely relevant 'digs' at contemporary society as Adams saw it at the time, as all good satire should be. It even came up with the 'secret of life, the universe and everything', something that I am vainly trying to do in writing this book. And what **was** his solution to the problem, arrived at by the 'supercomputer' 'Deep Thought' after a million years of pondering the matter? 42! I only wish real life could be so simple!

This is the first of six chapters that follow on directly from Chapter 11, each of them dealing with a different aspect of the 'scientific' world view. It shows how 'cosmology', our ideas regarding the large-scale structure of the universe, have developed since the triumph of the 'Copernican Revolution' in the early 18th century, and how it is currently going through a genuine 'golden age', just as Western philosophy did the in the 'classical' world of the Greeks and Romans. I will begin by looking at how the 'size' of the known universe has increased in a genuine 'mindbogglingly' way since the time of Newton, so much so that my opening quotation does not really do it justice. And that is just the 'known' universe, the part that we can actually 'see'! Some cosmologists believe that this is only a tiny part of what is 'out there', and that the universe may actually be infinite in extent, although I find that a bit 'hard to take'.

The progressive increase in the 'size' of the Universe after 1600

When I developed my original plan for the structure of this chapter, I intended to produce a 'fairly conventional' account of this topic, dealing with it in a systematic, 'historical' manner, as I have with all the other topics dealt with so far. Then I changed my mind, since I realised that an adaptation of a talk that I have been giving for well over 50 years now would give readers a **much** clearer idea of just how dramatically our picture of the **true** scale of the universe has changed since 1600. For many years, this was my 'flagship' talk, and I have now given it well over a hundred times (I have lost count of just how many), and have also given it to audiences of all ages, from the upper forms of primary schools, through all stages of secondary education, and to students of colleges and universities, as well as to a wide range of adult audiences. It is now entitled 'A Guided Tour of the Universe', and is delivered from a 'data stick' rather than with the 'carousel' slide projector that I used to have to lug around the country. Since the late 'noughties', I have also given all the teachers whose schools I visited in order to deliver my talk a personal copy of my PowerPoint presentation, together with a full script of the talk itself. I tried to make the latter as clear and succinct as possible, and have found that it was very easy to adapt it here. Since all the images that I used in my presentation (or the equivalent) are now readily available via the 'Internet', this will also enable readers to 'see' what I am writing about. This is the one chapter in the book that really would benefit from 'accompanying pictures', and, thanks to the 'Internet', readers can easily access them for themselves. I hope that many of you will do so!

The 'Title Frame' of my talk is superimposed on a dramatic photograph of the 'Hubble Extreme-Deep Field', and is on display while my audience is arriving. After being introduced by my host, I then open my talk with the following words:

'I am about to take you on a Guided Tour of the Universe, starting in the Solar System, then moving to the Stars and the Galaxy of which they form a part, and then travelling to the furthest reaches of the Extragalactic Universe – over 13 billion light years away.'

Then I use a 'bit of drama', showing them the launch of one of the NASA rockets and asking them to imagine that they are sitting at the top of this, and then showing them what they would see if they looked down from progressively greater heights, culminating in the glorious sight of the entire Earth, 'a beautiful blue cloud-covered planet nearly 8000 miles in diameter'. I then show them a composite photograph of the Earth and the Moon, showing their comparative sizes, and introduce the first piece of 'proper astronomy'.

'The Earth is actually part of a 'double planet' system, the other member being the Moon. This is roughly 2000 miles in diameter, and 240,000 miles from the Earth. We believe that it was formed when a 'proto-planet' roughly the size of Mars stuck the Earth a 'glancing blow' shortly after it was formed 4,600 million years ago. The resulting debris condensed to form the Moon.'

(I will skip the next six frames of my talk, since they deal exclusively with the nature of the Moon's surface and with the 'Apollo 11' lunar mission in 1969, topics with which I am sure most readers are thoroughly familiar.)

The next part of my 'guided tour' takes my audience away from the Moon into the 'inner regions' of the Solar System, showing them 'Venus' and 'Mercury', and then describing our approach to the Sun, accompanied by a dramatic image showing the comparative sizes of the Earth and the Sun, which I tell them 'is a huge flattened sphere of hot gas roughly 860,000 miles in diameter – over 100 times as big as the Earth'.

I then introduce a 'bit of astrophysics', with a schematic cross-section of the Sun, showing the structure of the interior: 'The temperature at the surface of the Sun is 6000°C, and gets higher and higher as we move towards its centre, where it reaches 15million°C. This is hot enough for the hydrogen of which the Sun is mainly composed to 'burn' to form helium by thermonuclear fusion – the same thing that happens when a hydrogen bomb explodes. The Sun is converting roughly 4 million tonnes of its mass into energy **every second**, and has been doing this for 5000 million years. This energy travels out to the Sun's surface, and is radiated into space, providing all the energy needed to support life on Earth'.

After talking about other images of the Sun, including a 'solar flare' and the 'solar corona', photographed during a 'total eclipse', we leave the Sun and travel outwards through the Solar System, passing Mercury, Venus and the Earth, then spending some time looking at Mars, passing through the 'Asteroid Belt', and then visiting the four outer 'gas giants' – Jupiter, Saturn, Uranus and Neptune, and so on to the outermost reaches of the Solar System, which is occupied by a second 'Asteroid Belt' known as the 'Kuiper Belt'. Its members include Pluto (recently 'demoted' from 'full planetary status' to that of a 'dwarf planet') and Sedna, which was discovered in 2004, and is the most remote body in the Solar System, currently being roughly 5000 million miles from the Sun.

Next, I show them a schematic map of the stars in the immediate vicinity of the Sun, accompanied by the following words:

'To reach the nearest stars, however, we would have to travel **very** much further. The nearest one is 'Proxima Centauri', which is over 4 'light years' away – roughly 25 million million miles from the Sun. If the stars were 'scaled down' to the size of peas, and the Sun was placed in

Aberdeen, Proxima Centauri would be located in Perth, roughly **80 miles** away.'

I then introduce a second 'bit of astrophysics', with the aid of the 'Hertzsprung-Russell diagram', astronomy's equivalent of chemistry's 'periodic table' (look it up on the Internet):

'There are many different types of star, and astronomers find it useful to illustrate this by plotting their **brightnesses** against their **surface temperatures** (as indicated by their **colours**) on what is called the **Hertzsprung-Russell diagram**. Most stars lie on the **main sequence** of this diagram, taking up a position that depends on their **mass** as soon as they are born (heavy stars at the top left-hand end; light ones at the bottom right-hand end). As you can see, the Sun is roughly halfway up. When they get older, and have used up all the hydrogen fuel in their cores, they move off to the right of the main sequence, becoming **red giants** and eventually losing most of their mass in an explosion of some sort. They then move to the left of the main sequence, becoming **white dwarfs**, **neutron stars** or **black holes**'.

That, in a nutshell, is what 'stellar evolution' is all about. I then use the next 21 frames to give a detailed description of the processes by which stars are 'born' (in places like the 'Great Nebula in Orion'), and eventually 'die', showing them photographs or computer images of what is going on. I will miss all that out, however, and move on to the part of my talk which deals with the structure and scale of the Galaxy in which we live (the 'Milky Way') and the structure and scale of the Extra-Galactic Universe, since these are what this chapter on 'cosmology' is really about.

I begin by showing them a photograph of the 'Milky Way', seen on a clear, dark night, and a second photograph seen through a large telescope, showing the countless millions of stars of which it is composed:

'If you look at the Milky Way through a large telescope, you will see that it consists of a vast number of individual stars – several hundred billion in all – that appear to be arranged in a flat disc completely surrounding the Earth.'

I then show them a computer image of the Milky Way as seen from well outside it, showing the details of its structure (find one on the Internet):

'Actually, the Milky Way is somewhat more complicated than this. It has a 'central bulge' of very old stars, from which two short straight 'bars' stick out. These are surrounded by a system of four 'spiral arms', roughly 100,000 light years in diameter. Our Sun is located on one of these spiral arms, roughly 30,000 light years from the centre of the Galaxy'.

I then show them photographs of the central region of our Galaxy, of the large cloud of gas and dust that is located there, and a computer-generated image of the super-massive 'black hole' that 'lurks' within it. This is 4 million times as heavy as the Sun, and similar objects are now believed to 'lurk' at the centres of nearly all other galaxies. Their presence was a comparatively-recent discovery.

Now, I take them on the final stage of their 'Guided Tour', showing them what exists **outside** our own Galaxy. I begin by showing them four successive black-and-white images of the 'Great Nebula in Andromeda', with the final one showing clearly how it is composed of individual stars, and then showing them a beautiful colour image of the full Nebula taken by the Hubble Space Telescope:

'For a long time, most astronomers believed that our Milky Way constituted the entire Universe. We now know that this is not the case, and that objects like the Great Nebula in Andromeda are in fact located well outside the boundaries of our Galaxy. This was discovered by Edwin Hubble in 1919, when he used the newly-opened 100inch Mt. Wilson telescope to take closer and closer images of the Nebula. These showed quite clearly that it consisted of countless billions of individual stars, and, by measuring the distances of some of the brightest of these, Hubble was able to prove that the Nebula was not located **within** our Galaxy, but is a separate galaxy in its own right. The Great Nebula is now known to be roughly 2.5 million light years away, and has also been found to be moving towards us at 300,000 miles an hour. It may collide with the Milky Way in roughly 2 billion years'.

I then show how we can see other galaxies whenever we look into the sky, and how they come in a wide range of shapes and sizes, including 'irregular galaxies' (with no definite shape), 'elliptical galaxies', 'barred-spiral galaxies' (like our own Milky Way), and 'simple spiral galaxies' (with no straight bars). I show them photographs of all these types, as well as photographs of collisions between galaxies.

I then go on to describe the overall structure of the Extra-Galactic Universe, with beautiful illustrative 'Hubble' images:

'The observable Universe is thought to contain several hundred **billion** galaxies, arranged in a hierarchy of structures of increasing size. First, there are 'small' **groups** a few million light years across, containing up to a few dozen individual galaxies. Our Milky Way and the Andromeda Nebula are members of such a group – the so-called 'Local Group'. Next, there are **clusters** a few tens of light years across, typically containing several hundreds or thousands of galaxies. Then there are **superclusters** roughly 100 million light years across, typically containing 10,000 or more galaxies. These are sometimes found to be part of even larger structures known as **supercluster complexes**.

I then show them three images of the very furthest parts of the observable Universe:

'This is the Hubble Medium-Deep Field', which contains some galaxies (the small red ones) that are up to 6 million light years away – halfway to the edge of the observable Universe. And this is the 'Hubble Extreme-Deep Field', which includes galaxies roughly 12 billion light years away, right at the edge of the observable Universe. Beyond these, all we can see is the 'Cosmic Microwave Background', the radiation that is left over from the 'Big Bang' itself. It varies slightly in temperature from place to place, and has told us a great deal about the structure, composition and age of the observable Universe'.

I then review what we have learned in the course of our 'Guided Tour' with the aid of three 'closing frames' – the 'Earth seen from space', the computer image of the 'Milky Way', and the 'Hubble Extreme-Deep Field':

'First, we have seen that the Earth is not the 'Centre of the Universe', as had long been assumed. It is merely a small, fairly insignificant planet, one of many thousands of planets, moons and asteroids that make up the Sun's family. Then we have seen that our Sun is itself a fairly insignificant star, one of several hundred thousand million that make up the Milky Way. And it is not even at the **centre** of the Milky Way, being located roughly 30,000 light years out, in one of its 'spiral arms'. Finally, we have seen that our Milky Way is only one of several hundred thousand million galaxies that make up the observable Universe – the part that we can see. This contains more stars then there are grains of sand on all the beaches on the Earth's surface. Since we now believe that most of these have their own planetary systems, many of which are probably capable of supporting life, I leave you with this final thought:

How can we possibly be alone in the Universe?'

Before these last nine words, I flip to a fourth and final 'closing frame', with the words superimposed on the 'Hubble Extreme-Deep Field'. I leave this in view during the subsequent 'question and answer' session. It certainly leaves the audience 'thinking'!

The systematic study of our own Galaxy and its contents

Before the time of Copernicus, it was generally believed that the Solar System constituted the entire Universe, the stars being 'lamps' that were situated on the surface of the 'celestial sphere', which rotated round the Earth once a day and marked the 'boundary' of the Universe. After the overthrow of the Ptolemaic System, however, it was realised that the stars must be situated at enormous distances from the Earth, otherwise their apparent positions would change as the Earth moved round the Sun because of 'parallax effects'. (To demonstrate how these occur, stretch your right arm out in front of you, raise your middle finger, close one eye, and move your head from side to side; you will see that your finger appears to move in the **opposite** direction against the background.) In actual fact, the nearer stars **do** show a very small parallax movement as the Earth moves round the Sun, but the apparent change in position is so small as to be virtually undetectable. Indeed, it was not until the 1830's that telescopes became powerful enough to detect stellar parallax movements, and use them to measure the distances of stars. The first such measurement was carried out by the German astronomer, Otto Struve, in 1837, when he showed that Vega is 26 light years away from the Earth (a 'light year' is the distance light travels in one year, and is equivalent to 5.88 million million miles). Almost simultaneously,

Friedrich Bessel (in Germany) and Thomas Henderson (a Scot working in South Africa) reported similar successful measurements of 61 Cygni and Alpha Centauri. Since then, the distances of all the closest stars have been measured by the same method. The nearest star is Proxima Centauri, which is 4.27 light years away, and shows an annual change in position of only 1.52 seconds of arc (1 'second' is one-sixtieth of a 'minute' of arc, which is itself one-sixtieth of a 'degree'). The 'parallax method' can be used to measure the distances of stars up to roughly 150 light years; beyond this distance, other, less-accurate methods such as comparing the apparent luminosities of stars of the same spectral type must be employed.

The first person to make a serious attempt to determine the way in which stars are distributed throughout space was Thomas Wright of Durham, who, in 1750, realised that the Milky Way was a cross-section of a 'flat' disc. During the latter part of the 18th century, William Herschel (1788-1832) greatly extended his work, showing that the stars of the Milky Way were distributed in the form of a huge 'flattened bun' – the 'Galaxy' – with the Sun being located near its 'central plane'. Herschel, who was born in Hanover but later moved to England, where he became a British citizen and was later knighted, was probably Britain's greatest-ever observational astronomer. He built a succession of ever-larger telescopes in the grounds of his various houses, the largest being a 48inch reflector – the largest telescope in the world at the time. With these, he made a succession of important discoveries, the most important of which were the discovery of the seventh planet in the Solar System (Uranus) in 1781, and the systematic mapping of the part of the Galaxy that can be seen in the northern sky. Later, his son John Herschel (1792-1871), working in South Africa, repeated his work for the part of the Galaxy that can be seen in the southern sky. Between them, they built up a fairly good qualitative picture of the Galaxy, a picture that was steadily improved during the remainder of the 19th century. During this period, attempts were made to estimate the size of the Galaxy, but these were hampered by the fact that there was no reliable method of measuring the distances of very remote stars. They believed that the Galaxy was roughly 10,000 light years in diameter, an estimate that turned out to be an 'order of magnitude' too low. (As we saw in the previous section, we now know that the Galaxy is roughly 100,000 light years in diameter.)

The 'distance' problem was eventually solved in 1912, when Henrietta Leavitt (1868-1921), one of a group of female astronomers working at Harvard College Observatory, made one of the most important discoveries in the history of observational astronomy. She had been studying a class of extremely-bright stars known as 'Cepheid variables', and found that their 'periods' were linearly dependent on their 'absolute luminosities'. Thus, if the 'period' of a Cepheid could be measured (a simple task), measuring its 'apparent' luminosity (another simple task) then allowed its 'absolute' luminosity to be calculated, and, by comparing the two, allowed its 'distance' to be calculated with high accuracy. Since 'Cepheid variables' are all 'extremely bright', as we have seen, this discovery provided a method of measuring the distances of extremely remote stars for the very first time, and enabled 'great advances' in astronomy to be made. In 1918, Harlow Shapley (1885-1972), an American astronomer then working at the Mt. Wilson Observatory, used its 60inch telescope (then the largest in the world) to measure the distances of Cepheid variables located in large spherical collections of roughly 100,000 stars known as 'Globular Clusters', which, at the time, were thought to be located well **within** the Galaxy. Shapley showed that this was not the case, and that they were in fact located **outside** of the disc of the Galaxy. He also showed that the Globular Clusters formed a sort of 'spherical exoskeleton' for the Galaxy, being evenly distributed throughout a sphere which was divided in half by the plane of the Galaxy. He also showed that the size of the Galaxy was roughly ten times larger than had hitherto been believed, and that the Earth was not located at the centre of the Galaxy, but roughly 3/5 of the way out.

During the last hundred years, our knowledge of the structure and composition of the Galaxy has increased enormously, partly due to advances in optical astronomy, partly due to the equally-impressive advances that have been made in radio astronomy since the end of the Second World War, and partly due to the fact that astronomers are now able to use virtually all other parts of the electromagnetic spectrum to make observations since we became capable of putting instruments into space. We now know that the Galaxy consists of three main parts. The first is the 'central bulge', which contains the great majority of the hundred thousand million or so stars that are now thought to make up the Galaxy. The second part is the 'disc' of the Galaxy, which has a diameter of roughly 100,000 light years, and a thickness of 2,500 light years. This consists mainly of a set of four 'spiral arms' that radiate outwards from the 'central bulge' and its two short, straight 'bars', and contains only a tiny fraction (500 million) of the stars in the Galaxy. The stars in the disc all rotate slowly about its centre, with the stars at the 'edge' taking longer than those nearer the 'centre', so that they tend to 'trail behind', thus giving the arms their 'spiral' shape. The disc of the Galaxy contains large amounts of gas and dust as well as stars, whose presence made it extremely difficult to determine its detailed structure before the development of radio astronomy made this possible. The third part of the Galaxy is the 'halo', a much-more-sparsely populated 'sphere' of stars 100,000 light years in diameter that forms an extension of the tightly-packed central bulge. The halo also contains the 'Globular Clusters', of which over 100 are known.

The stars that make up the Galaxy are of many different types, are at various stages in their evolution, and are grouped together in all manner of ways. There is, however, an important difference between

287

the kind of stars that populate the central core and halo of the Galaxy, and the kind that populate the spiral arms of the disc. The former are found to be much older than the latter, and form a completely different pattern when plotted on a Hertzsprung-Russell diagram (see last section). The 'young' stars of the disc are known as 'Population I', while the 'older' stars of the core and halo are known as 'Population II'.

The investigation of the Extra-Galactic Universe

The first person to appreciate the full extent of the Universe in which we live was our old friend, Immanuel Kant, who had carried out important work in astronomy before he turned to philosophy. In 1755, he postulated that the faint, luminous 'nebulae' that had been discovered by Maupertuis and others were actually 'galaxies' similar to our own. Kant envisaged a Universe consisting of an unlimited number of such 'galaxies', stretching for an indefinite distance in all directions. His theory went virtually unnoticed, however, since Kant was 150 years ahead of his time. From 1764 onwards, the French astronomer, Charles Messier, carried out the first systematic study of all the different bright nebulae that could be seen, and produced the 'catalogue' of these that still bears his name; the 'Great Nebula in Andromeda', for example, is known as 'M31', since it was the 31st nebula listed in this catalogue. The next person to make a serious study of the 'spiral nebulae', as objects like M31 came to be known, was the Irish Astronomer William Parsons, the 3rd Earl of Rosse, who constructed a huge 72inch reflecting telescope in the grounds of Birr Castle, his Irish home, and used this to carry out the most detailed study of such nebulae so far. Seen through his telescope, the 'spiral shape' of these nebulae was now obvious. Most astronomers still believed that they were located **inside** our own Galaxy, however.

All this changed in 1923, when the American astronomer, Edwin Hubble (1889-1953) used the recently-opened 100inch Mt. Wilson telescope to prove conclusively that the Great Nebula in Andromeda was located **well outside** our Galaxy. He had been using the new telescope, then the largest and most powerful in the world, to search for Cepheid variables **inside** the Andromeda Nebula, and eventually found six of them. He was able to calculate their distances, which turned out to be roughly 750,000 light years away from the Earth, a distance that he later revised upwards to 900,000 light years. (This was in fact still far too low, with the distance to the Andromeda Nebula being further revised upwards to 2 million light years in 1952, and, later, to the currently-accepted value of 2.5 million light years.)

The 'Cepheid variable' method only allows the distances of the **nearest** galaxies to be measured, since they eventually become too faint to see. Beyond this distance, other methods had to be used, one being based on the comparison of the apparent luminosities of even brighter stars known as 'supergiants'. It was assumed that all supergiants of the same spectral type had roughly the same absolute luminosity, so that the distance of such a star could be determined by measuring its **apparent** luminosity and determining its spectral type. This method could be used for distances up to several tens of millions of light years. When the distance became too great for even the supergiants to be visible, the distance of a galaxy could be estimated by measuring its **apparent** luminosity and **apparent** size, since Hubble had shown that galaxies of the same type have roughly the same absolute luminosity and size. This method allowed the distances of extremely remote galaxies to be estimated. During the 1920's and 1930's, Hubble and his colleague, Milton Humason, carried out extensive distance measurements using these methods, and thereby confirmed the earlier discovery by Vesto Slipher, working at the Lowell Observatory in Arizona, that practically all of the galaxies whose spectra he had been studying had spectra that were 'shifted' towards the red (long wavelength) end of the spectrum. This discovery, which was given the name 'red shift', was assumed to be caused by the 'Doppler effect', the same effect that causes the apparent pitch of a police car siren to fall as the car approaches us, passes us, and then moves away from us. It means that all galaxies that display such a 'red shift' in their spectra are **moving away** from us, so that they are **getting further and further apart**, which means that the Universe is **expanding**, rather than being **static**, as had hitherto been generally supposed. In 1929, Hubble announced that the **amount** of this 'red shift' was **directly proportional to the distance of the galaxy**, a result that is now known as 'Hubble's Law'. The 'constant of proportionality' between the **velocity of recession** and the **distance** is now known as the 'Hubble Constant', and plays a vital part in all modern cosmological theories. Although its **exact value** was not measured until comparatively recently, this has now been done. The latest value, calculated from data obtained from the Planck satellite in 2013, is '71km per second per megaparsec' (the 'parsec' is the 'official' astronomical unit of distance, being equivalent to 3.26 light years).

As we saw in the first section of this chapter, astronomers now have a pretty clear idea of the overall structure and composition of the Extra-Galactic Universe – or, at least, the **observable** part of this. This is now thought to contain several hundred billion galaxies, each containing up to several hundred billion stars, according to their size, arranged in a hierarchy of groups, clusters, superclusters and supercluster complexes of progressively increasing size. These surround us in all directions, the furthest ones being over 12 billion light years away. What (if anything) lies **beyond** these is still a matter for speculation, as we will see later.

The development of the 'Big-Bang' theory of the origin of the Universe

The work of Vesto Slipher, Hubble and Humason led directly to the development of what has now become the 'standard model' of cosmology – the so-called 'Big-Bang' theory. (It was actually given this name sarcastically by Fred Hoyle during a radio broadcast in 1949, and, much to his annoyance, the name stuck!) Let us now examine this theory in some detail.

The origins of the theory can in fact be traced back to 1927, when the Belgian astrophysicist, George Lemaitre (1849-1966) proposed that the Universe originated as a 'primeval atom' which subsequently expanded explosively. Two years later, Hubble demonstrated the linear relationship between galactic distance and rate of recession ('Hubble's Law'), but predicted an age for the Universe (1.8 billion years) that was much less than the geological age of the Earth (4.5 billion years), a 'discrepancy' that became known as the 'timescale problem'. In 1933, the American physicist Fritz Zwicky (1898-1974) predicted the existence of 'dark matter' by studying the motion of galaxies in the 'Coma' cluster, a prediction that was later confirmed by other work. In 1946, Hoyle, Bondi and Gold presented a rival theory to the 'big-bang' theory that apparently resolved the 'timescale problem' – the 'steady state' theory that was described in Chapter 11. Two years later, the Russian-born American physicist, George Gamow, (1904-1968) proposed that 'nucleosynthesis' had taken place during the early stages of expansion of Lemaitre's 'primeval atom', and predicted the existence of the 'cosmic microwave background radiation' (CMB), 18 years before it was eventually discovered. In 1958, the American astronomer Walter Baade (1893-1960), using the new 200inch Mt. Palomar telescope, 'resolved' the 'timescale problem' by showing that the Universe was much bigger (and older) than had hitherto been believed, much to the relief of supporters of the 'big-bang' theory. And in 1961, the British radio astronomer, Martin Ryle, (1900-1976) published his long-awaited survey of 'radio galaxies', providing convincing proof that the 'big-bang' theory was correct and the 'steady state' theory was wrong. Further corroboration of the theory was produced in 1965, when two engineers working at the Bell Telephone Laboratories in the USA, Arno Penzias and Robert Wilson, 'accidentally' discovered the CMB, for which they were subsequently awarded the 1978 Nobel Prize in Physics. In 1980, the American physicist Alan Guth presented a possible solution to three of the most worrying problems then associated with the 'big-bang' theory (the 'horizon problem', the 'flatness problem' and the 'magnetic monopole problem') by suggesting that the Universe had gone through a phase of 'inflationary expansion' during the early stages of the 'big-bang', after which 'cosmic inflation' became a key part of the theory. In 1992, data from the 'Cosmic Background Explorer' (COBE) satellite revealed exactly the variations in intensity needed to support the 'big-bang' model. And in 1998, study of Type 1a supernovae by two independent research teams came up with the astonishing result that the expansion of the Universe is **speeding up** rather than **slowing down**, driven by a completely new form of energy known as 'dark energy', now known to constitute roughly 68% of the 'mass-energy' that the Universe contains. Four years later, data from the 'Wilkinson Microwave Anisotropy Probe' (WMAP) satellite 'tied down' the rate of expansion, age and composition of the Universe, providing further confirmation of the 'big-bang' model. Finally, in 2013, data from the 'Planck' satellite 'tied down' these values even more accurately, and provided further strong confirmation of the theory, if any was needed.

So much for the **history** of the 'big-bang' theory. Let me now try to give you some idea of what it tells us about the way in which the Universe **evolved** after the 'big-bang' event that we believe brought it into being, eventually giving rise to the gigantic Universe that we see around us today.

Let us say that the 'big-bang' started at 'time zero', reflecting the views of St. Augustine that 'the Universe was born **with** time, not **in** time.' About its development during the first 10^{-43} seconds of its existence, known as the 'Planck era', we know absolutely nothing, although some cosmologists and physicists believe that all four of the basic forces of physics (see next chapter for details) were 'unified' as a 'single force', possibly in 'higher-dimensional' space/time of some sort. After 10^{-43} seconds, we believe that an 'embryonic bubble' roughly 10^{-33}cm in diameter 'emerged' from the 'background vacuum state' and embarked on a short period of 'inflationary expansion', driven by an 'unknown force' ('dark energy'?), and increasing in size by a factor of up to 10^{50} during the following 10^{-34} seconds. During this expansion, 'gravity' separated from the other three basic forces, after which 'inflation' ended, and the 'Universe' entered a lengthy period of decelerating 'Friedman' expansion, slowed down by the now-independent force of gravity. During the following three minutes, virtually all the 'matter' in the Universe mutually-annihilated with 'antimatter', leaving a small residue of 'matter' in the form of 'quarks' and 'leptons' (again, see next chapter for information about these), together with a large amount of radiation in the form of high-energy 'photons'. The 'strong' force then separated from the 'weak' and 'electromagnetic' forces, after which the temperature became low enough for 'quarks' to combine to form 'light nuclei' (hydrogen; helium; lithium; beryllium; boron). The Universe was now composed of a hot 'photon gas', positive nuclei, negative electrons, and neutrinos (again, see next chapter for further information about these). After a further 380,000 years, the temperature had fallen to roughly 3000K, cool enough for electrons to combine with nuclei to form stable, neutral atoms. This eventually made the Universe 'transparent', since the 'photons' in the 'comic background radiation' were no longer absorbed by charged particles (this is the oldest stage of the Universe that we can 'see' by observing the present 'cosmic background radiation'). After expanding for a further billion years or so, the temperature had fallen to roughly 18K. Now, quasars, galaxies, stars and planets begin to form by 'gravitational contraction', made possible by the presence of 'quantum ripples' in the original fireball. Stars then begin to 'cook' the medium-mass elements up to iron, and supernova explosions to 'cook' the heavy elements throughout the galactic interiors. Once the Universe was roughly 6.5 billion years 'old', **decelerating** 'Friedman' expansion gradually gave way to **accelerating** 'de Sitter' expansion, driven by 'dark energy' ('Friedman' and 'de Sitter' expansion are two of the forms of expansion that are permitted by Einstein's 'general theory of relativity'). Stars and planets continued to form in the clouds of gas and dust that are found in the 'discs' of all galaxies (our own Sun and Solar System was formed in such a cloud roughly 5 billion years ago). Eventually, 13.8 billion years after the 'big-bang' event, we arrived at the present day. As we have seen, the Universe now consists of a hierarchy of stars and planetary systems, galaxies, galactic 'groups', 'clusters' 'superclusters' and 'supercluster complexes', and continues to expand at an ever-increasing rate. We believe that it will continue to do so indefinitely.

So what is the 'current state' of the 'big-bang' model of the 'creation' and 'evolution' of the Universe that I have just described? 'Pretty good', according to all the evidence that has been found so far. This takes four key forms.

1. The observed 'red shift' of all but a few of the very nearest galaxies, and its relationship to distance from us, which shows conclusively that the Universe is 'expanding', and at an ever-increasing rate.
2. The evidence from radio astronomy, and from the amazing images produced by the Hubble Space Telescope, that the nature of the Extra-Galactic Universe appears to have changed significantly over the course of its lifetime.

3. The observed relative abundance of the 'light elements' up to boron, which agree almost perfectly with the predictions of the 'big-bang' theory.
4. The discovery of the 'cosmic microwave background radiation' (CMB) and its subsequent detailed study, which 'strongly corroborate' the big-bang theory.

So, for so long as it continues to 'fit the facts', and until someone comes up with a **better** theory, we shall continue to use it, and to believe that it provides an accurate description of the wonderful Universe in which we live. That is all that we, as, 'good scientists', can do.

What questions about cosmology have still to be resolved?

Well, there are quite a lot, as it happens.
1. What was there **before** the 'big-bang'?
2. What **caused** the 'big-bang'?
3. What caused **cosmic inflation** to start and stop (assuming that it actually happened)?
4. Why does the Universe contain **matter** but not **antimatter** (as far as we are aware)?
5. How did **galaxies form**?
6. What is the nature of **dark matter** and **dark energy** (which respectively constitute 27% and 68% of the mass/energy in the Universe)?
7. Is the Universe **finite** or **infinite**?
8. Are there more than **four dimensions** (three of space and one of time)?
9. Is our Universe part of a larger **multiverse**?
10. Why is our Universe so suited to the **development of life**?

There ought to be a few future 'Nobel Prizes' among that lot, I would think!

Some of the sources of information on material covered in Chapter 12

Once again, I was on 'home territory' here, since I am thoroughly familiar with most of the material covered, and have in fact 'taught' or 'given talks on' quite a lot of it. I did, however, have to refer to many of the books and other materials in my personal library for some details, and found the following particularly useful:

- 'The Story of Astronomy', by Patrick Moore (once again!)
- 'Big Bang', by Simon Singh (still probably the best book on the subject, although slightly dated now).
- 'The Beginning and End of Everything', by Paul Parsons (a recent book that provides a large amount of up-to-date information).
- 'Chambers Biographical Dictionary' (yet again!)
- The various 'handouts' that I have produced over the years to support teaching and giving talks on the material covered.

Chapter 13: Exploring the microscopic world

'To see a world in a grain of sand
And a heaven in a wild flower
Hold infinity in the palm of your hand
And eternity in an hour'

- William Blake ('Auguries of Innocence')

When looking for a suitable quotation with which to begin this chapter, I was trying to find one that drew attention to the connection between the 'macroscopic world' of everyday reality, and the 'microscopic world' that underlies and underpins it. I thought of using the title of the Dalai Lama's wonderful book, 'The Universe in a Single Atom', but eventually settled on what is probably the best-known quotation from William Blake, another of the people whose work I greatly admire. I even have a large print of his artistic masterpiece, 'The Ancient of Days', in my front hall, so that I (and all my visitors) see it when we come into my house. It shows a wind-swept 'God' using a large set of 'dividers' to show how he was bringing 'design' and 'rationality' into the world he was 'creating', and is one of the most striking and impressive paintings with which I am familiar. It certainly 'makes a powerful statement' to all my visitors, since it is literally 'in their face'.

Just as the last chapter dealt with the 'very large', so this one deals with the 'very small', showing how modern scientists have been just as successful in exploring the latter as they have been in exploring the vast Universe in which we all live. It begins by looking at how the invention of the microscope, and its increasingly-widespread use during the last 400 years, totally transformed biology, and brought it into the 'modern era'. The rest of the chapter shows how physicists started to 'probe the inner structure of matter' in ever-finer detail during the 20th century, leading to the tremendous discoveries that were made during the 'golden age' of particle physics in the latter half of the century, discoveries that have completely revolutionised our ideas about the 'fine structure' of reality. I lived through all of these developments, and always followed them with tremendous interest; I still do.

How the invention and use of the microscope transformed biology

Modern anatomy and modern biology are said to have begun with work of the Italian anatomist, Heironymous Fabrizzi (1537-1619), and his brilliant English 'student', William Harvey (1578-1637), who, between them, discovered the way in which blood was pumped round the body by the heart. Harvey's detailed work on the circulation of the blood was, however, greatly hampered by the fact that he could not show where the 'arteries' and 'veins' actually 'met'. He could only **suppose** that the connections existed, but they were far too small to see with the naked eye. All this changed with the invention of the **microscope** at the start of the 17th century, shortly after the invention of the telescope. Just as the latter 'totally transformed' observational astronomy, as we saw in Chapter 7, so the former 'totally transformed' observational anatomy and biology; neither of them ever looked back.

As the early, primitive microscopes were steadily improved during the 17th century, so their use by anatomists, naturalists and biologists was broadened and extended. They enabled 'naturalists' to describe small creatures with a detail that would have been impossible without them, enabled 'anatomists' to discover structures that could otherwise never have been seen, and, eventually, enabled biologists to discover and explore the 'cellular' and 'sub-cellular' structures of living things in ever-increasing detail. One of the first to do so in a systematic way was the Dutch naturalist, Jan Swammerdam (1637-1680), who spent his time observing insects under the microscope, and producing beautiful drawings of tiny details of their anatomy. He also discovered that blood was not a uniform red liquid, as it appeared to the naked eye, but contained countless tiny bodies that lent it its colour – what we now call 'red blood corpuscles'. Later, the English botanist, Nehemiah Grew (1641-1712), studied plants under the microscope, and, in particular examined their reproductive organs, describing the individual pollen grains that they produced. A Dutch anatomist, Regnier de Graaf (1641-1673), performed similar work on animals, studying the fine structure of their testicles and ovaries. In particular, he described little structures within the ovary that are still known as 'Graafian follicles'. Even more dramatic was the work of the Italian physiologist, Marcello Malpighi (1628-1694), who produced final confirmation of Harvey's theory of the circulation of the blood by tracing the connections between arteries and veins in great detail. Nearly all of the early microscopists, including all the ones that I have mentioned so far, made use of instruments that incorporated linked systems of lenses (just as all the early 'telescopists' had done until the invention of the 'reflecting telescope' by Newton). One, however, the Dutch merchant, Anton van Leeuwenhoek (1632-1723), for whom microscopy was merely a 'hobby', used single lenses, tiny enough to be made from small pieces of flawless glass. He ground these with meticulous care, to the point where he could get clear magnification of up to 200-fold. With these lenses, he made many important discoveries, including the presence of tiny creatures, later called 'protozoa', in stagnant ditch water. One of his assistants was also the first to observe the spermatozoa in male semen. The only other discovery of the era to match van Leeuwenhoek's work, at least in terms of its future significance, was that of the eminent English scientist, Robert Hooke (1635-1703), whom we have already encountered in Chapter 7. He was 'fascinated' by microscopes, and did some of the best of the early work in the field. In 1665, he published a book, 'Micrographia', in which some of the most beautiful microscopic drawings ever made are to be found. His most important single drawing was that of a thin slice of cork, which he noted to be made up of a 'fine pattern of tiny rectangular chambers', which he called 'cells'. (Thus, he had anticipated the development of the 'cell theory' of biology by Schleiden and Schwann by over 170 years.)

The development of microscopy in the biological sciences languished during most of the 18th century, mainly because the instruments available at the time had reached the limits of their effectiveness. Indeed, it was not until 1773, nearly 100 years after van Leeuwenhoek's original discovery of protozoa, that further significant advances in this area became possible because of progressive incremental improvements in microscope design. It was in that year that the Danish microbiologist, Otto Friderich Muller (1730-1784), could see bacteria (creatures even smaller than protozoa) well enough to describe the shapes and forms of their various types. The power and effectiveness of microscopes was given a further major boost by the development of 'achromatic microscopes' around 1820. Just as the development of 'achromatic objective lenses' had transformed 'observational astronomy' during the 18th century, so the invention of 'achromatic microscopes' transformed 'observational biology' during the 19th, leading the way to many revolutionary discoveries and advances. I have already described the best-known of these 'biological revolutions' (the so-called 'Darwinian Revolution') in Chapter 9. Well, the discovery by two German biologists, the botanist, Mathias Jacob Schleiden (1804-1881) and the physiologist, Theodor Schwann (1810-1882), that all plants and animals were made up of collections of individual 'cells', each surrounded by a membrane separating it from the rest of the world, was probably just as important, possibly even more so. Although Schleiden and Schwann are generally jointly credited with the development of the 'cell theory', many others also contributed, and thus began the science of 'cytology' – the study of cells and their components. Much of modern biology and medicine is largely based on work in this area. And none of it would have been possible without the development of the modern 'optical microscope'. (Just over 100 years later, the invention of an even-more-powerful instrument, the 'electron microscope', enabled further major advances to be made, as we will see later.) The invention of the 'achromatic microscope' also gave a tremendous boost to the development of the 'germ theory of disease', and to the burgeoning science of 'bacteriology'. Indeed, we subsequently discovered that such creatures are by far the most abundant form of life on Earth. Our digestive systems, for example, are now known to be totally reliant on them for the processing and absorption of food.

When the 'germ theory of disease' was being developed by Louis Pasteur (1822-1895), Robert Koch (1843-1910) and others, it was believed that most diseases were caused by bacteria, and, in due course, most of the bacteria involved were identified and studied, with a view to finding cures for, or at least alleviating the symptoms of, such diseases. There were, however, some diseases, such as rabies, for which Pasteur and his successors failed to find the 'infective agent', possibly, as Pasteur had suggested, because they were caused by a micro-organism that was 'too small' to be detected by the techniques available at the time. The idea that an infectious agent might be much smaller than ordinary bacteria was shown to be true in connection with a disease involving the tobacco plant ('tobacco mosaic disease'). It was known that juice from diseased plants could affect healthy ones, and, in 1892, the Russian botanist, Dmitri Iosifovich Ivanovski (1864-1920) showed that the juice remained infective even after it had been passed through filters fine enough to stop any known bacterium. Three years later, the Dutch botanist, Martinus Willem Beijerinck (1851-1931), named the infective agent a 'filterable virus', where the word 'virus' simply meant 'poison'. This marked the beginning of the science of 'virology', the study of such organisms. It was not until the 1930's, however, that an instrument powerful enough to 'detect' and 'study' such viruses in detail was developed. This was the 'electron microscope', which works by focussing beams of **electrons** rather than light waves, and can produce magnifications several 'orders of magnitude' greater than optical microscopes. Modern biology and virology are now strongly dependent on the use of such microscopes, which can now be found in virtually all laboratories and research establishments. (I well remember when such a microscope was acquired by RGIT's 'School of Physics' in the late 1960's, as a result of a large grant from the Scottish Education Department. An entire 'mini-department' was built around this amazing machine, which soon achieved widespread use by many of the rest of RGIT's 'School's, such was its power and versatility.) The investigation of the viruses that caused recent diseases such as 'AIDS' and 'Covid19' would simply not have been possible without these amazing instruments.

The discovery of the atom and study of its structure

As we saw earlier in the book, the existence of 'basic particles of matter' called 'atoms' had been postulated since Greek and Roman times, and had been firmly established as part of the modern scientific 'world picture' by Newton. During the 19th century, most scientists assumed that these particles existed, especially chemists, who based their entire subject on the assumption that matter consisted of such 'atoms', usually combined with other 'atoms' to form 'molecules'. Some physicists, however, refused to believe that 'atoms' actually existed, since there was no incontrovertible 'experimental evidence' for this. Not, that is, until Einstein's 'annus mirabilis' of 1905, when his 'Brownian motion' paper finally provided evidence for the existence of atoms and molecules that no rational scientist could doubt.

Until the final years of the 19th century, however, most scientists still believed that 'atoms' were 'indivisible particles' of the type that Newton had proposed, since there was no evidence that this was not the case. All this changed in 1897, however, when the English physicist,

J.J. Thomson (1856-1940), working in the Cavendish Laboratory at Cambridge, postulated the existence of the first 'fundamental particle', the **electron**, a particle that was subsequently shown to be an integral part of the atom. In 1898, Thomson went on to propose the first theory of the **structure** of the atom, the so-called 'plum pudding' model, in which negatively-charged electrons were embedded in a hard, uniform sphere of positive charge, thus making the atom 'electrically neutral' (i.e., 'uncharged') overall. Between 1909 and 1913, however, Thomson's picture of a 'hard, solid atom' was demolished forever by a brilliant series of experiments carried out by the New Zealand-born British physicist, Ernest Rutherford (1871-1937), working at Manchester University. Between 1909 and 1913, he attempted to investigate the interior structure of the atom by 'firing' beams of 'alpha particles' (heavy particles that are produced during one form of radioactive decay) at thin sheets of gold foil, and studying the resultant 'scattering'. Rutherford found that virtually all the alpha particles passed through the gold foil without undergoing any significant deflection, but that a few were scattered through large angles, up to 180°. From his experiments, he eventually came to the conclusion that the mass of an atom was virtually all concentrated into a very small volume at the centre of the atom, rather than being spread throughout its entire volume, as proposed by Thomson. He had thus discovered the **atomic nucleus**, one of the most important discoveries in the history of modern physics. He proposed that this central, positively-charged 'nucleus' is surrounded by a 'cloud' of negatively-charged electrons, with most of the volume of the atom consisting of 'empty space'. Rutherford's model of the atom was later developed by Niels Bohr (1885-1962), Erwin Schrodinger (1887-1961) and others, and is basically the model that we use today. Physicists still had to solve the problem of the **composition** of this positively-charged nucleus, however.

Evidence for the existence of a second 'fundamental particle', the positively-charged **proton**, gradually accumulated during the first two decades of the 20th century, mainly through the study of 'gas discharges', and, in particular, from the study of the so-called 'canal rays' that were produced by employing a 'perforated cathode' (negative electrode) in such studies. This work was carried out by Thomson, Rutherford and several other workers, who, by 1920, had succeeded in showing that the proton was an integral part of the atom. Physicists had already succeeded in measuring the 'mass' and 'charge' of the electron, and they had now managed to do the same thing for the proton. They had found that the proton and the electron had exactly the same **electric charge**, but with opposite 'sign', but that the **mass** of the proton was very much greater than that of the electron – 1836 times as great, in fact. They now believed that all matter was composed of 'protons' and 'electrons', and that an atom of 'mass number' A and 'atomic number' Z consisted of a positively-charged 'nucleus' containing A 'protons' and (A-Z) 'electrons', surrounded by a 'circumnucleus' containing Z electrons. There were, however, a number of 'theoretical problems' regarding this simple model of the atom, since it could be shown by several different arguments (which I will not go into here) that it was highly unlikely that electrons could have separate physical existence **inside** the nucleus. The observed fact that nearly all of the 'chemical elements' had 'atomic weights' that were clearly **not** integral multiples of the mass of the proton also posed 'problems'. According to the 'Rutherford-Bohr' model of the atom, the experimentally-measured value of the 'atomic weight' of the atoms of each element should be very nearly **equal** to the combined masses of the protons in the nucleus, but this was clearly not the case.

The problem of determining the composition of the atomic nucleus was eventually solved in 1934, when the English physicist, James Chadwick (1891-1974), working at the Cavendish Laboratory with

Ernest Rutherford (who was now Director of the Cavendish), finally confirmed the existence of a third 'fundamental particle' – the **neutron**. This had a **mass** that was almost equal to that of the proton (very slightly larger, in fact) but was **electrically neutral**. (The existence of such a particle had in fact been postulated by Rutherford in 1920, but he had no 'direct evidence' of this at the time.) This discovery solved all the outstanding problems relating to the composition of the atomic nucleus at a stroke, since it removed any need for the presence of electrons **within** its structure. Now, an atom of 'mass number' A and 'atomic number' Z was assumed to have a 'nucleus' containing Z **protons** and (A-Z) **neutrons**, with the 'circumnucleus' containing Z **electrons**, as before. The new model of the nucleus also solved the 'atomic weight' problem, since it was realised that the atoms of a given chemical element could have **different numbers of neutrons** in their nuclei, thus producing the different **isotopes** of each element with which we are so familiar today. Some of these 'isotopes' are 'stable', having the correct proton/neutron ratio for this to be the case. If this ratio is too high or too low, the isotope is 'unstable', returning to stability by changing one or more protons into neutrons, or vice versa, by undergoing a form of 'radioactive decay' known as 'beta emission' (I will not go into the details of this now).

The discovery and explanation of the 'particle zoo'

With the discovery of the neutron in 1934, physicists thought they had all the 'fundamental particles' that they needed to explain the basic structure of the 'atoms' of which all matter in the Universe was believed to be composed. These consisted of the **protons** and **neutrons** that made up the 'atomic nucleus', and the **electrons** that made up the 'circumnucleus'. In the years leading up the outbreak of the Second World War, however, several 'new' fundamental particles were discovered (or, if not actually 'discovered', had their 'existence' convincingly demonstrated by powerful theoretical arguments). Let me now deal with each of these in turn.

The first 'new' particle to be 'discovered' was the **neutrino**. The existence of this particle (the 'little neutral one') was proposed by the brilliant Italian physicist, Enrico Fermi (1901-1954), in 1932, in an attempt to explain some physical 'anomalies' that had been discovered in the theory of 'beta decay'. I will not describe them here, but Fermi's idea that an as-yet-undiscovered neutral particle was emitted along with an electron during beta decay turned out to be completely correct, and such a particle was eventually discovered many years later. (The 'neutrino' is now an integral part of the 'standard model' of particle physics.)

The next 'new discovery' was the **positron**. In 1928, the brilliant English physicist, Paul Dirac (1902-1984), of whom we will hear much more about later in the book, had predicted the existence of **antiparticles**, particles that had the opposite electric charge to their corresponding 'real' particles, and would 'mutually cancel each other out' if they ever met, releasing the energy equivalent of their combined 'rest masses' when they did so. The first such particle of this type, the positively-charged 'antiparticle' of the negatively charged electron, was discovered by the American physicist Carl Anderson in 1931, in the course of his study of cosmic rays.

Finally, there were the **mesons**. The existence of such particles was predicted by the Japanese physicist, Hideki Yukawa (1907-1981), in 1935, as part of his theory of the 'strong nuclear force'. This was the force that was needed to 'bind' protons and neutrons together within the atomic nucleus, and 'mesons' were the 'exchange particles' that he believed 'mediated' this force. Physicists thought they had discovered Yukawa's postulated particle in 1937, but this eventually turned out to be a completely different type of particle – the 'muon', a 'heavy' form of the electron. The particle predicted by Yukawa (the 'pion') was eventually discovered after the end of the Second World War, in 1947.

Until 1947, it was still possible to think of the Universe as being 'constructed' from a fairly small number of 'fundamental particles', namely, the ones discussed above. In that year, however, the first of the so-called **strange particles** was discovered, particles that were so named because they had anomalously long half-lives, roughly a **million million** times too long, in fact. They were also found to decay by the so-called **weak interaction** (the one by which 'beta decay' occurs) rather than by the **strong interaction** (the one that controls the force between protons and neutrons within the atomic nucleus). During the next 20 years or so, 'strange particles' were discovered in ever-increasing numbers, using the increasingly-more-powerful **particle accelerators** that were now being built in different parts of the world, particularly in Europe and the USA. These were found to be of two distinct types, namely, **mesons**, with masses less than that of the proton, and **hyperons**, with masses **greater** than that of the proton. Both classes of particles were found to interact strongly with matter. All the 'hyperons' have a 'mass number' of 1, and, together with the two 'nucleons' (the 'proton' and the 'neutron') are collectively known as **baryons** (heavy particles). All **mesons**, on the other hand, have a 'mass number' of 0. Because of the large numbers of these particles, physicist started to refer to them as the 'particle zoo'. It was also becoming increasingly recognised that there were so many of them that it was not realistic to describe them **all** as being truly 'fundamental', and physicists started looking for a way of developing a 'simpler' system for describing the basic nature of the physical world.

Following a period of some confusion, the man who eventually came up with an acceptable solution was the American physicist Murray Gell-Mann (1929-), one of the greatest physicists of the recent modern era. To simply say that he is 'very bright' is probably the understatement of the century; he is 'bright' in the 'Newton' or 'Einstein' class. He is also a true 'polymath' in the 'Diderot' class. Indeed, it is said that he knows more about many subjects than **specialists** in these subjects! But be that as it may, he has undoubtedly made more major contributions to the field of 'particle physics' than any other physicist who has ever lived, work for which he received the 1969 Nobel Prize in Physics – one of the very few people to have been the 'sole recipient' of such an award in the post-war era; most are now awarded to two or three people, 'three' being the maximum permitted number. His most important contribution to the field was undoubtedly his development of the 'quark theory' that eventually solved the problem of the 'particle zoo'. Let me now try to explain this as simply as I can, before describing how it subsequently became the basis of the highly-successful 'standard model' of particle physics.

Basically, what Murray Gell-Mann did during the late 1950's and early 1960's was develop a theory which showed that **all** the known baryons and mesons could be divided into 'supermultiplets' containing either eight or ten individual particles, by plotting a quantity known as 'hypercharge' (designated by 'Y') against their 'electric charge' (designated by 'Q'), a system that he described as the 'eightfold way', in an allusion to the 'Eightfold Way' of Buddhism that I described in Chapter 5. The formation of these 'supermultiplets' was governed by the principles of 'group theory', the branch of mathematics that deals with the different 'symmetries' that can exist between members of 'systems' of all types, and also between 'systems' themselves. One of the most important applications of the 'eightfold way' was its ability to predict the **existence** of hitherto-undiscovered fundamental particles, and, furthermore, to predict their **properties** with considerable accuracy. The most striking example of such a 'successful prediction' was the discovery of the 'omega minus' particle, the 'missing particle' at the top of the first 'baryon decuplet', in 1964. Gell-

Mann had predicted that it should have a 'spin' of 3/2, zero 'isotopic spin', a 'hypercharge' of -2, a 'charge' of -1, positive 'parity', and a 'rest mass' of about 1680MeV (1680 million 'electron volts'). When a particle with **exactly** these properties was discovered at the Brookhaven National Laboratory, the case for Gell-Mann's 'eightfold way', and the 'SU3' group symmetry on which it was based, was clinched. I was working at Harwell at the time, and well remember the excitement among the physics community, who fully recognised the significance of the discovery. (The only comparable event in the 'particle physics' field so far was the discovery of the 'Higgs boson' at CERN in 2012.) Gell-Mann subsequently provided a purely 'physical' explanation of this 'eightfold way', as opposed to his purely 'mathematical' one via the 'SU3 symmetry group', by developing his 'three-quark theory' of the composition of all the existing known baryons and mesons. (The name 'quark' was, incidentally, taken from a quotation from James Joyce's 'Finnegans Wake': 'three quarks for Muster Mark', one of the few example of a 'scientific' concept being derived from 'literature, as opposed to the other way round.) As it turned out, the number of 'quarks' needed to explain the basic nature of the physical world was gradually increased from three to six during the ensuing years, and it is six such entities (the maximum number allowed by current theory) that form the basis of the 'standard model of physics', whose development and basic content I will now describe in some detail.

The development of the 'standard model' of particle physics

I have already described the events that led to Murray Gell-Mann's development of the 'eightfold way' and the 'three quark theory' that provided a physical explanation for it, so I will move on from where I left off at the end of the previous section. Once again, I will try to describe and explain these subsequent developments as simply as I can, albeit at the cost of gross oversimplification, and missing out what some people would regard as 'key features' of the standard model. Readers who wish to read more deeply about these matters can find all the information they need on the 'Internet'.

As we have seen, Gell-Mann was able to explain the structures and properties of **all** the baryons and mesons that were known at the time by postulating the existence of only **three** quarks – the 'up quark', the 'down quark' and the 'strange quark', all of which had fractional electric charges - +2/3 in the case of the 'up quark' and 'strange quark', and -1/3 in the case of the 'down quark'. The two 'nucleons' (the proton and the neutron) were respectively composed of two 'up quarks' and one 'down quark', and two 'down quarks' and one 'up quark', thus giving them net electric charges of '+1' and '0', as the experimental evidence had shown. All **baryons** were shown to consist of 'three quark' combinations of various types, this being one of the combinations 'allowed' by the underlying theory. All **mesons**, on the other hand, were shown to consist of 'two quark' combinations of various types, this being the second of the 'allowed combinations' that the underlying theory permitted. Furthermore, each meson has to consist of a combination of a 'quark' and an 'antiquark' in order to satisfy the 'rules' of the theory. Within each of these different types of particles, the 'quarks' were bound together by what was now called the 'strong force', which was 'carried' or 'mediated' by a new type of particle called the 'gluon', of which there were eight different types.

The simple 'three quark' model of the 'basics' of the physics of the 'strongly-interacting' particles did not last long however. Among other things, it predicted that certain particles should 'break up', or 'decay', in specific ways, and there was increasing experimental evidence that some of these simply did not happen in the way the 'three quark' theory predicted. The most promising theory involved the prediction of the existence of a **fourth** type of quark, which was eventually called the 'charm quark'. The hunt for evidence that such a quark existed began, and, in 1976, its existence was 'verified' by the independent 'discovery' of a completely new type of particle, containing the postulated 'charm quark', by two American research teams, one working at the Brookhaven National Laboratory and the other at the Stanford Linear Accelerator Center (SLAC). Following this discovery, the existence of two further 'quarks', the 'bottom quark' and the 'top quark' were predicted by theorists. Both were eventually discovered by the 'experimentalists', at different 'accelerator centres'. If the 'standard model' proves to be correct in its predictions, as it always **has** been so far, these will be the **last** quarks to be discovered, since it only 'allows for' **three** 'pairs' of quarks and these have now all been found.

During the 1970's, detailed study of the 'strong' force that bound baryons and mesons together, and the 'weak' force that controlled radioactive decay by 'beta emission' led to the development of what eventually came to be known as the **standard model** of particle physics. This 'unified' the theories of the **electromagnetic force** and the **weak force** to produce what became known as the **electroweak force**, and also predicted the existence of two completely new 'types' of particles – the **W bosons** and **Z bosons**, the 'carriers' of the weak force. These were both 'discovered' at CERN during the 1980's. The modern theory of the **strong force**, the so-called **colour force**, or **quantum chromodynamics** (QCD), was also developed at this time. This was found to be extremely complicated, so I will not attempt to describe it here. The 'standard model' also included another completely new type of particle, whose existence had been predicted by the theoretician, Peter Higgs, and others, during the 1960's – the **Higgs boson**. Among other things, this was needed to give 'mass' to quarks and other fundamental particles such as the electron. It was eventually discovered at CERN in 2012, thus justifying the vast cost of its recently-opened 'Large Hadron Collider' at a stroke. Its discovery provided the final 'missing link' in the 'standard model', which was now thought to be 'complete'. Had the Higgs boson **not** been discovered at CERN, the theory would have been 'falsified', and the theoretical particle physicists would have had to go back to 'square one', and start again. **That** was why its discovery was so important. Peter Higgs had been waiting patiently for his 'Nobel Prize' for roughly 50 years, and its almost-immediate award was richly deserved. He must have been a very relieved man!

Let me now conclude this discussion of the 'standard model' by describing the **different types** of particle that it includes, and the **different roles** that these play in the theory. The standard model involves three different **classes** of fundamental particles – particles that make up **matter**, particles that 'carry' (or 'mediate') the four basic **physical forces**, and the **Higgs boson**.

The particles that make up **matter** consist of three different **generations** of particles of progressively greater mass, each generation consisting of two **quarks** (one with charge +2/3 and one with charge -1/3), a **lepton** with charge -1, and an uncharged **neutrino**. I have given details of each of these below. Note that their **masses** are all given in **MeV** (millions of electron volts) or **GeV** (billions of electron volts), representing the 'energy equivalent' of their masses; this is 'standard practice' in particle physics.

First-generation

up quark (mass 2.3MeV)
down quark (mass 4.8 MeV)
electron (mass 0.511 MeV)
electron neutrino (mass?)

Second-generation

strange quark (mass 95MeV)
charm quark (mass 1.27GeV)
muon (mass 0.105GeV)
muon neutrino (mass?)

Third-generation

bottom quark (mass 4.18GeV)
top quark (mass 178GeV)
tau (mass 1.78GeV)
tau neutrino (mass?)

All these 'matter quarks' have so-called **antiparticles**, with which they mutually annihilate if they come into contact, converting their combined mass into **energy** in the process. The other particles in the standard model do **not** have antiparticles.

Each of the four basic forces of physics (the **electromagnetic force**, the **weak force**, the **strong force** and **gravity**) has its own specific type of **force-carrying particle**, as shown below.

The **electromagnetic force** is 'carried' ('mediated') by the **photon**, which has zero mass and travels at the speed of light.

The **weak force** is 'carried' ('mediated') by three different types of **intermediate vector bosons** – the W^+ (mass 80.4GeV), the W^- (mass 80.4GeV) and the Z^0 (mass 90.1GeV); according to **electroweak theory**: these are all essentially 'heavy versions' of the photon.

The **strong force** (QED) is 'carried' ('mediated') by eight different types of **gluon**, which, like the proton, have zero mass, and travel at the speed of light; they themselves also 'feel' the strong force, unlike the photon, which does not 'feel' the electromagnetic force.

The fourth force, **gravity**, is thought to be 'carried' ('mediated') by a further massless particle called the **graviton**, which has yet to be discovered; gravity has still to be incorporated in the 'standard model', as we will see later.

The third type of particle that makes up the standard model, the **Higgs boson**, is uncharged, and was found to have a mass of 126GeV. It is the 'quantum particle' of an all-pervading 'field' called the **Higgs field**, which 'interacts with' all non-zero-mass fundamental particles by a process known as the **Higgs mechanism**, which is too complicated to describe here (look it up on the Internet if you are interested). It is this 'interaction' that gives such particles their mass, and thus makes the existence of 'matter' possible. If these particles did **not** have 'intrinsic mass', they would all travel at the speed of light, like the photons and gluons, and 'stable matter' could not exist. **This** is why the 'Higgs boson' plays such a 'key role' in the 'standard model', and why it was so important that it should be found.

The search for physics beyond the 'standard model'

In Chapter 12, I described the development of the 'standard model' of cosmology, the 'Big-Bang' theory, and showed how it gives an accurate explanation of virtually all the observed large-scale features of the vast Universe in which we live. At the very end of the chapter, however, we saw that there are still a few 'puzzles' that cosmologists have been unable to answer so far, including the questions of what 'dark matter' and 'dark energy' really are, and why the Universe only contains 'matter' and not 'antimatter'. In this chapter, I described the development of the 'standard model' of particle physics, and showed how it has so far been able to explain all the observed features of the 'particle zoo'. In doing so, I may have given the impression that there are no 'puzzles' left in the field of particle physics. Unfortunately, this is not the case, for there are still some very serious 'puzzles' that have yet to be resolved. One is the 'hierarchy problem', the failure to explain why 'gravity' is so very much weaker than the other three forces of nature, the 'strong' force, 'electromagnetism' and the 'weak' force. Linked to this is the total failure of theorists to develop a 'quantum theory of gravity', and thus incorporate 'gravity' into the 'standard model' that I have just described. Another is the failure to find experimental evidence for a phenomenon known as 'supersymmetry', which was one of the things that it was hoped that the 'Large Hadron Collider' at CERN would be able to do. Let me now end this chapter by saying a little about this.

Back in the early days of quantum theory, it was found that 'particles' were of two different basic types, depending on the sort of 'particle statistics' they obeyed – **fermions** and **bosons**. 'Fermions' obeyed 'Fermi-Dirac statistics', had 'half-integral spin', and obeyed the 'Pauli exclusion principle', which specifies that no two particles in a 'system' can occupy the same set of 'quantum states'. All 'quarks' and 'leptons' were later found to be 'fermions'. 'Bosons', on the other hand, obeyed 'Bose-Einstein statistics', had 'integral spin', and did not obey the 'Pauli exclusion principle', so that there was no limit on the number of particles in a 'system' that could occupy the same set of 'quantum states'. All the 'force-carrying particles' in the 'standard model' were later found to be 'bosons'. For a long time, it was thought that 'fermions' and 'bosons' were completely different in virtually every respect, and were not connected by any 'fundamental symmetry', as were the 'proton' and the 'neutron', for example. During the 1970's, however, a group of European and Russian theoretical physicists showed that fermions and bosons **could**, in principle at any rate, be 'linked' by such a symmetry, to which they gave the name 'supersymmetry'. Under this scheme, each 'fermion' would have a 'boson' as a 'supersymmetric partner', and vice versa. These were given strange names, such as 'sleptons' and 'bosinos', but, if they could be shown to exist, would solve many of the current 'puzzles' in particle physics. 'Supersymmetry' also became a key component of 'superstring theory', which, as we will see in Chapter 15, once seemed to be by far the most 'promising candidate' for a 'theory of everything'. (Some 'string theorists' still think it is, but many other physicists are not convinced by their arguments.) At any rate, particle physicists have been looking for evidence for the **existence** of 'supersymmetric partners' ever since, and have so far failed to do so, even with the help of the 'Large Hadron Collider'. There are two possible reasons for this failure. **Either** the concept of 'supersymmetry' is completely wrong, and should be abandoned, **or** the masses of the lightest 'supersymmetric partners' are too large to allow them to be detected by the 'particle accelerators' that have been available so far. Following the successful discovery of the 'Higgs boson', finding evidence for the existence of such 'supersymmetric partners' remains one of the main 'tasks' for the 'Large Hadron Collider'. If the search is successful, this will represent the first 'new physics' to have been discovered 'beyond the standard model'. I wish them all success!

Some of the sources of information on material covered in Chapter 13

Yet again, I found myself very much on 'home territory' here, since I was thoroughly familiar with most of the areas to be covered, and, indeed, had either 'taught' or 'given talks on' quite a lot of it. I did have to refer to quite a few of the books and other materials in my personal library to fill in details, however, and found the following particularly useful:

- 'A Short History of Biology', by Isaac Asimov (an extremely-informative book that I purchased in 1965 through the 'Scientific Book Club', which, unfortunately, no longer exists.)
- 'Great Physicists', by William H. Cropper (once again).
- 'Chambers Biographical Dictionary', 1990 edition (yet again).
- My own 'lecture notes' and 'handouts', which cover a great deal of the content of the chapter; I have not looked at most of the former for decades, since I stopped teaching 'advanced physics' at RGIT a very long time ago!

Chapter 14: The 'weirdness of the quantum world'

'Anyone who **thinks** he understands quantum theory – **doesn't**'

- Richard Feynman

It is now generally recognised that quantum theory is probably **the** most important single development in the history of physics. With the exception of gravity, **all** physical phenomena are now effectively described by the theory at a fundamental level. Everything from the processes within the atom to the workings of the Sun follow the laws of quantum theory. And **all** the electronic devices on which modern society depends (computers, mobile phones, television sets, audio equipment, and so on) **rely totally** on the many **applications** of quantum theory. Despite all this, we still do not know how quantum theory **works**, as the above quotation from Richard Feynman shows, and have very little understanding of the strange picture of 'reality' that it reveals to us. Indeed, many features of the 'quantum world' are so counter-intuitive that they seem to defy 'common sense', as we will see later. Let us therefore take a close look at this strange theory, starting by describing how it began, and how it subsequently developed.

The discovery and development of quantum theory

Quantum theory is one of the two 'foundations' upon which modern physics is built, the other being **general relativity**. As we saw in Chapter 11, it had its origins in 1900, when the German physicist, Max Planck (1848-1947), came up with a revolutionary solution to a problem that had been worrying physicists for many years, the so-called 'ultra-violet catastrophe'. Planck was born in Keil and studied in Munich, and then under Gustav Kirchoff and Hermann von Helmholtz at Berlin University, where he succeeded the former as Professor of

Physics in 1889. There, his work on the laws of thermodynamics and black-body radiation led him to abandon 'classical dynamical principles' in attempting to explain the latter, and to postulate that such radiation was emitted in discrete 'packets' or 'quanta' rather than continuously, as had hitherto been universally assumed. By so doing, he not only succeeded in giving an accurate description of the black-body emission spectrum, but founded a completely new branch of physics – **quantum theory**. As we saw in Chapter 11, his ideas were taken forward by Albert Einstein in 1905, when he showed that the electromagnetic radiation that was emitted by black bodies took the form of **photons**, a name for 'particles of light' that has been used ever since. In so doing, he formulated the basic concept upon which 'quantum theory' was subsequently built. Thus, he and Max Planck are now regarded as the two 'founding fathers' of quantum theory, and both continued to play a key part in its development for many years.

The subsequent early development of quantum theory took place in two main phases. During the first, which lasted until roughly 1920, what became known as the 'old' quantum theory gradually evolved, with the 'key players' being Planck, Einstein, Niels Bohr (1885-1962) and Arnold Sommerfeld (1868-1951). Following Rutherford's discovery of the 'atomic nucleus', Bohr developed the first 'mathematical model' of the atom in 1913 (the so-called 'Bohr atom'), and used this to give an accurate explanation of the hydrogen emission spectrum. Sommerfeld later extended Bohr's basic model, using it to explain the spectra of other, heavier elements. By 1920, however, the 'Bohr-Sommerfeld' model of the atom was getting into serious difficulties, difficulties that led to the development of what became known as the 'new' quantum theory during the 1920's.

The 'key players' in these developments included Planck, Einstein, Bohr, Werner Heisenberg (1901-1976), Erwin Schrodinger (1887-1961), Louis de Broglie (1892-1987), Max Born (1882-1970), Wolfgang

Pauli (1900-1958), Paul Dirac (1902-1984) and many others. They were based on two radically-different approaches – the **matrix mechanics** of Heisenberg, a highly-mathematical model which used 'matrices' to describe the 'input' and 'output' of quantum processes, and the **wave mechanics** of Schrodinger, which described quantum processes in terms of a 'wave function', which was 'controlled' by an equation that subsequently became known as the 'Schrodinger equation'. Dirac then showed that the two approaches were equivalent, and, in the mid-1920's, produced a 'new' version of the basic equation of quantum mechanics (the 'Dirac equation') that incorporated the principles of 'special relativity', and became the basis of most subsequent developments in the field. It is now regarded as one of the most important equations in the history of physics.

A third phase in the development of quantum theory began in the mid-1940's, with the development of modern 'quantum field theory' by Richard Feynman, Julian Schwinger and Shinichiro Tomonaga, working largely independently, for which they subsequently shared the 1965 Nobel Prize in Physics. Richard Feynman (1918-1988) is generally acknowledged to have been one of the most brilliant theoretical physicists who ever lived; the widely-acclaimed biography that James Gleick wrote in 1992 is simply entitled 'Genius – Richard Feynman and Modern Physics', and is a truly amazing 'read'. Born in New York, he was a leading figure in the wartime 'Manhattan Project' that developed the atomic bomb. He subsequently taught at Cornell University from 1945 till 1950, after which he became a Professor at California Institute of Technology, where he had an office next to Murray Gell-Mann for a time. The theory of 'quantum electrodynamics' ('QED') that he played a leading part in developing was (justly) described by him as 'the jewel of physics – our proudest possession' in the book on the subject that he subsequently wrote for the 'general reader' in 1985 ('QED – The Strange Theory of Light and Matter'). I have a well-thumbed copy in my personal library, next to the James Gleick biography, which I have now read three times. The theory has been found to be one of the most successful ever produced, predicting the results of experiments with astonishing accuracy. It layed the foundations for virtually all subsequent developments in quantum theory and its many applications.

One of Richard Feynman's most important contributions to the development of quantum theory, and to sub-atomic physics in general, was his invention of what became known as the **Feynman diagram**. In Chapter 11, I told you how one of the early outcomes of Einstein's 'special theory of relativity' was the development of the concept of 'four-dimensional space-time', and the representation of 'objects' by 'world lines' through such space-time. Well, a 'Feynman diagram' is simply a two-dimensional 'representation' of such a 'world line', thus allowing it to be drawn or printed on a two-dimensional surface such as a sheet of paper or a computer screen. In such a diagram, 'movement through space' is represented by **horizontal movement**, and 'movement through time' by **vertical movement**. Feynman based much of his version of quantum electrodynamics (QED) on such diagrams, the simplest of which represented the basic process that occurs therein – the repulsive force that occurs between two **electrons** when they exchange a **photon**. In the Feynman diagram that describes this process, the two electrons are represented by solid lines, marked with arrows, moving **upwards** through time, and **converging** as they do so. When they reach their point of closest approach, they exchange a photon, represented by a 'wiggly line', and then continue their upwards journey through time, now **diverging** as they do so. Feynman showed how **all** the interactions that take place in quantum electrodynamics can be represented by combinations of more complicated versions of this simple diagram, and can be used as the basis of **all** the calculations that QED involves. It was later found that Feynman diagrams could be used to represent virtually all the interactions that take place in the standard model of particle physics, thus providing clear, easily-understandable pictorial representations of what was going on in them. The decay of a **muon** (a heavy form of electron) into an **electron** and an **antineutrino** via the **weak interaction**, for example, is represented thus. A muon is shown travelling vertically upwards through time, and, at the time when it decays, changes into a **muon neutrino** and a **W- boson** (represented by a wiggly line), which continue moving upwards through time, **diverging** as they do so. After a short interval, the W- boson disappears, turning into an **electron** and an **anti-electron neutrino**, which continue to move upwards through time, **diverging** as they do so. Feynman diagrams can even be used to describe the complicated process by which matter particles acquire mass via the 'Higgs mechanism', executing a zig-zag vertical path through space-time as they do so. I have given talks on the 'standard model' and on the 'Higgs mechanism' with the aid of such diagrams. If you want to learn more about them, look them up on the Internet.

Let us now take a detailed look at four of the main ways in which quantum theory seems to 'defy' common sense, starting with the essentially 'random nature' of quantum processes.

The 'random nature' of the quantum world

Science has shown that the 'macroscopic world' (the world of everyday objects) appears to be essentially **deterministic** in nature. In other words, we can usually assign definite **causes** to specific phenomena, although it is often difficult to predict their **future development** with any accuracy (the weather is a good example). On the other hand, it has been clearly shown that the 'microscopic world' (the world of atoms, subatomic particles and photons) appears to be almost totally **random** in nature. This means that it is not possible to predict exactly **when** and **how** particular quantum events will occur, only to determine the **probabilities** that such things will happen. Einstein (who, as we have seen, was one of the 'founding fathers' of quantum theory), was never able to accept this finding, stating famously that 'God does not play dice with the Universe'. To which Stephen Hawking later replied that 'not only does God play dice, he throws them where we cannot see them!' Hawking seems to have been closer to the truth regarding this matter.

The random nature of quantum events is well illustrated by the phenomenon of **radioactive decay**, so it is well worth taking a detailed look at this. Most of the early work on such decay, which had been discovered late in the 1890's, was carried out by Ernest Rutherford (who I introduced you to in the last chapter) while working at the Cavendish Laboratory at Cambridge University. He found that there were three different types of such decay, which he named 'alpha decay', 'beta decay' and 'gamma decay', names that are still used today. In alpha decay, a radioactive atom moves to a more stable state by emitting an 'alpha particle' (now known to be a 'helium nucleus' of 'mass number' 4). In beta decay, it does so by emitting a 'beta particle' (now known to be either a negative electron or its positively-charged 'antiparticle', the 'positron'). In 'gamma decay', it does so by emitting a 'gamma ray' (now known to be a very-high-energy 'photon'). When systematic study of all three of these decay processes was subsequently carried out, it was found that it was impossible to predict exactly **when** a given unstable atom would decay, only to state the **probability** that it would do so in a given time. Physicists began to describe this process in terms of the **half life** of the radioactive species, this being the time after which **half** of a large number of such atoms would have undergone decay. Suppose, for example, that you started with a small radioactive sample that contained 100 million of such atoms (a **very** small sample indeed). After one 'half life', the number of undecayed atoms would have fallen to 50 million, after two half lives to 25 million, after three half lives to 12.5 million, and so on until the number of undecayed atoms had decreased exponentially to zero.

It was found that these 'half lives' varied from billions of years in the case of some 'alpha' emitters, to much shorter times for most 'beta' and 'gamma' emitters. Following the pioneering work of Rutherford, all the 'laws' that describe radioactive decay, and describe the 'transformation chains' by which an initially-unstable radioactive species eventually ends up as a stable, non-radioactive species were discovered. One of the useful 'by-products' of such work was the development of techniques for the 'radioactive dating' of very old rocks by measuring the relative abundances of the various components of such 'chains'. Geologists have been making systematic use of such techniques for a long time now.

While all the early work on the study of radioactive decay and radioactive chains was going on, physicists still had no real idea of the **underlying mechanisms** by which such decay occurred. This had to wait until the science of 'nuclear physics' got properly underway. The first type to be explained was 'alpha decay', for which a satisfactory theory was first developed by George Gamow (who we met in Chapter 12 in connection with his work on the 'big-bang' theory) in 1928. He pictured the 'alpha particle' as having a 'separate existence' inside the atomic nucleus, and being 'trapped' within a 'potential well' from which it could not escape by simply 'climbing over' the 'energy barrier' that surrounded the 'well'. Gamow showed that an alpha particle could eventually escape from the nucleus by a process known as 'quantum-mechanical tunneling', which was permitted by the 'new laws' of quantum theory that had recently been developed. The next type to be explained was 'beta decay', for which a 'tentative theory', that later turned out to correct, was developed by Wolfgang Pauli and Enrico Fermi during the early 1930's. Beta decay was later fully explained by the development of the standard model of particle physics, which showed how 'conversion' of a neutron into a proton or a proton into a neutron could be fully explained at the 'quark level'. Beta decay is now seen to involve either the 'conversion' of a 'down quark' into an 'up quark', with the emission of a 'negative beta particle' (an 'electron'), or the conversion of an 'up quark' into a 'down quark', with the emission of a 'positive beta particle' (a 'positron'). Both processes can be beautifully and clearly described with the aid of appropriate 'Feynman diagrams'. A satisfactory explanation of gamma decay had to await the development of the 'shell model of the nucleus' during the late 1940's. This pictures the nucleus as having a range of discrete 'internal energy levels', through which an unstable nucleus moves to a more stable state by emitting a high-energy 'gamma ray' photon. When a nucleus finds itself in an 'excited state', it generally moves to a 'lower-energy state' extremely rapidly, in a time that may be as short as 10^{-14} seconds. In some cases, however, the excited state may be 'metastable', because transitions to states of lower energy have a lower probability of occurring. Some excited states can exist for a long time (up to several years in some cases), thus giving rise to 'gamma emitters' with comparatively long 'half lives'. All three radioactive decay processes are now more-or-less fully understood, in so far as processes happening at the quantum level **can** be 'fully understood'!

The 'principle of superposition' of quantum states

One of the key features of quantum theory, and one that many people find hard to believe, is the **principle of superposition**, which holds that **quantum objects** can be in **many different states** at the same time. Indeed, the **normal condition** of such objects is to **be** in such a superposition of states. For example, it has been clearly shown that quantum objects can be in **many different places** simultaneously, rather than being definitely located **in a single place**, as is the case with the 'macroscopic' objects that we see and feel all around us. This phenomenon is clearly illustrated by the behaviour of the **electrons** that surround the nuclei of atoms. According to the 'old' quantum model of the atom that was developed by Bohr and Sommerfeld, such electrons were pictured as moving in well-defined, 'classical' orbits around the nucleus, just as the planets move in well-defined 'classical' orbits round the Sun. Bohr and Sommerfeld pictured the electrons 'jumping between' these orbits when they emitted or absorbed a 'quantum of light' (a 'photon'), with the 'allowed' orbits being determined by the 'laws of quantum mechanics' that had been developed up to then. As we saw earlier, the Bohr-Sommerfeld model of the atom described the 'hydrogen spectrum' with almost perfect accuracy, but did not work so well with the 'heavier' atoms. As we again saw earlier, it was only when the 'new' quantum theory was developed during the 1920's that a model of the atom capable of describing the spectra of these multi-electron atoms was produced. This was based on Schrodinger's 'wave mechanics', which pictured the electrons that surrounded the atomic nucleus as diffuse **probability clouds**, in which the electrons did not have their positions clearly defined, but effectively occupied a **whole range of positions at the same time**. This new model of the atom proved extremely effective in explaining the spectra of **all** heavier atoms. It also enabled the structure of the 'Periodic Table of the Elements' that had formed the basis of chemistry since the time of Mendeleev (1834-1907) to be explained with perfect accuracy. This was based on the 'aufbauprinzip', or 'atom-building process' that had first been suggested by Bohr, which only became possible once the 'Schrodinger' model of the circumnucleus appeared. This pictured the cirumnuclear electrons as being arranged in a series of ever-larger 'shell clouds', with the maximum number of electrons that were 'allowed' in each 'shell' being determined by the laws of the 'new' quantum theory. By using this model, the 'periodic' nature of the periodic table followed logically from the 'shell cloud structure' that was specified by the new theory. In my opinion, this effective explanation of virtually the whole of chemistry by a model of the atom developed by physicists was one of the greatest achievements in the history of science. I thoroughly enjoyed teaching it to my students during my time as a physics lecturer. (My **students** were also 'suitably impressed' by it, as they jolly well **should** have been!)

Another aspect of the 'principle of superposition' is the well-established fact that 'quantum objects' such as photons and electrons do not 'move' from one place to another by following **well-defined paths**, as the 'macroscopic' objects we see around us do. Rather, they move along **many different paths**, which have to be 'added together' mathematically in order to produce the **apparent path** that the object follows when moving from one place to another. This was one of the things that was predicted by Richard Feynman's 'quantum electrodynamics'. Indeed, Feynman showed that such an object effectively follows **all possible paths** between the two points in question. When such a 'sum over histories' or 'path integral' calculation is carried out, it is found that nearly all the **possible paths** 'cancel out', producing something close to the path that **would** be followed if the object moved in a more conventional, 'classical', manner. Nevertheless, quantum physicists now believe that a quantum object **actually does** follow all the possible paths between the two points. Feynman's 'path integral' theory explains the apparently-'crazy' results of the notorious **two-slit experiment**. Here, a beam of monochromatic light is allowed to fall on a barrier containing two closely-spaced narrow slits, and the resulting 'interference pattern' of alternating light and dark bands is observed by allowing the light to fall on a screen or array of detectors of some sort. Numerous experiments have demonstrated conclusively that such an interference pattern is formed even when the intensity of the light beam is reduced to such a low level that **only one photon passes through the system at a time**! This means that each photon is effectively **interfering with itself**, something that can only be explained if the individual photons are indeed passing through **both** slits on their way to the detecting system, as predicted by Feynman's theory. As I said, this astonishing experiment has been carried out many times by different teams of experimentalists, always with the same result.

The impossibility of finding the 'true nature' of quantum systems

Another key feature of quantum theory is that we can never tell what 'quantum objects' or 'systems' are **really like**, since they behave in **different ways** in **different situations**. This is manifested in the strange phenomenon of **wave-particle duality**, in which both **electromagnetic radiation** and **matter** sometimes behave like **waves**, and sometimes behave like **particles**, depending on the nature of the **experimental system** that is set up to examine them. Take **light**, for example. From the start of the 19th century onwards, this was generally regarded as being a type of **wave**, since it demonstrated **wave-like properties** in situations like the 'two-slit experiment' described above. Early in the 20th century, however, Einstein showed conclusively that light could also behave like **particles** in other situations, e.g., when it was used to produce **photoelectric emission**. As we saw earlier, it was his 1905 paper on this that introduced the concept of the 'photon', or 'particle of light', into physics. We also saw that it was his work on explaining the 'apparent anomalies' in photoelectric emission by introducing this idea that won him the 1921 Nobel Prize in Physics, **not** his much-more-important work on special and general relativity, which the Nobel Committee regarded as 'too controversial' at the time! It is now recognised that light is something whose **real nature** we do not understand, but which behaves **as if it was a wave** under **some** experimental conditions, and behaves **as if it was made up of particles** under **other** experimental conditions. **Strange**, but **true**!

Exactly the same appears to be true of **matter**. Until 1924, everyone assumed that this was made up of **particles**, as had been postulated by the Greek 'atomists' and by Isaac Newton. Once the first 'sub-atomic particle', the **electron**, was discovered in 1897, it was assumed that all such 'particles' **were indeed 'particles'**, and had no wave-like properties associated with them. In that year, however, Louis de Broglie, one of the 'founders' of the 'new' quantum theory, made the seemingly-ridiculous suggestion that **matter** might also have a dual, 'wave-particle' nature. His suggestion would probably have been laughed out of sight, or ignored, had he not also predicted what the **effective wavelength** of his hypothetical 'matter waves' might be, something that made it possible to **test** his theory experimentally. This was soon done – independently – by G.P. Thomson (1892-1975), working at Aberdeen University, and by Clinton Davisson (1881-1958) at the Bell Telephone Laboratories in the USA, showing that **electrons** underwent 'diffraction' when passed through crystals, thus 'verifying' de Broglie's idea. Louis de Broglie won the 1929 Nobel Prize in Physics in recognition of his work, and Thomson and Davisson subsequently shared the 1937 Prize. Once again, it is now recognised that matter is something whose **real nature** we do not understand, but which behaves **like particles** under **some** experimental conditions, and which behaves **as if these particles also have wave-like properties** under **other** experimental conditions. Once again, **strange** but **true**.

Related to 'wave-particle duality' is another key feature of quantum theory (and one of which most people have **heard**, even if they do not **understand** it!) – **Heisenberg's uncertainty principle**. This states that it is **intrinsically impossible** to carry out **precise simultaneous measurements** of certain 'pairs of properties' of 'quantum objects' known as **conjugate variables**. Take, for example, the **position** and **momentum** of such an object, which constitute a 'linked pair of variables' of this type. Heisenberg showed that the **product** of the **uncertainty in the position** of a quantum particle such as an electron, and the **uncertainty in its momentum** could **not** be greater than **Planck's constant, h** (a tiny 'fundamental constant' in quantum theory, equal to 6.6×10^{-34} joule seconds). If the **speed** of such an electron is found to have a value of 300 metres per second, accurate to plus or minus 0.01%, then it can be shown that its **position** cannot be known with an accuracy better than plus or minus **2.4 centimetres**. The 'classical concept' of the electron as a 'tiny dot' is not very valid under these circumstances!

Heisenberg also showed that there is a similar 'uncertainty relationship' between **time** and **energy**, with the product of the uncertainty in the **energy** of a 'quantum object' or 'quantum system', and the uncertainty in the **time** for which it **has** that energy again being no greater than Planck's constant, h. One important consequence of this second form of the 'uncertainty principle' is the formation of **virtual particles**, which play a key role in many quantum processes. Consider, for example, the **weak force**, in which certain types of subatomic particles interact by exchanging massive force-carrying particles known as **W** and **Z bosons** (I told you about these in the last chapter when I described the 'standard model' of particle physics). Such particles can 'appear' out of the 'vacuum state' (effectively appearing **out of nothing**), **travel** between the two interacting particles, and then 'disappear' back into the vacuum state **without violating the principles of conservation of mass-energy** provided that the time taken to do so is **less** than the time allowed by the 'time-energy' form of the uncertainty principle. The creation and subsequent disappearance of such 'virtual particles' has now been 'verified' in countless experiments, and they play an absolutely key role in the standard model of particle physics.

Because of the tiny value of Planck's constant, h, Heisenberg's uncertainty principle imposes **no effective limits** on the simultaneous measurements of pairs of 'conjugate variables' in respect of objects or systems in the **macroscopic** world. Thus, tennis players can safely plan to hit the ball without worrying that their racket will miss it because of the 'intrinsic uncertainty' in its position; this is **far** too small to have any effect on the game! There is, incidentally, no truth in the rumour that there is a 'blue plaque' on the wall of Heisenberg's birthplace in Wurzburg stating that 'Heisenberg **possibly** lived here', but it would be nice if there were! (The Germans are not particularly noted for their 'sense of humour, however.)

The 'intrinsic interconnectedness' of the Universe

I have left the best till last, here. What I am about to tell you about **quantum entanglement**, and its implications for the **intrinsic interconnectedness** of the Universe in which we live, is, I believe, giving us a **very broad hint** about the nature of **ultimate reality**, tying in, as it does, with the ideas of Kant and Schopenhauer, and with the much-earlier ideas of the Hindus and Buddhists. But more of that in the 'Conclusion', where I will discuss these matters at much greater length. Let me now simply concentrate on the **facts** as we currently see them.

During the last 40 years or so, it has been **firmly established** that **some** quantum systems, such as pairs of fundamental particles or photons emitted during radioactive decay, or by the decay of other fundamental particles, remain **intimately linked** to one another **no matter how far they are separated in space**. Consider, for example, the decay of an unstable atom that emits two photons that are 'polarised' in opposite ways, and which travel off in opposite directions. Until we carry out an **actual measurement** of the polarisation of one of the photons, we do not know exactly **how** it is polarised, since each photon is effectively in a **superposition** of all possible polarisation states. (As I showed you earlier in this chapter, it is the normal situation for a quantum system to be in such a superposition of states.) All we know is that if **one** of the photons is polarised in a certain way, the other member of the pair **must** be polarised **in the opposite way**, because of the 'laws of physics' that controlled their original emission by the unstable atom. This is not a matter over which there is **any possible doubt**. Now, suppose that we wait for several years, thus allowing the photons to separate by a corresponding number of light years (twice that number, in fact, because they are moving in opposite directions), and then measure the polarisation of **one** of the photons. Because of 'quantum entanglement', we **know, for certain**, that the other photon **must** acquire **exactly the opposite polarisation** at **exactly the same time**. Since there is **no known way** in which a **physical signal** of any conceivable type can pass **instantaneously** between the two photons, because of the absolute 'speed limit' imposed by the laws of special relativity (remember what I told you about this in Chapter 11), we **have** to conclude that the Universe **must** be **intrinsically interconnected** at some deep level that we do not understand at the moment, and, if we believe Kant, may **never** be able to understand. During the 1930's, Einstein and his two colleagues, Boris Podolsky and Nathan Rosen, wrote a famous paper (the so-called 'EPR paper'), in which they dismissed the idea of such 'intrinsic interconnectedness' as 'impossible'. Indeed, Einstein described it as 'spooky action at a distance'. Subsequent developments have **proved** that Einstein and his colleagues were **wrong**, however, since the interconnectedness of such entangled pairs of photons was **verified experimentally** by Alain Aspect and his team in a classic series of experiments carried out in Paris during the early 1980's. Numerous subsequent experiments have **confirmed** their findings, and Einstein's 'spooky action at a distance' is now a firmly-established feature of reality. A 'strange world', indeed!

These, then, are just a few of the 'weird' features of the quantum world that have been discovered during the last hundred years or so. There are many others, some of which are even more weird than those that I have just described (**delayed-action switching experiments**, for example, and **quantum erasure experiments**, which cast doubt on the very **existence of time** as we currently understand it). Interested readers can find out about them in any up-to-date popular book on quantum theory, or by looking them up on the 'Internet'. In the meantime, let me end this chapter by taking a look at some of the main **interpretations** of quantum theory that have been produced to date. As you will see, there is currently **no agreement** regarding which, if any, of these is the **correct** interpretation, and I doubt if there ever will be. But perhaps I am being over-pessimistic; I leave it for you to judge after you have read the final section.

Attempts to 'interpret' quantum theory

The physicists who started to develop the 'new' quantum theory during the early 1920's spent a lot of their time arguing about how to **interpret** the marvellous new theory that was gradually emerging in all its glory. Three of them, Bohr, Born and Heisenberg, championed what became known as the 'Copenhagen interpretation' (Copenhagen was where Bohr worked, and later 'held court'). Three others, Einstein, Schrodinger and de Broglie, became increasingly unhappy with this 'interpretation' as it gradually became the 'accepted orthodoxy', largely because of the influence of the forceful Bohr, and never in fact accepted it. They all favoured some form of 'hidden variables' interpretation of quantum theory. Let me now try to explain what each of these rival 'interpretations' involved.

Explaining exactly what Bohr's 'Copenhagen interpretation' involved is not an easy task, since he never actually gave a complete and full account of it. Also, quotations from Bohr's published papers on the subject are not always 'consistent', which is not really surprising, since his ideas were 'constantly evolving' as the articles were being written. Nevertheless, there are several key features which are generally believed to characterise it. First, it stresses the notion of 'complementarity', whereby 'particle' and 'wave' interpretations 'complement' each other, with one or the other manifesting itself depending on the type of 'experiment' being carried out. Second, it only allows 'classical' physical principles to enter via the so-called 'correspondence principle', which says that the results of 'quantum theory' **must** agree with the predictions of 'classical physics' in areas where the latter is still expected to work. This idea, originally used by Planck, played an important role in the discovery of the 'correct' form of quantum theory. Third, the underlying philosophy is strongly 'anti-realist' in tone. Bohr said that 'there **is** no quantum world, only an abstract quantum physical **description** of what is there'. He also said that 'it is wrong to think that the task of physics is to find out what nature **is**'; rather, 'physics is concerned with what we can **say** about nature.' He also maintained that the only things we were allowed to discuss were the **results** of experiments, not what actually happens **during** the experiments. Fourth, his entire 'interpretation' was essentially based on the **'measurement problem'**, characterised by the 'collapse of the wave function' during such a 'measurement'. Fifth, Bohr maintained that the 'new' quantum theory was 'complete', and needed no underlying 'hidden variables' to make it work. He spent over 20 years arguing with Einstein over this matter, and usually got the better of such arguments. Despite his success in these, he never managed to give a satisfactory explanation of what **actually happens** during a 'quantum measurement', which involved dividing the world into the 'observed system', which obeyed the rules of 'quantum theory', and the 'measuring device', which obeyed the laws of 'classical physics'. Despite these problems, Bohr's 'Copenhagen interpretation' of quantum theory remained the 'orthodox position' for many years, although very few people who think about the subject today would be likely to find it satisfactory. I certainly do not think it is, mainly because Bohr's views on the impossibility of investigating the 'true nature of reality' are totally incompatible with the 'Enlightenment vision' so eloquently expressed by David Hilbert in the quotation that I included in Chapter 9 (Wir **mussen** wissen, Wir **werden** wissen.')

The 'hidden variables' interpretations of quantum theory that were advocated by Einstein, Schrodinger, de Broglie and many later workers try to get around the problem of the intrinsic 'randomness' of quantum processes, which, as we saw earlier, Einstein was **never** able to accept. All such theories assume that what we see around us is not the whole of reality, and that what **appear** to be identical initial systems are in fact 'different', distinguished by having different values of certain new 'variables', not normally specified, and therefore referred to as 'hidden'. The main weakness of all such theories was that their proponents were unable to say much **about** these 'variables', presumably because they **were** 'hidden'. Such theories were also subsequently dealt an apparently fatal blow by the work of the Irish theoretical physicist, John Bell, during the early 1960's. In 1964, he published a remarkable new theorem based on what became known as the 'Bell inequality', which enabled experiments to be carried out in order to determine whether 'hidden variables' theories were compatible with the rest of physics. When such experiments were carried out, they provided fairly conclusive proof that they were not. As a result, the 'hidden variables' interpretation of quantum theory effectively vanished from the 'physics world', although one notable theoretician, David Bohm, continued to support it. He believed that the world that we see around us (what he called the 'explicate order') is underpinned by a deeper, undetectable level of 'reality' which he called the 'implicate order'. He also developed a highly-plausible version of a 'hidden variables' theory based on 'pilot waves', which predicted the same basic results as conventional quantum theory. Bohm died in 1992, but I have to say that I found his ideas 'highly plausible' and will have more to say about them later in the book.

One of the most remarkable interpretations of quantum theory ever produced was the 'many worlds' theory developed by the American physicist, Hugh Everett III, which was first presented to an astonished world in 1957. He began by noting that the orthodox 'Copenhagen interpretation' of quantum theory required the 'wave functions' that describe quantum systems to change in two distinct ways, first, in a continuous, 'deterministic' way, as described by the Schrodinger equation, and second, in a discontinuous, 'undeterministic' way during the 'collapse of the wave function' that takes place during measurement. Everett's proposed solution to this 'wave function reduction' problem was to claim that it **never actually happens**. Instead, **all possible outcomes** of the measurement actually happen, with the 'world' separating into a 'collection of worlds', one for each possible result of the measurement. Although this idea may seem bizarre, Everett's 'many worlds' theory could be shown to produce exactly the same 'results' as conventional quantum theory, and was therefore taken very seriously indeed by many workers in the field. I myself find it difficult to give credence to, since I find the idea of the 'world' dividing into a 'multitude of worlds' every time an event takes place at the quantum level totally 'incredible', in the true sense of the word. Others, however, do not, and Everett's 'many worlds' interpretation of quantum theory is still regarded as one of the possible options. It is still described in all books on quantum theory.

For what it is worth, the 'interpretation' of quantum theory that I find most attractive is the less-well-known 'transactional theory' that was proposed by John Cramer during the 1980's. I will not describe it here, because it would take far too long, but interested readers can find a detailed description in the 'Epilogue' of John Gribbin's excellent book, 'Schrodinger's Kittens'. John Gribbin is a highly-qualified scientist who is also a best-selling author of 'popular science' books. **He** certainly takes Cramer's ideas seriously, and I suspect that many of you would too. It is, however, well 'on the fringe' of 'mainstream' thinking.

Some of the sources of information on material covered in Chapter 14

Once again, I was on 'home territory' when writing this chapter, since I am thoroughly familiar with most of the areas that it deals with, and have also lectured on, or given talks on, several of these. I was also able to base most of the chapter on one of my articles that was published electronically by 'Quo Vadis Publications' in 2016, 'The Weirdness of the Quantum World'. I did have to refer to several of the books in my personal library, and also to my own lecture notes, for detailed information, finding the following particularly helpful:

- 'Great Physicists', by William H. Cropper (once again).
- 'Genius – Richard Feynman and Modern Physics', by James Gleick (probably the most fascinating and informative biography that I have ever read).
- 'QED – The Strange Theory of Life and Matter', by Richard Feynman (well worth reading, and highly readable, if you want to learn what modern quantum theory is **really** all about).
- 'The Mystery of the Quantum World', by Euan Squires (the source of nearly all the material in the final section of the chapter).
- 'Schrodinger's Kittens', by John Gribbin.
- 'Chambers Biographical Dictionary' (yet again).

Chapter 15: The search for a 'theory of everything'

'Is the current search for a 'Theory of Everything' a realistic project or an unattainable chimera?'

- Henry Ellington

I have always been interested in the search for a 'Theory of Everything', and, in the late-'noughties', started giving talks on the subject. In order to support these, I prepared a printed 'handout' and a PowerPoint presentation with the above title, which summed up my ideas on the matter at the time. It still does, more or less, although I have now moved closer to regarding the search for a 'Theory of Everything' as an 'unattainable chimera', as you will see as Chapter 15 unfolds. Make up your own minds once you have read it.

What do we mean by a 'theory of everything'?

The idea of what constitutes a 'theory of everything' means different things to different people, and has changed considerably since the start of the 20th century. Before then, no-one really used the term, although, for the previous 200 years or so, we had the 'nearest thing' to such a theory that we have ever had, and probably **will** ever have. I am, of course, referring to the 'Newtonian world picture' which dominated physics and astronomy until the end of the 19th century. As we saw in Chapter 7, this had effectively explained everything that was known in physics and astronomy at the time, the only problems being the two 'clouds in the sky' that had been identified by Lord Kelvin in his lecture at the Royal Institution in April, 1900. As we saw in Chapter 11, these two 'clouds' (the failure to detect 'motion through the ether' and the failure to explain the 'black-body emission spectrum') eventually brought the whole magnificent edifice of Newtonian physics crashing down, ushering in what subsequently became known as the 'Einsteinian Revolution' in physics. In many ways, we are still living the aftermath of this.

During the 20th century, it took a long time for the concept of a 'theory of everything' to develop, and nobody actually **used** the term initially. As we will see in the next section, they originally referred to the search for such a theory as the search for a 'unified field theory', an attempt to 'unify' the two basic physical forces that were known at the time – **gravity** and **electromagnetism**. As we will see, this attempt failed, and the term eventually started to be applied to the search for a theory that could unite electromagnetism and gravity with the two 'new' forces that were subsequently added to the list of 'basic physical forces' – the **'strong' nuclear force**, or 'strong interaction', and the **'weak' nuclear force**, or 'weak' interaction. (I told you about both of these in Chapter 13.) Since then, the term 'theory of everything' has come to designate a 'fundamental theory' that is capable of explaining **all** the 'basic features' of 'physical reality', particularly the nature of **space** and **time**, the nature of all the **basic forces** that underlie physics, and the nature of the **fundamental particles** that make up the physical world. If we **were** able to develop such a theory, it would effectively **underpin** and **inform** the whole of science, so it is claimed. It would certainly be a marvellous achievement, whatever its other benefits turned out to be.

Unsuccessful attempts to find such a theory to date

To date, there have been a number of attempts at develop such a 'theory of everything', but all eventually 'failed' for various reasons, or, at least, have not 'succeeded' so far. Let us now take a detailed look at four of the most important of these – **Unified Field Theory, 'Grand Unification', 'Supergravity',** and **'String Theory'**.

Unified Field Theory

As we saw in the previous section, the search for a 'unified field theory' had its roots in the ultimate failure of Newton's magnificent 'world picture', which had, during the final stages of the 19th century, seemingly offered the possibility of explaining **everything** that was known about physics. It had, after all, successfully 'taken on board' the two 'new' branches of physics that had grown to maturity during its early- and mid-decades – **thermodynamics** and **electromagnetism**. As we saw in Chapter 7, Newton's world picture was based on two core assumptions – that the world is made of nothing but **matter** (Newton's 'atoms', and larger 'aggregates' of these), and that the world exists within a **fixed framework** of three-dimensional, 'Euclidian' **space**, through which **time** flows inexorably, linearly and smoothly. With the eventual abandonment of the concept of 'absolute motion' from this picture, and the resulting abandonment of the ether itself, there was really only one place to go. This was to 'reverse' the theory that gravitational and electromagnetic fields were simply 'stresses in the ether', and accept that **fields** might be the 'fundamental stuff' of which the world was made. It followed from this that **matter** must be 'made from' such fields. Since there were already theories that pictured electrons and atoms as 'stresses' in these fields, this was not really such a 'big step'. But even as this idea gained adherents, there were still mysteries, including the 'big question' of why there were **two** fundamental types of field – the **gravitational field** and the **electromagnetic field** – and not merely **one**. It was this type of thinking that led physicists to start looking for ways in which the two fields could be 'unified'.

Since Einstein had already incorporated **electromagnetism** into his 'special theory of relativity' in 1905, the obvious way to proceed was to try to incorporate **gravity** into the same theory. In 1914, a Finnish physicist called Gunnar Nordström showed that this could be done very easily, by simply increasing the number of 'dimensions' of 'space' from 3 to 4. When he wrote down the equations that described electromagnetism in a 'world' with **four** dimensions of space and **one** of time, out 'popped' 'Newtonian gravity' as a 'natural consequence'. So, just by adding that one 'extra dimension' of space, you produced a 'unification' of gravity with electromagnetism that was also perfectly consistent with Einstein's special theory of relativity. But if this was true, why were we not able to 'see' this new, extra dimension, just as we can 'see' the three dimensions of Euclidean space? The proposed solution was to suppose that the new dimension was 'curled up' into a tiny circle at every point in four-dimensional space-time, so that if you travelled along it, you ended up back where you started. (This idea of 'compactification' of extra spatial dimensions was one that would be revived in two, much later, 'theories of everything' – **supergravity**, and **string theory**.)

Now, you might have thought that Einstein, of all people, would have embraced this new theory, but, as we saw in Chapter 11, he was already well on his way down a completely different road to explaining gravity. In 1915, he published his 'general theory of relativity', which described 'gravity' as an effect of the 'curvature of space' that was produced by the 'matter/energy' density that it contained. (Remember John Wheeler's beautifully-simple description of this process: '**Matter** tells **space** how to **curve**; **space** tells **matter** how to **move**'.) At any rate, there turned out to be a way of finding out which of the two theories was 'true' – by seeing whether 'light' was 'bent' when it passed close to a massive gravitating body such as the Sun. Nordström's theory predicted that no such 'bending' would occur; Einstein's theory predicted that it would, and also predicted the **amount** of bending that would take place. As we saw in Chapter 11, the matter was settled once and for all by the results of Eddington's 1919 expeditions. After these were reported, Nordström's theory was quietly forgotten, and Einstein's theory became one of the two 'foundations' of modern physics, along with quantum theory. **This** was an example of how a 'key experiment' could change the future of science in a 'big way'.

Following the triumph of general relativity, a German physicist called Theodor Kaluza revived Nordström's idea of uniting electromagnetism and gravity by adding an extra, 'hidden' dimension to space, but did this 'the other way round'. When this was done, he showed that Einstein's 'field equations' of general relativity 'naturally contained' the 'field equations' of 'electromagnetism'. Thus, if Kaluza's idea was correct, the 'electromagnetic field' was just another name for the 'geometry of the fifth dimension'. During the 1920's, Kaluza's idea was further developed by the Swedish physicist, Oskar Klein, resulting in what became known as the **Kaluza-Klein theory**. As Lee Smolin later observed in his 2006 book, 'The Trouble with Physics', 'their theory was beautiful and compelling indeed'. Gravity and electromagnetism are unified in one blow, and Maxwell's equations are explained as coming out of Einstein's equations, all by the simple act of adding a single 'dimension to space'. Einstein and many of his prominent contemporaries were greatly impressed by the Kaluza-Klein theory. One of them, George Uhlenbeck, remembered first learning about it in 1926, reporting that 'I felt a kind of ecstasy! Now one understands the world'.

Unfortunately, Einstein and the other enthusiasts for the Kaluza-Klein theory turned out to be wrong, and, as with Nordström's theory, the idea of unifying gravity and electromagnetism by adding a 'hidden dimension' to space failed. Let me now try to explain why as simply as I can. As we have seen several times in this book, if a 'new theory' is to succeed, and gain 'general acceptance' by the scientific community, it has to 'win its place' in the currently-accepted 'body of science' by making **predictions** that survive **rigorous experimental testing**. (This principle was clearly set out by Karl Popper in 1934, as we saw in

Chapter 11.) And, to prove **really successful**, a 'new theory' should also generate a plethora of **new insights** that lead to a wide range of further discoveries. Compelling as it was to some people, neither of these things happened in the case of the Kaluza-Klein 'unified field theory'. There was a simple reason for this, something that turned out to be the 'Achilles heel of the whole enterprise', as Lee Smolin so aptly expressed it in his 2006 book. This was that the theory not only predicted that the 'extra dimension' should be 'curled up' into a circle far too small for us to be able to detect it, but that its size should be **fixed** and **frozen**, changing in neither space nor time. This requirement made the Kaluza-Klein theory completely incompatible with the very essence of Einstein's general theory of relativity, which holds that the geometry of space-time is essentially **dynamical** in nature. And, as we saw in Chapter 11, Einstein's general theory has, so far, **survived every experimental test to which it has been subjected**. To make matters even worse, the Kaluza-Klein theory also turned out to be incompatible with many of the predictions of the 'new quantum theory'. Einstein continued to support the theory, however, and, as I stated in my 'handout paper' on the search for a 'theory of everything', 'effectively wasted the last half of his scientific career on the unified field project', with his reputation being 'severely damaged as a result'.

Grand unification

Following their failure to find a viable 'unified field theory', it took physicists quite a long time to start thinking about unification of the basic forces of physics once again. They had, after all, been kept quite busy discovering and explaining the 'particle zoo' (as we saw in Chapter 13), and developing 'quantum electrodynamics' (as we saw in Chapter 14.) They had also discovered two completely new forces, the **weak force** (or 'weak interaction') and the **strong force** (or 'strong interaction'), both of which only operated at 'subatomic level'). Once they started to think about 'force unification' once again, they decided to concentrate on the three 'strongest' of these, the 'strong force', 'electromagnetism' and the 'weak force', since 'gravity' was **many** 'orders of magnitude' weaker than any of these. There were also severe problems associated with producing a 'quantum theory of gravity', as I will explain later. It had also been found that the four basic forces behaved in their own characteristic ways. **Gravity**, being a 'distortion' of the very **fabric** of space-time, acts on **all** types of matter, and on **all** types of fundamental particles. **Electromagnetism**, on the other hand, only acts on electrically-charged particles such as positively-charged protons and negatively-charged electrons. The **strong force** is even more 'choosy', acting only on 'heavy' matter particles ('hadrons' and 'mesons' that are made up of 'quarks'), excluding a whole class of other 'matter' particles called 'leptons'. Finally, the **weak force** only participates in a limited group of particle transformations (beta decay, for example), although it does also play a key role in the ubiquitous 'Higgs mechanism' that gives matter particles their 'intrinsic mass'. (All these differences were described in greater detail in Chapter 13.)

As I explained in Chapter 13, it took particle physicists over 20 years to develop a satisfactory explanation of the 'particle zoo' that started to be discovered after the end of the Second World War. This culminated in the discovery that all the 'hadrons' (including the proton and neutron) and all the 'mesons' (including the 'pions' that mediated the force that held the atomic nucleus together) were in fact 'composite particles' rather than true 'fundamental particles', being made up of different combinations of 'quarks'. As I showed, the 'mastermind' behind this work was the 'super-genius' and 'super-polymath' Murray Gell-Mann, who also applied the principles of 'group theory' to explaining the 'symmetry relationships' that existed between these different groups of particles. During the 1970's, particle physicists also started to carry out detailed study of the 'strong' force that bound hadrons and mesons together, and the 'weak' force that controlled radioactive decay by 'beta emission', work that eventually led to the development of what became known as the 'standard model' of particle physics. I have already described this in some detail in Chapter 13, so will not repeat myself here. Rather, I will concentrate on the attempts that were made to develop the 'theory of everything' that became known as 'Grand Unification'. Initially, this showed great promise, and had a number of major successes, but eventually failed in its ultimate aim – to produce a theory that 'unified' the **electromagnetic force**, the **weak force** and the **strong force**, and also 'explained' the 'standard model' itself.

The attempts to develop a 'grand unification theory' of these three basic forces were built upon the great mathematical edifice known as **group theory**, which describes the 'symmetry relations' that exist **between** objects such as fundamental particles, and also **within** 'systems' of all types, including 'mathematical systems'. (I will discuss group theory again in Chapter 17.) They were also built upon a class of powerful physical theories known as **gauge theories**, and on the principles of a process known as **spontaneous symmetry breaking**. 'Gauge theories' are based on a 'beautiful mathematical idea' known as the 'gauge principle' that was 'discovered' ('invented'?) in 1918 by Herman Weyl, described by Lee Smolin as 'one of the deepest mathematicians ever to ponder all the equations of physics'. The 'gauge principle' is much too complicated for me to describe in detail here (even if I could!), but there are two basic things that you need to know about it. The first is that the forces it leads to are 'mediated' by particles called **gauge bosons**. The second is that the **electromagnetic**, **strong** and **weak** forces have each been found to be forces of this kind. (I introduced you to the 'gauge bosons' that 'mediate' each of these in Chapter 13.) 'Spontaneous symmetry breaking' is also quite difficult to explain to people who lack a deep physics and/or mathematical background. All you need to know is that it can happen to the 'symmetries' that occur between the 'fundamental particles' that make up the natural world. And when it occurs for those symmetries that, through the 'gauge principle', give rise to the 'forces of nature', it leads to the observed 'differences in their properties'. Conversely, use of the theory of 'spontaneous symmetry breaking' also allows us to 'unify' fundamental forces that **appear** to have different properties.

This is exactly what the American physicist, Steven Weinberg, and the Pakistani physicist, Abdus Salam, did in 1967, when, working independently, they discovered that the combination of the 'gauge principle' and 'spontaneous symmetry breaking' could be used to construct a 'beautiful theory' that 'unified' the **electromagnetic force** and the **weak force**. This theory now bears their joint names, being known as the **Weinberg-Salam** model of the **electroweak force**. Very quickly, their work led to prediction of several 'new phenomena', including the existence of the three 'gauge bosons' that 'mediate' the 'weak' branch of the electroweak force − the W^+, W^- and Z^0 'intermediate vector bosons' that I told you about in Chapter 13. These were subsequently discovered at CERN during the 1980's, thus producing a triumphant 'verification' of the first stage of 'Grand Unification'. Nobel Prizes soon followed for all those involved.

Now on to the next stage, it was hoped. All the work on the unification of the forces up to now had been based on three 'symmetry groups'. The first, known as **U(1)**, was used to describe the symmetries involved in electromagnetism, the '1' signifying that 'one' electrical charge was involved. The second, known as **SU(2)**, describes the 'isospin doublets' that quarks and leptons form, the '2' signifying the fact that 'two' particles are involved in each of these (e.g., the proton and neutron). Combining these two groups produced the U(1)xSU(2) theory of the 'electroweak' force. The third, known as **SU(3)**, was used to describe the 'colour force' ('quantum chromodynamics') that acts between quarks, the '3' signifying that the force involves 'three' colours. The 'combined theory' developed up to now was designated

U(1)xSU(2)xSU(3). In order to take the process of 'Grand Unification' further, however, it was necessary to employ an even more 'powerful' mathematical group. It was hoped that this would provide a 'deep symmetry' that would not only bring the three **forces** (**electromagnetic, weak** and **strong**) together, but would also bring **quarks** (the particles 'ruled' by the 'strong force') and **leptons** (the particles 'ruled' by the 'weak force') together under a 'single theory'. The simplest 'candidate' for such a 'Grand Unification' was the 'symmetry group' known as **SU(5)**. Here, the '**5**' is a 'code' for the 'five kinds of particles' re-arranged by the new 'symmetry group' – the 'three' coloured quarks of each 'generation', and the 'two' leptons of each 'generation', the 'electron' and the 'neutrino' (see Chapter 13 for details). SU(5) not only 'unified' quarks and leptons'; it explained, concisely and clearly, everything that went into the 'standard model', and made a **necessity** of much that was previously **arbitrary**.

SU(5) also made a number of **completely new predictions**, one of which was that the **proton** was intrinsically **unstable**, and should 'decay' with a 'half-life' of the order of 10^{33} years. Although this is an **enormously** long time, many 'orders of magnitude' greater than the 'age of the Universe', it is something that was well within the scope of 'experimental testing'. All you had to do was build a very large tank deep underground (to shield it from cosmic rays), fill it with water, surround it with suitable detectors, and wait for the few protons a year that the SU(5) theory predicted should decay. Such facilities started to go into operation almost 40 years ago now, and the number of proton decays so far detected has been precisely **zero**. We have now waited long enough to know, with something approaching **absolute certainty**, that SU(5) Grand Unification is **wrong**. It is a 'beautiful idea', but one that nature seems **not** to have 'adopted'. Once again, the results of a 'key experiment' had completely changed the course of a major branch of physics.

According to Lee Smolin, particle physics has never 'recovered' from the 'failure' of SU(5) Grand Unification, and is now probably past the peak of its 'golden age'. Only if the 'Large Hadron Collider' at CERN succeeds in discovering some exciting 'new physics' 'beyond the standard model' will it ever get back there. And, as I explained at the end of Chapter 13, the chances of this happening are becoming increasingly remote with every year that passes. We can all but hope, however, but do not bet 'serious money' on it happening in our lifetimes, since there are currently no plans to build a larger successor to the 'LHC'. When **it** reaches the end of its operational life, 'big' particle physics will effectively be 'dead', unless a **large** amount of 'new money' is found somewhere.

Supergravity

As I said in the previous section, the theoretical physicists who started looking for a theory that might unite the basic forces of nature decided to concentrate their efforts on the three most powerful of these forces – the **strong** force, the **electromagnetic** force and the **weak** force, at least initially. Trying to bring the weakest of the four basic forces, **gravity**, into the theory was considered to be 'just too difficult' at the time. For a start, gravity was not only **very** much weaker than the other forces, it was **unimaginably** weaker. Consider, for example, the forces that act between the single proton and single electron that make up an atom of hydrogen. These are subject to two attractive forces, the **electromagnetic force** (resulting from their opposite electric charges) and the **gravitational force** (resulting from their masses). Believe it or not, the former is 'stronger' than the latter by a **factor of 10^{40}**. This is why gravity can effectively be ignored when working at the 'atomic' and subatomic' scales; it is simply 'too weak' to have **any** noticeable effect. It is only when **very** large masses are involved (those of planets, or stars, or galaxies, or 'black holes') that gravity comes into its own, and, indeed, becomes the 'dominant force'. Indeed, when working at very large scales, with very massive objects, it is the **other three forces** that can effectively be ignored in most cases, because it is **they** that are simply 'too weak' to have any noticeable effect. (I said 'in **most** cases' rather than 'in **all** cases', because it has been found that **magnetic** forces do sometimes play a major part in processes that take place at such scales.) Another problem with gravity was that the 'gauge boson' that was thought to be responsible for 'mediating' the force at the 'quantum scale', the **graviton**, had twice as much **spin** as the gauge bosons that mediated the other three basic forces. For various technical reasons that I will not go into here, this made it impossible to develop a 'quantum theory of gravity' that produced 'finite answers' when things like the **strength** of the force were calculated using 'quantum methods'.

A possible way out of the problem of developing a 'quantum theory of gravity' started to appear in 1974, when the English theoretical physicist, Stephen Hawking (1942-2018), made a revolutionary break-through in the theory of **black holes**. He showed that 'quantum effects' appeared to operate at the **boundary** of such objects, an imaginary spherical surface known as the **event horizon**. According to Hawking's theory, this caused black holes to 'evaporate' by emitting so-called 'Hawking radiation', and, eventually, to 'disappear' altogether. (This only happens with '**very** light' black holes, however, and, to date, no such 'vanishing' black holes have ever been found. Had such objects been detected before Hawking's death, he would almost certainly have been awarded the Nobel Prize for Physics, and would have richly deserved it.) Hawking's work was continued by one of his research students, Jacob Beckenstein, and the two of them eventually developed a comprehensive theory of the **thermodynamics** of black holes, showing that they possessed properties such as **temperature** and **entropy**, and, because 'entropy, and 'information' were known to be intimately linked, also **contained** 'information', which a black hole gradually lost during the emission of 'Hawking radiation'. It was this work by Hawking and Bekenstein that prepared the way for the development of a 'quantum theory of gravity' that seemed likely to 'work', at least for a while. This was called **supergravity**, and was based on the idea of **supersymmetry** that I described in detail at the end of Chapter 13. This proposed that all 'fermions' and 'bosons' had 'supersymmetric partners' that could be 'converted' into one another by quantum processes controlled by this powerful new symmetry. It did, however, require a few 'extra space dimensions' to make it 'work', no fewer than six in the case of the most 'promising' version of the theory. This meant that 'space-time' possessed no fewer than ten dimensions in total, nine of 'space' and one of 'time'. As in the case of the one extra dimension required by the various 'unified field theories' that I described earlier, the six 'extra space dimensions' were pictured as being 'curled up' or 'compactified', so that they were far too small to detect. The ultimate aim of the 'supergravity' programme was to produce a 'theory of everything' that would unify all the basic **particles** and **forces** with **space** and **time**. For various technical reasons that are too complicated for me to go into here, it did not succeed in doing this, but effectively 'laid the foundations' for the development of **string theory** – the **next** major attempt to produce a 'theory of everything'. Indeed, 'supersymmetry' and 'supergravity' were eventually found to be integral parts of such a theory.

String theory

Although 'string theory' is probably **the** most complicated theory to be devised by the mind of man, surpassing even Einstein's 'general theory or relativity' in the difficulty of the mathematics that it involves, it can actually be **described** in very simple terms. It postulates that **all** the 'truly fundamental particles', all the **quarks** and **leptons**, all the **gauge bosons**, and also the ubiquitous **Higgs boson**, are in fact composed of **extremely** tiny, one-dimensional objects known as 'strings', which can either be 'open-ended' or 'joined up' to form loops. These 'objects' are so tiny that they make all these 'fundamental particles' look positively **gigantic** by comparison, their 'size' being comparable with the so-called **Planck length** – the smallest conceivable distance that can be meaningfully talked about in physics. As we saw in Chapter 12, it is believed that the **size** of the Universe was roughly equal to this 'Planck length' immediately after the start of the **big-bang**, having a diameter of the order of 10^{-35} metres. Because of their unimaginably-small size, it is extremely unlikely that we will **ever** be able to detect strings or investigate their properties by any conceivable type of experimental procedure. All we can do is investigate their properties **theoretically**, and hope that this leads to 'predictions' that **can** be 'tested' experimentally. So far, 'string theory' (which, like 'supergravity', requires no fewer than ten dimensions in which to operate, six of them 'compactified'), has made no such predictions, and so cannot really be tested.

Nor has the more 'advanced' version of the theory that was subsequently developed. This is known as **M-theory**, and replaces the one-dimensional 'strings' in the original theory by 'objects' in higher dimensions known as **branes**. M theory requires eleven dimensions in which to operate, seven of which are 'compactified' in this case. The 'mastermind' behind this latest version of string theory was the American mathematical physicist, Edward Witten, who is reckoned to be one of the cleverest men who has ever lived. It is interesting to note that he has won the 'Fields Medal' (the mathematical equivalent of the Nobel Prize) for his work on string theory, but has never been awarded the Nobel Prize in Physics. This is only awarded to 'theorists' whose work is 'verified' 'experimentally', something that is **extremely unlikely** to happen in the case of 'string theory'. Because of this on-going failure to make 'testable' predictions, 'string theory' has been heavily criticised by many prominent physicists in recent years. Indeed, in 2006, Peter Woit published a scathing attack on string theory entitled 'Not Even Wrong', thus echoing the damning words that were used by Wolfgang Pauli to describe a theory that he **really** did not like! Having read several books on the subject, I tend to agree with Peter Woit.

Why we may never be able to find such a theory

As we have seen, **all** the attempts to produce a 'theory of everything' have so far proved unsuccessful. This has led a number of scientists and philosophers to question the whole idea of developing such a theory. Some say that it will **never** been possible to develop a 'theory of everything', and have produced powerful arguments as to why this is the case. Others have argued that such a theory would have extremely limited applications even if it **could** be developed, so would not really warrant being described as a 'theory of **everything'**. Let us now take a closer look at these various arguments, which can be loosely described as **'epistemological'** arguments, the **'Gödel'** argument, and the **'emergence'** argument.

Epistemological arguments

As I explained earlier in the book, **epistemology** is the branch of philosophy that deals with the **nature of knowledge**, and has been the subject of much discussion since the time of the 'Pre-Socratics'. It addresses such basic questions as 'what **can** we know?' and '**How** do we know that we know it'? As I showed you in Chapter 8, the German philosopher, Immanuel Kant, published what was unquestionably the greatest ever book on epistemology, 'Critique of Pure Reason, in 1781. In this, he demonstrated, by **purely rational arguments**, that **scientific knowledge** is limited to what we can learn about the **phenomenal world** that we perceive to lie around us and in which we live our lives (what we now call the **empirical world**). We do this by gathering data about this world via our physical senses, and then **processing** and **integrating** this using our **mental faculties**. Since both our physical and our mental 'apparatus' are **strictly limited** in what they can gather and process because of their **intrinsic nature,** Kant went on to argue that we can **never** discover the **true nature** of **ultimate reality**, which he called the **noumenal world**. His ideas regarding the **possible** nature of this permanently-hidden, underlying world were further developed by Schopenhauer, as we again saw in Chapter 8. Many of Kant's successors, including Bryan Magee and myself, have accepted this basic epistemological doctrine, and believe that this rules out the possibility of **ever** being able to develop a true 'theory of everything'. All we can do is try to develop **provisional models** of 'reality' and **test** these experimentally to see if they 'work'. We can, however, **never** know whether even the most successful of these models represents a genuine picture of what **ultimate reality** is like, since, in the immortal words of the semanticist, Alfred Korzybski, 'The **map** is not the **territory**'. (This is probably the best description of the 'limitations' of scientific theories and models that I have ever read.)

Another version of the 'epistemological argument' against the possibility of ever developing a true 'theory of everything' is based on the work of one of Kant's most famous and influential successors, Ludwig Wittgenstein. In his 'Tractatus Logico-Philosophicus', published in German in 1921 and then in English is 1922, he tried to 'complete' the 'epistemological project' by determining, once and for all, just what we **could** and **could not** know about the 'empirical world', which he defined as the 'totality of **facts**, not of **things**'. As a result of detailed analysis, he came to a number of definite conclusions about what we can and cannot know about this 'world of facts', the one most relevant to the present problem being his statement that 'The **sense** of the world must lie **outside** the world'. Let me try to explain what Wittgenstein was saying here. First of all, he believed that we live in a **contingent** world (one where things **might** be different from what they are) rather than in a **necessary** world (one where things **must** be as they are). Then, he was presenting the undisputable philosophical 'truth' that such a contingent physical world cannot contain **within itself** the explanation **for itself**, something that follows, logically, from the meaning of the word 'contingent', and is therefore what philosophers call an **analytical, 'a priori'** truth. If you agree with this argument, it again leads you to the inescapable conclusion that we will **never** be able to develop a true 'theory of everything'.

The Gödel argument

To help you to understand this argument, I will have to tell you a little bit about the history of mathematics (I promise it will just be a **little** bit, because I do not want to lose all my readers at this point!). In the early part of the 20th century, mathematicians believed that they would eventually be able to develop a **fully-complete, fully self-consistent** mathematical 'edifice' by **proving theorems** derived from the **basic axioms** (self-evident, fundamental 'truths') of the field. The purpose and scope of this mammoth 'project' had been set out at the start of the century by the great German mathematician, David Hilbert (1862-1943), one of whose most-famous statements has already been referred to twice in this book. By the start of the 1930's, the 'project' appeared to be well underway, but, in 1931, the hopes of Hilbert and his followers were completely shattered by the work of the brilliant Austrian mathematical logician, Kurt Gödel (1906-1978). What subsequently became known as 'Gödel's incompleteness theorem' conclusively demonstrated that Hilbert's hope of developing a **fully-complete mathematical system** that was, at the same time **completely free from self-contradictions**, was impossible. What Gödel **proved**, using the **rigorous methods of mathematics**, was that **any** 'formal' mathematical system that was based on 'axioms' and 'rules of procedure', and was free from 'internal contradictions' of any type, **must** contain some 'statements' which are neither **provable** nor **disprovable** by the **means allowed within the system**. Such 'statements' were in fact **undecidable** by the methods inherent in the

354

'system', although they could sometimes be 'proved' or 'disproved' by using methods taken from **outside** the system. The similarity to Wittgenstein's statement that 'the sense of the world must lie outside the world' is obvious, and Gödel's revolutionary theorem had the same devastating impact on the 'theory or everything' project as it had on Hilbert's 'axiom-based mathematics' project. One of the key features of Gödel's theorem was that it only applied to mathematical systems that were 'rich' enough to contain all the features of 'basic arithmetic' (what mathematicians called 'Peano arithmetic'). Since it was clear that any worthwhile 'theory of everything' would **have** to be **considerably richer** than this if it was to be capable of explaining **anything**, let alone **everything**, many 'thinking people' came to believe that the 'Gödel argument' ruled out any realistic possibility of developing a full 'theory of everything' just as effectively as the two 'epistemological arguments' that I described earlier. This did not stop theoretical physicists going on **trying** to develop such a theory, however. (As we saw earlier in this chapter, most of the 'serious work' in this area happened **well after** the publication of Gödel's work in 1931.)

The emergence argument

It is now becoming increasingly recognised that science is **hierarchical** in nature, with each successive layer being **underpinned** by all the layers below it, but with each layer containing **concepts** and **laws** that **emerge** from that layer alone, and which therefore cannot be **proved** or **derived** from more 'fundamental' concepts or laws associated with lower layers. Starting at the very bottom of this hierarchy, we have the really basic things which a 'theory of everything', as we conceive it today, is concerned with – the nature of **space** and **time**, and the various **forces** and **particles** that operate at the bottom layer of the empirical world. Above this, we have the **atomic world**, which is still the concern of physics, and, above this, the **molecular world**, which is largely the concern of **chemistry**. Moving higher, we enter the world of **biology**, starting with **sub-cellular biology**, and **biochemistry**, then moving on to **cellular biology**, and then to the biology of **multicelled organisms**, which, for historical reasons, is still usually divided into **botany** (which deals with **plants**) and **zoology** (which deals with **animals**). The biological sciences get more complicated after this, with some, (such as **anatomy** and **physiology**) dealing with **individual** organisms, and some (such as **psychology** and **ecology**) dealing with them **collectively** in most cases. At the very top, we have the various social sciences such as **sociology, economics** and **history**. Note that I have greatly 'oversimplified' this hierarchical structure, missing out some extremely important 'hybrid' subjects such as **geology, geography** and **astronomy**, as well as important **subdisciplines** of all the major subjects, but I think you will have got the idea by now.

The point that I am trying to get across is that it is simply no longer possible to believe that we live in a **totally deterministic** world, where **everything** that happens is **completely predetermined** by events that happened in the past, and **everything** that happens at each of the different 'layers' of the hierarchy is **completely controlled** by things that happen at each lower level. Yet this is what most people believed at the time of Laplace, when the Universe was thought to be entirely composed of Newton's 'atoms', whose behaviour was completely controlled by the 'basic laws of physics' that he had discovered. There **are** still some people who continue to believe that we live in such a 'deterministic world', in which there is no room for 'freedom of will, and 'individual choice', but I find such an idea ridiculous, as well as totally undermining concepts such as 'ethics', 'morality' and 'justice'. I could also give you several good reasons why it is no longer possible to believe in such a world, one of the most telling being the discovery that the quantum processes that operate at a **microscopic** level, and effectively control what happens at a **macroscopic** level, are **totally random** in nature, as I showed you in Chapter 14. Because of this, it is simply **not possible** to predict **exactly what will happen** in such a quantum event; all we can do is predict the **probabilities** of the various possible outcomes, and wait to see what happens. Thus, even if we **could** develop a 'theory of everything' that **completely describes** the field of fundamental physics, it would be **extremely limited in scope**, and would therefore not justify its name. Ladies and gentlemen, I rest my case. The 'jury' may now retire.

Where, then, does all this leave us? First of all, we have seen that **all** the attempts to develop a 'theory of everything' have so far failed. I believe that they will continue to do so, for the reasons given in the 'epistemological' and 'Gödel' arguments that I have just described. And even if one of them **did** eventually succeed in producing an accurate description of the basic reality that underpins the **empirical** world, I believe that we would **never** be able to **know, for sure**, that this was indeed the case, because certain knowledge of the nature of 'ultimate reality' appears to be **intrinsically inaccessible** to us, if we believe Kant, Schopenhauer and Wittgenstein. Also, such a theory would only be able to describe **a very small part** of the vast, hierarchical edifice of science because of the phenomenon of 'emergence'. For all these reasons, I have come to the conclusion that the current search for a 'theory of everything' is indeed a search for an 'unattainable chimera' rather than a 'realistic scientific project'. That, however, is only **my** opinion; you may disagree, and I would welcome hearing your reasons for doing so. As a 'good Popperian', I am **always** willing to change my opinions if anyone convinces me that they are wrong.

Some of the sources of information on material covered in Chapter 15

This chapter is a greatly-expanded version of the 'handout' that I prepared to support my talks on the 'theory of everything' back in 2008. I did, of course, have to draw on several of the books in my personal library in order to obtain the detailed information that enabled me to produce this version. I found the following particularly useful.

- 'The Trouble with Physics', by Lee Smolin (an excellent survey of the field, written in 2006 by someone who was personally involved in much of the work described).
- 'The Cosmic Onion' – Quarks and the Nature of the Universe', by Frank Close (a 'blow-by-blow' account of the 'Grand Unification' project, written in 1982, **before** the project was 'falsified' by the failure to detect proton decay).
- 'Superforce – The Search for a Grand Unified Theory of Nature', by Paul Davies (a 'blow by blow' account of the 'Supergravity' project, written in 1984, **before** it was finally abandoned).
- 'The Elegant Universe – Superstrings, Hidden Dimensions, and the Quest for the Ultimate Theory', by Brian Greene (the classic work on the early and middle stages of 'string theory', written in 1999 by someone who was heavily involved in the project).
- 'The Fabric of the Cosmos – Space, Time and the Texture of Reality', by Brian Greene (the 2004 'follow up' to his 1999 book, describing the development of 'M theory').
- 'Theories of Everything', by Frank Close (written in 2017, this is probably the best recent survey of the field; I learned a lot from it).

Chapter 16: The 'biofriendliness' of the Universe

'The Goldilocks Enigma'
'Why is the Universe Just Right for Life?'

- Paul Davies

I have chosen the 'title' and 'subtitle' of Paul Davies's ground-breaking book as the opening quotations for this chapter because they capture, in eleven well-chosen words, the very essence of the chapter, and do this far better than I could ever do. I read the 'Sunday Times' review of the book when it was published in 2006, purchased a copy immediately, and found it absolutely fascinating, since it looked at the problem of the 'origin of life' from a completely new angle, examining the question of why the laws of physics, and the constants that are built into them, **appear** to be 'finely tuned' in order to allow life to have developed in the Universe.

Six years later, I decided to add a talk on this topic to my 'repertoire' of talks to schools and adult bodies, re-read the book, and produced a detailed 'handout' backed up by a 'PowerPoint' presentation in order to help me to do so. My talk was extremely well received, and my 'handout' was subsequently published electronically by Quo Vadis Publications in 2016, along with five other articles, under the title 'The Goldilocks Effect'.

This chapter is an expanded version of my article, and I hope that readers find it interesting, since it includes some **very** challenging ideas. I regard my article, and the present chapter, as my 'personal tribute' to Paul Davies, who is one of my favourite authors. I have most of his books in my personal library, and refer to them regularly – particularly his seminal work on 'The Mind of God'. This was published in 1992, but is still probably the best general introduction to the relationship between science, philosophy and religion, which is, of course, the 'core theme' of the present book. (It was probably largely because of 'The Mind of God' that Paul Davies was awarded the prestigious 'Templeton Prize' several years ago; its value was deliberately set by the 'Templeton Foundation' in order to give its recipients more money than each of the six 'Nobel Prizes' is worth!) Last year, my copy of this excellent book literally 'fell apart', and I had to order a new one. I hope this will 'see me out'!

All I can hope to do in this chapter is give readers a broad, general introduction to the topic, and I only hope that I have done justice to Paul Davies's ideas. I strongly recommend that you follow this up by reading his book yourselves. I guarantee that you will thoroughly enjoy it, and will get a great deal out of it. I did!

The anthropic cosmological principle

Let me take as my starting point the so-called **anthropic cosmological principle**, which was first introduced by the British astrophysicist, Brandon Carter, in the 1970's, and was subsequently developed by a number of other people, as a result of which many different versions were produced. (The use of the word 'anthropic' in this principle was perhaps an unfortunate choice, since it implies that it is mainly concerned with 'human life', which was **never** Carter's intention. Indeed, he once remarked that if he had known the trouble it would cause, he would have suggested something else – the 'biophilic principle', perhaps. But Carter's name for the principle 'stuck', and is the one that virtually everyone uses today). As I explained, several different versions of the principle have been produced over the years, but the one that is most widely quoted is the **weak anthropic principle (WAP)** which states that:

'The nature of the Universe **must** be such as to allow life to develop, otherwise we would not be here to observe it'.

This is clearly a 'self-evident truth' that is accepted by virtually everyone who has thought seriously about the matter. The other main version is the **strong anthropic principle (SAP),** which states that:

'The nature of the Universe **must** be such that the appearance of life is **inevitable** at some stage in its development'.

Unlike the WAP, this is clearly **not** a 'self-evident truth', being more akin to a 'statement of faith', and it is generally agreed that there are no compelling reasons why it should be true. The same is true, 'a fortiori', of all the other, even 'stronger' versions of the anthropic principle, the details of which I will not bother you with. (My absolute favourite among these is the 'completely ridiculous anthropic principle', because it has such a delightful acronym!) But to return to more serious matters, let us adopt the 'weak' form of the anthropic principle, the 'WAP', as the starting point of our further discussions, since this is not only totally acceptable to practically all workers in the field, but also provides us with a considerable amount of useful guidance on how best to proceed. As we will see in the next section, Paul Davies has examined the **implications** of the WAP in some detail, and has found that three very basic requirements **must** be satisfied in order to permit life to develop in at least one place in the Universe – which we **know** it has, because **we** are here. Let us now spend some time examining these in detail, since they are absolutely fundamental to the rest of the chapter.

Some of the things that can be deduced from the principle

The three 'basic requirements' that Paul Davies has shown to follow directly from the WAP can be very simply stated:

(i)   The 'laws of physics' **must** be such as to allow **stable, complex structures** to form **somewhere** in the Universe.

(ii) The Universe **must** contain the **sort of substances** (such as **carbon**) that biology employs to **construct** such structures.

(iii) An **appropriate setting** (or settings) **must** exist in which the vital components can **come together** in order to allow this to happen.

Restrictions on the form of the laws of physics

It has long been recognized that we live in a world with three 'space' dimensions and one 'time' dimension, although it is now accepted that this may not have always been the case. As we saw in Chapter 12, some cosmologists believe that our Universe may have had **more** than three space dimensions during the early stages of the 'big bang', although this is still a highly-controversial matter. Certainly, the various versions of 'string theory' and 'M-theory' **require** such higher dimensions, but, if they **do** in fact exist, they have long since been 'compactified', so that they are now far too small to detect by any currently-conceivable physical means. Thus, whatever happened in the past, the Universe now contains only the three 'large' space dimensions that we see today.

We now recognize that this was a **necessary pre-requisite** for the development of life, since it was **only** in a world containing three large 'space dimensions' that the laws of physics **could** have taken the form necessary for this to happen. If space had **fewer** than three 'large dimensions', there would simply not have been 'room' for structures sufficiently complex to support life to have been developed. The possibility of life developing in a world containing only **two** space dimensions was explored in a delightful book called 'Flatland', written by a Victorian headmaster and Shakespearian scholar named E.A. Abbott in 1884. The 'inhabitants' of this world were geometric figures such as 'triangles', 'squares' and 'pentagons', and the 'extreme difficulties' that they encountered through living in a two-dimensional world were made clear. Life, as we know it, would simply be impossible in such a world. And if space had **more** than three large dimensions, it can be shown that **stable planetary systems** and **stable atoms** – both absolutely **essential** for the development of life – could simply not have formed. Both depend on the forces that make them possible (**gravity** and **electromagnetism**) obeying **inverse-square laws** of attraction, something that can **only** happen in a 'world' that has three 'large' space dimensions. It can also be shown that such structures would again be unstable if there were more than one **time** dimension. In addition, the **principle of causality** that underpins so much of physics would also cease to operate if this were the case. We do not really understand the **nature** of time, and probably never will, but we **do** know, **for certain**, that any 'world' that had more than a single 'time dimension' would be full of 'contradictions' and 'anomalies', and would therefore be totally incapable of 'operating' in a systematic, rational way. Thus, it appears, without any **possibility** of doubt, that the 'dimensional structure' in which we live is the **only one** in which physical laws capable of supporting life as we know it **could** exist.

Production of the various substances necessary for life

All living things are built of **molecules** of different types, and these molecules, in turn, are made up of different types of **atoms** – those that constitute the different chemical **elements**. There are well over 100 of these elements, and, for life to have been developed, it was necessary for the **full range** of these to have been produced in the course of the evolution of the Universe. It is believed that the very **lightest** chemical elements (hydrogen, helium, lithium, beryllium and boron) were produced by progressive **nucleosynthesis** during the very early stages of the 'big bang'. As we saw in Chapter 12, the fact that we can use the big-bang model to explain the relative abundances of these five elements with almost perfect accuracy is one of the key pieces of evidence for **belief** in the big-bang theory. All **heavier** elements, on the other hand, were produced in the interiors of massive stars, which subsequently underwent violent 'supernova' explosions which spread them throughout the Universe. Indeed, we believe that the heaviest elements of all (those above iron in the Periodic Table) were produced **during** these supernova explosions. As we saw in Chapter 11, one of the people largely responsible for showing how all the heavy elements were produced was the British astronomer, astrophysicist and mathematician, Fred Hoyle (1915–2001). During the 1950's, working in collaboration with Margaret and Geoffrey Burbidge and Willy Fowler, he produced one of the most important papers in the history of astrophysics. This massive 'paper', Synthesis of the elements in stars', was published in 'Reviews of Modern Physics' in 1957, under the alphabetical names of its four authors, and is generally known as 'B^2FH'. It laid the foundations for virtually all subsequent work on the creation of the 'heavy' elements, which, like the creation of the 'light' elements, is now more-or-less fully understood.

Now one of the key stages in the creation of the heavy elements is the production of **carbon** by the fusion of three **helium nuclei** in the interiors of stars, a process known as the 'triple-alpha' reaction. During the early 1950's, Fred Hoyle had shown that this process could only work if the carbon nucleus possessed a particular excited energy state known as a 'resonance'. This would enable the 'triple alpha' reaction to take place in 'stages', beginning with the combination of **two** helium nuclei, which would later be joined by a third to produce a carbon nucleus. No such resonance was known of, or even **suspected**, at the time, since the study of nuclear physics was still in its infancy, and there were very few laboratories which were capable of carrying out experiments to see if it **did** exist. As it happened, Fred Hoyle was paying an academic visit to 'Caltech' in 1951, which just happened to be one of the few places where such a laboratory existed. Hoyle spoke to a group of young American nuclear physicists who now worked there, including Willy Fowler, telling them about his prediction of such a resonance in the carbon nucleus. To cut a long story short, they agreed to modify their equipment in order to try to detect Hoyle's resonance, and soon found it at **exactly** the energy level that had been predicted by Hoyle. It was this discovery that led Hoyle (who was a well-known atheist) to make his famous observation that 'the Universe was beginning to look like a put-up job'. Certainly, **without** Hoyle's resonance, there would be no **carbon** (or any heavier elements), and hence no **life** as we know it.

Development of suitable settings for life to appear

As we saw in Chapter 12, the Universe that we observe to lie around us consists of vast numbers of **galaxies** (at least several hundred billion in the part we can see), each of which contains up to several hundred billion individual **stars**. During the past few decades, astronomers have detected hundreds of **planets** orbiting stars in the nearest parts of our own Galaxy, and now believe that a very high proportion of stars possess their own planetary systems. Thus, there could well be something of the order of 10^{22} planets in the part of the Universe that we can see, and goodness knows how many in the part that we **cannot** see, which some cosmologists now believe may be **infinite** in extent. (I, myself, very much doubt this, for what it is worth). But be that as it may, we now know that there are **vast numbers** of planets in the Universe where life **could** have developed, assuming that the development of life here on Earth was not a highly-unlikely statistical 'fluke', which most biologists think it was not. Most now believe that life **will** eventually develop on planets where the conditions are suitable for this to happen. After all, we now know that life did not take very long (in geological terms) to develop on Earth, once it had 'settled down' after the violent events that led to and followed on from its birth roughly 4.6 billion years ago. So why should it not also have developed on many other planets, in other parts of the Universe?

So we now know that it was necessary for **planets** to form in order to produce suitable 'settings' for life **as we know it** to develop. (There may be **other** 'settings', where **different** forms of life can develop, but we cannot be sure of this. Back in 1957, the same year in which 'B^{2}FH' was published, Fred Hoyle wrote a famous science-fiction novel called 'The Black Cloud' in which he described a race of super-intelligent beings that had evolved in interstellar space, inside such 'black clouds'. Among the general public, Hoyle is certainly much better known for writing this novel than he is for his astronomy work!) And for **planets** to form, it was necessary for **galaxies** to form, since, without them, there could be no **stars** as we know them today, and without **stars** there could be no **planets.** The first key stage in this process was clearly the formation of **galaxies**. We still know comparatively little about the detailed process (or processes) by which this happened, but we **do** know that the early Universe had to be slightly 'clumpy' for galaxy-formation to happen at all, with the density varying from one place to another by roughly 1 part in 100,000. When the 'cosmic microwave background' (the radiation left over from the 'big bang') was discovered in 1965, and its detailed structure subsequently studied by the 'COBE' satellite , it was found in 1992 that the CMB had **exactly** this amount of 'clumpiness', much to the relief of cosmologists . This could not have happened if the laws of quantum mechanics had been significantly different from what they are.

It has also been found that the formation of stable, long-lived stars would not have been possible if the relative strengths of the four basic forces of nature (gravity, electromagnetism, the strong nuclear force, and the weak nuclear force) had been significantly different from the values that we actually observe. If **gravity** had been significantly **weaker**, for example, stars would never have been able to form at all, since the gravitational forces that tended to make the clouds of gas and dust from which they formed collapse into individual 'protostars' would not have been able to overcome the various 'dispersive forces' (such as heat production) that tended to prevent this. And if gravity had been significantly **stronger**, the temperatures in the cores of the resulting stars would have been so high that they would have 'burned up' their hydrogen fuel far too quickly for them to have lasted long enough for life to have developed and evolved on any of their planets, since the rate at which 'thermonuclear fusion' takes place in the cores of stars is very strongly temperature-dependent. We know that life took several **billion** years to develop to the stage that we observe today on Earth, so, depending on just how much stronger the force of gravity was, life would either not have developed at all, or would have been 'snuffed out' by the death of the Sun before it got past a very primitive stage of its subsequent evolution. In either case, **we** would not be here today.

There are many other 'cosmic coincidences' of this type, all of which were necessary for life to have developed and evolved here on Earth, and, indeed, anywhere else in the Universe. It thus appears that we are very lucky to be here at all, and that the Universe, does **indeed** begin to look as if it is a 'put-up job', to repeat Fred Hoyle's memorable words.

Attempts to explain the Universe's 'biofriendliness'

Let us now summarize where we have got to so far. We have now examined, in some detail, the 'Goldilocks Effect' that was identified by Paul Davies back in 2006. This, of course, is based on the story of 'Goldilocks and the Three Bears', with which I assume that most readers are familiar. You will recollect that when Goldilocks entered the Bears' cottage and tasted each of the three bowls of porridge that she found there, she found the first one 'too hot', the second 'too cold' and the third 'just right', so she ate it all. This, said Paul Davies, was a perfect analogy for the 'state of the Universe' in which we find ourselves today. When it was formed 13.8 billion years ago, the conditions were 'just right' for life to develop. It took some time for the Sun and the Earth to form far out in one of the spiral arms of the Galaxy, but, once this eventually happened, the conditions were still 'just right' for this to happen, since the **laws of physics** and the **constants** that are 'built into' them are not thought to have changed since the time of the 'big bang'. And we **know** that these 'laws' and 'constants' are, indeed, just right to have enabled life to develop and evolve. We will now look at some of the possible **reasons** why this should have been the case, and thus solve the problem of 'The Goldilocks Enigma' that Paul Davies chose for the title of his book. Four such possible reasons have been offered so far, and I will now try to give you a broad overview of what each of these involves. If you want more detailed explanations, you will, of course have to read the book itself.

1.   The Universe is as it is, and that is that!

In 1948, the philosopher, Bertrand Russell, took part in a famous radio debate with Father F.C. Copleston, a prominent Roman Catholic theologian, on the Third programme of the BBC. In this, Father Copleston argued that the observed nature of the Universe, including the nature of physical laws, could only be explained if you believed in a 'creator God'. Russell argued that such a being was 'not required' in order to provide an explanation of these matters, and that we, as 'rational human beings', should simply accept these as 'brute facts' that **required** no deeper explanation. This is probably what most practising scientists still believe. According to this point of view, the Universe 'is at it is' for reasons that we cannot possibly begin to understand, and 'just happens' to be suitable for life to have developed. It **could** have been otherwise, but 'what we see is what we get', and **had** it been 'significantly different', we would not be here to argue about it. The Universe **may** or **may not** have a 'deep underlying unity', but there **appears** to be no **design, purpose** or **point** to it all – at least, none that would make sense **to us**. Indeed, it may simply be a result of 'pure chance'. As Steven Weinberg, a well-known atheist, famously remarked: 'The more the Universe seems **comprehensible**, the more it also seems **pointless'**. And many people, including many other scientists, fully agree with him regarding this matter.

The advantage of holding this position is that it its easy to hold – easy to the point of being a 'cop-out', in fact. If there **is** no 'deeper scheme' or 'deeper meaning' to the 'world', then there is absolutely no point in **searching** for one. Bertrand Russell made **exactly** this point during his debate with Father Copleston. When the latter said the following: 'But your general point then, Lord Russell, is that it's illegitimate even to **ask** the question of the cause of the world?' Russell simply replied: Yes, that's my position'. He could not have made this any more clear, and, once again, many people would probably agree with him. In particular, there is, according to the people who hold such views, no point in seeking links between 'life', 'mind' and 'cosmos'. If there **are** such links, we have absolutely no prospect of **finding** them, at least by **scientific methods**. As Wittgenstein pointed out in his 'Tractatus', 'The **sense** of the world must lie **outside** the world', and is, therefore, **totally beyond the reach** of such methods. This is a point that he later reinforced, in his own memorable manner, with the very final words of the 'Tractatus' ('Proposition 7'): '**Whereof** one cannot speak, **thereof** one must remain silent'. According to him, that was absolutely 'the last word' on the matter, and there was no point in discussing it any further. People **did** continue to discuss it, however, as we will now see.

2.   The Universe is as it is because this is the only way it could be

This point of view, which is supported by many prominent scientists, holds that there is a 'deep underlying unity' in physics, and that there is a mathematical theory 'out there' that will 'pull it all together' – if only we are smart enough to formulate it. It could be 'string theory', 'M theory', or something else. **Whatever** is is, however, it will turn out to be founded on a 'deep mathematical principle' which leaves 'no room' for **adjustment** or **improvement**. All the **laws of physics**, the various **constants of nature**, the existence of **four-dimensional space-time**, the **origin** of the Universe – the 'whole shebang' – will follow **logically** and **inevitably** from this one, final 'unified theory', which will truly be the long-sought-after 'theory of everything'. In fact, it goes **well beyond** the things that physicists were looking for when they were trying to **find** such a theory. If we **could** find it, it would actually be the solution to the problem of 'life, the Universe and everything' that Douglas Adams's supercomputer 'Deep Thought' was given a million years to try to solve in 'The Hitchhiker's Guide to the Galaxy' (see Chapter 12). You will remember that 'Deep Thought' **did** eventually come up with a 'mathematical solution' to this ultimate problem ('42'), but that this really did not satisfy anyone. Nor was it meant to, since Adams was making a 'big joke' of the matter, as only he could.

The **advantage** of this 'necessary Universe' position is, of course, that it holds out the dream of a **complete understanding of physical existence**. If the project were to succeed, **nothing** would be left unexplained, and **nothing** of a fundamental nature would be **arbitrary**, or a result of **chance**, or would need 'fixing' by an unknown 'designer'. The position does, however, have a number of serious weaknesses – not the least of which is the **total failure** of scientists to have developed such a theory so far, despite the claims to the contrary by the advocates of 'string theory' and 'M-theory'. As I showed in Chapter

15, physicists have not even managed to develop a 'theory of everything' that manages to unite the four basic 'physical forces' – **gravity, electromagnetism,** the **weak nuclear force,** and the **strong nuclear force,** let alone develop a 'super-theory of everything' of the type that believers in the all-explaining 'necessary universe' solution of the 'Goldilocks Enigma' problem hope that they will eventually discover. And this is **before** we take account of the 'epistemological arguments', the 'Gödel argument', and the 'emergence argument' against the 'theory of everything' concept that I introduced you to in that chapter. On the basis of the 'case' against the 'theory of everything' project that I presented there, I hope that I have convinced you that the even-more-ambitious 'necessary Universe' project does not have a 'bat-in-hell's' chance of succeeding. Once again, this is only my **opinion,** and you are fully entitled to **disagree** with it if you wish. But if you do, you will have to produce **very convincing arguments** if you want me to change my mind on this matter.

3. Our Universe is part of a very-much-larger 'multiverse'

A minority of scientists, but a steadily-growing one, now support the **multiverse** theory in one form or another. These include some extremely prominent and distinguished figures in the field of cosmology and astronomy, including Sir Martin Rees, the former astronomer Royal. In 'Just Six Numbers', his best-selling 1999 book on 'Cosmic Coincidences' and 'The Deep Forces that Shape the Universe', he explains the best-known version of the 'multiverse' theory in some detail, showing how some recent cosmological models pointed strongly towards the existence of a multiplicity of **cosmic domains** as a natural result of the events that brought the cosmos into being. According to these models, the 'Universe' in which we live is only **one** of a (possibly infinite) number of such 'domains', and the 'big bang' that produced **our** 'Universe' was only one of a (possibly infinite) number of 'big bangs' that have taken place throughout the life of the cosmos. Some of these 'multiverse' theories suppose that the values of the basic constants that are built into the laws of physics – or even the laws of physics themselves – **vary significantly** throughout this 'range of domains'. In the great majority of them, the conditions are almost certainly unsuitable for life, but, purely by chance, we just happen to find ourselves in one where the conditions are 'just right' for it. If this is the case, the 'Goldilocks effect' can be explained by a purely-natural 'selection process'.

The great strength of 'multiverse' theories of this type is that they provide a **natural** and **easy explanation** of why **our** Universe **appears** to have been ideally designed for life to appear, and removes any need for an **intelligent designer** of any sort (see the next section for a detailed discussion of this possible explanation of the 'Goldilocks effect'). They do, however, also have a number of weaknesses, the main one being that they appear to be virtually 'untestable' by any currently- conceivable physical process. If a possibly-infinite number of 'other Universes' lie beyond the effective 'edge' of **our** 'observable Universe', the maximum distance from which light has had time to reach us since the 'big bang' 13.8 billion years ago, there is absolutely no way in which we are able to find out what is going on 'out there'. Such theories also go completely against the 'principle of parsimony' advocated by William of Ockham (c1285-c1349) roughly 700 years ago ('entia non sunt multiplicanda praeter necessitatem'); they do, after all, require an 'awful lot' of Universes! Finally, they also require a lot of **unexplained** and **very inconvenient** physics to make them 'work'. What, for example, is the nature of the **universe-generating** and **law-changing** mechanism that makes them possible? Supporters of the 'multiverse theory' have still to give a satisfactory answer to this question.

There is, however another, completely-different group of 'multiverse theories' that effectively 'get round' the last of these difficulties, in much the same way that Hugh Everett's 'many worlds' interpretation of quantum theory 'gets round' the problem of the 'collapse of the wave function' (see Chapter 14). These assume that our 'Universe' is only one of a possibly-infinite number of other 'Universes' that occupy **the same 'phase space'**, defined as the 'set' of 'all conceivable states' of what is called the '**manifold**'. These ideas may seem to be completely bizarre, but they do in fact fit in well with one of the 'models of reality' that I find to be highly convincing – the 'holographic model' that I will introduce you to in Chapter 20. They have also been brilliantly explored by the British science-fiction writer, Steven Baxter, in the three novels in his 'Manifold' series ('Space', 'Time' and 'Origin') and in the accompanying collection of short stories ('Phase Space'). I regard him as by far the 'deepest thinker' among the 'new generation' of science-fiction writers, and his books provide an excellent introduction to this 'second group' of multiverse' theories. He certainly 'knows' his physics, cosmology, mathematics and philosophy, as well as being an excellent writer.

4. Our Universe was deliberately designed to be the way it is

This is the traditional 'monotheistic' religious view – that the Universe was **created by God**, and was **designed** to be **suitable for life**, because the emergence of **sentient beings** was part of **God's plan**. It was succinctly and brilliantly presented by Father F.C. Copleston in his 1948 radio debate with Bertrand Russell, the 'full text' of which was included in Russell's 1957 book 'Why I am not a Christian'. This is a 'paradigm case study' in how two highly-articulate people, who happen to hold diametrically-opposite views on an important issue, can debate these in a **civilized** and **highly-informative** way. I commend it to all readers who want to see how such matters **should** be debated. Most of our current 'class' of politicians would also learn a lot from it. The 'intelligent designer' explanation of the 'Goldilocks theory' has the great advantage of providing a simple explanation of cosmic 'fine-tuning' and 'biofriendliness' for those people who have already decided, for other reasons, that 'God exists' – and there are billions of these in the world today, as we saw in Chapters 5 and 6. It also attributes the 'design-like' qualities of the Universe to an actual designer, which, to many people, is a perfectly reasonable and rational point of view. The development of the **anthropic cosmological principle** during the latter part of the 20th century, and its use by people like Paul Davies to demonstrate how 'cosmic fine tuning' was an **essential pre-requisite** for the development of life in the Universe, has also given 'new life' to the once-seemingly-discredited 'teleological argument' for the existence of God that I discussed in Chapter 9. Many theologians and philosophers of religion seem to have been slow to appreciate this, however, but I am sure they will all do so soon.

The 'intelligent designer' explanation of the 'Goldilocks enigma' does, however, also have a number of serious problems associated with it. The simple claim that 'God did it!', for example, provides no actual **explanation** for **anything**, unless one can also say **how** and **why** God 'did it'. And religious supporters of the 'creator God' idea have not really managed to answer **either** of these key questions in a convincing way. They have certainly not managed to convince many scientists, and, since most 'thinking' members of the general public now have a knowledge of science that would have been unimaginable 50 or 60 years ago, many of these are now coming to reject the teachings of the Christian church regarding these matters – hence the steady fall in church attendance and church membership that I described in Chapter 9. We also run into the fundamental problem of 'who **designed** the **designer?'**, unless we accept the highly-dubious concept of 'God' as a **necessary being**. This leads to all sorts of logical and philosophical anomalies, and I think it is fair to say that theologians have yet to produce satisfactory answers to these. The other main problem with the 'intelligent design' solution to the 'Goldilocks enigma' is that the

identity of the designer need bear no relation at all to the God of traditional monotheism. It might, for example, be a **committee** of Gods, in which case the definition of a 'camel' as a 'horse designed by a committee' immediately comes to mind! Or, the 'designer' might be a 'superintelligent **natural** being', or an extremely 'advanced civilization' of some sort. Both are possibilities that cannot be dismissed 'a priori'. The designer might even have been some sort of 'supercomputer' that produced a 'Matrix-type' model 'simulating' our Universe. Thus, simply invoking an 'intelligent designer' to explain 'the sense of the world' appears, to many thinking people, to create more problems than it solves, despite the fact that it is still believed by billions of members of the world's various religious faiths.

These, then, are probably the four most serious attempts to explain the remarkable suitability of our Universe for the development of life. All four have their strengths and weaknesses, but it is probably true to say that **none** of them gives a **completely satisfactory** explanation of the 'Goldilocks effect' – at least from a **scientific** point of view. Thus, it is probably best to let the scientists get on with their 'day jobs' of trying to explain these aspects of the 'phenomenal', 'empirical' world that they **are** capable of investigating using the methods at their disposal, and, in the words of Paul Davies, 'leave the big questions to the philosophers and priests'. They will almost certainly have no more success than the scientists, however, so that the 'Goldilocks enigma' is likely to be with us for some considerable time.

Some of the sources of information on material covered in Chapter 16

I found that I had to refer to many of the books in my personal library in order to write this chapter, but by **far** the most important was Paul

Davies's book, 'The Goldilocks Enigma', as I explained in the 'preface'. Other important sources included the following:

- 'The Anthropic Cosmological Principle', by John Barrow and Frank Tipler.
- 'Why I am not a Christian', by Bertrand Russell.
- "Just Six Numbers', by Martin Rees.
- 'Tractatus Logico-Philosophicus', by Ludwig Wittgenstein.

Chapter 17: The 'unreasonable effectiveness' of mathematics

'The miracle of the appropriateness of the language of mathematics is a wonderful gift which we neither understand nor deserve.'

- Eugene Wigner

In 1960, the eminent Hungarian physicist, Eugene Wigner (1902 - 1995), published a ground-breaking paper entitled 'the Unreasonable Effectiveness of Mathematics in the Natural Sciences.' In this, he posed a number of interesting questions about the relationship between mathematics and the natural sciences, particularly physics and astronomy. He observed that 'the enormous usefulness of mathematics in the natural sciences is something bordering on the mysterious, and there is no rational explanation for it.' In this chapter, I will examine the ideas developed by Wigner and the various people who later followed up on his work in some detail, since they are highly relevant to the main theme of this book - trying to gain a deeper understanding of the nature of reality. As we have seen in many other chapters, mathematics has played a key role in this since the time of Pythagoras. I will begin by discussing the 'mysterious power of mathematics' in general terms, after which I will look at some specific examples of the **application** of this power. I will end by reviewing some of the attempts that have been made to **explain** 'the unreasonable effectiveness of mathematics', rounding these off with a few comments of my own.

The mysterious power of mathematics

Since the time of Galileo, it has been realised that a large amount of mathematics is needed to understand the physical world. Indeed,

Galileo himself summed up the matter rather well when he wrote the following:

'Philosophy is written in that great book which continually lies open before us (I mean the Universe). But one cannot understand this book unless one has learned to understand the language and to know the letters in which it is written. It is written in the language of mathematics.'

This leads to a number of obvious questions: **Why** is mathematics so **essential** to an understanding of the 'physical world' in which we live out our lives? **Why** does mathematics **work** so well when applied to this world? And, looking at the matter from a somewhat different point of view, **why** does the physical world seem to **obey** mathematics?

All three of these apparently-simple questions have exercised the minds of some of the greatest scientists, mathematicians and philosophers in all succeeding generations. One of the very greatest of these was the English physicist, Paul Dirac, who, as we saw in Chapter 14, played a leading role in the development of the 'new quantum theory' during the 1920's. He wrote the following about the matter:

'It seems to be one of the fundamental features of nature that fundamental physical laws are described in terms of mathematical theory of great beauty and power, needing quite a high standard of mathematics for one to understand it. You may wonder: Why is nature constructed along these lines? One can only answer that our present knowledge seems to show that it is so constructed. We simply have to accept it. One could perhaps describe the situation by saying that God is a mathematician of a very high order, and He used very advanced mathematics in constructing the Universe.'

Einstein had a somewhat different view of mathematics and its relationship with the physical world, but again summed up the problem rather well when he wrote the following:

'At this point, an enigma presents itself, which in all ages has agitated inquiring minds. How can it be that mathematics, being after all a product of human thought which is independent of experience, is so admirably appropriate to the objects or reality? Is human reason, then, without experience, merely by taking thought, able to fathom the properties of real things?'

Einstein certainly believed that **he** was able to do so, since he maintained that his greatest intellectual achievement, the development of his 'general theory of relativity', was **indeed** a product of 'pure thought' - his own!

And, as we have seen, Wigner himself brought the matter to a head with his 1960 paper, which he concluded with the following words:

'The miracle of the appropriateness of the language of mathematics for the formulation of the laws of physics is a wonderful gift which we neither understand nor deserve. We should be grateful for it, and hope that it will remain valid in future research and that it will extend, for better or for worse, to our pleasure, even though perhaps also to our bafflement, to wide branches of learning'.

Some specific examples of the power of mathematics

Let now look at some specific examples of the 'mysterious power of mathematics' in **explaining** the physical world, and **predicting new features** thereof.

1. Use of the mathematics of 'conic sections' to explain planetary motion

The ancient Greeks loved geometry, and effectively laid the foundations for the detailed study of the subject. One of the greatest of the Greek geometers was Apollonius of Pergo, who, virtually single-handedly, developed the mathematics of **conic sections** during the 3rd century BCE. 'Conic sections' are the curves that are generated when a flat plane cuts through the surface of a cone, producing circles, ellipses, parabolae or hyperbolae depending on the angle that the plane makes with its axis. He wrote the 'basic textbook' on the subject, presenting roughly 400 'theorems' describing the different properties of such curves. 1800 years later, the Polish astronomer, Johannes Kepler, was trying to make sense of Copernicus's radical new idea that the Earth and all the other planets known at the time revolved around the Sun, rather than the Earth being the 'the centre of the Universe', as was taught by the Church. As I showed in Chapter 7, Kepler had found that Copernicus's 'heliocentric' model failed to give an accurate description of the actual **movements** of the planets, which had been studied in great detail by the Danish astronomer, Tycho Brahe. These discrepancies arose because Copernicus had retained the Ptolemaic idea that the planets moved in combinations of **circles** known as 'cycles' and 'epicycles', a system that had singularly failed to explain Tycho's observational results. Kepler eventually realised that the problem could be resolved by postulating that the planets moved in **ellipses** rather than in combinations of circles, with the Sun being at one 'focus' of each elliptical orbit. Being familiar with the work of Apollonius on the geometry of such curves, and being a highly-skilled mathematician, he was eventually able to show that such a theory matched Tycho's results with perfect accuracy, and enabled him to develop his 'three laws of planetary motion'. Later, Isaac Newton was able to complete the 'Copernican Revolution' by using his newly-established 'laws of motion' and 'law of universal gravitation' to show why the planets moved in elliptical orbits, and to **derive** all three of Kepler's laws of planetary motion from 'first principles'. Writing about the vital role that Apollonius's work played in the 'Copernican Revolution', one eminent historian of science observed that 'if the Greeks had not cultivated conic sections, Kepler could not have superseded Ptolemy'.

2. The discovery of Neptune

The mathematical theories that Kepler and Newton used to describe the movements of the planets and other heavenly bodies transformed astronomy into an 'exact, mathematical science', as we again saw in Chapter 7, and also enabled a number of important new 'discoveries' to be made. One of the most important of these was a prediction of the existence of the **eighth** planet in the solar system - **Neptune**. In 1781, the **seventh** planet - Uranus - had been discovered by the great German-born English astronomer William Herschel, in the course of a comprehensive 'survey of the skies' that he carried out at his own private observatory. During the next 65 years, astronomers studied the movement of the new planet with great accuracy, using the increasingly-powerful telescopes that were now becoming available. They eventually found that Uranus did not appear to be moving in exactly the way predicted by the Kepler/Newton theory. Sometimes, it appeared to move **faster** than the theory predicted, and sometimes **slower**. Working completely independently, the English astronomer, John Couch Adams, and the French astronomer, Urbain Leverrier, came to the conclusion that these apparent discrepancies in Uranus's orbit could be explained if there was **another** planet further away from the Sun than Uranus, a planet whose gravitational pull would 'slow Uranus down' if it was **behind** it in its orbit, and 'speed it up' if it was **ahead** of it. By comparing the **actual** movement of Uranus with its **predicted** movement, both men were able to calculate the **exact position** in the sky where the 'new planet' should then be located.

Adams actually completed his calculations first, and got in touch with the British Astronomer Royal, George Airy, to tell him where to look. Unfortunately, the weather at the Greenwich Royal Observatory was bad at the time, making observation impossible for several nights. Shortly afterwards, Leverrier completed **his** calculations, got straight in touch with the Berlin Astronomer Royal, Johann Galle, and told **him** exactly where to look for the new planet. Since the sky over Berlin was clear at the time, Galle was able to discover the new planet on the very same night - September 23rd, 1846. The discovery of Neptune, for which Adams and Leverrier are now giving joint credit, was made purely as a result of mathematical prediction, and was one of the 'greatest triumphs' of Newtonian physics. The one big 'loser' was George (later Sir George) Airy, who was always remembered as 'the Astronomer Royal who missed out on discovering Neptune'!

3.   Non-Euclidean geometry and general relativity

By far the most famous of the ancient Greek mathematicians was Euclid, who, as we saw in Chapter 4, set up a mathematical school in Alexandria during the 4th century BCE, and went on to write a textbook on geometry which effectively defined the practice of the subject for over 2000 years. At the start of the 19th century, however, European mathematicians began to study what eventually became known as **non-Euclidean geometry** by extending their work from **plane** surfaces to **curved** surfaces of different types, and eventually extending it to more than the three dimensions of **Euclidean geometry.** (Navigators had in fact been using a **form** of 'non-Euclidean geometry' for centuries, since the 'the spherical trigonometry' that they used to plan their voyages round the world was a limited form of this; nobody **called** it 'non-Euclidean geometry', however.) The early work on 'non-Euclidean geometry' was carried out by several mathematicians, including the great German astronomer, mathematician and physicist, Carl Friedrick Gauss (1777 - 1855), the

Hungarian mathematician, Janos Bolai (1802 - 1860), and the Russian mathematician, Nikolai Ivanovitch Lobachevsky (1793 - 1856) (who was later immortalised by being the subject of one of Tom Lehrer's 'satirical songs' during the 1950's; I still know the words of nearly all of these!). The work was effectively completed by another great German mathematician, Bernhard Riemann (1826 - 1866). His work was based on the use of complicated mathematical objects called **tensors**, the study of which became known as **tensor calculus**. As we saw in chapter 11, Albert Einstein developed his **special theory of relativity** in 1905, and then spent several years trying to extend it to more 'general situations' involving both **acceleration** and **gravity.** Although he had formulated most of the basic ideas that **underpinned** this new theory in a **qualitative** way, he had completely failed to develop a **mathematical model** capable of 'articulating' his new ideas so that they can be put to 'practical use'. Not, that is, until his friend and former teacher, Marcel Grossman, suggested that he 'take a look' at the 'tensor calculus' that had been developed by Riemann in the middle of the previous century, of which Einstein was obviously totally unaware at the time. To Einstein's surprise and delight, he found this was **exactly** what he had been looking for, and was soon able to produce the detailed, **mathematical** statement of his **general theory of relativity** that has been one of the two 'foundations' of physics ever since. Had Riemann's 'tensor calculus' **not** been available at the time, Einstein's revolutionary new theory would probably never have seen the light of day.

4.   The use of 'complex numbers' in quantum mechanics

Back in the 16th century, the Italian mathematician, naturalist, physician, philosopher, gambler and astrologer, Gerolamo Cardano (1501 - 1576) developed a completely new method of 'solving' certain types of 'polynomial algebraic equations' which mathematicians believed **had** no solutions. He did this by introducing the concept of imaginary numbers into mathematics, one of the greatest-ever 'leaps forward' in the field. The 'basic' imaginary number is 'i', the 'square root' of '-1'. Clearly, such a number cannot actually **exist** in the same way that 'real' numbers such as 2 and 5 exist, but Cardano asked his fellow-mathematicians to **imagine** that it did, and think about the consequences, and this is **exactly** what they did during the years and centuries that followed Cardano's apparently ridiculous suggestion. First, they **multiplied** 'i' by 'real numbers', creating a full range of other 'imaginary numbers' such as 2i and '1.47i'. Then, they **added** 'real numbers' to 'imaginary numbers' to create **complex numbers** of the form '8 + 3i'. Mathematicians then spent many 'long, lonely years' developing 'mathematical systems' **based** on these 'complex numbers', and even developed a branch of 'analysis' based on what they called 'functions of a complex variable'. I had to study both of these areas of mathematics during my 'honours degree' in 'natural philosophy' at Aberdeen University during the early 1960's, by which time they had become a 'key part' of subjects like physics and electrical engineering. This had taken a long time to happen, however, since it was only when physicists started to study 'the strange world of the quantum' during the early decades of the twentieth century that 'complex numbers' **really** 'came into their own'. It was found that the 'principal of superposition' that I described in Chapter 14, and the 'wave functions' that I introduced to you in the same chapter, required 'complex numbers' in order to describe them properly. As a result, number systems that had once been regarded as 'strange curiosities' were found to be **absolutely essential** features of the 'strange new theory' that was developed in order to **describe** the world in which we live, and to learn how to **control** that world by developing all the different 'electronic devices' on which it now so totally depends. Cardano, I think, would have been 'absolutely delighted' to find out just how useful this apparent 'crazy idea' turned out to be.

5. The use of 'noncommutative operators' in quantum mechanics

During the middle decades of the nineteenth century, the Irish mathematician, William Rowan Hamilton (1805 - 1865), was working on 'complex numbers' and, in particular, at how they effectively extended the 'real numbers' into **two** dimensions, by plotting them on a so-called **Argand diagram.** Here, the 'real' part of a complex number is plotted along the 'horizontal' ('x') axis, and the 'imaginary' part along the 'vertical' ('y') axis. Hamilton wondered if it would be possible to extend this system to **three** dimensions, and, in 1843, invented the concept of **quaternions**, or **Hamilton numbers.** Whereas 'complex numbers' are all of the form 'a + bi' (where 'a' and 'b' are 'real numbers'), 'quaternions' are all of the form 'a + bi + cj + dk', where a, b, c and d where are 'real numbers', and 'i', 'j' and 'k' are so-called 'special numbers'. He went on to develop the 'quaternion' concept into a full mathematical 'system', just as earlier mathematicians had done with 'complex numbers'. And that, I think, is all that you need to know about 'quaternions', except for one important thing - 'quaternions' do **not** obey the **'commutative law of multiplication'**, as do 'regular' types of 'numbers'. Thus, quaternions are said to be **'noncommutative'**, which means that the **answer** you get when you multiply two of them together depends the **order** in which the multiplication is carried out. The 'detailed mathematics' of such 'noncommutative operations', and the 'noncommutative operators' that controlled them, were later further developed by Hamilton and other mathematicians such as Hermann Gunther Grassman (1809 - 1877) and Arthur Cayley (1821 - 1895), but were largely ignored by physicists and 'non mathematicians' for a long time, just as 'complex numbers' themselves had been. Once again, it was only with the development of 'quantum mechanics' during the early decades of the 20th century that such 'noncommutative operators' started to play a 'key part' in physics. In particular, physicists found that they could not formulate 'Heisenberg's uncertainty principle' in formal, mathematical terms **unless** they expressed these in terms of 'noncommutative' operators'. Suppose you have two such 'quantum operators', 'X' and 'Y', that you wish to apply to a 'quantum system' as parts of a 'measurement process' of some type. Applying these to the system in the order 'X' then 'Y' will give you a different answer than if you apply them in the order 'Y' then 'X'. This may seem very strange to you, but I can assure you that this is **exactly** what happens in the 'weird quantum world'. As with Cardano, I am sure that Hamilton would have been 'absolutely delighted' to find just how important his ideas eventually turned out to be.

6. The discovery of 'antimatter'

I have already described how the great English physicist, Paul Dirac, played a key role in the development of the 'new quantum theory' during the 1920's by developing what became known as the 'Dirac equation'; this is now regarded as one of the most important equations in the history of physics. It effectively completed work on the 'new quantum theory', and 'laid the foundations' for virtually **all** future developments in quantum theory. Most people who know about these things now regard Dirac as the third greatest physicist that Britain has ever produced - after only Isaac Newton and James Clerk Maxwell. (I have an original copy of his classic textbook on 'Quantum Mechanics' in my personal library, and it is one of my most treasured possessions. It must now be worth quite a lot of money, but I would never **think** of selling it!) Once he had produced his amazing new equation, Dirac examined the various possible solutions that it could give rise to. One of these described the **electron**, whose existence had been known since 1897, and which had a **negative** electric charge. The equation also had a second possible solution, however, describing a particle **identical** to the electron except that it had a **positive** electric charge. Such a particle was actually discovered by the American physicist, Carl Anderson, in 1932, and became known as the **positron** (the **positive electron**). This was the first discovery of a so-called **antimatter** particle. It has now been found that **all** the 'fundamental particles' that make up matter (the **quarks** and **leptons**) possess similar antiparticles, particles that have **opposite electric charges**, and which **mutually annihilate** with them when they come into contact, converting their combined mass into energy. The prediction of the existence of 'antimatter' on purely mathematical grounds, and its subsequent experimental discovery, was yet another triumph for theoretical physics. And, of course, the 'warp drive' of the 'Starship Enterprise' would have been impossible without it.

7. Group theory and particle physics

In 1832, the young French mathematics student, Evariste Galois, developed a highly-novel method of investigating the solubility of 'polynomial algebraic equations', and sent a summary of this to a friend before he fought a duel, as hot-blooded young men **did** in those days. He was killed the next day, but his ideas laid the foundations for a completely new branch of mathematics - **group theory**. This deals with the various 'symmetries' that can exist between objects, parts of objects, or parts of mathematical systems, and has proved to have important applications in many branches of physics and chemistry. As we have seen in earlier chapters, much of the theory of modern **particle physics**, for example, is based on the structure of different mathematical 'groups'. This has led to many important advances being made in the field, including the discovery of several new types of particles. In the early 1960's, for example, Murray Gell-Mann used group theory to develop a revolutionary classification of all the known **strongly-interacting particles**, based on different combinations of completely new particles which he called 'quarks'. Using this system, which he called the 'Eightfold Way', after the Buddhist doctrine of the same name, he predicted the existence of an as-yet-unknown particle called the **omega minus**. This was duly discovered in 1963, thus confirming the existence of quarks. During the 1970's, Steven Weinberg, Sheldon Glashow and Abdus Salam used group theory to develop a unified model of the **weak** and **electromagnetic forces**, a model that predicted the existence of three massive new force-carrying particles - the **W^+**, **W^-** and **$Z^°$**. These were duly discovered in the 1980's, with **exactly** the properties predicted by the new **electroweak theory**. And group theory also played a major part in the prediction of the existence of the **Higgs boson**. This was eventually discovered in 2012, after decades of searching for it, effectively completing the 'standard model' of particle physics. **None** of this work would have been possible without the powerful mathematical 'tools' that group theory made available to physicists.

Some attempts to explain the extraordinary success of mathematics

These, then, are just a few of the ways in which mathematics has been used to make major advances in physics and astronomy. Many other examples of such use can be found in the scientific literature. I will now try to explain just **why** mathematics has proved to be so effective in these areas, I will do so by examining three of the most plausible explanations that have been given so far, plus an interesting 'alternative view' on the matter.

1.   The whole system is a result of 'intelligent design'

We have, of course, been here before. In the previous chapter, we took a detailed look at the idea that the 'biofriendliness' of the Universe is the result of such 'intelligent design'. I will now present similar arguments for the explanation of the 'unreasonable effectiveness of mathematics', arguments that have been presented by people of a 'religious persuasion' for a very long time. This maintains that the 'entire system' - the Universe **and** the set of physical and mathematical laws that underpin it - is the **deliberate result** of

intelligent design of some sort. Traditionally, the 'designer' has been assumed to be the God of monotheistic religion, or the 'creator Gods' of other religions such as Hinduism.

More recently, it has been recognised that the 'designer' might have been some other type of 'entity' - a 'committee' of Gods, for example, or a 'super-intelligent being' or 'advanced civilization', or even a 'supercomputer', as I showed in the previous chapter. Whatever the **nature** of the 'designer', however, it is assumed that he/she/they/it created the Universe with **perfect laws**, and that these 'laws' were written in a **perfect mathematical language** that we would be able to **understand** and **use**. Kepler expressed this 'intelligent design' argument 'clearly and succinctly' when he wrote the following back at the start of the 17th century, when **everyone**, scientists and mathematicians included, believed in 'God', without really giving the matter much 'deep thought', in most cases:

'The chief aim of all investigations of the external world should be to discover the rational order and harmony that has been imposed on it by God, and which He revealed to us in the language of mathematics'.

In other words, **'science follows mathematics because both** emerge from the **mind of God, within which** they were **originally formed'**, as Noson Yanofsky so clearly put it much more recently (in 2013, in fact). While this solution is perfectly acceptable and rational to people who already believe in a 'creator deity' for other reasons, it poses many problems for those who do not. For example, it does not really banish the 'mystery' at all, since a 'creator God' or other 'superintelligent designer' is even **more** 'mysterious' than Wigner's 'unreasonable effectiveness of mathematics'. People who are looking for a **scientific** explanation of the connection between 'mathematics' and 'science' find the possible existence of such an 'intelligent designer' to be well beyond the limits of 'rational explanation'. They would prefer an explanation that is more 'related to human experience', and, more 'testable'. Let us now see whether such an 'explanation' can be found.

2. Mathematics exists in a 'Platonic realm' that we can 'access'

One of the oldest explanations of this type goes right back to the ancient Greeks. As we saw in Chapter 3, the 'Pythagorean School' of philosophy believed that 'numbers' and the 'relationships between them' had some sort of 'mysterious control' over the 'physical world', and that the 'very essence' of the Universe was 'mathematical'. As we saw in Chapter 4, part of this 'ideology' was taken up and developed by Plato, and came to be known as **Platonism**. To Plato and his many subsequent followers, abstract entities such as 'mathematical objects' and 'physical laws' exist in a 'transcendental' **Platonic realm**, to which 'suitably-trained' and 'conditioned' minds (such as that of Plato himself) can somehow 'gain access'. To Plato, the 'physical world' that we perceive through our 'senses' was a **mere shadow** of this 'real' 'Platonic world'. Thus, to a 'Platonist', mathematics is **not a human invention** (as Einstein so firmly believed), but something that **exists independently** within this 'Platonic realm'. **All** its 'laws' and 'systems' are thus **waiting for us to discover them** - if only we are clever enough to do so. This idea is supported by the undoubted fact that the same mathematical 'laws' and 'principles' have been arrived at by **different people**, working in **different places**, and at **different times**, something that would be **highly unlikely** if they were mere 'human inventions'. The 'Platonic realm' does also pose a number of problems, however. How, for example, can we **know**, for **certain**, that such a 'realm' **actually exists**? And **who** (or **what**) 'set up', this wonderful, 'magical' realm? If we invoke the idea of a 'creator God' or some other type of 'intelligent designer', we are back where we started in the previous section. And **how** does this 'mystical realm' **interact with** the 'physical world' in which we live? Finally, how are **some** people (such as Plato and his close followers) able to **access** this 'world', while **many others** (the 'great majority' of the population, in fact) are clearly **unable** to do so? Thus, postulating the existence of a 'transcendental Platonic realm', where the 'laws' and 'principles' of mathematics are simply 'waiting for us to discover them', probably introduces more problems than it solves, at least for 'non- Platonists'. Fortunately for such people, there is another, **much** less 'metaphysical' possible explanation for the 'mysterious power of mathematics, and this is the one that we will examine next.

3.   Mathematics comes from our 'experience of the world'

Probably the most popular answer that philosophers, mathematicians and scientists give to explain the 'mystery' of Wigner's 'unreasonable effectiveness of mathematics' is that mathematics actually **arises from our experience of the physical world itself.** Our concept of the 'counting numbers', for example (the 'positive integers' from 1, 2, and 3 upwards) are thought to **come directly** from our **everyday observation** that if we combine **two** 'discrete objects' (say) with **two** similar 'discrete objects', we end up with **four** such objects. Other 'mathematical concepts' (it is claimed) arose in similar ways, albeit 'much more complicated' in some cases. Thus, according to advocates of this 'explanation', there is really **no mystery** in the fact that we can describe the 'physical world' using mathematics, since it was **in that same physical world** that we **learned mathematics** in the first place. In other words, mathematics is nothing more than a series of **abstractions** and **generalizations** of things that we (or others) have **actually observed** or **experienced** in the 'physical world'. Mathematics is thus a **human invention** rather than **existing in its own right**, as the 'Platonists' believe. While this 'explanation' of Wigner's 'mysterious power' of mathematics certainly **seems** to make sense to many people, it is, on deeper reflection, clearly far from perfect. If, for example, we **provisionally accept** that **all** mathematics comes directly from the 'normal world' of 'everyday experience', how is it that the mathematics that we developed in this way often gets **applied** in **situations** and **places** that are **very far** from such 'normal experiences' - and **seems to work just as well in such situations**? Why, for example, should 'mathematical laws', derived from 'everyday experience' in the 'macroscopic world' in which we live out our lives, 'work' at speeds **close to the speed of light** (as in 'special relativity'), or in the weird, **'microscopic world' of 'quantum mechanics'**, where, as we saw in Chapter 14, things happen that are **totally alien** to 'everyday experience'? Another problem is that not all mathematics **is** a 'generalisation of everyday experience'. Some occurs as a result of a clear, creative leap **away** from such experience, examples being the development of ' negative', 'imaginary' and 'complex numbers', which have **absolutely no basis** in the everyday world. For thousands of years, we got on perfectly well **without** the need for such concepts, but, as we saw earlier in this chapter, we found many of them 'extremely useful' when they **did** eventually appear on the 'mathematical scene'. The development of modern 'quantum theory', for example, could simply not have happened without 'complex numbers' and 'non-commutative operators', as we saw earlier in the chapter. And all the great advances of modern 'particle physics' could **certainly** not have happened unless the highly-abstract mathematical system known as 'group theory' had been available to the physicists working in the field.

4.   Mathematics is not really effective in most areas of science

One of the most intriguing positions regarding the 'mysterious connection' between science and mathematics is based on the assertion that the connection is, in fact, 'rather questionable' in **most** areas of science. Whereas **some** physical phenomena undoubtedly **can** be accurately described and explained using mathematics, many others clearly **cannot.** It has long been known, for example, that a physical system as simple as three astronomical bodies moving under the influence of their mutual-gravitational fields cannot have its future behaviour predicted by the basic laws of mechanics. It is true that astronomers **can** and **do** manage to make such predictions in **some** situations, but they have to resort to 'approximations' and so-called 'numerical methods' in order to do so. Indeed, it can be shown that the **vast majority** of physical systems cannot be accurately described purely by applying the 'mathematical laws' that are 'known' to describe such systems. Our future **weather**, for example, can only be 'predicted' a few days in advance, even with the most comprehensive data-gathering systems and most powerful computers at our disposal. Such systems have been studied using a completely new branch of mathematics known as **chaos theory**, which has provided considerable insights into the behaviour of intrinsically 'chaotic systems' such as the weather, in which a tiny change **somewhere** in the system can give rise to massive, virtually-unpredictable changes **elsewhere**. This is the famous 'butterfly effect', whereby a butterfly flapping its wings in Africa (say) can later give rise to a massive storm in South America. There are also many branches and sub-branches of science where mathematics plays very little part in explaining behaviour or predicting future patterns. This is true in **biology**, in the so-called **'social sciences'** (history, psychology, anthropology, sociology, etc.) and even in **economics**, which has always been regarded as the 'most mathematical' of the non-physical sciences. Here, the attempted use of 'mathematical models' of great 'power' and 'complexity', **totally failed** to predict catastrophic events such as the 1929 crash of the American stock market, or the near-total-collapse of the entire Western banking system in 2008. Indeed, the world-famous mathematician, Israel Gelfand, has been quoted as saying the following:

'Eugene Wigner wrote a famous essay on the unreasonable effectiveness of mathematics in the natural sciences. He meant physics, of course. There is only one thing which is more unreasonable than the unreasonable effectiveness of mathematics in physics, and this is the unreasonable **ineffectiveness** of mathematics in biology'.

There are also vast tracts of mathematics that **never** get applied to the physical world - many parts of **number theory** and **set theory**, for example. Indeed, it is probably true to say that the great majority of 'papers' in 'pure mathematics' are never so applied. Some 'purists' in this branch of mathematics actually take great pride in this, and get very annoyed if someone finds a 'useful application' for their work!

These, then, are four of the different positions that people have adopted regarding Wigner's (alleged) 'unreasonable effectiveness of mathematics'. While it is undoubtedly true that mathematics has proved extremely effective in **some** branches of science, particularly physics and astronomy, it is also clear that it has proved **much less effective** in **other areas**, such as biology and the 'social sciences'. It is also clear that **none** of the three attempted explanations of the phenomenon has proved totally convincing, to say the least. Thus, although we are really not much further forward in solving the 'mystery' identified by Wigner, we **do** know a great deal more about the 'strengths' and 'weaknesses' of his doctrine, and of the different 'explanations' that have been put forward. This is a 'perfectly respectable' position for **philosophers** to find themselves in after long periods of reflection and debate, so perhaps it is all that we can hope for!

Let me now bring this chapter to a close by sharing with you a few thoughts of my own regarding the key question of whether we **discover** or **invent** mathematical principles, laws and systems. After a great deal of reading and thinking about this, I have come to the conclusion that we **do both.** I tend to agree with (most of) the famous observation by the great German mathematician, Leopold Kronecker (1823 - 1891), that 'God made the integers; all the rest is the work of man', I would, however venture to **modify** this statement in one important way. I believe that we **invent** 'mathematical systems' such as 'group theory', by developing the 'axioms' on which they are based, but that we subsequently **discover** untold and unexpected 'riches' **within the bounds** defined by these axioms. As someone who spent a large part of my professional life working on the theory and design of 'academic games' of a wide range of types, I have come to realise that there is a strong relationship between 'games' and 'mathematics', as did many other thinkers **much** more intelligent than me - the great Hungarian-born American mathematician, John von Neumann (1903 - 1957), for example. Take **chess** as a case in point. No-one would deny that the 'rules of chess' are a purely 'human invention', albeit one that 'evolved' over a long period of time. It is also true that what is actually a comparatively 'simple' game contains within these basic 'rules' the possibility of a lifetime of study by some of the 'cleverest people' who have ever lived - the chess 'grand masters'. They 'discover' untold 'richness' within the game that they love, including new 'strategies' and 'tactics' that no one has thought of before. All this 'richness', I would venture to suggest, lies **latent** within the 'rules of chess', just **waiting** to be 'discovered'. The close parallels with areas of mathematics such as 'group theory' are self-evident, I would suggest. I would love to hear what readers think.

Some of the sources of information on material covered in Chapter 17

I decided to add a talk on the 'unreasonable effectiveness of mathematics' to my 'repertoire' at roughly the same time as I decided to add one on the 'Goldilocks effect', and 'prepared' for this in exactly the same way. I began by producing a 'PowerPoint presentation' for delivering the talk, backed up by a detailed 'handout'. As with the one on the 'Goldilocks effect', this was eventually published electronically by Quo Vadis Publications in 2016, under the title, 'The unreasonable effectiveness of mathematics'. This chapter is an expanded version of this published article, and, once again, I had to consult several of the books in my personal library in order to obtain the additional information that I needed to do this. The most useful of these were the following:

- 'The Outer Limits of Reason', by Noson S Yanovsky (which was also the source of much of the information that I used in preparing my 'handout' for my talk).
- 'The Great Physicists', by William H Cropper (once again).
- 'The Story of Astronomy', by Patrick Moore (once again).
- 'Chambers Biographical Dictionary', 1990 edition (once again).

Chapter 18: The spread of 'new-age thinking' and related activities

'This is the dawning of the Age of Aquarius'

- James Rado and Jerome Ragni

This is the third line of the opening chorus of 'Hair', a cult musical of the 1960's, which introduced many people to the new 'hippie' culture. It was infamous for its (then highly shocking) final scene, when the entire cast, male and female, appeared entirely naked, and members of the audience were 'invited to join them' - fully clothed in their case. I and a colleague from the School of Physics at RGIT attended a performance of 'Hair' in Aberdeen's 'His Majesty's Theatre' in the late 1960s, and did in fact do so. It was an extremely 'interesting' experience! (Our respective wives, incidentally, were, like Queen Victoria, 'not amused'.) 'Hair' was, in fact, a manifestation of the 'Generation War' that took place during the 1960's, following the staid, 'conservative' days of the 1940's and 1950's in which I was brought up. To the young, it was a 'breath of fresh air'; to the middle-aged and old, it seemed to be a very real threat to virtually everything they had been brought up to believe in. The person who 'captured the mood' of these turbulent and exciting times was probably the American singer and songwriter, Bob Dylan, who was actually born in the same year as me - 1941. Here is the most-famous verse of his most-famous song, 'The Times They Are A-Changing', which he wrote in 1964, - at the height of the 'the youth rebellion':

'Come mothers and fathers,
Throughout the land
And don't criticize
What you can't understand.
Your sons and your daughters

Are beyond your command
Your old road is
Rapidly agin'
Please get out of the new one
If you can't lend your hand
For the times they are a'changing!'

The importance of Bob Dylan's work was later recognised by the recent award of the Nobel Prize for literature, an event that caused a large number of 'apoplectic fits' among some of the more 'reactionary' elements of the literary establishment. For what it is worth, I fully supported the award, partly because I recognised the 'sheer genius' of the man, and partly because he represented, in a way no-one else did, the 'spirit of his age'.

As someone who lived through early-1960's and the even-more-violent events of the late-1960's and 1970's, I have tried, in this chapter, to provide an outline of the four aspects of 'new-age thinking' that are of greatest relevance to the subject of this book - the investigation of the 'the nature of reality'. First, I will look at the use of 'mind-altering drugs' to explore the 'true' nature of reality, something that so-called 'primitive cultures' had been doing for a **very** long time. Second, I will examine the explosive increase in the use of 'Eastern' meditation techniques, something in which I became actively involved myself during the late-1970's, as we saw earlier in the book. Third, I will look at how some 'Westerners' and 'Easterners' started to identify parallels between 'spiritual' and 'scientific' world pictures, an area in which I again started to take an active interest during the late-1970's. Finally, I will show how there has been a very significant increase in interest in all aspects of the 'paranormal', a subject that was largely ignored by science prior to the 'Age of Aquarius'.

Exploring reality using mind-altering drugs

As I explained in Chapter 1, a large proportion of what we know about the 'hunter-gatherer' societies that lived in 'Palaeolithic' times comes from the study of the few remaining 'pre-agricultural societies' that managed to survive into the 'modern age', particularly in Australia, Africa and South America. These are nearly all disappearing, however, as the 'benefits' of 'Western civilization' reach them. Soon, there will be no such 'primitive societies' left for anthropologists to study, which will be a great pity, since **we** have almost certainly **much** more to learn from **them** than **they** have from **us**, in my opinion. Since I started taking a serious interest in such societies during the 1970's, I have come to the **firm conclusion** that they have a **much** better idea of the **true nature** of reality than we do, and have an **infinitely greater** idea of how humankind can live **in harmony** with the natural world. I also believe that the same can almost certainly be said of the so-called 'primitive societies' who lived in the 'Paleolithic Era', although I have, of course, no **proof** of this. This was, I believe, particularly true of the 'shamans', or 'spiritual leaders', who played a key role in such societies, and still do so today in the few that survive. It is also a well-established fact that such 'shamans' nearly always make use of 'mind altering drugs' in order to enhance their natural ability to 'see reality in a different way'. The literature is full of accounts of such use, and I will now tell you about one of these.

In 1960, the American Museum of Natural History sent the anthropologist, Michael Harner, to live among the Conibo Indians, in part of the Amazon Rain Forest, for a year. Once he had settled in, and was starting to be 'accepted', he asked the Indians to tell him about their 'religious beliefs'. They told him that if he **really** wanted to learn, he had to take a 'shamanic secret drink', made from a 'hallucinogenic plant' known as 'ayahuasca', the 'soul-vine'. He eventually agreed, and, after drinking the bitter concoction, had an out-of-body experience in which he travelled to a 'level of reality' populated by what appeared to be the 'gods' and 'devils' of the 'Conibo's mythology', some of which 'told him things' about 'reality' and the 'origin and evolution of life' that truly amazed him. After he had 'emerged' from this 'experience', Harner sought out a blind Conibo shaman noted for his paranormal talents, to talk to him about what had happened. Here is Harner's own account of this. 'I was stunned. What I had experienced was already familiar to this barefoot, blind shaman, known to him from his own explorations of the same hidden world into which I had ventured'. This was not the **only** shock that Harner received, however. He later recounted his experiences to two Christian missionaries who lived nearby, and was intrigued when they seemed to know what he was talking about. After he finished, they told him that some of his 'descriptions' were virtually identical to certain passages in the 'Book of Revelation', passages that Harner, an atheist, had never read. So it is 'possible' that Harner and the old Conibo shaman might not have been the 'only people' to explore this 'inner realm'. Some 'Old' and 'New Testament Prophets' **might** also have done so. (Readers who want to read a more detailed account of Harner's experience can find it in Chapter 8 of Michael Talbot's fascinating book, 'The Holographic Universe', of which I will have **much** more to say in Chapter 20.)

One of the first modern 'Westerners' to realise the potential role of mind-altering drugs in increasing our awareness of the 'true nature of reality' was the eminent author, Aldous Huxley. In a hugely-controversial book published in 1954, he vividly described his personal experiences with the drug mescaline, and suggested that hallucinogenic drugs of this type might prove useful in helping people to achieve 'transcendental' and 'mystical' experiences. The use of **natural** preparations of marijuana, mescaline and psilocybin in 'religious rituals', and for 'pleasurable effects', had been known since the earliest times, but it was only when the purely **artificial** hallucinogenic drug, **LSD**, came onto the scene that things really started to 'take off' in this area. It was found that this not only had some extremely-useful **medical** and **psychiatric** applications, but also turned out to be **by far the most powerful hallucinogenic drug** ever discovered up to then. To say that it was 'marijuana on steroids' was the understatement of the century. During the 1960's, many research teams started to investigate its amazing properties in a systematic way, and, once they found out about it, and found that it was (at the time) perfectly legal to use it, more and more members of the general public (especially the young) started to 'try it out' for themselves. Many 'unreligious' people who were given their first dose of LSD for 'medical purposes' were often 'quite indignant' when told that the most important outcome of their session might well be 'spiritual', but this is what actually **happened** in many cases. More and more people reported that taking the drug gave them an 'enhanced view of reality' that they would never have believed possible, and, even highly-religious people found its effects 'quite amazing'. As one American pastor, who was clearly a follower of American football, so memorably put it:

'The drug seems to make an end-run around Christ and go directly to the Holy Spirit'.

And two other commentators clearly pointed out the potential **danger** that LSD represented to **conventional religion** with the following joint comment:

'Undoubtedly, it would be the supreme irony of the history of religion should it be proved that the ordinary person could, by the swallowing of a pill, achieve those states of exhaulted consciousness, that a lifetime of spiritual exercises rarely brings to the most ardent and adept seeker of mystical enlightenment'.

But possibly the most famous (notorious?) plea for the increased, and free, use of LSD by ordinary people was made by the American psychologist, Timothy Leary, in a lecture in 1968:

'If you take the game of life seriously, if you take your nervous system seriously, if you take your sense organs seriously, if you take the energy process seriously, you must turn on, tune in and drop out'.

This proved a bit too much for the 'establishment', and, despite the pleas from the 'young' that they be allowed to continue to use LSD without restriction, its use for both personal **and** for medical and research purposes was eventually made illegal. I now regard the latter to have been a great mistake, for reasons I will explain later in the book. I was **never** a user of illegal drugs, but, looking back, am sorry that I never had the chance to 'see what LSD could do' under **carefully-controlled laboratory conditions**. I am sure that I would have learned a **great deal** from the experience. Now, I almost certainly never will.

Readers might have gained an impression from what I have written so far that I am a supporter of the **de-criminalisation** of the use of **all** drugs, which a large number of people are now suggesting. I certainly support this in the case of marijuana, which is now widely recognised as being less dangerous than alcohol if it is not too strong, and **much** less dangerous than tobacco, but I think the legalisation of the use of some of the most **dangerous** and **addictive** drugs, such as heroin and cocaine, would be a total disaster. And, as few people are probably aware, use of drugs was one of the main reasons why America eventually **lost** the Vietnam War. Last year, I was given a signed copy of Max Hastings's brilliant book on this tragic war as a birthday present, and read all its 650+ pages with increasing shock and horror. Hastings attributes the loss of the war to a number of factors - America's inability to fight what are now known as 'asymmetric wars'; collapse of support for the war 'at home'; racial strife, powerfully influenced by the 'Black Power' movement; and a decline of 'discipline' and the 'will to fight', greatly aggravated by virtually-uncontrollable 'drug abuse' by the largely 'conscript' army. It was only when I read Hastings's book that I realised just how catastrophic this drug use had been. As one US general observed later, 'We went into Korea with a rotten army, and came out with a fine one; we went into Vietnam with a great army, and finished with a terrible one'. And, as Hastings explains, a large part of this decline was due to drug use by the 'grunts' - the 'ordinary soldiers', of whom a 'disproportionately high number' were 'coloured'. These did not **want** to be in Vietnam anyway, and while they **were** there, took the only consolation they could - by remaining as 'permanently high' as they possibly could be. Anyone who reads Hastings's 'horror story' can see how **all** armies now try to 'stamp down' on drug use as hard as they can. **None** of them want 'another Vietnam'.

The spread of Eastern meditation techniques

One of the most important and most wide-ranging manifestations of 'new age thinking' during the 1960's, 1970's and 1980's was the explosive increase in the use of 'Eastern' meditation techniques and related activities in other parts of the world. And many people who became involved in their use did through so the **Transcendental Meditation (TM) Movement**, which grew even faster than Islam did during its early years. Even then, Islam took some time to move out of its 'birthplace' in Arabia, and even longer to spread to the surrounding areas, and, eventually, to spread throughout the world. TM did this in **under 20 years**!

Just as **Buddhism** was effectively the result of the work of one remarkable man (Siddhartha Gautama), and **Islam** was also the result of the work of another remarkable man (Mohammed), so with **TM**. Here, the 'remarkable man' was **Maharishi Mahesh Yogi**, who 'came out of India' in order to 'bring TM to the rest of the world' in 1958. He had been a 'disciple' of the renowned Indian 'sage' Brahmananda Saraswati, who Maharishi always referred to as 'Guru Dev', which can simply be translated as 'Divine Teacher'. Maharishi met Guru Dev while he was studying physics and chemistry at Allahabad University, and, after a few exploratory meetings, asked if he could become his 'disciple'. Guru Dev agreed to accept him as such, on the condition that he first completed his science studies. This he duly did, and then spent the next twelve years studying, learning, and working with Guru Dev. During this time, Maharishi had become Guru Dev's closest disciple, and, on his master's death, inherited all the knowledge of an apparently-long-lost Hindu meditation technique that Guru Dev had 'rediscovered'. This was subsequently 'adapted' by Maharishi to become the basis of TM. With this knowledge, he retired to live in solitude in an isolated mountain cave deep in the Himalayas. He had no particular plans at this time, and only wanted to be 'alone' and 'still'.

He eventually decided that he was 'duty bound' to 'give TM to the world'. So, after teaching TM in India for some time, and establishing the 'Spiritual Regeneration Movement' ('SRM') in Madras, he moved out of India in 1958, first to Singapore, then to Hawaii, reaching California in 1959. He stayed there for several months, teaching TM, and establishing a permanent 'residential centre' for the SRM, before moving on eastward to New York and Europe. By the end of one year, so many people were wanting to learn TM that Maharishi realised that he could no longer handle this on his own. He therefore decided to embark on the 'training' of 'teachers of meditation' - first on a small scale, and then on an increasingly-large scale. To cut a long story short, by 1975, he had trained nearly **10,000 people** as 'TM teachers'. Realising that people in the 'West' were a little wary of anything 'spiritual', and were often 'put off' TM by the **name** of his organisation, he decided to 'change its image'. So, in 1960, he established the more neutral-sounding 'International Meditation Society' ('IMS'), and, in 1965, the 'Student's International Meditation Society' ('SIMS'), to cope with the rapidly-increasing demand for TM among the student population and others of that age group.

At roughly the same time, scientists in the West began to take a greater interest in the **physiological** and **psychological** effects of meditation, and, as a result, TM started to acquire 'academic respectability'. This led to the establishment of two more major organisations, the 'Maharishi International University' ('MIU'), which integrated the study of TM with conventional academic disciplines, and the 'Foundation for the Science of Creative Intelligence', which was primarily concerned with introducing the 'benefits of TM' to business and industry. TM continued to spread rapidly, attracting followers from many walks of life - doctors, politicians, businessmen, academics, students, housewives, and, by 1976, it was estimated that roughly **1.5 million people** were practising the technique throughout the world, with the number growing by roughly **40,000 a month**. Nor was this rapid growth of interest confined to America and Europe. By the late-1970's, it was being taught in almost every country of the world, except in Russia and its 'sphere of influence', and China. Some of the **greatest** interest was actually in India, to which TM eventually returned 'wearing the clothes of the West', as Peter Russell so eloquently put it in 1978. Talk about 'taking coal to Newcastle!'

But what, you might ask, does TM actually involve its practitioners in **doing**? It simply involves sitting down in a (preferably) quiet place for 20 minutes early in the morning and in the late afternoon, closing your eyes, and letting your 'personal mantra' 'take over your mind'. Once you have been shown how to do so by a properly-trained TM teacher, this enables your 'relaxed mind' to go through a series of 'cycles', in which it first sinks into a state where all 'conscious thought' disappears, allowing you to 'make contact with' what Maharishi calls 'pure consciousness', the 'source of thought'. After spending some time in that 'blissful state', your mind returns to 'normal waking consciousness', and, after some time, the cycle begins again, quite naturally. After your '20 minutes are up' (you check the progress of the session by opening one eye and glancing at your watch or at a convenient clock), you 'shut down' your mantra, and simply sit quietly for a further two minutes, before opening your eyes fully, and returning to the 'real world'. If you come out of meditation **too** quickly, or if your session is 'interrupted' for any reason, you can end up with a 'nasty headache' that takes some time to 'go away'. And that is all there is to TM! I have now been practising it for well over 40 years, and, although I have never had any 'profound spiritual experiences' as a result, it has certainly produced **all** the other benefits that are claimed for it - reduction of stress, renewal of 'mental energy', and so on. If I have spent a day involving 'strenuous mental activity', and am feeling 'mentally exhausted', my 'afternoon TM session' invariably leaves me 'raring to go' once again, and greatly increases the effective length of my 'working day'. TM also makes me **feel better**, and, I hope, makes me a **better person** as a result. And, as I know from speaking to 'fellow meditators', my experience of TM is 'fairly typical'.

Something akin to the 'blissful state' of 'pure, transcendental consciousness' has apparently been experienced by many 'creative writers' over the years. Probably the most famous of these is what the great 'Romantic Poet', William Wordsworth, referred to as 'a happy stillness of the mind..... a wise passiveness'. In his poem, 'Tintern Abbey', he memorably describes one brief, but clear, moment of 'transcendental consciousness':

' - that serene and blessed mood,
In which the affections gently lead us on,
Until, the breath of this corporeal frame,
And even the motion of our human blood,

Almost suspended, we are laid asleep
In body, and become a living soul'.

I have never experienced anything **quite** like that, but many other people clearly have. I can only assume that I am not 'sufficiently far down my spiritual journey' (as the Hindus would say) to enable me to do so! This is also probably why Christianity did not 'work for me' during my early 20's, as I explained in Chapter 10. People tell me that I am too 'locked into the rational world of concepts' to be a 'truly spiritual' person. I can only reply that I am 'perfectly content' to be so 'locked', and have done **very nicely** in this 'world of concepts', thank you very much. But, having said that, I have still found TM to be sufficiently beneficial to have continued practising it since I received my 'initial training' in 1978, and will continue to do so for as long as I am around.

Identifying parallels between spiritual and scientific world pictures

Since the 'dawning of the Age of Aquarius' in the 1960's, this has been done from **both** sides. One of the most influential books to appear in this era was 'The Tao of Physics', written in 1976 by Fritjof Capra. He studied physics as an undergraduate, and later obtained a Ph.D. in theoretical physics from the University of Vienna, before carrying out research in particle physics in several European and American universities. As we saw earlier, particle physics was in 'a bit of a mess' following the discovery of the 'particle zoo', and there were several theories as to how this might be explained. As we saw in Chapter 13, this was eventually achieved by Murray Gell-Mann, when he developed his 'Eightfold Way' and 'quark theory' of the strongly-interacting particles, but, before this was accepted by the particle-physics community, another theory attracted some support for a while. This was the so-called 'bootstrap hypothesis', whose main advocate was the physicist, Geoffrey Chew. To put it very simply, this rejected the idea that fundamental particles were composed of other, even-more-fundamental entities, and maintained that they constituted a self-supporting set of entities that, quite literally, 'pulled themselves up by their own bootstraps'. According to this view, **all** the so-called 'fundamental particles' depended on **all** the other particles for their existence, so that **none** of them could have existed **without all the others.** Chew extended his 'bootstrap hypothesis' to the entire natural world, claiming that the Universe was a 'dynamic web of interrelated events', **none** of which were truly 'fundamental', and **all** of which followed naturally from the properties of all the other parts. Readers will recognise that this 'world view' bore a close resemblance to the 'Hindu' and 'Buddhist' 'world-views', which also held that the 'phenomenal world' of 'appearances' is simply an 'interconnected set' of such 'relationships', and is, in fact 'essentially illusory'.

As I showed in Chapter 13, the eventual success and universal acceptance of Gell-Mann's 'quark' model of the strongly-interacting particles turned this into the 'new paradigm' of particle physics. This meant that 'alternative theories', such as Chew's 'bootstrap hypothesis', were quietly forgotten, so much so that very few people now have even **heard** of it. It did, however, lead directly to the publication of Fritjof Capra's 'The Tao of Physics' and several other books of this type, including 'The Dancing Wu Li Masters', by Gary Zukav (another physicist). Each of these books drew attention to the fact that **both** the world of contemporary 'particle physics' **and** the world of traditional 'Eastern mysticism' were in fact manifestations of the same 'ultimate reality', which was seen as being 'essentially dynamic' in nature. This was clearly, and powerfully, expressed in the front cover of the original paperback version of 'The Tao of Physics', which shows the traditional Hindu image of 'the dance of Shiva' superimposed on a bubble-chamber photograph of the complex interactions of 'fundamental particles' that had been recorded thereon. This image made a strong impression on everyone who saw it, including myself, as can be seen by the cover that I chose for this book. I subsequently replaced my copy of the 1975 'Fontana', paperback edition of 'The Tao of Physics' with the updated 1982 'Flamingo' edition, but retained the former in my personal library, purely because of this memorable image, which is still one of the 'icons' of the 'Age of Aquarius'. I also have a beautiful brass statue of 'the dance of Shiva' in a prominent position in my study. As I said earlier, the 'bootstrap hypothesis' that **prompted** the 'writing' of 'The Tao of Physics' has long since been consigned to the 'dustbin of history', but the **ideas** regarding the strong links between the 'spiritual' and 'scientific' world views are just as true today as they were when Capra wrote his book. At least, that is what I firmly believe. Try reading 'The Tao of Physics' for yourselves, and see what **you** think. It requires no 'specialist knowledge' of physics.

Roughly 30 years after the publication of 'The Tao of Physics', one of the world's leading representatives of the 'Eastern' position, His Holiness the Dalai Lama, wrote an amazing book entitled 'The Universe in a Single Atom'. This took, as its opening 'quotation', the following extract from an ancient Buddhist scripture:

'In each atom of the realms of the Universe,
There exist vast oceans of world systems'

Let me now quote, in its entirety, the opening paragraph of the 'Prologue' to this book, since it sums up his position extremely well.

'I was never myself trained in science. My knowledge comes mainly from reading news coverage of important scientific stories in magazines like 'Newsweek', or hearing reports on the BBC World Service and later reading text books on astronomy. Over the last thirty years, I have held many personal meetings and discussions with scientists. In these encounters, I have always attempted to grasp the underlying models and methods of scientific thought as well as the implications of particular theories or new discoveries. But I have nonetheless thought deeply about science - not just its implications for the understanding of what reality is but the still more important question of how it may influence ethics and human values. Specific areas of science that I have explored most over the years are subatomic physics, cosmology and biology, including neuroscience and psychology. Given that my own intellectual training is in Buddhist thought, naturally I have often wondered about the interface of key Buddhist concepts and major scientific ideas. This book is a result of that long period of thinking and of the intellectual journey of a Buddhist monk from Tibet into the world of bubble chambers, particle accelerators and fMRI (functional magnetic resonance imaging).'

And what a journey it is! In his amazing book, this amazing man (surely one of the most important figures of the 'modern age') shows that 'science' and 'spirituality' are not rivals, but are simply 'different ways' of 'looking for the same thing'. As he says later in his 'Prologue':

'This book is not an attempt to unite science and spirituality (Buddhism being the example I know best) but an effort to examine two important human disciplines for the purpose of developing a more holistic and integrated way of understanding the world around us, one that explores deeply the seen and the unseen, through the discovery of evidence bolstered by reason. I am not attempting a scholarly treatment of the potential points of convergence and difference between Buddhism and science - I leave that to professional academics. Rather, I believe that spirituality and science are different but complementary investigative approaches with the same greater goal, of seeking the truth. In this, there is much each may learn from the other, and together they may contribute to expanding the horizon of human knowledge and wisdom'.

When I re-read this passage in preparing to write this chapter, I was struck by the similarity between **his** aims in writing **his** book, and **my** aims in writing **my** book. I learned **many** things from it, including the importance of investigating key aspects of reality both by **objective** study of the **external world** by 'scientific methods', and by **subjective** study of the **inner world** by 'spiritual methods'. His Holiness uses the investigation of the nature of 'consciousness' as a paradigm case study here. He points out that the 'scientific' approach to this 'hard problem of psychology' has been to investigate the 'the mechanics' of the 'inner workings of the brain' by studying the 'electrical', 'chemical' and 'physiological' processes that take place therein, work that has led to some spectacular results and insights, but (as I showed in Chapter 10) has not, so far, managed to give a satisfactory explanation of the 'causes' and 'nature' of consciousness. He maintains that the alternative, 'introspective', approach to the study of consciousness appears to have had somewhat greater success in some areas. For example, the deep understanding of the 'mind's' capacity for 'transformation' and 'adaptation' that it has produced over the centuries has recently been confirmed by the 'scientific' discovery of the remarkable potential for 'changeability' in the human brain, long after childhood and adolescence. This 'plasticity', he claims, demonstrates that the two approaches to such studies should be regarded as 'complementary', and that **both** have an important part to play in studies such as these. I could not agree more!

The increased interest in the 'paranormal'

Traditionally, the 'paranormal' has been a 'taboo subject' among the scientific community. Most of them dismiss it as 'impossible', because it clearly does not fit in with the 'highly- materialistic' 'world picture' that many of them still believe in, despite the increasing evidence that this does **not** give an accurate picture or reality. Others simply ignore it, and refuse to take seriously the vast amount of literature which suggests that it really **does** happen. A few, on the other hand, have now started to take it seriously, and some have even carried out 'scientific experiments' on such things as 'precognition' and 'remote viewing'. Ever since I read Lyall Watson's ground-breaking book, 'Supernature', in the early 1970's, and followed this up by buying and reading nearly all of his subsequent books, I have taken the 'paranormal' **very** seriously, since there is so much evidence that 'paranormal events' **can** and **do** happen, that no rational person can **ignore** this evidence any longer. I now have quite a large collection of books on various aspects of the subject, possibly the most important being Michael Talbot's book on 'The Holographic Universe', which I will discuss in much greater detail in Chapter 20. Suffice to say, this provides a perfectly rational explanation for many so-called 'paranormal' phenomena, provided you accept the possibility that we **may** live in such a 'holographic universe' - and I am becoming increasingly convinced that this **may indeed** be the case.

Dr Lyall Watson, a professional life scientist of considerable repute, has possibly done more to promote interest in, and serious study of, all things 'paranormal' than anyone who has ever lived. In 'Supernature', he presented a 'natural history of the supernatural', which, in his own words, was 'an attempt to fit all of nature, the known and the unknown, into the body of supernature and to show that, of all the faculties we possess, none (was) more important at this time (1973) than a wide-eyed sense of wonder'. The book was written in four parts, respectively dealing with the 'cosmos', 'matter', 'mind' and 'time', and taking readers on a 'rich' and 'thoroughly researched and referenced' journey through all these different areas. It had a tremendous impact at the time, both among the general public, and (increasingly) among the scientific community. He followed this up with 'Gifts of Unknown Things' in 1976, with 'Lifetide, A Biology of the Unconscious' in 1979, and with 'Supernature II' (an extension of his original book) in 1986. I have all of these in my personal library, as well as several of his other books, and found them all highly impressive and extremely convincing.

One of the first 'serious' scientific books to be published on the paranormal was 'ESP Beyond Time and Distance', by T. C. Lethbridge, of which I purchased the 'Scientific Book Club Edition', in 1965 (I was a member of this excellent organisation at the time, and was sent a new book every month). At the time, the Russians were claiming that they had 'proved' the existence of 'extra-sensory perception' ('ESP'), that man had a 'sixth sense', and that 'telepathy' was allied to the 'means of communication' used by the animal world. Lethbridge took a 'deep and critical look' at these Russian claims, and, indeed, took them 'even further'.

An even more influential book was published in 1977 by Russell Targ and Harold Puthoff, two senior researchers at the world-famous Stanford Research Institute (SRI) in Menlo Park, California. This was entitled 'Mind-Reach - Scientists Look at Psychic Ability', and described an extremely-impressive research programme on '**remote viewing**', carried out under the most rigorous protocols, and providing detailed information on how other researchers could repeat their work. Their 'historic findings' sparked a 'torrent of discussion in scientific circles' that even reached that most prestigious of all scientific journals, 'Nature'. These concluded that 'remote viewing' was an 'established fact', although some people **still** dispute this finding.

The aspect of the 'paranormal' that is probably **most** widely accepted as an 'established fact' is **dowsing**, which has been practised since time immemorial. 'Dowsers' (as they are called) are widely employed to seek out underground water, minerals, buried artifacts or power cables. They usually do this by walking over the chosen site, holding a forked stick, two L-shaped rods, or a pendulum. At the key point, the 'divining rod' twists in their hand, or, if a pendulum is used, 'starts to twirl'. But it is now well established that these 'divining devices' are of secondary importance, only serving to amplify bodily responses to the 'subtle forces' involved. These are probably magnetic in origin, and are, in varying degrees, registered by **all** living creatures on Earth. 'Natural' dowsers appear to be particularly sensitive to them.

One aspect of the 'paranormal' that has aroused considerable interest during the last few decades is '**psychokinesis**', also known as **telekinesis**, or simply **PK**. This is defined as 'the movement of physical objects by mental influence without physical contact', or 'the power of **mind** over **matter**'. The ability of certain people to perform such feats has been well-recorded throughout history, but by far the most famous exponent was undoubtedly Uri Geller, who made a 'profession' out of it during the 1980's. He was best known for his 'spoon bending', but he had in fact a whole 'range of talents' in this area. These were 'tested' under stringent scientific conditions at the Stanford Research Institute, where his 'remarkable powers' disturbed the US Intelligence Agencies, not merely for what he accomplished, but for the 'almost limitless list of equipment failures' that invariably accompanied his visits, including the 'wiping of computer programs'. Both the Russians and Americans are thought to have carried out 'experiments' on the possible use of 'PK' in warfare as a result.

Another well-established aspect of the paranormal is **precognition** - 'knowledge' or 'vision' of an event **before** it actually occurs. This 'baffling phenomenon' is extremely well-attested. 'Second sight' in Gaelic culture is (or was) 'taken for granted', and there are countless records of people who had this ability to an advanced degree. Lord Kilbracken 'dreamed' of 'horse-race winners' who generally subsequently won. Mark Twain 'dreamed' of his brother's death. And, more recently, there were widespread 'premonitions' of the 'Titanic' and 'Aberfan' disasters. The subject was popularized in J. W. Dunne's 'An Experiment with Time' in 1927 (I have a copy), and particularly since 'new age thinking' came into vogue. Indeed, there is hardly anyone around today who does not 'know someone' with psychic ability, or (in a few cases) have such ability themselves. I certainly know (or knew) several such people.

Let me now end this brief account of the growth of interest in the paranormal since the 1960's by looking at **psychic healing** and **psychic surgery**. If we are to believe the Bible, Jesus regularly performed 'miracles' involving such healing, and there are many well-documented accounts of other people being able to do the same. The work of so-called 'psychic surgeons' in the Philippines, Brazil and elsewhere has been reported since the 1950's. Here, totally untrained 'healers', who lack any proper 'surgical facilities', perform 'complex surgery' on patients 'without anaesthetics', and with a 'high level of success'. The accounts of such 'psychic surgery' by Lyall Watson are particularly impressive. On three visits to the Philippines, occupying 8 months, Watson witnessed **over a thousand** such operations by 22 different 'healers'. In 1973, the Chicago journalist, Tom Valentine, saw many similar 'operations', and 'dismissed the possibility of sleight-of-hand, hypnosis or hoax'. There are so many other reliable reports of such 'surgery' that we can now safely regard it as an 'established fact', in my opinion. But exactly **how** it happens is quite another matter.

Some of the sources of information on material covered in Chapter 18

Here, I had to refer to many of the books in my personal library in order to obtain, or remind myself of, the information I needed. Some of the most important were the following:

- 'The Oxford Dictionary of Quotations', of which I own the 1996 edition (purchased in an 'Oxfam' shop, as are many of my reference books).

- 'The Holographic Universe', by Michael Talbot.
- 'Drugs of Hallucination', by Sidney Cohen (the 1964 'Scientific Book Club' edition).
- 'LSD in Action', by P. G. Stafford and B.H. Golightly (the 1970 'Scientific Book Club' edition).
- 'Vietnam - An Epic Tragedy, 1945 - 1975', by Max Hastings. (Superb!).
- 'Transcendental Meditation - Maharishi Mahesh Yogi and the Science of Creative Intelligence', by Jack Forem.
- 'The TM Technique', by Peter Russell.
- 'Seven States of Consciousness - A vision of possibilities suggested by the teaching of Maharishi Mahesh Yogi', by Anthony Campbell.
- 'The Tao of Physics', by Fritjof Capra.
- 'The Universe in a Single Atom', by His Holiness the Dalai Lama.
- 'Supernature', by Lyall Watson.
- 'Lifetide', by Lyall Watson.
- 'ESP Beyond Time and Distance', by T. C. Lethbridge (1965 'Scientific Book Club' edition).
- 'Mind-Reach - Scientists Look at Psychic Ability', by Russell Targ and Harold Puthoff.
- 'The Paranormal - An Illustrated Encyclopaedia', by Stuart Gordon.

Chapter 19: A broad look at atheism

'There is no God, and Dawkins is his prophet'

- (anon)

This is a very old joke that has been made about several militant atheists over the years. The earliest reference I can find is in Graham Farmelo's excellent biography of Paul Dirac, one of the founders of modern quantum mechanics, and one of the greatest physicists of all time (see Chapters 15 and 17). Farmelo ascribes the origin of the joke to the 'Punch' humourist, Douglas Jerrold, who, in the early 1850's, quipped about the controversial feminist writer, Harriet Martineau: 'There is no God, and Harriet Martineau is her prophet.' Farmelo reports that the same thing was said by Wolfgang Pauli about Paul Dirac, after the latter had launched a (totally unexpected) violent and prolonged attack on religion in all its forms. This happened during a discussion that took place in a hotel bar one evening, during the ground-breaking 1927 'Solvay Conference' for international physicists, where the future direction of the 'new quantum theory' was effectively decided. Throughout Dirac's diatribe against religion, Pauli had been 'uncharacteristically silent', but, according to Werner Heisenberg (another of the many prominent physicists present, which included Einstein), later made the following observation: 'Well, our friend Dirac, too, has a religion, and its guiding principle is: "There is no God, and Dirac is his prophet"'. Heisenberg reported that 'everyone laughed, including Dirac'. The same joke is apparently now being told about Richard Dawkins, and I am sure that he will not object to my using this version here. After all, it **does** sum up his own views on the matter rather well!

What do we mean by the terms 'atheism' and 'atheist'?

'Atheism' is actually a comparatively new concept, as is the term 'atheist'. In all early societies, everyone was expected to believe in the 'tribal' or 'local' gods, and anyone who refused to acknowledge these ran the risk of being put to death by their fellow-tribesmen. As we saw earlier, open dissent was **not** encouraged in such societies. Things became a **bit** more relaxed in most of the early civilisations that I described in Chapter 1, and in the religious communities that emerged and developed during the 'Axial Age', but people were still expected to believe in the 'official gods' or 'state gods', although, in many of the societies, they were afforded **some** choice as to **which** particular gods or goddesses they elected to give their allegiance to. In the Roman Empire, for example, which was so 'totalitarian' in many ways, its citizens and other subjects were given considerable freedom regarding these matters, provided that they also remained loyal to the Emperor. It was only when Constantine and Theodosius made Christianity the 'official state religion' in the 4th century of the 'Common Era' that things started to change. Once the increasingly-authoritarian 'Roman Church' started to take control over people's lives, everyone **had** to believe in the 'Christian God', and refusal to do so came to be regarded as 'heresy', of which the Church took a very dim view indeed. So, by the turn of the new millennium, nobody in the Roman Catholic world would have **dared** to say that they did not believe in God, and the term 'atheist' simply did not exist.

This remained the case right up to the time of the 'European Enlightenment', when for the very first time, a few brave people started to **question** the existence of God. They did not dare to express such doubts **openly**, however, since **everyone** was still expected to 'believe in God'. As we saw in Chapter 9, this situation did gradually change, and, by the start of the 19th century, it actually became possible to describe oneself as an **atheist** without risking imprisonment, torture or death, at least in **some** European countries. Much later in the 19th century, T.H. Huxley ('Darwin's bulldog') invented the term **agnostic** to describe someone who was **uncertain** about the question of God's existence, and this name stuck. So now there were **three** types of people in Christian Europe – people who **did** believe in God **(theists** and **deists)**, people who **were not sure** **(agnostics)**, and people who did **not** believe in God **(atheists)**. Of the two groups who did believe in God, the 'theists' believed in a 'personal God', who 'took an interest' in human affairs, and the 'deists' believed in an 'impersonal God', who simply created the Universe, and then left it alone to 'run by itself'. As we saw in Chapter 9, this was a term that started to be used **during** the 'Enlightenment', many of whose supporters did not believe in the 'personal God' of the 'theists', but could not bring themselves to abandon belief in God completely. As we saw, Voltaire was a typical example of such a 'deist'.

Fast forward to 2006, when Richard Dawkins published his notorious book, 'The God Delusion'. In this, he launched a ferocious attack on all aspects of religion, which I will come to later in this chapter, but also helped to clarify the 'terminology' regarding the belief (or disbelief) in God. Dawkins suggested that the terms 'atheist', 'agnostic' and 'theist' were not sufficiently 'discriminating' to describe the full range of modern people's beliefs/disbeliefs. He suggested using a 'seven point scale', ranging from **certain belief** in God at one end, to **certain disbelief** in God at the other, with five intermediate stages. Here is the full version of this scale, as given on pages 50-51 of the 'The God Delusion'.

1. Strong theist, 100 percent probability of God. In the words of C. G. Jung, 'I do not believe, I **know'**.
2. Very high probability but short of 100 percent. 'De facto' theist. 'I cannot know for certain, but I strongly believe in God, and live my life on the assumption that he is there'.

3. Higher than 50 percent but not very high. Technically agnostic but leaning towards theism. 'I am very uncertain, but I am inclined to believe in God'.
4. Exactly 50 percent. Completely impartial agnostic. 'God's existence and non-existence are exactly equiprobable.'
5. Lower than 50 percent but not very low. Technically agnostic but leaning towards atheism. 'I don't know whether God exists but I'm inclined to be sceptical'.
6. Very low probability, but short of zero. 'De facto' atheist. I cannot know for certain, but I think God is very improbable, and I live my life on the assumption that he is not there'.
7. Strong atheist. 'I know there is no God, with the same conviction as Jung 'knows' there is one'.

When I first read this 'seven point scale' back in 2006, I thought it was a **great** improvement on the previous crude, three-point 'theist/agnostic/atheist' scale, but felt that it 'could be improved'. I was starting to deliver talks and run seminars on the 'conflict between science and religion' at the time, so decided to produce my own version of Dawkins's scale for use as a 'handout' in these. In doing so, I decided to remove Dawkins's 'percentage probabilities', since I did not think that these were particularly useful. I also introduced **names** for the two categories for which Dawkins did not do so, which I felt would enable users of my scale to 'identify more closely' with the category that they believed they belonged to. I also tried to make the scale look 'more symmetrical' in terms of its presentation. Here is what I eventually came up with.

1. **Strong theist**: 'I **know**, with **absolute certainty**, that there is a God who participates in human affairs (i.e., a **personal God**), and feel **morally bound** to do as He wills.'

2. **De-facto theist:** 'I **cannot know for certain**, but **strongly believe** in a **personal God**, and live my life on the assumption that such a being exists and takes an interest in me.'

3. **Theistic agnostic:** 'I am **very uncertain**, but am **inclined to believe** that a **personal God** exists, and tend to live my life accordingly.'

4. **Pure agnostic:** 'I believe that God's **existence** or **non-existence** are **equally (im)probable**, so it is **impossible to decide** either way.'

5. **Atheistic agnostic:** 'I am **very uncertain**, but **am inclined to believe** that there is no **personal God**, and tend to live my life accordingly'.

6. **De-facto atheist:** 'I **cannot know for certain**, but believe that the existence of **any** type of God is **highly improbable**, and live my life on the assumption that there is no such being'.

7. **Strong atheist:** 'I **know**, with **absolute certainty**, that there is no God, so the question of whether I should **obey** such a 'being' becomes **totally irrelevant** to me.

All the people to whom I gave my 'handout' said that they found it 'extremely clear', and 'extremely helpful'. One point that readers might find interesting is that Richard Dawkins placed himself at 'point 6' on his own scale, since even **he** could not bring himself to say, with 'absolute certainty', that there is no God, although he admitted that he was 'pretty close' to that position. I placed myself at exactly the same point on mine, for the same reason, although I was not **nearly** so close to 'absolute certainty' as he was. As I remarked to people at the time, this was one of the few things about which Richard Dawkins and I were in (almost) complete agreement, although we also agreed that the then-fashionable idea of **non-overlapping magisteria (NOMA)** was deeply flawed. This held that 'science' and 'religion' were so radically different that there could be no 'overlap' between them, and therefore no 'conflict'. Dawkins contended that there **was** such an 'overlap', so that there **was** a possibility of conflict. I fully agreed, and later developed my own 'model' of the conflict between science and religion, which I used as the basis of the main 'handout' that I subsequently developed for use in my talks and seminars. This was later published electronically by 'Quo Vadis Publications' under the title: 'Science and Religion: Possible Areas of Conflict'.

Although I was quite happy to describe myself as an **atheist**, and then as a **de-facto atheist** for many years, I have now ceased to do so, describing myself as a **pagan** instead. The 1993 edition of the 'The Chambers Dictionary' contains three 'religious' definitions of this term:

- 'A person following any (especially polytheistic) pre-Christian religion'.
- 'A person who is not a Christian, Jew or Muslim, regarded as uncultured or unenlightened, a heathen'.
- 'More recently, someone who has no religion'.

The last of these describes my own position regarding religion perfectly. Indeed, I am now finding that more and more people are describing themselves as 'pagans' rather than 'atheists', and I hope that this trend continues. I think it is a **much** better name for people like me, who do not subscribe to the teaching of any **organised religion**, but still have some sort of **spiritual** beliefs. I will have more to say about **why** I now describe myself as a 'pagan' in the final section of this chapter.

Some of the different forms that atheism has taken to date

When I wrote the original versions of the 'Introduction' and 'Contents Section' of this book back in May, 2020, I intended to call this chapter 'The Atheistic world view', and include a section on 'The purely materialistic picture that atheists have of reality'. Once I started carrying out really detailed research on atheism, however, I decided that it would not be possible to do so, for the following reasons. Firstly, I found that there is no such thing as a generally-accepted 'atheistic world view', and that there are probably as many 'atheistic world views' as there are 'atheists'. Second, I found out something that I had long begun to suspect – that not all atheists **do** have a 'purely materialistic picture of reality'. I, myself, certainly do not, as I hope I have made clear in the previous chapters of this book. So what I decided to do instead was to move straight on from a discussion of what the terms 'atheism' and 'atheist' mean, to a survey of 'some of the different forms that atheism has taken to date'. This, I think, will be much more helpful to readers. I will then attempt to describe the current conflict between the 'hard atheist' movement that Richard Dawkins initiated in the mid-'noughties', and the 'back-lash' that this subsequently gave rise to.

In preparing to write my broad survey of the historical development of atheism, I was greatly helped by a book called 'Seven Types of Atheism' that was written by the free-lance author, John Gray, in 2018. I bought a copy as soon as it was published, read it almost immediately, and returned to it when I was preparing to write this chapter. Gray identified **seven** different types of atheism, but I have added **three** more, as you will see. I have also slightly changed the order in which I describe Gray's 'seven types', which is an 'author's privilege'. I am, however, extremely grateful to John Gray for writing his excellent and highly-insightful book at what was exactly the right time for me. I could not have written this section of the chapter before it appeared. Let me now try to outline the 'ten different types of atheism' that I have identified by synthesising our joint ideas on the matter. I would stress that these **are** just **outlines**, and would refer readers who want to learn more about any of John Gray's 'seven types of atheism' to his book. It is well worth reading.

1. The 'new atheism' that appeared in the 19th century

I have already explained how atheists only started to feel safe to express their views openly once the 'European Enlightenment' got properly underway, a process that continued throughout the 19th century. The so-called 'new atheists' that started to make their voices heard then directed their attacks against a comparatively narrow section of religion, and, in John Gray's opinion, 'failed to understand even that small part'. Seeing 'religion' simply as a 'system of beliefs', they 'attacked it' as if it was no more than an 'obsolete scientific theory'. Gray clearly did not think much of the 'new atheists', claiming that they said little that was 'novel' or 'interesting', so, after describing their 'activities' for purely historical reasons, never referred to them again in his book.

2. The 'atheism of silence' inaugurated by Schopenhauer

If Nietzsche shouted 'the death of God' from the rooftops, his fellow-German 'mentor', Arthur Schopenhauer (who we have already met in Chapter 8) gave the Deity a 'quiet burial'. Far more than his 'wayward disciple', Nietzsche, ever could, he left 'Christian monotheism' behind 'without regret', and developed a 'highly mystical' form of atheism that had considerable subsequent influence, what Gray described as the 'atheism of silence'. Schopenhauer was particularly noted for his 'extreme pessimism', despite enjoying a 'extravagant lifestyle', paid for by his huge 'family inheritance', which ensured that he could live in luxury for most of his life. As we saw in Chapter 8, notable figures who took his ideas on board included Wagner, Tolstoy and Freud.

3. 'Secular humanism' and John Stuart Mill

This had its roots deep in classical philosophy and early Christianity, and also in 'Enlightenment' thinking, but was effectively 'born' in

'Victorian' times, when John Stuart Mill (1806-1873) founded what became known as 'liberal' or 'secular' humanism. For all his 'secular upbringing' by his dictatorial Scottish father, James Mill, his 'liberal humanism' was always strongly influenced by Christian ethical principles, and, as we saw in Chapter 8, had a tremendous influence on the development of Victorian society, making it more 'humane'. Although he apparently never actually **described** himself as an 'atheist', he clearly was one, and also influenced prominent future atheists such as Nietzsche and Russell. The 'modern secular humanism' that I will describe later incorporates many of his ideas.

4.   'Atheism without progress': Santayana and Conrad

Next, Gray described the atheism of George Santayana and Joseph Conrad, which he collectively described as 'atheism without progress'. Both rejected the idea of a 'creator-god', but also had no 'feelings of piety' towards 'humanity'. Both produced their initial ideas during the latter part of the 19th century, and continued to develop them during the early decades of the 20th. Santayana (1863-1952), a Spanish philosopher, poet and novelist, was born in Madrid, moved to the USA in 1872, taught at Harvard, and returned to Europe in 1912. Conrad (1857-1924) was a Polish-born British novelist who wrote many books and established an international reputation.

5.   Making a 'religion out of science'

The increasing influence of science during the latter decades of the 19th century led to the emergence of a form of 'scientific racism' among non-religious 'rationalists' during the early part of the 20th. Prominent British writers such as H.G. Wells, George Bernard Shaw and Julian Huxley (grandson of 'Darwin's bulldog', Thomas Henry Huxley) openly advocated what we now regard as odious 'eugenics' programmes, justified by what became known as 'Social Darwinism'. If you want to get a flavour of what they were proposing, have a look at Shaw's play, 'Man and Superman'. All in all, this was not exactly the 'finest hour' for some of Europe's leading 'intellectual atheists', and undoubtedly sowed the seeds for the later horrors of Hitler's genocidal racist policies.

6.   The 'political religions' of the 20th century

These had their roots in the 'Jacobinism' that almost destroyed France soon after the French Revolution that had initially promised so much (see Chapter 9). They really took off towards the end of the First World War with the 'Bolshevic Revolution' in Russia. This was followed by the rise of 'Fascism' in Italy and the rise of 'National Socialism' in Germany, and, later by the development of what John Gray calls 'contemporary evangelical liberalism'. Ironically, all these movements had their roots in 'Christian monotheism', with its faith in gradual, but inevitable, movement towards a 'perfect' society, but these ideas were totally perverted by them. The last of them also perverted the idealistic 'liberal humanism' that John Stuart Mill had hoped would be the 'saviour of the world'.

7.   'God-hating atheists'

The seventh and final form of atheism that John Gray identified had its origins with 'God-haters' such as the Marquis de Sade, and Dostoevsky's fictional character, Ivan Karamazov. It attained its greatest fruition in the ideas of William Empsom, during the middle decades of the 20th century, however. Born in 1906, Empson had an 'interesting life', which, in 1961, led to the publication of 'Milton's God', one of the 'great books of criticism in the English language', in Gray's professional opinion. Among other things, this claimed that what Christians were **really** worshipping, with their 'incessant advertisements for torture', was, quite literally, the Devil. His image of 'God as a Belsen Commandant' was also highly memorable.

These, then, are the 'seven type of atheism' that John Gray identified in his admirable book of the same name. Surprisingly, he stopped at this point, and did not look at what I would regard as the most important types of 'contemporary atheism', so I will attempt to do this now. As I see it, these consist of what we might call 'modern **secular** humanism', 'modern **spiritual** humanism', and 'strong atheism'. Let us now take a brief look at each of these, before taking a detailed look at the rise of 'strong' atheism since the mid-'noughties', and the 'backlash' that it subsequently provoked.

8.   Modern 'secular humanism'

In my opinion, this is by far the most significant, and most welcome, development that has ever happened in the history of atheism. It started as a minority view, held by people who were unhappy with the doctrines of the established Christian churches, and, in Scotland, started to develop into a genuine movement, with a clear, albeit loose, supporting organisational structure, at around the time that 'organised Christianity' started to go into its current progressive decline. (I described my own experience of that decline in Chapter 9.) Now, there are probably almost as many 'humanist' funerals as traditional 'religious' funerals in Scotland, and more and more couples are now opting to hold 'humanist weddings', although traditional 'church weddings' are still popular. Many years ago, one of the stipulations that I made in my will was that my funeral should be of the former type. Since my new son-in-law, George, as of October, 2018, is the Funeral Director who will be responsible for organising this, I can be sure that my wishes will be followed 'to the letter'. When he married my daughter, Pamela, they also elected to have a 'highly-personalised' humanist ceremony, which was by far the most beautiful and moving that I have ever attended, despite the absence of traditional hymns. I was so impressed by the way the lady-in-charge conducted the ceremony that I told George that I would like her to conduct my own funeral, but not for some time, I hoped! All 'humanist' ceremonies are purely 'secular' affairs, since the 'secular' branch of 'contemporary humanism' is effectively based on what I would call 'soft atheist' principles, and bans any 'religious trappings' from all their 'ceremonies'. I have now attended many of these, especially funerals, and have never ceased to be impressed by the 'quiet dignity' with which they are conducted. These are **very** nice people.

9.   Modern 'spiritual' humanism

As far as I am aware, this is still a very long way from being systematically organised in the way that 'secular humanism' now is, and is probably in the same state that the latter was in 50 or 60 years ago. I am a great admirer of the 'secular humanist' movement, and will continue to make use of them as long as they are 'the only game in town', but, as a 'pagan' with a strong belief that there is 'something spiritual' underlying the empirical 'world of appearances' in which we live out our lives, would describe myself as a natural 'spiritual humanist' rather than a totally-non-believing 'secular humanist'. I am sure that there are **many** people like me around, and I get the sense that this number is increasing all the time. I look forward to the day when 'spiritual humanists' like me have access to the same sort of organisational facilities that 'secular humanists' currently enjoy in Scotland, although I accept that this may not happen in **my** lifetime. In the meantime, I am perfectly happy to have my funeral run on 'secular humanist' lines.

10. Strong atheism

This form of 'extreme atheism' really started to 'take off' in the latter part of the 'noughties', following the publication of Richard Dawkins's ground-breaking, and **highly** controversial book, 'The God Delusion', in 2006. The other main figure in the 'movement' was probably Christopher Hitchens, whose equally-explosive book, 'God Is Not Great', appeared a year later. Several other books of a similar ilk followed, and the 'hard atheist' movement soon came to provide a 'natural home' for all the other 'natural hard atheists' who had obviously been around before then. Since I will be dealing with this 'movement' in some detail in the next two sections of this chapter, I will say no more about it here.

The 'hard atheist' movement that developed during the mid-'noughties'

Until Richard Dawkins and the 'boys in the band' came along, most atheists were perfectly reasonable and polite people. They made it clear that they did not accept the 'religious world picture' that had dominated Western society for so long, but did so in a dignified, reasoned way, without deliberately trying to offend people. Richard Dawkins and his fellow 'hard atheists' behaved in a completely different way, and it seemed to many people that they were **deliberately** setting out to be offensive. How else are we to interpret Dawkins's suggestion that 'atheists' should call themselves 'brights', because they were clearly 'much cleverer' than most religious people, and knew it. Their suggestions that providing a 'religious upbringing' was tantamount to 'child abuse' also did not go down very well, as did their persistent claims that 'organised religion' did a great deal of harm, and hardly any good. All in all, they really did not have anything **good** to say about religion, which caused a lot of anger among the countless millions of ordinary people who had clearly got a 'great deal' out of religion. Their repeated claims that it was only **their** ideas that were 'truly scientific' also caused considerable annoyance among many other scientists. I remember meeting an **extremely** distinguished British scientist at one of RGU's graduations, prior to the award of an honorary degree, mentioning Richard Dawkins, and being told, in no uncertain terms, that 'he gives science a bad name'. I agreed, and said that he also gives **atheism** a bad name. We both laughed at this!

Let me begin by telling you a little bit about the two men who were the 'founding fathers' of the 'strong atheist' movement. Richard Dawkins was born in 1941 (again, the same year as myself), was educated at Oxford University, and taught at the University of California before returning to Oxford in 1970. He went on to become one of the world's leading evolutionary biologists, writing a string of best-selling books that had a tremendous influence on subsequent thinking. These included 'The Extended Phenotype' (1982), 'The Blind Watchmaker' (1986), 'The Selfish Gene' (1989), 'Climbing Mount Improbable' (1996), 'The Ancestor's Tale (2004), 'The God Delusion' (2006) and 'The Greatest Show on Earth' (2009), all of which I have in my personal library. Dawkins is a brilliant writer who is capable of explaining his ideas **clearly** and **simply**, which, combined with his encyclopaedic knowledge of his subject, has made him one of the best 'popular science' writers ever. He was well known for his 'anti-religious' views long before 'The God Delusion' appeared. Born in 1949, Christopher Hitchens was also one of Britain's leading intellectuals, combining a glittering career as an author with academic work (he was a Visiting Professor in Liberal Studies at the New School in New York), and with various other activities (e.g., as a 'contributing editor' to 'Vanity Fair'). He was once named as one of the world's 'Top 100 Public Intellectuals' by 'Foreign Policy and Prospect'. His books include 'Love, Poverty and War', 'Blood, Class and Empire', and, of course, 'God Is Not Great'. He died in 2011, so is no longer around to campaign for the movement he helped to found. He is greatly missed by many people.

Let me now try to summarise the main points that Dawkins and Hitchens made in their sustained attack on religion, as presented in their 2006 and 2007 books, which are now considered to be the joint 'Bibles' of the 'hard atheist' movement. I will do so by considering the two books as an 'integrated whole' rather than dealing with them separately, since the same points are often made in each of them, albeit in slightly different ways in some cases. Taken together, they certainly constitute an extremely formidable assault, reminiscent of the series of coordinated offensives that Germany launched all along the Western Front in the spring and summer of 1918, and which very nearly won the 'Great War' for them. As everyone knows, those offensives were all eventually 'stopped', and the 'Entente' forces then began the brilliant 'hundred days' of virtually-continuous offensives which drove the German army back to its own borders, and won the War for **them** in November, 1918. It remains to be seen if the current 'fight back' against 'hard atheism' will have a similar result in the long run. In some ways, it reminds me of the 'science wars' I described in Chapter 9.

As I see it, here are the eight most important points that Dawkins and Hitchens made against religion. There are many more, as anyone who reads their books will find out.

First, they presented what was probably the strongest case ever made by **anybody** that God does not exist. This included a systematic demolition of the three main 'traditional proofs' of God's existence, which I have already dealt with myself in Chapter 9. This was backed up by a wide range of other arguments, many of which they claimed to be based on sound 'scientific' principles, although the validity of these was often subsequently challenged by other scientists, and also by theologians.

Second, they launched an equally-formidable attack on the various 'metaphysical claims' of religion, arguing that many of these were based on totally-discredited 'primitive' ideas about the nature of the world. Once again, they cited the subsequent findings of science in support of this line of attack, claiming that these had effectively rendered all 'religious metaphysics' obsolete.

Third, they launched savage assaults on both parts of the Judeo-Christian Bible, claiming that both the 'Old Testament' and the 'New Testament' were in fact 'evil documents'. Readers who want to find out more about these attacks can find them in Chapter 7 of Dawkins's book, and in Chapters 7 and 8 of Hitchens's book, and they do not make 'pleasant reading' for people who regard the Bible as 'sacred'.

Fourth, they make equally-savage assaults on Islam (the possibility of a few 'Fatwas' here, I would have thought). Among other things, they claim that much of the contents of the Koran, their 'holy book', is 'borrowed' from 'Jewish and Christian myths' (even more Fatwas?). They then turn their attention to the various 'Eastern religions', saying that these are 'no better', and that 'there is no Eastern solution'.

Fifth, they claim that religion, in general, does **not** constitute the 'roots of morality', as its supporters claim, or make people 'behave better'. Indeed, they claim that most 'religious teachings' make them behave **worse**. Among other things, they cite the 'paroxysms of hate' that they arouse against people who do not share their particular beliefs, and the vast loss of life that 'wars of religion' have caused throughout history. They have a point here, I think.

Sixth, they make the general claim that, taking everything into account, religion actually does more **harm** than **good**. Indeed, they really do not think that organised religions do much good at all, despite the claims by their 'leaders' and 'priests' that they do.

Seventh, they make what they believe is a very strong case that 'indoctrinating' a child into **any** form of religious belief during their 'formative years' is tantamount to 'child abuse'. Chapter 9 of Dawkins's book is in fact wholly devoted to this topic, as is Chapter 16 of Hitchens's book. Bertrand Russell had in fact made much the same point in some of his writings.

Finally, they both make the claim that people would be **much** happier, and probably also better off, if they lived their lives according to 'purely-rational, atheistic principles' rather than on those based on religion. This, they firmly believe, could constitute a genuine 'new enlightenment'.

So, there you are, readers, the basic 'articles of faith' of the 'hard atheist' movement. I have almost certainly not done them 'full justice' in the limited amount of space I have available, but can only try to remedy this by recommending that you read the books themselves if you want to get a 'fuller picture'. They are both extremely well written, and are well worth reading, in my opinion, even if you do not agree with most of what they say. Now, let me try to describe the inevitable 'backlash' that the two books gave rise to.

The fightback against the 'hard atheists'

As I explained at the start of the last section, the 'hard atheist' movement has aroused a large amount of vehement opposition, mainly from the members of the 'religious establishment' and from 'theologians' of all faiths, but also from many scientists, who, like the eminent recipient of an honorary RGU degree that I spoke to at the awards ceremony, feel that people like Richard Dawkins 'give science a bad name'. I have met several other prominent scientists who share these views. The 'hard atheists' have also given considerable offence to millions of ordinary people, not only because of what they are **saying** and **writing**, but also because of the **manner** in which they express themselves. In this section, I will limit myself to examining two of the most important books that have been written to express such opposition, one written by an eminent academic theologian who also has a scientific background, and the other by one of the world's most distinguished, and most-respected, theological authors.

Alister McGrath, Professor of Historical Theology at Oxford University and a 'world-renowned theologian', wrote a book entitled 'Dawkins' God: Genes, Memes and the Meaning of Life' in 2005, a year **before** the publication of 'The God Delusion'. (You could therefore say that he was following the rugby maxim that you should always try to 'get your retaliation in first.') Since he also had a scientific education, holding a Ph.D. in molecular biophysics, among other qualifications, he was uniquely qualified to attack Dawkins, both from a theological **and** from a scientific angle, and this he did brilliantly in his book. I heard about this soon after I acquired 'The God Delusion', and was extremely impressed by the way in which he refuted most of Dawkins's key arguments against religion, and, in some cases, completely demolished them – but did so in a clinical, dispassionate way.

Working in a progressive, systematic manner, McGrath examined all the main 'scientific' arguments that Dawkins had presented in the various books that he had written so far, and addressed these 'head on', starting with 'The Selfish Gene', probably his most famous and influential book. McGrath offered a somewhat different interpretation that I found highly plausible. Then, he moved on to 'The Blind Watchmaker', in which Dawkins claimed to have totally discredited the 'teleological' argument for the existence of a 'creator God'. McGrath claimed that the 'scientific method' was incapable of delivering 'a decisive argument' on this issue, and that those who claimed that it did were pressing that method 'beyond its legitimate limits', and ran the risk of 'abusing or discrediting it'. He believed that 'natural science' leads '**neither** to atheism **nor** to Christianity'. He then went on to discuss the question of 'proof and faith', and the 'place of evidence in science and religion', again challenging the validity of many of Dawkins's arguments. Next, he moved on to question the validity of one of Dawkins's most controversial ideas, what he called the 'flawed analogy' between **memes** (**supposed** vehicles for 'cultural evolution') and **genes** (**proven** vehicles for 'biological evolution'). In my opinion, McGrath dealt Dawkins's 'meme theory' a blow from which it will probably never recover. He ended his book with one of the best surveys of the 'conflict between science and religion' that I have ever read, again disagreeing with several of Dawkins's ideas on the subject. Overall, I thoroughly enjoyed reading Alister McGrath's book, and was extremely impressed with his systematic, clinical refutation of many of the key arguments presented by the 'hard atheists'. I thoroughly commend it to everyone who is interested in the subject.

Karen Armstrong is one of the world's 'leading commentators on religious affairs', and, as I said earlier, is my very favourite theologian. I now have five of her excellent books in my personal library, and I am sure that more will follow. Brought up as a Roman Catholic, she spent seven years as a nun in the 1960's, but then left her teaching order in 1969 to read English at St. Anne's College, Oxford. (Why she did so is explained in one of her early books.) In 1982, she became a full-time writer and broadcaster, producing over 15 best-selling books by 2009, when she wrote 'The Case for God: What Religion Really Means', her 'reasoned reply' to 'The God Delusion' and the other attacks on religion by the 'hard atheists'. I found out about this book through the review that Christopher Hart wrote for the 'Sunday Times', and I will now quote the opening of this in full, to show you **why** I immediately ordered a copy.

'Karen Armstrong is a former Catholic nun who has written highly acclaimed biographies of Muhammed, Buddha, and, most recently, the Bible. Her new book, with its crucial subtitle, is more of a polemic, albeit of the gentlest sort. It is clearly intended as a riposte to all those blasts of aggressive atheism from the likes of Richard Dawkins and Christopher Hitchens. Reading Armstrong after these boys is like listening to a clever and kindly adult after a bunch of strident adolescents.

Both Bible-bashing fundamentalists and dogmatic atheists have a similar idea of what "God" means, she points out, and it is an absurdly crude one. They seem to think the word denotes a large, powerful man we can't see. Such a theology is, she says, "somewhat infantile". The only difference between the fundamentalists and the atheists is that the former affirm this God's existence; the latter deny it, and try to demolish it.

The new atheists, Armstrong says with impeccable restraint, "are not theologically literate", and "their polemic...lacks intellectual depth". In contrast, she usefully reminds us, both Galileo and Darwin, supposed icons of modern atheism, were adamant that their discoveries had no impact on religious faith. Equally humble in a different way, Socrates pushed rationality and intellect to the point where they fail: you reach his famous 'aporia', and realise you really know nothing at all. The new atheists do the opposite. Their rationality and intellect bring them to a place of absolute knowledge, a height from where they survey all history, and pronounce with finality on pretty much everything. Never trust anyone who knows this much.'

When I bought and read her book, it did not disappoint me. She shows that ideas of God and the Bible were, for centuries, **far** more subtle and profound than today's atheism or fundamentalism can conceive, claiming that "we have lost the 'knack' for religion". It seems as if the success of science in the material world has 'rewired our brains', making us tone-deaf to myth. "Is this true?", we constantly ask, meaning "Did it **really** happen? Is it **literally true**? If not, we're not interested." Armstrong draws on 2000 years of Christian theology and mysticism to demonstrate rich, alternative ideas about the 'divine'. The fact that Dawkins and his fellow 'hard atheists' think that pointing out the Bible's imperfections undermine Jewish or Christian faith only "demonstrates their ignorance of the traditions they presume to undermine". **Of course**, it is not meant to be "**understood literally**", the early Christians seem to "sigh across the centuries". Armstrong goes on to show how the words "I believe" have also changed and become 'scientised', now meaning "I assert these propositions to be empirically correct". Quoting the great German theologian, Rudolf Bultman, she points out that Jesus himself saw God "not as an object of thought or speculation, but as an existential demand". Yet, thanks to the 'misapplication of science to religious faith', she claims we remain 'literal-minded' and 'spiritually immature'. She says that we need to think of God not as **a being**, but as **Being** itself. She points out that, in most religious traditions, you can ultimately say **nothing** about God, since God is **no thing**. And she says much, much more in her magnificent book, but I hope you have now 'got a flavour' of its contents. Let me now conclude by quoting the final, short paragraph of Christopher Hart's superb and highly-penetrating review:

''The Case for God' simmers with a quiet spiritual optimism. It is dense and brilliant, chastening and consoling. Whether or not it sells as well as the latest Hitchens or Dawkins will be a measure of us, not the book.'

Why I now describe myself as a 'pagan'

I promised earlier that I would explain **why** I now describe myself as a 'pagan', and **why** I place myself at 'point 6' on the seven-point theist/atheist scale, right next to the 'strong atheists' who are **certain** that there is no such thing as a 'personal God'. I have two main reasons for this, one based on 'personal experience', and the other arrived at after a long period of 'philosophical pondering'.

First, the 'argument from personal experience'. As I explained in Chapter 9, I was born into a 'Christian family' (albeit a not particularly 'devout' one), was baptised as a baby, and was subsequently brought up as a 'practising Christian'. I even joined the Christian Church while at University, and transferred my membership to a small 'local' Scottish Church when I moved to England for two years, after graduating. During my time in England, however, I gradually lost what little I ever had of any 'Christian faith', partly because I found it increasingly hard to accept the main aspects of 'Christian doctrine', and partly because I found that 'Christianity' simply 'was not working for me'. I **did** attempt to pray, after a fashion, but found that it did not 'bring me into contact with God', let alone 'into contact with Jesus', as my Church told me it was **supposed** to do. Indeed, in all my years as a 'practising Christian', I had **never** experienced any such 'sense of contact'. This was why I never joined another Christian Church on returning to Aberdeen in 1965, leaving my 'papers' with the Church that I had joined while in England. I have never felt any inclination to **join** another Church since, although I have always remained in close contact with the two Churches of which my wife was a member, and sometimes even attended services along with her. I was also happy to have my two children 'christened', although I told the Minister that I would be unable to actually 'take the vows' as I stood alongside my wife. The Minister was perfectly happy with this, since he fully accepted that I had 'no religion'. He was just happy to see me stand beside my wife during the ceremony. My wife also fully understood my position, although she was never exactly happy with my lack of religious beliefs; she called me 'the family heathen'.

Second, the 'philosophical arguments'. These are partly based on the fact that I found that I could not accept the validity of **any** of the three 'traditional philosophical proofs' for the existence of God – the 'ontological' 'cosmological' and 'teleological' arguments that I described in Chapter 9. During the last 20 years, I have studied these in great detail, and have also participated in 'seminars' on them for senior pupils of 'Religious Studies' and 'Philosophy' in Secondary Schools. I even prepared detailed 'handouts' on all three of the 'proofs', handouts that the teachers involved subsequently used in their own teaching. I would also point out that **all** these 'proofs' only deal with a 'creator God' of the **deist** type, **not** with a 'personal god' of the **theist** type, something of which few people seem to be aware. And it is with such a 'personal', 'theist' God that I found that I had by far my most serious 'philosophical problems'. To put it as simply as I can, I could not accept that 'God' could be both **transcendental** and **immanent** without introducing what I came to regard as **insurmountable logical contradictions**. To be 'transcendental', God had to be **completely separate from** and **completely beyond any possibility of contact with** the 'phenomenal', 'empirical' world in which we live out our short lives. To be 'immanent', on the other hand, God had to be **constantly involved in** the affairs of this 'phenomenal world', and, to be a truly 'personal God', had to **take an interest in** and **be in contact with** individual 'human beings'. I simply could not see how 'God' could have **both** of these clearly-irreconcilable characteristics. And that is the essence of my 'philosophical problem' with the very **concept** of a 'personal God'. Taken along with the fact that I have **never** had any experience of 'being in contact with' such a God, I hope it explains why I now describe myself as a 'pagan', and place myself on the sixth point of the 'seven-point scale' that Richard Dawkins invented.

Some of the sources of information on material covered in Chapter 19

Once again, I found that I had to consult quite a lot of the books in my personal library when writing this chapter. The most useful were the following.

- 'The God Delusion', by Richard Dawkins.
- 'God Is Not Great', by Christopher Hitchens.
- 'Seven Types of Atheism', by John Gray.
- 'Atheist Universe', by David Mills.
- 'The Atheist's Guide to Reality', by Alex Rosenberg.
- 'Dawkins's God', by Alister McGrath.
- 'The Case for God', by Karen Armstrong.

Chapter 20: 'Information-based' pictures of reality

'The stream of knowledge is heading towards a non-mechanical reality; the Universe begins to look more like a great thought than a great machine.'

- James Jeans

During the first half of the 20th century, Sir James Jeans (1877-1946) was one of Britain's most prominent physicists, astronomers and popular science writers. His best-known books were 'The Universe Around Us' (1929), and 'The New Background of Science' (1933). He was at the peak of his powers during the development of the 'new quantum theory' in the 1920's, and fully recognised its significance for our understanding of the 'nature of reality', as the above quotation shows. He was in fact 'well ahead of his time', here, and science has been 'catching up', ever since, as I will try to show in this final chapter of my book. As you will see, we have indeed been steadily moving away from the 'matter-based', Newtonian model of the world, and are now fully recognising the importance of 'information' in gaining a deeper understanding of reality. I firmly believe that this is where the future lies, and am extremely excited about where it might lead us. Be ready to have your 'minds blown' when you reach the final section of the chapter. Mine was, when I first read the book on which it is based fifteen years ago.

The progressive move away from a 'matter-based' model of reality

In Chapter 7, I gave a highly-detailed description of how the mechanistic, matter-based 'Newtonian world picture', or 'Newtonian paradigm', was gradually developed between the mid-16th and mid-18th centuries, and how this totally dominated the way the Western world thought about 'reality' until the end of the 19th century. I also showed you how this led to what is now called the 'First Industrial Revolution', which started in Britain in the middle of the 18th century, and subsequently spread throughout Europe, and also to the USA and Japan. This not only brought immense power and wealth to all the nations involved, starting with 'Great Britain' (as it came to call itself), but also began to change the face of the Earth itself. This Industrial Revolution was a time of fantastic confidence, and was, indeed, 'the triumph of materialism' in every way. As Paul Davies and John Gribbin showed in their 1991 book, 'The Matter Myth', however, this happy state of affairs did not last, and, by the later stages of the 20th century, people like them were beginning to realise that they were in the middle of a 'Kuhnian paradigm shift' that was gradually 'throwing off the shackles' of three centuries of accepting the mechanistic 'Newtonian' paradigm without seriously questioning its underlying validity.

This had, of course, begun at the beginning of the 20th century, with the 'Einsteinian Revolution' that I described in detail in Chapter 11. This had dealt the comfortable 'Newtonian' paradigm two severe blows, blows from which it never really recovered. The first came from Einstein's theories of 'special relativity' (1905) and 'general relativity' (1915), which completely changed our ideas regarding the nature of 'space', 'time' and 'gravity', and the complex relationship between them. By demonstrating the equivalence of 'mass' and 'energy', the former also made physicists start to think about the possible 'dematerialisation' of the concept of matter for the very first time. This process was accelerated by the development of the 'new quantum theory' during the 1920's, and by the development of 'quantum field theory' during the 1940's, as I showed in Chapter 14. These showed that 'matter' was much more 'ephemeral' than had hitherto been supposed. Not only did 'atoms' (the foundation of Newton's 'world picture') consist largely of 'empty space', but the very 'fundamental particles' of which they were composed also appeared to have a 'ghostly', highly 'insubstantial' character, popping into and out of existence via the 'quantum processes' that seem to underly and underpin the macroscopic world. Later in the 20th century, the concept of a purely 'material world' based on 'hard matter' was dealt a further severe blow by the tremendous advances that took place in 'evolutionary and molecular biology', and in the so-called 'new information sciences', from the 1940's and 1950's onwards. Indeed, it later came to be argued that, at a molecular level, the biological sciences could be regarded as essentially **based** on 'information' of one form or another. All these developments gradually brought about the move from the 'materialist, matter-based' age of the 'Newtonian paradigm' to the 'information age' that we are currently living through.

In 'The Matter of Myth', Paul Davies and John Gribbin cited **Australia** as a notable example of a country that had successfully confronted the challenges posed by such a transition to the 'information age'. For most of its short history, the Australian economy had been dominated by the export of 'commodities' such as wood, coal, wool and other agricultural products, and, later, uranium. For reasons of history and geography, Australia had essentially 'missed' the Industrial Revolution that had so transformed the societies of Europe, North America and Japan, and, by the 1930's, very little manufacturing industry had been developed. Now, the Australian Government, led by Prime Minister Bob Hawke, made the extraordinarily-enlightened and far-reaching policy decision to 'leapfrog' over the 'industrial phase', and embrace a 'new economic order', based on the marketing of 'ideas, information and education'. He told his fellow-countrymen, and the world, that Australia could no longer be content to be 'the lucky country', because of its abundance of 'natural resources', but had to become 'the clever country'. One of the first tangible results of this policy was the decision to built a 'new type of city', known as a 'Multi-Function Polis' (MFP), near Adelaide, containing research institutes, scientifically-designed environmental schemes and social organisations, and advanced health, leisure and recreational facilities. But perhaps the most far-sighted aspect of the new policy, as represented by the MFP, was the recognition that **education** and **scientific research** were **highly-valuable resources** that could be **marketed** like any other 'commodity'. Such futuristic plans for Australia subsequently spread throughout the developing world, with Malaysia following Singapore's earlier example by going down a similar route, and becoming one of the 'tiger economies' of South-East Asia as a result. I have worked in both of these countries, and have seen for myself just what can be achieved by adopting such far-sighted policies.

What do we mean by 'information'?

Before looking in detail at some of the ways in which this new 'information age' is changing our ideas about the 'nature of reality', let me pause for a few moments and explain what we **mean** by the term, **information**. As with so many things, our old friend Aristotle was one of the first people to think seriously about the matter. Indeed, his concept of 'patterned information' is still often referred to as 'Aristotelian information'. When I was running training courses for new lecturers in RGIT and RGU during the 1980's and 1990's, I used to run a session on 'Collecting, Processing and Presenting Information', which, latterly, had the following overall structure. Each of the 'subheadings' under each 'main section heading' had several 'bullet points', which I have not shown here for reasons of space. I imagine that the contents of this session cover much of what most people (other than specialists in the different areas of 'information theory' and related fields) would regard as 'information'. See what you think.

Some reasons for collecting information

- To increase your own knowledge
- To prepare for delivering teaching, training, etc.

- To prepare for writing a paper or book
- For delivery to an employer or outside body
- As part of a research programme

The different sources of information

- Your own books, journals, etc.
- Conventional libraries
- Electronic databases
- The World Wide Web
- Original research

The different ways of collecting information

- Examining existing sources of information
- Talking to people
- Direct observation
- Questionnaires
- Specialised research instruments
- Scientific experiments of various types

Processing raw information and data

- Qualitative processing of information
- Determining the overall distribution of data
- Determining the central tendency of data
- Determining trends and correlations
- Determining reliability

The different ways of presenting information

- By producing written material
- By giving a live presentation

- By producing a media package of some sort

Some features that can be incorporated in presentations

- Tables
- Scattergrams and graphs
- Bar charts and pie charts
- Diagrams, drawings, cartoons etc
- Photographs in various formats
- Video material, animated material, etc.
- Audio material

In retrospect, I now realise that this was a somewhat simplified and limited picture of what was meant by 'information', in a purely-academic context, but it did meet the needs of young, newly-appointed lecturers at the time. Feedback that I received from them indicated that they found my sessions on 'Collecting, Processing and Presenting Information' extremely useful. Now, of course, I realise that there is **much** more to 'information' than what I had covered, far too much, in fact, for me to include in the limited space that I have available to me in this section of the chapter. I would need **several books** to do full justice to the topic! Let me therefore confine myself here to introducing readers to a few of the key concepts that underpin modern 'information theory'.

The most important of these is the distinction that is made between **semantic information** and **syntactic information**. To put it as simply as I can, the first category includes all the different types of information that are clearly **about** something, i.e., have genuine **semantic content**. Examples are the information contained in a novel or film, or, indeed, any of the types of information that I included in my teaching session on the topic. The second category, on the other hand, includes all the different types of information that do **not** possess such semantic content, but are purely 'syntactic' in nature. There are many examples of such information, the one with which most people are probably most familiar being the strings of binary digits ('bits') that are processed by digital computers. Although these can be used to **represent** 'real things' or 'real situations', they have, **in themselves**, no **semantic content**. This is one of the reasons why digital computers will **never** be able to 'think' in the same way that human beings and other sentient creatures 'think'. For a long time, members of the 'strong AI' (artificial intelligence) community maintained that digital computers probably **could** be made to 'think' in this way, but most of them now admit that this will probably never happen. There have been tremendous advances in computing during recent years, including the development of 'expert systems' that can carry out 'medical diagnoses' far better then any 'human' doctors, but it is now admitted by the 'AI community' that they do this purely by processing vast amounts of data more quickly and more effectively than any human being possibly could. The fact that computer programs capable of beating even the most brilliant chess 'grand masters' have now been developed has the same basic explanation. Such programs are successful because they can determine the outcomes of all the various possible 'moves' that a given situation can give rise to far more effectively and more quickly than a mere human can, because the computers on which they run now have a virtually-unlimited capacity for processing digital information. They do not, however, have any idea of **what** they are doing, because such programs have no 'semantic content'. Other examples of purely syntactic information are the 'DNA codes' that control the production of proteins within living cells. These 'do their job' in a purely **mechanical** way, again with no 'understanding' of **what** they are doing, or **why** they are doing it.

Another key aspect of modern information theory is what is known as **Shannon information**. This is based on work that was carried out by Claude Shannon at the Bell Laboratory in the USA during the 1940's, work that used a statistical approach to the analysis of electrical and electronic signals and their capability to carry information. His work laid the foundations for the entire modern telecommunications industry, but his analysis excluded any reference to 'semantic content' or 'significance', treating 'information' purely in 'engineering terms'. Thus, although his work has brought untold benefits to modern society, it has little relevance to our present discussion of the role of information in understanding 'reality'. Readers who want to learn more about it can find ample information on the Internet.

Is 'information' the key to understanding the 'nature of reality'?

In August, 2006, a highly-significant Symposium was held in the Consistorial Hall of Copenhagen University, under the joint aegis of the 'John Templeton Foundation' and the 'Copenhagen University of Research Priority Area on Religion in the 21st Century'. The overall aim of this Conference was to 'explore fundamental concepts of matter and information in current physics, biology, philosophy and theology with respect to the question of ultimate reality'. It probably played the same important role in the development of thinking in this area as the 1927 'Solvay Conference' in Brussels did in the development of modern quantum theory. A book describing what was discussed at the conference was later produced jointly by Paul Davies and Niels Henrik Gregersen in 2010. This was entitled 'Information and the Nature of Reality: From Physics to Metaphysics', and was undoubtedly the most important book yet published in this area. I purchased a copy as soon as I found out about it, and have read it twice, although it is pretty 'heavy going' in places. It was also my main source of information for this section of the present chapter. Although it would clearly be impossible for me to cover the entire contents of a 382-page book in a few pages of my own book, I will try to give readers a general idea of what it contains.

Following a nine-page 'Introduction' by Davies and Gregersen posing the question 'does information matter?', and concluding that it clearly **does**, the main body of the book is divided into four parts.

Part 1, **'History'**, consists of two chapters.

The first, written by Ernan McMullin, O'Hara Professor Emeritus of Philosophy at the Notre Dame University in Paris, is entitled 'From matter to materialism and (almost) back', and covers the same broad areas as the first section of the present chapter, but in much greater detail – and in a highly erudite way that I could never hope to match. It made very enjoyable reading.

The second, written by Philip Clayton, Ingraham Professor of Theology at Claremont School of Theology, and Professor of Religion and Philosophy at Claremont Graduate University, is entitled 'Unsolved dilemmas: the concept of matter in the history of philosophy and in contemporary physics', and provides a clear, comprehensive and insightful review of this key area, setting the scene for what is to follow in Part 2. Clayton came to two main conclusions. First, he suggested that 'idealist' thinkers, who sought to 'dispense with the notion of matter altogether', are 'misguided', and that 'the conundrums are not resolved by turning one's back on the mysterious nature of objects and particles in physics'. Second, he argued that 'physics suggests theories of reality in which **information** takes over the roles that **matter** once played', and also suggests 'an entanglement of matter and meaning'. However, he also felt that, 'in recent years, the baton has passed to the biological sciences, where new insights into the nature of information are now receiving empirical support'. He concluded his chapter with the following words:

'Taken together, I suggest, these new lines of inquiry are putting the final nails in the coffin of the materialist world once touted as science's crowning glory'.

Part 2, **Physics**, consists of three chapters.

The first is written by Paul Davies himself, who held various University positions in Cambridge, London, Newcastle and Sidney before joining Arizona State University as Professor and Director of the Centre for Fundamental Concepts in Science. It is entitled 'Universe from bit', and directly challenges some widely-held assumptions about the nature of physical reality. For example, he asks what happens if we do **not** assume that the mathematical relations of the so-called 'laws of nature' are 'the most basic level of description', but regard **information** as the 'foundation on which physical reality is constructed'. Davies suggested that, instead of taking **mathematics** to be primary, followed by **physics** and then **information**, the 'picture should be inverted in our explanatory scheme', so that the 'conceptual hierarchy' becomes **information → laws of physics → matter**. He concludes his chapter with the following remarkable observation:

'Whether reality does lie in a quantum realm, to which human beings have no access, or whether it lies in the realm of bits and real observations, could therefore be put to the test with a sufficiently complex quantum system. If the quantum computation optimists are right, it may be that within a few years a new discipline will emerge: **experimental ontology**.'

Now **that** would **really** be something!

The second is written by Seth Lloyd, Professor of Quantum-Mechanical Engineering at Massachusetts Institute of Technology. It is entitled 'The computational universe', and shows how the 'information-processing revolution', based on electronic computers and optical communication systems has 'transformed work, education and thought', and has 'altered the life of every person on Earth'. Lloyd's view of the 'computational nature of the Universe' builds on Paul Davies's suggested 'conceptual hierarchy' by treating quantum events as 'quantum bits', or 'qubits', whereby the Universe 'registers itself'. He approached this subject from the viewpoint of 'quantum information science', which, at the time of the 2006 Symposium, was attempting to construct a 'quantum computer' – a device that would be able to process information 'at the quantum level', thereby achieving a spectacular increase in computational power. This ambitious project has made considerable progress since then. Lloyd went much further than this 'practical programme of research', however, using the concept of 'quantum information science' as the basis of an 'entire world view', declaring that the Universe as a whole is a 'gigantic quantum computer'. In other words, nature 'processes quantum information' whenever a physical system 'evolves'.

The third and final chapter in Part 2 is written by Henry Stapp, a theoretical physicist at the University of California's Lawrence Berkeley Laboratory, where he specialises in the conceptual and mathematical foundations of quantum theory, and, in particular, on the quantum aspects of the relationship between our 'streams of conscious experience' and the 'physical processes occurring in our brains'. (I have one of his excellent books on this topic, 'Mindful Universe: Quantum Mechanics and the Participating Observer', in my personal library, and found it **extremely** interesting.) The title of his chapter is 'Minds and values in the quantum universe'. It takes us into totally new areas of the 'quantum world', arguing, for example, that 'the replacement of classical mechanics by quantum mechanics opens the door to religious possibilities that formerly were rationally excluded'. I found **this** idea particularly exciting.

451

Part 3, Biology, consists of five chapters.

The first was written by John Maynard Smith, who died in 2004, two years before the actual Symposium. In the late 1950's and early 1960's, he carried out pioneering work on the genetics of aging in fruit flies, and went on to become one of Britain's leading geneticists and evolutionary biologists. His chapter is entitled 'The concept of information in biology', and provides a fascinating review of the field. He argues that the biological sciences should now be regarded as essentially based on **information** of one form or another, and on the **processing** of this at various levels within living organisms. In the 19th century, such organisms were regarded as some sort of 'magic matter' infused with a 'vital force'. Today, the cells that form the basis of all living systems are regarded as 'supercomputers' that operate with unbelievable fidelity, and we all rely on them continuing to do so throughout our lives.

The second was written by Terrence W. Deacon, who taught for many years at Harvard University and Boston University, before moving to the University of California, where he carried out research on the links between human evolutionary biology and neuroscience, and the evolution of 'human cognition'. His chapter is entitled 'What is missing from theories of information?', and tries to find an answer to this question. His starting point is that we still do not know what **information** really is, and, until we do, problems will always arise. Like so many of the 'hard problems' in philosophy, he believes that we have been asking 'the wrong sorts of questions'. Talking about 'cognition' in terms of the 'mind-brain' system, (implying a 'metaphysically-primitive identity'), or talking about the 'mind' as the 'software of the brain' (implying that 'mental contents' can be reduced to 'syntactic relationships embodied in and mapped to neural mechanics') both 'miss the point'. He favours a more complex relationship between 'mind' and 'brain', in which 'semantic information' plays a key part. All in all, I found his ideas extremely interesting and thought-provoking, as I did with virtually **all** the chapters in this excellent book.

The third was written by Bernd-Olaf Küppers, Professor of Natural Philosophy at the Friedrich Schiller University of Jena. It is entitled 'Information and communication in living matter'. He not only believes that information is 'a key concept in understanding living matter', he also believes that communication, 'the flow of information at all levels of the living system', plays an equally-important role. This means that 'information stored in the genome of the organism is expressed in innumerable feedback loops', a process through which the genetic information is 'continually re-evaluated by permanent interactions with the physical environment to which it is exposed'. In this way, he believes, the living organism 'is built up, step by step, into a hierarchically-organised network of unmatched complexity'. Thus, the processes of life would 'implode into a jumble of chaos' if they were not 'perpetually stabilised by **information** and **communication**'. As someone who knows a 'little bit' about 'cybernetics', this all makes a great deal of sense to me.

The fourth was written by Jesper Hoffmeyer, Professor Emeritus in the Department of Molecular Biology at the University of Copenhagen. It is entitled 'Semiotic Freedom: an emerging force', and questions the 'overarching role of genetics' in biology, opting instead for 'the importance of the cell-centred view'. His ideas are based on the comparatively-recent concepts of 'semiotic emergence' and 'downward causation', which are the very opposite of the 'upwards causation' that dominated the 'reductionist' view of biology that held sway for so many years. Overall, Hoffmeyer takes a very 'holistic' view of biological development, and believes that 'biosemiotics' may potentially account for the appearance of 'conscious human beings with moral feelings' by purely 'natural processes'. He believes that such an approach 'overturns the need for, or legitimacy of', the argument for 'intelligent design', a suggestion that I found extremely interesting.

The fifth and final chapter in Part 3 is written by Holmes Rolston III, University Distinguished Professor and Professor of Philosophy Emeritus at Colorado State University. Like Paul Davies, he has been awarded the 'Templeton Prize' in recognition of his work on the relationship between 'science' and 'religion', which is one of his main interests. His chapter is entitled 'Care on Earth: generating informed concern', and fully reflects this interest. In it, he offers a 'natural history' of the emergence of an 'informed concern' for others. Evolution is generally regarded as a 'notoriously selfish process', but, eventually, it produces creatures that display 'altruism', and exhibit 'concern for others'. With the increase in 'sense perception and the top-down capacity of mammalian brains', Rolston shows how 'an ethical dimension of nature' eventually arrives on the 'evolutionary scene'. In his opinion, a 'cell-centred view' is not necessarily a 'self-centred view'.

Part 4, Philosophy and Theology, again consists of five chapters.

The first was written by Arthur Peacocke (another winner of the prestigious Templeton Prize), a biochemist and theologian who taught at both Oxford and Cambridge Universities in the course of his long and distinguished career. He died in 2006, and the book on the proceedings of the Copenhagen Symposium was 'dedicated to his memory'. His chapter is entitled 'The sciences of complexity; a new theological resource?', and presents his 'integrative view' about how an 'emergentist monism', informed by the 'sciences of complexity', must be 'sensitive to the uniformity of the material world' as well as to the 'distinctive levels that come up at later stages of evolution'. Peacocke's distinctive 'theological synthesis' thus combines 'naturalism' and 'emergentism' with a 'pantheistic concept of God', that is, 'a God that permeates the world of nature **from within**', while, at the same time, being '**more** than the world of nature in its entirety'. (Baruch Spinoza, who we met in Chapter 8, held similar views.) He concluded his highly-impressive chapter with the following words:

'Hence, in responding to one of the questions this volume poses – "What is ultimate?" one does, now, not have to choose between "God, matter and information", but can hold them together in a new kind of synthesis that obviates the false dichotomies of the sciences/humanities, matter/spirit and science/religion that have plagued Western culture for too long'.

The second was written by Keith Ward, Emeritus Regius Professor of Divinity at Oxford University, and one of Britain's greatest-ever theologians. It is entitled, 'God as the ultimate informational principle', and (along with John F. Haught, author of the following chapter) explores novel ways for understanding God as a 'source of information' for a 'self-developing world'. Specifically, he presents a case for what he calls a 'supreme informational principle of the Universe', without which the combination of the 'lawlessness of the world' and its 'inherent value' would be 'inexplicable'. Such an 'informational code' for the construction of an 'actual Universe' logically precedes material configurations, by containing 'the set of all mathematically-possible states', plus a 'selective principle of evaluation that gives preference to the actual world that we inhabit'. Ward suggests that this 'primary ontological reality' may be 'identified with God', especially if the 'given laws of nature' can be seen as 'providing space for qualities such as goodness and intrinsic value'.

The third was written by John F. Haught, a Senior Fellow of the Woodstock Theological Centre at Georgetown University. As we have seen, he joined Keith Ward in exploring novel ways for understanding God as a 'source of information' for a 'self-developing world'. Haught argues that 'information' must 'walk the razor's edge' between 'redundancy' (too much order) and 'noise' (too much contingency). He believes that it is this 'felicitous blend of order and novelty' that transforms the Universe from a 'mere physical system' into a 'narrative of information processing'. While reminding us that all 'God language' must be regarded as 'analogical', Haught argues that the concept of God as an 'informational principle at work in the entire cosmic process' is 'far richer' than the idea of a 'designer God' at the 'edge of the Universe'.

The fourth was written by Niels Henrik Gregersen, Professor of Systematic Theology at Copenhagen University. It is entitled 'God, matter and information: towards a Stoicizing Logos Christology', and, as in the case of the last two chapters, effectively forms a 'matched pair' with the final chapter in Part 4 by Michael Welker. Both argue that 'new scientific perspectives' regarding the relationship between 'matter' and 'information' described in earlier chapters give fresh impetus to the 'reinterpretation of important strands of the Biblical traditions'. Specifically, Gregersen shows how the New Testament concept of a 'divine Logos becoming Flesh' (John 1, 14) has structural similarities to the ancient Stoic notion of 'Logos' as a 'fundamental organising principle of the Universe', and 'should not prematurely be interpreted in a Platonic vein'. The Johannine vision of 'divine Logos' being 'co-extensive with the world of matter' may be 'sustained and further elucidated' in the context of 'present-day concepts of matter and information', where the co-presence of 'order' and 'difference' is also emphasised.

The fifth and final chapter in Part 4 is written by Michael Welker, who held Faculty positions at the Universities of Tübingen and Münster before taking up the Chair of Systematic Theology at Heidelberg University. As we have seen, he joined Niels Gregersen in showing how important aspects of 'Biblical traditions' can be 'reinterpreted' in the light of new scientific ideas regarding the relationship between 'matter' and 'information'. In particular, he suggests that 'interdisciplinary discussions' between practitioners of science, philosophy and theology should be able to move between 'more general metaphysical proposals' and the 'more scientific semantic Universes', which are often 'more attentive to the particulars'. As an example, he cites Paul's distinction between the perishable 'Flesh' and the possibility of specific 'bodies' being filled with 'divine energy'. Such distinctions, he believes, may also be able to 'catch' the 'social dimensions of material coexistence', which tend to be left out of 'more generalised forms of metaphysics'. According to Paul, the 'Divine Spirit' may 'saturate the spiritual bodies of human beings', and 'bring them into communication', when 'transformed' in 'God's new creation'.

When I was writing this summary of the contents of 'Part 4', I could not help wishing that 'hard atheists' like Richard Dawkins and Christopher Hitchens could have been locked up for a week with the brilliant theologians who wrote the five chapters therein. As Karen Armstrong has pointed out, these people are 'not theologically literate', and I felt that exposing them to the sort of 'deep thinking' that is carried out by **real** theologians might, just might, make them moderate their extreme, and, in my opinion, highly-bigoted views. I now realise that this would probably be a complete waste of time, however, since such people are so firmly entrenched in their views that they are completely beyond the reach of 'reasoned argument'. They are, in many ways, very similar to the 'religious bigots' and 'extreme fundamentalists' that they excoriate with such superb literary skill. They are all clearly highly-intelligent and highly-informed people (well, **most** of them, anyway) but, as I showed in Chapter 3, even a man as highly intelligent as Pythagoras can do extremely 'stupid things' at times. Let me simply ask them to ponder on one of the wisest things ever said by the great German poet, Schiller, who knew a little bit about 'wisdom' and its opposite:

'Against stupidity, the Gods themselves contend in vain'.

Do we live in an information-based 'holographic Universe'?

In this, the final chapter of my book, I have shown you how we have now moved far down the road away from the purely-mechanistic 'Newtonian world picture' that dominated our thinking about the 'nature of reality' for almost 300 years, and are now well into the 'information age'. I have tried to give you an idea of some of the ways in which living in such an age is currently changing our views on the nature of reality. I hope that you have found the different views expressed in the last section as interesting and thought-provoking as I did, and thoroughly commend the book in which they were presented to the world in 2010, which seems a long time ago now. I thought at the time that this could well turn out to be one of the most important books ever written on the 'nature of reality', and have not changed my mind since. As you will have seen, it claims to show that the basic 'entity' on which the Universe and everything in it is built is not 'matter' but 'information' of various types, and presents a range of possible 'models' for such an 'information-based Universe'. I am about to introduce you to another 'model' of this type, the so-called **holographic Universe** model. I myself was introduced to this roughly 15 years ago, when I purchased a copy of Michael Talbot's book, 'The Holographic Universe', read it, and, metaphorically at least, had my 'mind blown away' by what I had read. I thought at the time that 'this could well be true', and, every time I have read it since, (and I have now done so four more times) become more and more convinced that this **might** be the case. As I will show in the 'Conclusion' to my book, I would need **much** more evidence to become **fully** convinced, but then, I am a 'very hard man' to make firmly convinced of **anything**, as I hope this book has shown. When I was planning the structure of my book, I planned to write my own description of the 'holographic Universe' concept. Having re-read the 'Introduction' to Michael Talbot's book, however, I have decided that I could not possibly improve on what he wrote in the opening sections of this. I have therefore included all of these here, without altering a word. If you want to learn more about the ideas outlined therein, read the book itself; I guarantee that you will not regret it.

'In the movie 'Star Wars', Luke Skywalker's adventure begins when a beam of light shoots out of the robot Artoo Detoo, and projects a miniature three-dimensional image of Princess Leia. Luke watches spellbound as the ghostly sculpture of light begs for someone named Obi-wan Kenobi to come to her assistance. The image is a hologram, a three-dimensional picture made with the aid of a laser, and the technological magic required to make such images is remarkable. But what is even more astounding is that some scientists are beginning to believe that the Universe itself is a kind of giant hologram, a splendidly-detailed illusion no more and no less real than the image of Princess Leia that starts Luke on his quest.

Put another way, there is evidence to suggest that our world and everything in it – from snowflakes to maple trees, to falling stars and spinning electrons – are also only ghostly images, projections from a level of reality so beyond our own that it is literally beyond both space and time.

The main architects of this astonishing idea are two of the world's most eminent thinkers: University of London physicist David Bohm, a protégé of Einstein's and one of the world's most respected quantum physicists; and Karl Pribram, a neurophysiologist at Stanford University, and author of the classic neuropsychological textbook, 'Languages of the Brain'. Intriguingly, Bohm and Pribram arrived at their conclusions independently, and while working from two very different directions. Bohm became convinced of the Universe's holographic nature only after years of dissatisfaction with standard theories' inability to explain all the phenomena encountered in quantum physics. Pribram became convinced because of the failure of standard theories of the brain to explain various neurophysiological puzzles.

However, after arriving at their views, Bohm and Pribram quickly realised that the holographic model explained a number of other mysteries as well, including the apparent inability of any theory, no matter how comprehensive, ever to account for all the phenomena encountered in nature; the ability of individuals with hearing in only one ear to determine the direction from which a sound originates; and our ability to recognise the face of someone we have not seen for many years, even if that person has changed considerably in the interim.

But the most staggering thing about the holographic model was that this suddenly made sense of a wide range of phenomena so elusive that they generally have been categorised outside the province of scientific understanding. These include telepathy, precognition, mystical feelings of oneness with the Universe, and even psychokinesis, the ability of the mind to move physical objects without anyone touching them.

Indeed, it quickly became apparent to the ever-growing number of scientists who came to embrace the holographic model that it helped to explain virtually all paranormal and mystical experiences, and, in the last half-dozen years or so, it has continued to galvanise researchers, and shed light on an increasing number of previously-inexplicable phenomena'.

(Three detailed examples too long to include here are then given.)

'These are only a few of the thought-provoking ideas that will be explored in this book. Many of these ideas are extremely controversial. Indeed, the holographic model itself is highly controversial, and is by no means accepted by the majority of scientists. Nonetheless, as we shall see, many important and impressive thinkers do support it and believe it may be the most accurate picture of reality we have to date.

The holographic model has also received some dramatic experimental support. In the field of neurophysiology, numerous studies have corroborated Pribram's various predictions about the holographic nature of memory and perception. Similarly, in 1982, a landmark experiment performed by a research team lead by physicist Alain Aspect, at the Institute of Theoretical and Applied Optics, in Paris, demonstrated that the web of subatomic particles that compose our physical Universe – the very fabric of reality itself – possesses what appears to be an undeniable 'holographic' property. These findings will also be discussed in the book.'

And if **that** does not whet your appetite to learn more about this fascinating concept, I do not know what will!

Some of the sources of information on material covered in Chapter 20

Practically all of the information on which I based this chapter comes from the following 'four sources':

- 'The Matter Myth', by Paul Davies and John Gribbin.
- My own loose-leaf 'teaching folder' of materials related to 'Information Technology and Communications' (which I have not looked at since I retired almost 20 years ago).

- 'Information and the Nature of Reality', edited by Paul Davies and Niels Henrik Gregersen.
- 'The Holographic Universe', by Michael Talbot.

Conclusion

'Left Wondering'

- Bryan Magee (Confessions of a Philosopher)

This is the title that Bryan Magee chose for the final chapter of his brilliant intellectual autobiography, which was published in 1997 – a book that I have now read nine times, at the last count. In this chapter, he admitted that he was no further forward in discovering the ultimate secrets of reality, but offered a number of personal ideas on where and how some of these secrets **might** ultimately be arrived at. This is precisely the position that I now find myself in, after a lifetime of thinking about such matters, so I will end this 'personal survey' of the 'nature of reality' by offering a few of my own ideas on what we have learned so far, and where such ideas **might** lead in the future. Bryan died in 2019, but I am sure he would have approved of my use of his words. I owe him a great debt of gratitude for guiding and informing my own philosophical development. As you will have seen, I actually dedicated this book to him.

In order to give my 'Conclusion' some sort of systematic structure, I have decided to base it in the following six questions:

1. What do we know about the **nature of the Universe** in which we live?
2. What do we know about the **different sorts of 'things'** of which it is ultimately composed?
3. Do we live in a **completely deterministic world**?
4. Is the **empirical world** that we see around us all that there is?
5. What do we know about any **underlying layer of reality**?
6. How can we try to **find out more**?

As you will see, these follow a natural progression from aspects of reality about which we **do** now know a great deal, to aspects about which we clearly **do not** know very much with any degree of certainty. Let me now try to answer the six questions as best as I can.

1.   The nature of the Universe

This is, in my opinion, the aspect of reality about which we probably now know the most – and furthermore, can now claim that **much** of our 'provisional knowledge' (as **all** 'scientific knowledge' ultimately is) is 'very probably true'. We still have a lot to learn about 'cosmology', and are adding 'new knowledge' every year, but, as I showed in Chapter 12, the progress that we have made since the time of Newton, and, in particular, in the last 50 or 60 years, has been positively spectacular. It must be 'great fun' and 'highly rewarding' to be a cosmologist right now, because cosmology is **truly** going through a 'golden age'. So let me now try to summarize our **current** state of knowledge of the 'nature of the Universe', and indicate areas where some uncertainty still exists – quite a lot, in some cases, as is inevitable in a discipline that is at the very 'cutting edge' of science.

As I explained in Chapter 12, we now have a pretty clear idea of the **size** and **structure** of the 'observable Universe' (the part that we can actually **see**), are pretty certain that we know its **exact age**, and also believe, with a great deal of confidence, that we know how it **originated**, and how it subsequently **evolved**. With regard to its **size,** we believe that the **cosmic light horizon radius** (the furthest distance from which light has been able to reach us since the time of the 'big-bang' event that we believe marked its beginning) is of the order of 45 billion light years. This is the figure that was recently given by Professor Brian Cox, who knows quite a lot about these matters. Note that this distance is considerably greater than the 13.8 billion light years that is obtained by multiplying the **age** of the Universe by the **speed of light** (the **lookback**, or **light travel time** distance). This is a direct result of the **expansion** of the Universe, which has caused the **true** distance of the 'cosmic light horizon' from us to increase considerably since photons from the horizon that are reaching us now set out on their journeys. We also 'know', with a reasonable degree of accuracy, that the 'observable Universe' probably contains at least a hundred billion **galaxies**, each of which can contain up to several hundred billion individual **stars**. As I showed in Chapter 12, these galaxies appear to be arranged in a hierarchy of structures, ranging from 'small' **groups** a few million light years or more across, through **clusters** and **superclusters** of varying sizes, up to **supercluster complexes** that can be up to a billion light years or more in length. Thanks to recent data on the **cosmic microwave background radiation** produced by the Planck Satellite, the **age** of the Universe has now been pretty well 'tied down' to 13.8 billion years. And, as I also showed in Chapter 12, cosmologists are now highly confident that the Universe did indeed **begin** with a 'big-bang' event, and also have a pretty clear idea of how it has **evolved** since the event happened. They still have no idea of what things were like **before** the big-bang, however, or of what actually **caused** the big-bang. These are things that we may possibly **never** know. We also have no idea of what there is **beyond** the edge of the observable Universe. Some cosmologists believe that it is probably 'more of the same'. Others believe that **our** Universe is only part of a very-much-larger **multiverse**, which some believe could be 'infinite' in extent. This is again something that we may **never** be able to investigate empirically.

2. The 'basic things' of which it is composed

This is another aspect of reality about which we now know a great deal, although, as in the case of cosmology, there are still quite a lot of things that we do **not** know. As I explained in Chapter 20, we have now moved almost entirely away from the **matter-based** model of reality, which pictured it simply as 'particles' and 'aggregates of particles' moving in the 'void', blindly obeying the 'laws of motion' and 'law of gravitation' that Newton had discovered. As we also saw in that chapter, **information** is now coming to play a much more important role in our models of reality, although we are still trying to establish exactly **what** role or roles it plays. Let me now try to give you a broad picture of the different 'types of things' that we now believe constitute the 'basic fabric' in the world in which we live.

First, we believe that the Universe contains two basically different types of 'stuff' – **radiation** and **matter**, although not the 'type of matter' that Newton had envisaged. You will note that I said 'radiation' and 'matter' rather than 'matter' and 'radiation', because there is in fact **far** more radiation than matter – roughly a billion more photons than there are matter particles. This radiation was originally created during the very early stages of the 'big bang', when virtually all the 'matter particles' in the embryonic Universe mutually annihilated with their corresponding 'antiparticles', turning into **very** high-energy photons. Before this happened, we believe that there were 10^9+1 'particles' for every 10^9 'antiparticles' (we do not yet know why), so that there was **one** particle of **matter** for every 10^9 particles of **radiation** (photons) after the process had 'run its course'. This radiation has now 'cooled down' from its original temperature of roughly 10^{32}K (degrees Kelvin), to the 2.725K that we observe today (yes, we now know the temperature of the cosmic microwave background to **that** degree of accuracy, again thanks to data recently produced by the Planck satellite).

Second, we now know that the **composition** of this matter is **very** much stranger than had long been supposed. Until the late 1930's, it was assumed that it consisted of **ordinary matter**, of the type found here on Earth. Since then, however, we have discovered that most of the 'matter' in the Universe takes the form of so-called **dark matter**, whose exact nature we have so far been unable to determine. Furthermore, work carried out towards since the end of the last millennium has shown that the Universe also contains a large amount of another mysterious substance, known as **dark energy**. This is responsible for the recently-discovered **acceleration** of the expansion of the Universe (until that discovery, we had always assumed that the rate of expansion was **slowing down** due to gravitational attraction). We have even been able to measure the **relative proportions** of the total mass/energy of the Universe that these different components represent. Again thanks to recent data from the Planck satellite, we now know the Universe is made up of 68% **dark energy**, 27% **dark matter,** and only 5% **ordinary matter**, which physicists refer to as **baryonic matter.**

Third, we now have a pretty good idea what that **ordinary matter** is like. I recently prepared a talk for delivery at Aberdeen Business and Professional Club (which meets every Thursday for a lunch, followed by a 20-minute talk, or at least **did** until 'COVID 19' arrived). This one was entitled 'A Simple Guide to Particle Physics', and, as is my custom, I prepared a detailed 'handout' to accompany it. Here is the opening section of the handout, which describes 'the different layers of matter as we currently understand them'.

Matter	is made up of	**molecules**	which are made up of	**atoms**	which consist of a	positive **nucleus** surrounded by a cloud of negative **electrons**
The **nucleus**	is made up of	positive **protons** and uncharged **neutrons** bound together by **mesons**	all of which are made up of	**quarks** bound together by **gluons**	and **may**, together with all other particles, be made up of	**strings** or **branes**

That, I think, is about as clear and simple a picture of the composition of matter that I could possibly give you. You may wish to remind yourselves of the meaning of all these terms by referring back to Chapter 13, which also provides a much-more-detailed description of the overall scheme; this is now described as the **standard model** of particle physics. To date, this model has passed **every** experimental test carried out to try to verify its validity.

3. Is the Universe completely 'deterministic'?

Well, many people certainly used to **believe** that it was. Newton himself had told us that it was, claiming that his 'mindless world' of hard, 'inert atoms' moving in the 'void' was rather like a **clock**, and, once it had been 'created' by 'God', it would carry on running **forever**, without further intervention by its 'creator'. Many people also came to believe that we live in a **wholly deterministic world**, in which **all** our actions and thoughts are the inevitable result of **chains of casual links** stretching indefinitely backwards through time. The strongest statement of this 'deterministic doctrine' was possibly given by Pierre Laplace, at around the start of the 19th-century. He believed that an omniscient and omnipotent being who knew the **exact positions** and **detailed motions** of all the particles in the Universe at **any given time** would be able to determine the **complete past history** of the Universe, and predict its **detailed future evolution**, purely on the basis of this knowledge. According to this doctrine, human beings had **no real control** over their thoughts and actions, so that the concept of **free will** was an illusion.

Three 20th-century developments have now effectively demolished this 'extreme deterministic' position, however. The first was the formulation of the **'new' quantum mechanics** during the 1920's. As we saw in Chapter 14, these showed that the 'microscopic events' that underpin and control the behavior of all 'macroscopic systems' appear to be completely **random** and **unpredictable** in nature. Thus, we can only predict the **probabilities** that quantum events will produce particular results, and can only find out what **actually happens** by carrying out appropriate **physical measurements**. The second was the development of **chaos theory**, from the 1970's onwards. This began with the study of complicated systems like the **weather**, which was notoriously difficult to predict more than a few days ahead. It showed that no physical system that incorporates **any** trace of 'non-linearity' in its 'internal dynamics' (ie, no **real system**) can have its behavior predicted indefinitely far into the future unless its **initial conditions** can be defined with **infinite precision**, something that is clearly impossible. The third was a discovery made theoretically by Jacob Bekenstein, one of Stephen Hawking's 'brightest' research students. This showed that the number of 'bits' ('binary digits') of 'information' that a given volume of space can contain is determined by the **area of its surface** divided by the square of the so-called **Planck length** (10^{-35} metres). Based on this criterion, which is now known as the **Bekenstein bound**, it can be shown that the **amount of information** that the very early Universe could have contained was **insignificantly small** compared with the information content of the **present** observable Universe, calculated to be roughly 10^{120} bits. Clearly, this would make the detailed predetermination of **all aspects** of the former's **future** development impossible.

Taken together, these three developments showed that the doctrine of a 'completely deterministic world' was ruled out purely on physical grounds.

Bryan Magee has also produced powerful arguments, based on Kant's doctrine of an undetectable 'noumenal' world underlying the empirical, 'phenomenal' world in which we believe we live. He believes that part of our 'minds' actually **exist** in this 'noumenal world', thus putting them effectively 'beyond the reach' of events that take place in the 'phenomenal world', and restoring the possibility of our having **free will** and being in **control** of our thoughts and actions. I find his ideas and arguments, which can be found in 'Confessions of a Philosopher', extremely plausible and convincing. **If they are true**, which we cannot yet say with **certainty**, they clearly deal a 'killer blow' to the doctrine of a completely deterministic Universe. I always found that idea 'completely daft' anyway, since I could **not** accept that I was nothing more than a 'robot', with no control over how I behaved.

4.   Is the 'empirical world' all that there is?

The possibility of there being more than one 'layer' of 'reality' is something that has been discussed since 'Pre-axial Age' times. A few years ago, I prepared another talk for delivery to the Aberdeen Business and Professional Club, entitled 'Three Alternative Pictures of Reality', and again produced a detailed 'handout' to support this. After a short 'general introduction' to the topic, it outlined the main features of these 'three alternative pictures', one developed by **Eastern philosophers**, one, much more recently, by **Western philosophers**, and one, **very** much more recently, by **Western scientists**. Since these descriptions contain all the information about the three 'pictures of reality' that you will need in order to consider their possible validity, I have simply included them here, in their original form.

The 'Eastern philosophical' picture

Hindus and Buddhists regard reality as having two aspects – the **phenomenal world** (the world of **appearances** that we experience through our senses), and the **ultimate reality** that they believe to lie beneath and beyond it. They believe that the phenomenal world (which Hindus call **samsara**) is essentially **illusory**, although it **appears** to most of us to be **real** in every way, and is also **constantly changing**.

They believe that the 'ultimate reality' that underlies it is a unified 'something' (which Hindus call **Brahman**), that cannot be understood through **reason**, but only through **direct experience**. They also believe that it is possible to **make contact with,** and even **become part of**, this ultimate reality through **deep meditation**, and that many people (such as the Buddha) have been able to do so throughout the ages. It is this belief that effectively differentiates **Eastern** philosophy from the two **Western** traditions that we will now examine.

The 'Western philosophical' picture

Western philosophy began with the so-called Presocratic Greeks, reached a first peak with the work of Plato and Aristotle in the fifth century BCE, and (according to many scholars) reached a second peak with the work of Kant and Schopenhauer between 1781 and 1818. Like the Hindus and Buddhists, they believed that reality has **two aspects**, the **phenomenal world** that we experience through our senses, and the **noumenal world** that lies beneath and beyond it, although they came to this conclusion by a totally different route – through **rational reflection**, rather than by **direct experience**. Like the Hindus and Buddhists, they also believed that the phenomenal world is **illusory**, in the sense that **we ourselves construct it**, using our innate sensory and mental 'apparatus', although it again **appears** to us to be real in every way. They believed that the noumenal world which lies beyond it is **completely** and **permanently inaccessible** to us, because of the **intrinsic limitations of our 'apparatus'**. According to Schopenhauer (who took Kant's original ideas into 'new areas'), this consists of an un-self-aware, undifferentiated 'something', to which he gave the (highly-confusing) name of **will**. He believed that the phenomenal world developed through **progressive manifestation** and **objectification** of this 'metaphysical will', first as **pure energy**, then as **inanimate objects**, then as **living things**, and finally as **self-aware beings** (us). This is very similar to the modern scientific picture of how the world and its contents developed.

The 'Western scientific' picture

The Western scientific tradition lay in the shadow of the Christian Church for many centuries, and did not really start to 'take off' until the work of men like Galileo, Descartes and Newton in the 16th and 17th centuries. For a long time, the scientific 'world picture' was highly **materialistic** in nature, being based on the assumption that the **physical world** that we perceive to lie around us, and in which we live, is all that there is. During the 20th century, however, the development of quantum theory led some scientists to suspect that there **might** be more to reality than the material world of atoms and molecules.James Jeans, for example, observed that 'the stream of knowledge is heading towards a non-mechanical reality', and that 'the Universe begins to look more like a great thought than a great machine'. This progressive movement **away** from materialism culminated in the work of the controversial quantum physicist, David Bohm, who, in the second half of the century, developed a **double-aspect** model of reality that was very similar to that previously developed by Eastern philosophers, and then by Kant and Schopenhauer. He believed that reality consisted of an **explicate order** (comprising the **phenomenal world** that we perceive to lie around us), and an **implicate order** (representing a deeper, more fundamental level of reality that underlies and underpins it). Furthermore, he believed that the phenomenal world was analogous to a **moving holographic image** that is stored on the **underlying matrix** of the implicate order, to which we can again never have direct access. Bohm and his followers were able to show that this two-level model of reality was able to explain many phenomena (such as paranormal activities) that had hitherto been completely beyond the reach of traditional materialistic science. If his ideas eventually gain general acceptance, they will constitute the greatest and most important **paradigm shift** that has **ever** taken place in science.

5. What do we 'know' about any underlying reality?

As we have just seen, these three 'alternative pictures of reality' are remarkably similar in many ways. This suggests to me that the ideas of Eastern philosophers, Western philosophers and Western scientists, just **might** be beginning to converge at long last. Let us hope that this trend continues. In the meantime, let us try to evaluate what we **really know** about any possible underlying level of reality. Let me begin by saying that I have now come to a fairly firm conclusion that there **is** such an underlying level, although I have **no incontrovertible evidence** that this is indeed the case, just a great deal of **highly-suggestive cumulative evidence**, together with a **gut feeling** that I simply cannot ignore.

First, the **Eastern** idea that the only **truly real** level of reality is the one that **underlies** and **underpins** the essentially **illusory** world in which we live out our short lives (or **succession of short lives,** as both the Hindus and the Buddhists firmly believe). As we saw in Chapters 2 and 5, there are a **vast number** of **first hand accounts** from people who have claimed to have **gained direct contact with**, and, in some cases, **actually become part of** this underlying level of reality, which Hindus call **Brahman**, and is, in many ways, similar to what Christians call the **Holy Spirit**, or **Holy Ghost**, the third 'person' of their 'triune God'. Although, I do not believe in any form of 'personal God' for the reasons I gave in Chapter 19, I am firmly convinced that there is **some form** of 'underlying force' or 'creative principle' or 'organizational principle' that **underpins** and **supports** the empirical world in which we live. I simply cannot believe that this is **all** a result of 'pure chance', even though I fully accept that 'chance' played a **significant part** in its development, as the evolutionary biologists have clearly shown. I myself have never had any experience of **direct** or even **indirect** contact with such an underlying force or principle, but this is almost certainly because of my own 'lack of significant spiritual advancement', rather than because such a force or principle does not exist. As the philosophers so correctly point out, 'absence of proof' is **not** 'proof of absence'. And there are just **too many people**, from virtually **all** religious traditions, who claim that they **have** had such contact, for me to deny the cumulative effect of their testimony.

Next, the **phenomenal/noumenal dichotomy** that Kant and Schopenhauer have postulated **on purely rational grounds**. When I first learned about this in my hotel bedroom in Saudi Arabia almost 20 years ago I was **extremely** impressed by it. I even took up Bryan Magee's challenge that a possible way forwards towards **understanding** this dichotomy might be to attempt to clarify the **position** and **nature** of the **boundary** between the 'phenomenal' and 'noumenal' aspects of reality. I then spent almost a year researching, drafting and revising a major, fully-referenced academic article entitled 'The Expanding Boundaries of the Empirical World' – some observations of a natural philosopher'. This questioned Kant's assertion that the boundaries between the two worlds were 'permanently fixed' because of the 'limited nature of our perceptual apparatus'. I showed that the 'effective size' of the 'empirical world' had in fact 'increased beyond all recognition' since the time of Kant and Schopenhauer – not because **we ourselves** have changed in any significant way, but because both the **range** of our **physical senses** and the **scope** of our **mental processes** have been **greatly expanded**, by developments that have taken place **outside our bodies and minds.** Specifically, I argued, our **senses** have been **greatly extended** by the development of **vastly improved equipment** such as modern **telescopes** and **microscopes**, and by our recent ability to **put the former into space**, in order to get past the barrier of our atmosphere. Our **mental faculties**, I argued, have also been extended in two main ways – first by the development of new **mathematical tools** and **scientific theories**, and then by the development of **electronic computers** of progressively greater power, speed and versatility since the mid-1940's. I worked on the article with the newly-appointed Principal and Vice-Chancellor of RGU, Professor Mike Pittilo, and with my former colleague, Dr. Alistair McLeish, who had completed a highly-impressive Ph.D. in philosophy while he was a lecturer in my Department. Mike was so impressed by my article that he arranged to have it typed (by his own Secretary), and published in-house as an A4 booklet. He subsequently gave copies of this to visitors to his office. Mike urged me to submit my article to an appropriate academic journal, and I did in fact do so; they turned it down because it was 'too long' (it ran to 18 pages). I still had my 'booklet', however, and was perfectly happy with that. I have given away many copies myself.

In addition to being extremely impressed by the distinction between the 'phenomenal' and 'noumenal' worlds that Kant had suggested in 1781, (which Bryan Magee had claimed to be 'the greatest single advance in the history of Western philosophy'), I was equally interested in the idea that part of us actually **lives** in Kant's noumenal world. Bryan Magee had a great deal to say about this in 'Confessions of a Philosopher', and has fully convinced me that this is probably indeed the case. If you accept this 'hypothesis', it throws a great deal of light on many puzzling aspects of our 'mental world', including the relationship between our 'conscious' and 'subconscious' minds, our 'freedom of will' and 'agency', and the possible 'location' of our 'long-term memory'. Once again, although I cannot cite any incontrovertible, empirical **proof** for the existence of Kant's 'phenomenal/noumenal dichotomy', I am as certain as I can be that there is a great deal of truth in it. The extended 'Kantian/Schopenauerian model' of reality also fits in very well with the 'Eastern model' advocated by the Hindus and Buddhists. Once Schopenhauer found out about this similarity, he read material from

Hindu texts every night, before going to sleep. And, as we saw in Chapter 19, Schopenhauer was a confirmed atheist!

Finally, the information-based **holographic Universe** idea developed jointly by David Bohm and Karl Pribram. As with the Kant/Schopenhauer phenomenal/noumenal dichotomy model, this one **really** impresses me, as it has a **real** 'ring of truth' about it. It explains so many features of the 'empirical world' in a genuinely 'scientific' way, and also gives a highly-plausible explanation of a wide range of so-called 'paranormal phenomena', that were hitherto thought to be completely outwith any possibility of 'scientific' explanation. Michael Talbot's amazing book also includes a large amount of 'empirical evidence' in support of the holographic model, from an extremely-wide range of sources. Indeed, he provides so much highly-convincing evidence of this type that I am very near to accepting that the case for a 'holographic Universe' has been proved 'beyond reasonable doubt', the level of proof required for a conviction in a **criminal** case in Britain. Talbot's 'case' is certainly now **well** past the corresponding 'burden of proof' for a **civil** case, which only has to be proved 'on the balance of probabilities'. All it requires is for a **really convincing, irrefutable** piece of 'empirical evidence' to be produced, preferably related to a **key aspect** of the model, and I will be 'right in there', giving it my **full public support**, for what it is worth. Like the Kant/Schopenhauer model, it also fits in well with many of the ideas of the Eastern philosophers. Indeed, I see no reason why a fully-integrated model of a 'double-layered reality', incorporating features of **all three** of the models that I have described in this Conclusion, could not be developed in due course. I will suggest some ideas on how this might be done in the next section.

6. How can we try to find out more

There is no question about how we should try to find out more about the **empirical world** that constitutes the 'upper layer' of all three of the two-layer models of reality that I have described in this 'Conclusion'. This is **fully accessible** to **systematic investigation** using the **well-established methods of science**, and scientists should continue to investigate it in this way. As I have shown in this book, science has already taught us a great deal about the empirical world, but there are still quite a lot of things we do **not** know. What, for example exactly **are** 'dark matter' and 'dark energy'? There are several Nobel Prizes waiting for the people that solve **those** problems, I would firmly predict. Also, is there still any **really** worthwhile physics to be done **beyond** the 'standard model' of particle physics? Some say that there is, but others are not so optimistic, believing that all the really important discoveries have now been made. To these people, I would only say one thing: remember what Lord Kelvin said about the 'state of physics' in 1900! There is, however, one major problem in physics that will **have** to be solved eventually if the subject is to retain its present high reputation. This is the fact that the **two key theories** on which the **whole of modern physics and cosmology are based** (**quantum theory** and Einstein's **general theory of relativity**) are **mutually incompatible**, and cannot possibly **both** be right. I will not try to explain **why** this is the case, because the matter is 'quite technical', but I can assure you that it **is indeed** the case. Thus, the problem of finding a satisfactory **quantum theory of gravity** must surely be the most pressing problem in physics, as it has been for some time now, as I showed in Chapter 15. This may require another 'Newton' or 'Einstein', but we should remember that there was a 237-year gap between the births of these two supreme geniuses, so we might have to wait a long time. I am confident that a solution **will** be found in due course, however, since it nearly always is. Thus, I think we can leave the 'empirical', 'phenomenal world' in the safe hands of the scientists.

This is truly **their** domain, and, although **philosophers** and **theologians** will probably have significant contributions to make, it is the **scientists** that will have to do the bulk of the work. Let them ignore the nonsense talked by the 'post-modernist' philosophers, and get on with it.

But what about the question of any 'ultimate reality' that lies **outwith** the empirical world? Here, I would suggest that the philosophers, and theologians of **all** religious traditions, can **really** come into their own, as in the pioneering work on 'information-based models of reality' that I described in Chapter 20. This could probably be 'kick started' by the establishment of a truly 'cross-disciplinary', international research facility by one of the big 'funding organization's such as the John Templeton Foundation, which has a proven 'track record' in this area. It would also require to be guaranteed funding for a very long period if it was to have any hope of making significant progress, so more than one major source of income would probably be required. It would probably be best for it to be a completely independent institution, free from the influence of any one country or closely-linked group of countries. This would clearly affect the question of where it should be located, but I am sure that many, highly-suitable 'hosts' would be 'queuing up' for the privilege.

I have, however, one more suggestion to make, and I am sure this will be **much** more controversial. Although I am confident that increased cooperation between scientists, philosophers and religious experts of all types **will** start to unravel the 'mysteries' of the 'nature of ultimate reality' in due course, I suspect that this will take quite a long time if carried out in a **conventional** way. There is, however, an extremely-powerful 'tool' available, that could, in my opinion, greatly speed up their work. I am, of course, referring to the psychedelic drug, LSD, which, as I showed in Chapter 18, was regarded by many people as a 'wonder drug' back in the 1960's and 1970's. Not only was it proving extremely effective as a 'therapeutic drug' in many clinical and psychiatric contexts, it also appeared to offer an incredibly effective 'fast track' to **highly** 'spiritual experiences', and also to an apparently **deep understanding** of the **true nature of reality** that was **totally unobtainable** by other means, except for a very few advanced Eastern 'mystics' such as Maharishi Mahesh Yogi. When I started work on Chapter 18, it was almost 50 years since I had read 'Drugs of Hallucination' and 'LSD in Action', and I had forgotten about most of their contents. Referring to them once again, with the **much** deeper understanding of subjects like philosophy, religion and history that I have now, made me convinced that this incredible drug (or whatever its modern successor is) **could** offer a truly 'royal road' to understanding reality. Remember, what the (unnamed) 'pastor' said about how it enabled users to 'bypass Christ completely', and gain 'immediate, direct access' to the 'Holy Ghost'. This, of course, will depend on the authorities **allowing** LSD to be used in this way. Its use is now totally banned in practically every country in the world, so steps will have to be taken to enable this ban to be relaxed in some cases. I would **strongly suggest** that its use for **medical** and **research** purposes be permitted once again, although this is obviously an area in which I have absolutely no influence. Possibly this book will help to change people's attitudes. I would like to think so.

Postscript

Having got all the 'really serious stuff' out of the way, I would like to end this book on a slightly lighter note, by pointing out how many of the ideas that I have presented therein were anticipated by Carl Sagan back in 1985, when he wrote his amazing science-fiction novel, 'Contact'. Carl Sagan, as many of my older readers will remember, was an extremely-distinguished American astronomer, writer and broadcaster, who probably did more to popularize science and astronomy than any other man or woman. His seminal book, 'Cosmos', was, for a long time, 'the best-selling science book ever published in the English language', and the accompanying television series was seen in over 60 countries. (Both the book and the DVD box set of the TV series are cherished items in my personal library.) 'Contact' is also one of my very favourite science-fiction books, right up there with Isaac Asimov's 'Foundation' series, Fred Hoyle's 'Black Cloud' and Stephen Baxter's 'Manifold' novels. I have now read it at least six times, and had to get my son to find me a second-hand 'hardback' copy on the Internet when my original 'paperback' copy literally 'fell apart'. The book is all about the 'first contact' with 'extra-terrestrial civilizations', through the medium of 'radio astronomy', and I will not spoil things for potential readers by telling you any details of the plot. Suffice to say that Sagan clearly used the book as a vehicle to present many of his own ideas on the nature of reality and the conflict between science and religion, and did so through the main character, an American radioastronomer called Eleanor Arroway. She became Director of 'Project Argus', which had been set up to look for any 'extraterrestrial civilizations' that might be 'out there', by systematically searching for radio signals from them. Eleanor was clearly a 'level 6' 'de-facto atheist' with distinct 'spiritual' tendencies (like me, and, I suspect, like Carl Sagan himself), and the book follows her through her entire life, right up to the aftermath of the epic events described in the novel. I would like to introduce you to two specific episodes. The first took place in the middle of a debate between Eleanor and a 'well-known' American 'religious fundamentalist' and 'evangelist' called Billy Joe Rankin (clearly a 'level 1' 'strong theist' of the 'most extreme' variety). This debate takes up no fewer than 15 pages of the book, with its climax starting with the following exchange, after a break for lunch:

Rev. Rankin
' I was struck by one or two things you said this morning. You called yourself a Christian. May I ask? In what sense are you a Christian?

Dr. Arroway

'I'm a Christian in the sense that I find Jesus Christ to be an admirable historical figure. I think the Sermon on the Mount is one of the greatest ethical statements and one of the best speeches in history. I think that "Love your enemy" might even be the long-shot solution to the problem of nuclear war. I wish he was alive today. It would benefit everybody on the planet. But I think Jesus was only a man. A great man, a brave man, a man with insight into unpopular truths. But I don't think he was God, or the son of God, or the grandnephew of God.'

Rev. Rankin

'You don't **want** to believe in God. You figure out you can be a Christian and not believe in God. Let me ask you straight out: **Do** you believe in God?

Dr. Arroway

'The question has a peculiar structure. If I say no, do I mean I'm convinced God **doesn't** exist, or do I mean I'm not convinced he **does** exist. These are two very different statements'.

And so the debate continued for another four pages, ending with the two still in total disagreement. Readers will have noted that Eleanor's ideas about Christ are very similar to those of Bryan Magee, which I outlined in Chapter 6. They will also have noted that Eleanor's statement about 'belief in God' is essentially the 'starting point' for the entire discussion of this key question that I have struggled my way through when writing this book.

I will now end by quoting the entire final page of 'Contact', at the end of the chapter entitled 'The Artist's Signature'. I will 'set the scene' for this by explaining that one of the methods that Eleanor and her colleagues had been using to investigate the nature of 'deep reality' was by exploring the 'deep structure' of 'transcendental numbers' such as 'pi', using the most powerful computers that were available to them. Here is the eventual outcome of this search. I think it is self-explanatory, and requires no further comment from me.

'The Argus computer was so persistent and inventive in its attempts to contact Eleanor Arroway that it almost conveyed an urgent personal need to share the discovery.

The anomaly showed up most starkly in Base II arithmetic, where it could be written out entirely as zeros and ones. Compared with what had been received from Vega , this could be at best a simple message, but its statistical significance was high. The program reassembled the digits into a square raster, an equal number across and down. The first line was an uninterrupted file of zeros, left to right. The second showed a single numeral one, exactly in the middle, with zeros to the borders, left and right. After a few more lines, an unmistakable arc had formed, composed of ones. The simple geometrical figure had been quickly constructed, line by line, self-reflective, rich with promise. The last line of the figure emerged, all zeros except for a single centered one. The subsequent line would be zeros only, part of the frame.

Hiding in the alternating patterns of digits, deep inside the transcendental number, was a perfect circle, its form traced out by unities in a field of noughts.

The Universe was made on purpose, the circle said. In whatever galaxy you happen to find yourself, you take the circumference of a circle, divide it by its diameter, measure closely enough, and uncover a miracle – another circle, drawn kilometres downstream of the decimal point. There would be richer messages further in. It doesn't matter what you look like, or what you're made of, or where you came from. As long as you live in this Universe, and have a modest talent for mathematics, sooner or later you'll find it. It's already there. It's inside everything. You don't have to leave your planet to find it. In the fabric of space and in the nature of matter, as in a great work of art, there is, written small, the artist's signature. Standing over humans, gods and demons, subsuming Caretakers and Tunnel builders, there is an intelligence that antedates the Universe.

The circle had closed.

She had found what she was searching for'.